Reflections on
Religious Literacy

Reflections on Religious Literacy

Paradox, Promise, and Politics in a Secular Age

Leo Van Arragon

Foreword by Peter Schuurman

WIPF & STOCK · Eugene, Oregon

REFLECTIONS ON RELIGIOUS LITERACY
Paradox, Promise, and Politics in a Secular Age

Copyright © 2026 Leo Van Arragon. All rights reserved. Except for brief quotations in critical publications or reviews, no part of this book may be reproduced in any manner without prior written permission from the publisher. Write: Permissions, Wipf and Stock Publishers, 199 W. 8th Ave., Suite 3, Eugene, OR 97401.

Wipf & Stock
An Imprint of Wipf and Stock Publishers
199 W. 8th Ave., Suite 3
Eugene, OR 97401

www.wipfandstock.com

PAPERBACK ISBN: 979-8-3852-5651-8
HARDCOVER ISBN: 979-8-3852-5652-5
EBOOK ISBN: 979-8-3852-5653-2

VERSION NUMBER 01/22/26

Scripture quotations marked ESV are taken from The ESV® Bible (The Holy Bible, English Standard Version®), © 2001 by Crossway, a publishing ministry of Good News Publishers. ESV Text Edition: 2025.

Scripture quotations marked KJV are taken from the King James Version and are in the public domain.

Scripture quotations marked NIV are taken from The Holy Bible, New International Version®, NIV® Copyright © 2011 by Biblica, Inc.® Used by permission. All rights reserved worldwide.

Scripture quotations marked NJPS are from the *Tanakh: The Holy Scriptures: The New JPS Translation according to the Traditional Hebrew Text*, copyright © 1985 by The Jewish Publication Society. Used by permission. All rights reserved.

"Our world is incredibly religiously diverse, from organized traditions to individuals who prefer science, nature, or atheism to those who find themselves somewhere in between. Religion education programs around the world reflect that diversity, to the point of confusion and marginalization in education. Into this breach steps Leo Van Arragon, with his bold assertion that religious education, and specifically religious literacy, is essential to education. After methodically defining and analyzing the terms 'religion' and 'literacy,' Van Arragon argues that religion is an 'interpretive screen' that enables humans—both individually and collectively within institutions, principles, rituals, and more—to make sense of the world and construct meaning. It is an embodied way of knowing, full of affects, experiences, narratives, rationality, and an element of wisdom. Religious literacy enables citizens to learn about themselves, each other, and the world, critically evaluating the world in its complexity and discussing how to live together well. Van Arragon rejects the common understanding that religion is a private affair, or that 'public' schools are religiously neutral. Arguing instead that all schools advance some vision of the good life and that religion is of public interest, he creates space for religious education for its own sake. Religious education contributes to civics and character education but cannot be reduced to either because religious literacy is a way of reading the world and living into one's most fundamental commitments of the head, heart, and hands."

—**MARGIE PATRICK**, Associate Professor of Education, King's University, Edmonton

"This book is the fruit of a deep commitment to education practice, scholarship on religion, and the well-being of students navigating a complex and uncertain world. In advocating for the inclusion of religious literacy as a component of critical thinking, Leo importantly unmasks the issues of power operating in all education systems, secular and religious alike. The questions raised are essential for everyone concerned about the purpose of education in times of deepening division, violence, and environmental collapse."

—**CATHERINE HOLTMANN**, Professor of Sociology, University of New Brunswick

"Carefully and rigorously researched, *Reflections on Religious Literacy* is a mind-expanding journey toward reshaping our thinking about religion and literacy, education, and the public square. With his finely honed perceptive mind and genuinely expansive and hospitable heart, Leo Van Arragon serves up a heaping helping of food for thought in a divisive and cantankerous world. Read this book slowly, savoring its wisdom and embracing its call to make this a better world for us and for the generations to come."

—**Dirk Buursma**, Senior Editor-at-Large

To Cathleen, my life partner

To my children and grandchildren, Lisa and Moses, Ben, Melody, Isabelle and Char, Christy, Dane, Arie and Annika, who keep me grounded in love and in their world

Contents

Foreword by Peter Schuurman | ix
Preface | xv
Acknowledgments | xxiii
Abbreviations | xxv

1   Introduction: A Case for Religious Literacy | 1
2   Religion | 24
3   Objections to Religion | 70
4   Literacy | 155
5   Religious Literacy: An Educational Paradox in Two Parts | 195
6   A Case for Religious Literacy as a Public Good | 229
7   Education as a Spiritual Exercise | 304

Bibliography | 317

Foreword

Few people will say, "I don't do economics" or "I'm against politics of any kind." Yet many believe they live without religion, and without any need to learn about religion. What will be so provocative about this book for the secular dominant culture in Canada—and to a lesser degree any cloistered religious minority—is that it argues quite rigorously that you cannot live without some sort of religious orientation, or without some need to understand such orientation in the lives of your fellow citizens. By defining religion with Beckford as "an interpretative category concerning the ultimate meaning"[1] there can be almost no one who does not fit this deeply human quest. As production and exchange are to economics, and power and authority are to politics, so is faith, trust, and ritual to religion. They are all constitutive of the human condition and thus human culture.

Some still resist religion because they perceive it to be exceptionally volatile and prone to antagonism, if not violence. Yet it is no more dangerous than politics or economics, the two cultural sectors we seem to take most for granted and that dominate our public discourse. In fact, religion is most dangerous when it is unacknowledged, ignored, or lumped into one universal mystical soup that leaves no cognizance of the deep differences that will continue to divide us. To switch metaphors, few would be content with understanding the forest without learning about the different trees, plants, and creatures that live there, especially if you had to live in the forest. Education demands a dive into difference so we can thrive together, and our increasingly diverse Canadian demographic demands more intentional public education around religion. Over the past five years (2020–2024), Canada has admitted approximately 2.1

---

1. Beckford, *Social Theory*, 4.

million immigrants across the border, and they are a religious rainbow of difference.

In fact, Van Arragon argues that religion needs to become the fourth R after reading, writing, and arithmetic in our public educational curriculum. If our ideal profile of an educated citizen is a person who understands the deepest commitments of our multicultural milieu, religion needs to be taught in schools so we can build bridges between our ethnic and religious communities and move beyond the mythical idea of a neutral public square. Canada has become increasingly pluralistic since the 1960s, and ignorance of the varieties of religious experience is a liability, especially in our polarized age.

Van Arragon knows that of which he speaks. We both come from a Dutch-Canadian Christian tradition that deeply values education—the Reformed branch of European Christianity. When post-war Dutch immigrants landed in Canada, they first built a church and then immediately set to building a primary school. This was followed by a high school, and then both universities and a graduate-level school of philosophy (the Institute for Christian Studies within the University of Toronto). In fact, Van Arragon has spent the better part of his life teaching at these schools and then leading three of them as the principal. As soon as he retired, he headed to the University of Ottawa to study the place of religion within our educational system with Lori Beaman, one of Canada's leading scholars in religious studies.

This background is truly an advantage: Van Arragon knows what it feels like to live in a religiously charged subculture and yet his offering in this book arises from a mind that is anything but parochial. He argues in a language and with conversation partners that are both academic and invitational—provoking a deeper thoughtfulness about religion and the pluralistic context in which we increasingly live. Electronic media makes the religious other unavoidable, even if you live in a sequestered community or isolated region of the globe.

Van Arragon and I both happen to be chairs of university campus ministry boards at this time—boards that oversee the work of a public university chaplain formed within our tradition. This means thinking deeply about what it means to be a person of faith among people of a diversity of faiths. For those who think public higher education is thoroughly secular, they need to investigate first the variety of religious student groups on campus (there are fifty-two such groups listed under Student Life at University of Toronto), and then see the diversity of chaplains and other clergy in the campus ministry office—now more often called the Faith and Life Center (Brock University) or Multi-Faith Resource Team (University of Guelph). Then, in a more creative way, come to see commitments to capitalism, socialism, Palestinian liberation, critical race theory, and feminism as often laced with a certain sacredness—with their own symbols, holidays, and language. This wider understanding of religion may even include such things as the nostalgic passion for singer Gord Downie, evolving feelings about the Canadian flag, or even fandom of the Edmonton Oilers as carrying unacknowledged quasi-religious commitments.

Like Van Arragon, I also did a PhD in religious studies (the Religious Diversity in North America program at University of Waterloo) after a first career, although my personal history was in the world of university campus ministry. I have now been teaching world religions to undergraduates, mostly at Redeemer University in Hamilton, for almost twenty years. I should add that my world religions textbook by Stephen Prothero, like a growing number of textbooks on religion today, includes an equal-length chapter on atheism. What religion is understood to be is less and less measured by the formerly dominant Judeo-Christian-Islamic traditions. In fact, my supervisor for my PhD, Doug Cowan, has lately published research on popular culture and its religious imagination—popular culture being a sub-discipline of religious studies that has been growing for decades already. Religion is everywhere—not just in temples, synagogues, and churches.

Van Arragon is not alone in his cry for greater religious literacy in Canada. One key example is Dr. Brian Carwana, executive director of World Religions Encounter in my hometown of Guelph, Ontario, otherwise known as the "religions geek." Through blogs, podcasts, webinars, training sessions and religious center tours, Carwana has been educating the public, the private sector, and students on religion, ethno-religious diversity, and what the meaning of that diversity is for our modern workplaces, schools, and societies. Quoting scholar Donovan Schaefer, Carwana explains that religion is not foremost about beliefs, but more of a "technology that makes us feel things." Religion is most often meaningful "in an emotional, experiential way."[2] Thus religious literacy helps us be moved to truly see people as people, beyond our biases, ready-made

---

2. Carwana, "Emotions, Politics & Religion," para. 6.

categories, and quick judgments. It makes space to form friendship and develop partnerships.³

Another example is The Institute for Religion, Culture, and Societal Futures (IRCSF), which just opened its doors in 2024 at the University of Waterloo. It seeks to share scholarship on religion and spirituality, as well as "emerging forms of communities of belief and practice" in order "to support undergraduate and graduate students, community organizations, faith groups, schools, the media, and the general public in better understanding the religious landscape of Canada and connections between religion, spirituality, secularity and other aspects of public and social life."⁴ They would be the first to acknowledge that Christian faith is waning in Canada (from 90 percent of Canadians in 1971 to 44 percent in 2023). Yet religion persists in a wide, colorful, and sometimes subtle variety.

So the time is ripe, especially post-9/11, to reconsider religious literacy and illiteracy and the educational curriculum around religion. Van Arragon is quite comprehensive—he responds to common criticisms about religion's public participation (it's a form of indoctrination, or it's irrational, pathological, or exclusive) and then goes on to offer a definition of religious literacy, address its common framing, and then make the case for religious literacy as a gift to our common life.

What is brilliant about Van Arragon's thesis is first of all that he has an eye to global conversations and examples while still focusing on the Canadian educational landscape. He draws on research from such places as Australia, Macedonia, Bosnia, and Haiti and provides examples from Zambia, Germany, and the UK. Yet he is attentive to difference in Quebec, British Columbia, and Ontario as well. Again, education is the development of an awareness of and respect for difference.

Second, while the definition of religion as "an interpretive category" gives the scope necessary for this apologetic for religion in education, Van Arragon doesn't get lost in abstractions. He is also able to write about religion as a spiritual quest or spiritual exercise, and that we all depend on "nested stories"⁵ to locate ourselves in the cosmos, including the sciences. Van Arragon can even become a little poetic when he describes the religious heart of the human creature:

---

3. Here Carwana draws on Diana Eck and the Harvard Pluralism Project at Harvard University. Carwana, "How Religious Literacy Helps."

4. University of Waterloo, "Institute," para. 1.

5. Greene, *Until the End of Time*.

FOREWORD

> It is our human burden and joy to ask questions about how we got here, but also why we did and what we are meant to do here in the immanent frame of our existence. In our darker moments we may conclude with Macbeth that it all comes down to sound and fury signifying nothing, but our getting up in the mornings to go to work, visit art galleries, get our children to soccer practice, pay our taxes, and mow our lawns signify something quite different. We do, in fact, live tales we believe to be true on some level, giving our lives their meaning, transcending the ups and downs inherent in human life. We do have faith that our tales are true, which is the basis for hope.[6]

Some may resist his universalization of such "religious" experience, but most will see something of themselves in this characterization of everyday life. Van Arragon can shift from the academic to a very clear and down-to-earth description after a single period.

We hope educators, policy-makers, politicians, and trustees will see the pressing need for a more intentional, more rigorous, and more sophisticated approach to religious literacy through reading this book. We ignore religion at our collective peril, and we ignore its diversity at the risk of our own educational poverty. The opportunity lies before us not only for a more responsible citizenship and more cooperative public life, but also for a deeper understanding of each other and our diverse spiritual quests. Such literacy can only mean greater well-being for all.

Peter Schuurman

---

6. Page 41 in the manuscript.

Preface

ON MY BOOKSHELF OCCUPYING a place of honor sits the Dutch, two-volume, children's story Bible titled *Groot Vertelboek voor de Bijbelse Verschiedenis* door Anne DeVries.[1] It has pretty much fallen apart, having travelled some distance over a long time, its pages yellowed and fragile, the binding broken. I have not yet decided if I should have it rebound but, on the whole, I think not. We have earned our scars, and I don't want to clean up the evidence of aging by cosmetic surgery and rebinding. The set has a lot of memories for me, its reading having been a staple of our family dinners throughout my childhood. The pattern of my father opening it after our lively dinners was invariable. I grew up in a family of nine, more or less, the number depending on who happened to be staying for dinner or for the night. Whatever the number, there were discussions, debates, bickering, territorial disputes, laughter that came to an end as my father moved his plate, fork, and knife to one side, got up, picked up the volume that contained the next story in the sequence, sat down, cleared his throat, waited for the us to settle down. Then he read. Actually, it was not a volume or a book that he picked up. It was the Bible, and its reading created a kind of sacred time and space during which we were expected to sit and listen, not pick up food or drink, fool around, or kick each other under the table. When my father was not home for dinner, particularly during his truck driving days, my mother would read. I cannot remember a dinner when this ritual was not followed.

I also cannot remember how often we went through the Bible retold by Anne DeVries, a wonderful storyteller, but it was often enough that the black and white pictures, the phrasing, and the narrative

---

1. *Big Storybook of Biblical History* by Anne DeVries.

PREFACE

sequence are part of my aesthetic, including my vocabulary. I assumed that everyone knew the stories that made up the big story of the Bible. It was not until I enrolled in a local public high school that I became consciously aware that most of my peers really did not know the stories I took for granted. I was baffled when the reference to Golgotha in *Macbeth* (act 1, scene 2) had to be explained or the recurring references to blood or the killing of MacDuff's children. I had heard about King Herod's slaughter of the innocents so often that Macbeth's fear and brutality seemed well within the range of what a ruler might do when feeling threatened. When I met Julius Caesar for the first time in grade nine, I knew about the Caesars, that they were at the peak of some kind of political hierarchy that included governors and kings, that they had power to order people around, disrupting their lives, including the lives of Joseph and Mary who ended up in Bethlehem after a difficult trip. The birth of Jesus in a stable was the focus of the trip and he, it turned out, was the Son of God, something we knew of course, having heard the story so many times we could have supplied the details but which still seemed new, told as it was in church, Sunday School, and at home, humble spaces turned into places of enchantment by trees decorated for the season, candles, the homecomings of sisters living far away, special foods, and the presents of an orange and a candy cane packaged in paper bags. The apostle Paul travelled around the eastern Mediterranean world, surviving shipwrecks, a snake bite, lynchings, visiting cities and islands and jurisdictions, exotic places where world-changing events took place. And, of course, there were pictures. We met people, good and bad, in high and low positions, in sickness and in health, for whom spirit quests were central to their lives and well-being. In some ways, Rome and Jerusalem were more real to me that Ottawa or Toronto as a kid. There were, after all, maps in the backs of the Bibles in church and in the ones we got as presents. I more or less understood why Brutus and his co-conspirators did not want to be dominated by somebody with the kind of power for which Julius was heading, the stories of the Israelites and the Jews and later Christians being stories of resistance that sometimes took violent and direct action. For example, you can look up Ehud and Eglon recorded in Judg 3:12–30 for a satisfyingly gruesome story, at least to an eight-year-old farm kid with a lot of imagination and resistant tendencies. Those trips into the dark side were what attracted me to William Shakespeare when I met him in a play that landed on my grade nine desk, and he lodged himself into who I am all these many years later when I am often troubled by the world.[2]

Besides the specific Biblical references, the Shakespearean worlds and the characters inhabiting them were not that different from the ones created by Anne DeVries. You had tragedy and comedy and hope and despair. You had deep human pain and folly, linked by complex motivations that often ended badly. I was not consciously aware at the time that I had absorbed a sense of history and historiography, of human drama, ways of looking at pictures. Deep loves and hatreds, deep longings for a better world, abuses of power with terrible results for human welfare, knowing that the good people do not always win were part of my daily diet, along with oatmeal porridge, cheese sandwiches, and our meat, potato, and vegetable suppers. I did not always like the fixed routines, my adolescent self chafing against ritual over which I had no say, wondering why my family was so weird, embarrassed by my father's Dutch accent and his obliviousness to trends I thought essential to my social survival.

The embarrassment is a thing of the past as is the unquestioned acceptance of the stories as true, or that their sequence was based on historical accuracy. For a variety of reasons, I am more detached from the faith of my mothers and fathers, but in other ways, it is more part of my spiritual and conceptual DNA. The religious vocabulary and ways of thinking about human nature, folly, hope, and despair, longings for a better world, skepticism of power and its abuses, trust that the story of history is bigger than me, that the universe is a place of wonder, the sacramental nature of all of reality. It's all still there in the way I read the world and my life in it. I read Donald Trump's puffing and blowing through the story of the response to King Herod's rousing speech, his hearers shouting, "It is the voice of a god, not a man." Of course, his moment (King Herod's, not Donald Trump's, so far at least) of glory is followed by the writer of the book of Acts telling us that "immediately the angel of the

---

2. I grew up in a Dutch-immigrant community in the 1950s, hearing stories of underground resistance to Nazi occupation of the Netherlands in the 1940s, which took what we now might call direct action. An uncle of my closest childhood friend was killed while attempting to free prisoners who had been picked up for various reasons. The Biblical, Shakespearean, and community stories were indistinguishable in their impact on my imagination about how the world worked, including the normalization of resistance to and collaboration with power. It also made me aware that no one is an unadulterated or simple hero. Resistance did not always make people better and people were attracted to resistance movements for different motives, not all of them noble. And sometimes it really did bring out astonishing nobility and courage in the most unexpected people and places.

PREFACE

Lord smote him, because he gave not God the glory: and he was eaten of worms and gave up the ghost" (Acts 12:21–23, KJV). You've got to love the way Jews tell a story! And it reassures me that this moment, too, will pass, although I am ambivalent about such a dreadful end for anyone, even those expressing overweening, self-serving, and destructive hubris. There's a lot of blood and guts and wonky sex in the unflinching look at the human condition that shocks my twenty-first-century, educated self, in the same way that the beheadings, shootings, and lynchings of infidels by various groups using a variety of means shock me. The shock and awe strategies of the Assyrians, Babylonians, and tribal Hebrews recorded for us in the Bible served purposes like the ones used by American forces in the Iraq War and the Israelis are using to wipe out the Palestinians. Different technologies, different names, same human nature. My religious self is not so surprised at what humans can do to each other but that doesn't mean it does not disorient me, especially on my bad days.

What reorients me is the essential comedy of the Biblical story and the tradition I inherited. It is a story of redemption, against impossible odds. The death of Jesus on the cross is followed by a resurrection, an open grave, and a sustaining passion to continue a life of redemptive activity. There is life after death. There is life in death. I no longer am as sure as I was as a kid that I will go to heaven when I die, or what that means, and I no longer believe that my neighbor, who does not share my religious tradition, will go to hell. But I have absorbed an essentially comic view of the world. That does not mean funny or even that things will be OK. What it has come to mean for me is that my life can be lived redemptively, that my life has meaning even though I am not one of the world's movers and shakers. I can live as a good neighbor, as a friend, as a husband because, while I may not understand the ultimate how and why, it is worth doing. Ecclesiastes is the book for my seventy-plus self, telling me that most of what seemed so important at one time is vanity, that my life is made whole through "enjoying life with the wife whom I love" (9:9), and the wisdom that warns me against being "too wise and too righteous" (7:16).

This is not to assert that my particular tradition and religious framework is the only one that stabilizes, frames meaning, and provides hope. It is not to argue that it is the right one or the only path to truth. Rather, religion is bodied in traditions, framed by sacred texts, so, when I write about religion and religious literacy, this is the one within which I think. My Muslim neighbors, the Sikhs who attended the gurdwara

PREFACE

in my Ottawa neighborhood, my Hindu fellow student, my Jewish colleagues, and my friends who self-identify as religious nones all have their ways of framing their meaning stories and life journeys. I cannot write in their voices. That does not mean that theirs do not intersect with my tradition, and hopefully they will be able to engage with my thinking about religious literacy and religion education.

I am thinking of my story as I consider questions about religion education and religious literacy: What is religious literacy? Am I religiously literate? Were my parents? Who decides these things and in what context are they decided? My parents were pretty easy to like in considering the question of literacy. They were mostly self-taught, without the benefits of formal education beyond grade six, but widely read, interested in what was going on in their world, embracing its increasing religious diversity. Having lived through the Nazi occupation in the Netherlands, they were skeptical of demagogues, thoughtful about the ways in which history can be reconstructed to create self-serving mythologies dividing the world between good and evil. So, religiously literate? Pretty easy to make the case. However, let's push this a little further. What about the person who is well versed in Biblical knowledge and theology, interpretations which lead them to conclude that "God hates fags" and is willing to act on that conclusion. Is that person religiously literate? What about the person who is tolerant of religious diversity, without knowing any particular form of religion in any depth, for whom tolerance masks a benign and patronizing contempt?

My question about religious literacy arises out of the creative tension inherent in the meeting of three worlds I inhabit. The family and communal world led with religion, religion providing the narrative for the disruptions of war and immigration as well as an anchor in times of health and prosperity. Religion is part of my DNA and, while I have reconsidered and struggled with its role in my life, continues to provide a world view and values orientation. A career as a professional educator working in independently Christian schools is the second world, one in which it was my professional duty to embody, practice, and teach religion and, in particular, a form of Christianity as a legitimate source of meaning to equip my students to navigate the world. Upon my retirement, I entered a third world when I enrolled in a PhD program in the Religious Studies department at the University of Ottawa, working under the supervision of Dr. Lori Beaman. My doctoral research project, from 2008 to 2015, was in the regulation of religion in public education systems, my case study being Ontario, the province where I have lived and worked and which I know well. My program coincided with Lori's having secured Social Sciences and Humanities Research Council (SSHRC) funding for the Religion and Diversity Project so, besides the benefit of her wonderful guidance, I got to meet and work with scholars from around the world who thought about religion, religious diversity, and religion education from a variety of perspectives. For six exciting years, I was absorbed in a world of religion very different from the one in which I had grown up and in which I had worked. It also created a stimulating dissonance as I navigated quite different ways of seeing religion and religious literacy.

Here's what I mean: while religion education and the delivery of religious literacy were the preoccupations of my personal and communal worlds, my professional life in Christian schools, and my academic life, what that meant was quite different in the three contexts. In my personal life, religion provided a coherent narrative of meaning and purpose, and a language to navigate the world. In my professional life, the goal of religious literacy was the perpetuation of a Christian faith tradition. For the parents of the students I served, religious literacy was primarily a matter of knowing the Bible and the outlines of a Christian worldview that would equip their children with a religious and conceptual platform of truth from which they could successfully navigate the world. For many of them, this truth has eternal implications, including the promise of heaven after their time on earth is over.

For my academic friends, the primary concern animating religion education was the delivery of religious literacy as part of the civic skills and attitudes essential for students to live well in a religiously diverse world. Many of my friends are sociologists and legal scholars so, in some ways, it is not surprising that the particulars of any one religion were less important than religious beliefs and practices guided by civic skills and attitudes of tolerance and respect for religious diversity.

I am an educator by profession, specializing in history and religion, which makes me sensitive to how education outcomes are written and expressed. I think in terms of what my students need to know but also what great story will animate their lives, providing guidance and an anchor in an increasingly confusing information world. In other words, educational outcomes of religion education programs stated in terms of civic skills and attitudes are part of what I want to see, but what is more important is what they know about history, religion, and science

PREFACE

and how that information and knowledge are translated into wisdom for their lives of service in the world.

The three approaches do not live in parallel universes without common ground. My Christian school friends want their children to live well in a religiously diverse world, be good neighbors, get good jobs, be good citizens. The schools in which I worked opened the day with students standing for the national anthem; we worked with community liaison officers, conducted fire drills, engaged with the Ministry of Education to ensure compliance with provincial academic standards required for the Ontario Secondary School diploma. My academic friends want students to be informed about specific religions, resulting in lively debates about which religions should be included in a program and what should be included about those religions. My public-school colleagues working in state-funded systems designed to deliver good citizens are highly committed to student success, which includes their commitment to a coherent system of values that would guide them in a complex and often confusing world.

This book lives at the intersection of common ground and differences in how religious literacy is conceptualized and embodied. It proposes a theoretical framework for religious literacy as a matter of public interest and investment, but it is equally an extended reflection on the conundrums and paradoxes inherent in education, religion, and religion education, as I have lived them in the three worlds in which I travel. I invite you, my readers, to travel with me.

Leo Van Arragon
Strathroy, Ontario, Canada
September 2025

Acknowledgments

My reflections on religious literacy are mine alone and, yet, in important ways, they are not. Hovering in the background is a cloud of witnesses, people in faith communities where I have been a member, schools, family and friend circles, students whom I taught who have shaped my experience and thoughts about religion. Most of them would have no idea of where their teaching and modeling would have led, nor should they. There is, thankfully, a statute of limitations on the responsibilities of teachers and other adults and their responsibilities for a mid-70s writer and thinker. I honor them and acknowledge that I live in a network of relationships, some of which I only vaguely remember.

There are, however, some in that cloud I need to name. Dr. Margie Patrick of King's University in Edmonton and Dr. Peter Schuurman of Global Scholars took the time to carefully read and offer both encouragement and valuable critique, as did Dr. Harry Fernhout.

Among the many teachers who have shaped my life, I honor the late Wayne Drost, principal and history teacher at London District Christian Secondary School, in 1968 a start-up school. He and the staff at LDCSS intervened in a time of personal trouble and disorientation, guiding me to see religion not as a fixed set of practices and beliefs (from which I was becoming increasingly alienated) but as a coherent way of seeing the world that could anchor me. At a much later stage, Dr. Lori Beaman took me on as a PhD student to guide my thinking about the role of religion in education in a more nuanced and disciplined way, respecting my religious commitments but challenging me to see beyond them. I joined Lori at the time she had secured funding for the Religion and Diversity Project, including me in a network of global scholars and fellow grad students. I loved the academic world through which she guided me, where I was a senior citizen and a junior scholar. These two were truly wonderful teachers who changed my life. Dr. Harry VanDyk, emeritus of Redeemer University, supervised my MA thesis back in the 1990s, which has continued to show up in the way I think about religion as a force in history. Dirk Buursma, friend and senior editor at Zondervan's, encouraged and guided me as I prepared to submit this project for publication.

Finally, I am blessed beyond measure by a family network who are in so many ways my life source. Foremost among them Cathleen, my life partner, and my children and grandchildren: Elizabeth and her late husband, Chris, and Moses; Ben and Melody, Isabelle and Char; Christy, Dane, Arie, and Annika; all of whom I am inordinately proud and who keep me grounded and in touch with the world. Then there are brothers, sisters, nieces, and nephews, lively company and fully engaged in living the religious diversity about which I think, and who remind me that there are few certainties, that we can live with ambiguities, that we do not need to panic when we do not have final answers.

The point of acknowledgments is that what you will see in this book are the outcomes of both academic and theoretical work that is embedded in the lived experience of pub nights, doing dishes and laundry, rock climbing, bike riding, and camping, the vicarious enjoyment of seeing my grandchildren and grandnieces and grandnephews develop skills and knowledge that elude me, church services where I absorbed a religious vocabulary, and where I developed a rich inner life during rituals and sermons that seemed to go on forever but whose wisdom became part of my spiritual DNA. And where enchantment and love flourish in surprising ways, feeding my spirit to this day.

Abbreviations

BBP: Building Bridges Program

CUT or GUT: Complete or Grand Unifying Theory (used interchangeably)

ERC: Ethics and Religious Culture

ODIHR: Office for Democratic Institutions and Human Rights

RE: Religion Education

SBNR: Spiritual But Not Religious

1

Introduction
A Case for Religious Literacy

RELIGIOUS LITERACY AS A MATTER OF PUBLIC INTEREST

IN 2007 THE OFFICE for Democratic Institutions and Human Rights (ODIHR) published the *Toledo Guiding Principles on Teaching About Religions and Beliefs in Public Schools*, the result of the collaborative work of the ODIHR Advisory Council of Experts on Freedom of Religion or Belief. Its purpose was to "discuss approaches to teaching about religions and beliefs in public schools in the 56-state OSCE [Organization for Security and Cooperation in Europe] region."[1] The *Toledo Guiding Principles* was only one of many policy statements, academic papers, books, and conferences addressing the intersection of religion and education after the 1980s and into the twenty-first century that have continued into the present day.[2] It seemed that the world's attention was focused on religion education (RE) after a long period in which the process of "secularization" and the marginalization of religion had seemed an inevitable result of modernization.

Examination of RE has been one theme among many in a body of literature examining the re-emergence of religion in public discourse and a reassessment of the secularization thesis in an array of academic

---

1. ODIHR, *Toledo Guiding Principles*, 11.

2. Jackson et al., *Religion in Education*; Clarke and Woodhead, *New Settlement*; Dinham and Shaw, *RE for REal*; Wertheimer, *Faith Ed.*; AAR, "Religious Literacy Guidelines"; CORE, *Religion and Worldviews*; Ellis, *Politics*.

disciplines after the 1970s.³ This book is not about the broad topic of secularization.⁴ Rather, the focus is the interest in religion and education, specifically on the politics of religious literacy and its partner, religious illiteracy, after 1990. The policy proposals and recommendations mentioned above emerged out of research initiatives around the globe about the role education might play in addressing the social role of religion and religious literacy in modern, religiously diverse societies.⁵ Religious literacy was seen as an antidote to religious illiteracy about which there had been relatively little interest until about the 1990s. Until then we did not seem to care that much whether people were religiously literate, at least not in public policy. So, what happened and what has been its impact on how we think about religion and religious literacy?

Rather than offering detailed analysis of broader cultural developments, I am asking a teacher question, which is, What is religious literacy? In other words, What does the religiously literate graduate of RE programs know that the religiously illiterate graduate does not?

WHY IS THIS IMPORTANT?

Two reasons make religious literacy an important matter of investigation. The first is that religious literacy is an element in critical thinking and therefore should be considered essential in any academic program. The second is that the advocacy for religious literacy depends on arguments that mobilize religion to achieve political and social ends that undermine its legitimacy as a partner in generating public wisdom. There is evidence that RE and religious literacy live on the margins of educational respectability in state education endeavors identified as modern and secular. This

---

3. In 1979, the Carter presidency in the USA in which President Carter identified his Christianity as an important element in his political identity and the Ayatollah Khomeini revolution in Iran were two important developments in the story of the re-emergence of religion as a political force.

4. Although it is very interesting. Much of the academic interest in the re-emergence of religion is focused on religious nationalism (after 2000), which brings together any number of factors, including a kind of religious literacy, providing narratives for historical interpretation, challenges to institutional stability, and economic competition to name a few.

5. Eickelman, "Mass Higher Education"; Jackson, *Rethinking Religious Education*; Starrett, *Putting Islam to Work*; Prothero, *Religious Literacy*; Bouma and Halafoff, "Multifaith Education"; McCowan, "Bridges"; Wertheimer, *Faith Ed.*; Hannam, "Religious Education"; Chan et al., "Recognition"; Moore, "Overcoming Religious Illiteracy."

book examines flaws in the advocacy for religious literacy that assume secularism as a normative characteristic of modernity. It proposes a more defensible rationale for religious literacy as a matter of public interest. The argument is that religious literacy is an important element in critical thinking and that we lose something valuable when it is marginalized.

WHAT IS RELIGIOUS LITERACY ANYWAY? TWO APPROACHES AND THE MARGINALIZATION OF RELIGIOUS LITERACY

The theoretical frameworks for religious literacy are provided by either the social sciences, primarily sociology, psychology, and ethnography, or by theology, which set the stage for defining preferred religious literacy outcomes. The outcomes defined within a social sciences framework are most likely to be expressed in terms of civic skills and attitudes and are most likely to be seen as secular and religiously neutral. Theological frames of reference identify outcomes in terms of familiarity with and commitment to the confessional statements, beliefs, and practices of the religion within which it occurs and are most likely seen as sectarian. The two ways of thinking about religious literacy live in a relationship of creative tension that can enrich each other but that can also be described as hostile in situations where their adherents compete for public space, legitimacy, and resources. In that sense, both theological and social sciences frameworks have political implications and, in some contexts, are political projects.

In the twenty-first century, any theoretical discussion of religious literacy, in either a social sciences or theological framework, is shaped by the malleable and contested concept of secularism in "the secular age" as examined by Charles Taylor. The acceptance of secularism as normative has implications for the legitimacy of religion as a knowledge category. The logic of secularism includes the idea that religion is primarily a private matter of choice, which means that the rationale for religious literacy as a matter of public interest cannot be sustained. There is evidence from jurisdictions around the world suggesting that the preferred civic attitudes and skills can be achieved without reference to religion and religious literacy.

Theological arguments for religious literacy are more logical but theology, the scientific study of beliefs and practices, is seen as a matter of sectarian interest. Therefore, theological arguments for religious literacy, while legitimate, cannot sustain an argument for religious literacy as a matter of public interest and investment. The logic of secularism is that in a secular age, although religion is clearly a presence in societies around the world, it cannot really be seen as a partner in generating public wisdom.

DEFINITION AS THE KEY AND AS A POLITICAL MATTER

While competition among groups about the definition of religion and religious literacy and their roles in the lives of individuals and society is usually conducted within the boundaries of civil discourse, such is not always the case when public recognition and access to resources are at stake. Competition, while normal and healthy in a democratic society, can include stereotyping of the other as a threat to social cohesion, morality, and individual self-actualization. For example, the representation of religious instruction delivered in *private faith-based* schools as disruptive threats to social cohesion and individual well-being, or the narrative that *secular public* schools are sinkholes of moral depravity, serve political purposes in conflicts over access to common space and resources but cannot withstand closer scrutiny.[6] The world is simply not that well organized along ideological and religious lines, despite the efforts to make it seem so to achieve political goals.

However, there are important differences in how religious literacy is conceptualized and defined and how those definitions are operationalized in education systems, and specifically in RE programs. Definitions of religious literacy are socially constructed, and RE programs are constructed to deliver a preferred graduate profile in which religion and religious literacy play a particular role. Definitions of religious literacy depend on definitions of literacy and of religion that have important implications for how religion is regulated and the roles it is given in the life journeys of people and in society.

---

6. I am writing this in the context of my experience in Ontario where the boundaries between "private," "separate," and "public" schools are more closely guarded and hostile than they are in other Canadian jurisdictions and on the global scene. Other jurisdictions have developed regulatory frameworks with more space for educational diversity.

INTRODUCTION

Definition is a political act of naming something that, besides stating what it is, also gives it social space, granting and withholding power and status. Timothy Fitzgerald, in his critique of religion as a legitimate knowledge category, says, "Meanings are not merely a question of definition but also of power."[7] He points to the political uses of definition in his examination of Japan and the imposition by the United States after World War II of Western Christian definitions of religion. The American interest in this exercise was to understand Japan and its imperialist adventures that collided with American imperial expansion in the Pacific. The imposition of a constitution that entrenched a religious-secular understanding of social organization was deployed as a strategy to bring Japanese institutions into line with American interests. Elizabeth Hurd identifies a similar pattern in the American definition of religious freedom, the distinctions between what counts as religion and what does not, depending on how they fit into American strategic interests.

This is not unique to America, of course. Canadian policies based on *reasonable accommodation* or the Indian Act 1876 (and it antecedent, the Gradual Civilization Act 1857)[8] are designed to bring all forms of religion into line with dominant Canadian interests. The research by Werner Schiffauer et al. on "civil enculturation" in four schools in Europe and the UK and Gregory Starrett's examination of mass education in Egypt provide further case studies of how the role of education in the management of religion relies on definitions that serve state purposes.

Definition grants permission for something to be treated in particular ways or for it to treat others in particular ways in the interest of establishing and protecting social order.[9] The global survey of RE in *The Routledge International Handbook of Religious Education* provides evidence that religion and the secular are malleable terms given content in historical and political contexts to achieve social harmony in states

7. Fitzgerald, *Ideology*, 19.
8. Hanson, "Indian Act"; CAID, "Act to Amend"; "Act to Encourage."
9. Emma Southon illustrates this in her examination of murder in ancient Rome titled *A Fatal Thing Happened on the Way to the Forum*. Her thesis is that what counted as murder (what might be considered a socially significant killing of a human being) depended on the social status of the person on the receiving end of violence. The killing of slaves amounted to property damage, sometimes necessary to keep a vast slave population in line, while the killing of family members was considered a private family matter, which might or might not attract the attention of state authorities. Her irreverent and often funny style is sobering and thought provoking, one take away being that all social and economic systems create hierarchies of status depending on definitions of who is fully human and what that might mean for permission.

and by state actors whose goal is to manage diversity. Definitions of religion and the secular serve purposes in networks of power to achieve a preferred form of society. Definitions are mobilized to achieve through persuasion accompanied by coercion, to achieve what Dalton McGuinty, erstwhile premier of Ontario, called *togetherness* in a provincial election in 2007, in which funding for non-Catholic faith-based schools became a wedge issue.[10]

The act of definition tells us what something is, but it also tells us what it is not. Definition creates its opposite. Defining religion in a particular way tells us what it is, at least in the view of the actor doing the defining. However, it also tells us what it is not, in language of "spirituality," the "secular," or "non-religion." Timothy Fitzgerald questions Ninian Smart's "conviction that 'religions' are distinctive objects in the world [which] can be found in all cultures except those that have been 'secularised.'"[11] What I understand him to be questioning is not the observation of practices and beliefs but rather what we call them or how we define them. In Fitzgerald's view, Smart's definitions create their own opposites that cannot adequately account for the cultural practices in Japan and India, forcing the complexities of Japanese and Indian life into European and Christian categories. In this case, definition is political in the sense that it is designed to achieve a longer colonial and imperialist project in a "West and the rest" tradition identified by Talal Asad, among others.

At one time in European history, Christianity was the imagined gold standard for religion, allowing the construction of non-Christian, non-European imaginaries as deficient in some way. However, within Christianity there were (and continue to be) ongoing disputes about what form of Christianity is the real gold standard, with terms such as *heresy*, *syncretism*, and *apostasy* applied to those forms that do not quite match up. In each case, definition creates its own opposite or its other with significant real-life consequences for those on either side of the fault lines. Forms of religion falling short of the gold standard are seen as threats to the social body, to be controlled in a variety of ways, some of them not all that pretty.

Social order is also served by literacy, however defined and operationalized. Johannes Fabian argues that "production signals the necessity to go beyond the confines of established sign systems; it evokes the labor

---

10. For an examination of *togetherness* see Van Arragon, "We Educate."
11. Fitzgerald, *Ideology*, 59.

INTRODUCTION

involved in creating knowledge and the elements of a discourse capable of conveying knowledge."[12] In other words, sign systems work to create and convey knowledge, but those systems also create boundaries between what counts and what does not count as knowledge with implications for what will have traction in social contexts. Literary practices are never just literary practices detached from their social contexts.[13] B. R. Ambedkar, calling for the "annihilation of caste" says that "the emancipation of the mind and the soul is a necessary preliminary for the political expansion of the people."[14] He links "reflective thought," which he says is "quite rare,"[15] to the emancipation of the mind and the soul to political change in India and the descriptions of what might happen to Dalits if they violate the restrictions of, among other things, access to the Vedas, providing a case study in demonstrating that literacy practices are never "just" literacy practices. Attempts to suppress Bible distribution by the Roman Catholic Church during the Middle Ages and by Chinese state actors suggest that literacy provides the tools and the furnishings essential to "reflective thought," which is disruptive.[16] Language and definition are among strategies used to manage disruptions to social order.

Definitions of literacy create categories of illiteracy, both of which are socially constructed, but often claim legitimacy appeal to universal principles that transcend time and space within either an immanent frame or appealing to a transcendent reality. However, Pierre Bourdieu and Jean-Claude Passeron, examining the education system in France, alert us to the implications of definitions of literacy for educational practice. They argue that definitions of literacy and the educational practices designed to deliver it cannot be seen apart from the power dynamics in the social context in which they occur.

In short, there are important issues of power involved in the act of defining religion, literacy, and religious literacy. What I am proposing is that religious literacy may, and probably should, include civic skills and attitudes and it may, and probably should, include familiarity with religious traditions. Linda Wertheimer is one of numerous voices alerting us to the consequences for communities whose members declare war

12. Fabian, *Time*, 79.
13. Fabian, *Time*, 81.
14. Ambedkar, *Annihilation*, 37.
15. Ambedkar, *Annihilation*, 89.
16. At the time of this writing, book banning is on the rise in the United States; see Stabile, "Book Banning"; Wikipedia, "Book Banning."

on each other over, among other things, religious diversity and religious literacy.[17] Civic skills and attitudes and familiarity with diverse ways of being in the world are important, essential to the creation of safe, harmonious spaces in which people can flourish.

However, the relevance of religious literacy will be marginalized if jurisdictions decide that they do not need religion to inculcate civic skills and attitudes. This is what the province of Ontario decided after 2000 when it dropped its *education about religion* initiatives developed after 1990 in favor of *character education*, issued in 2008. While I question this policy decision, it is rooted in Ontario's education history and does have a kind of logic to which Timothy Fitzgerald alludes when he observes that the concept of religion itself becomes irrelevant when detached from theology.[18]

DEFINITIONS AND THE MARGINALIZATION OF RELIGIOUS LITERACY

Here's why this is important: definitions and the differences between them have real-life consequences that deserve our critical attention. My questions about religious literacy are animated by concerns with its being defined either within the boundaries of a sectarian confessional, theological tradition, on the one hand, and in terms of civic skills and attitudes, on the other. Outcomes of religious literacy stated in terms of civic skills and attitudes leaves questions about religion itself. Is there anything about religion itself that makes it a worthwhile field of investigation? What if the preferred civic values and outcomes can be achieved

---

17. Zorica Kuburić and Christian Moe, introducing a collection of papers on RE in the Balkan states in *Religion and Pluralism in Education*, draw our attention to volatility around RE in a region where social tensions and political instability are ever present. I am always aware of the limitations of my perspectives in reading the work of scholars from different regions of the world where the social and political contexts are quite different from my own. While I have experienced some negative consequences of the politics of RE and religious literacy, I have been fortunate to live in a stable, prosperous country and region of the world and, in Isabel Wilkerson's analysis in *Caste*, I enjoy upper caste protections not available to others. Even people who disagree with me are usually pretty nice about it. Canada does have its tensions, its social and economic inequalities and injustices, but I am able to think about religious diversity without the shadow of war and violence hanging over my study. Humbling, really. However, despite the great variety in the contexts in which the research happens, there is a lot of common ground in publications from around the world about the conundrums inherent in RE.

18. Fitzgerald, *Ideology*, 8.

without reference to religion? And then, what might we lose or what are we missing if we follow the marginalization of religion in education to its logical conclusion, which is that we are not losing very much and so can make it optional or drop it all together? What are the implications of re-categorizing religion into language that contributes to its marginalizing? Quoting the author of *Ms. Muslamic* in her critique of "solidarity hijab," Liz Bucar suggests that "hijab tourism is offensive because hijab singly isn't the same without its religious context."[19] What I hear Bucar saying is that detaching practices from their religious roots has implications for our understanding the weight of their meaning in our lives. In chapter 5, I share evidence that one of the (perhaps) unintended consequences of RE programs defined in terms of civic attitudes and skills is that students and educational institutions take religion less seriously.[20]

Timothy Fitzgerald argues that "the more the researcher distances himself or herself from the explicit or implicit theological domination of 'religion,' adopting for example sociological or anthropological critical perspective, the more irrelevant the concept of religion will become."[21] Religious literacy might address social and therapeutic needs, but it is not essential if those benefits can be delivered in other ways. Taylor, discussing the history of the link between religion and a particular social and moral order, says, "The history I have just been resuming might be summed up in social science language by saying that the (latent) function of the faith in these cases has been the inculcation of a productive, adaptive character structure. This might explain why faith declines once the function has been fulfilled."[22]

On the other hand, religious literacy defined within the framework of a theological and confessional tradition raises questions of how to live well in a religiously diverse world where the goals of religion and religious literacy are invitational rather than exclusionary. Creating a world of insiders and outsiders defined along the lines of religion can marginalize outsider observations of those who might take a critical stance in relationship to religion. Insiders have a certain kind of knowing but they

---

19. Bucar, *Stealing*, 69.

20. I am using *unintended* cautiously because I am not so sure the marginalization of religion is unintended. Unacknowledged, maybe, but not unintended, perhaps. But I also know and respect friends and colleagues who advocate for religious literacy within a civics skills and attitudes framework who take religion very seriously and are frustrated by its marginalization. So, cautious about *unintended*.

21. Fitzgerald, *Ideology*, 8.

22. Taylor, *Secular Age*, 452.

are going to miss some things about their own traditions and practices that may have become normalized through familiarity and insider power politics. Foregrounding a particular confession as the ultimate source of truth can lead insiders to ignore or gloss over inconsistencies between stated confessions and social and personal behaviors that provide evidence for functional values. Insider politics and defensiveness can cover a multitude of sins as we have seen from the astonishing moral latitude given religious highflyers who have perfected the art of the public apology, invoking the language of God's forgiveness when they are caught in abuses of power and privilege.[23]

In addition, religious traditions can too rigidly control the outcomes of a spirit quest, managing doubt in a way that closes and limits rather than opening and expanding a religious imagination. In a series of lectures delivered in the 1930s, Muhammad Iqbal argued that doubt was an essential component of knowledge in Islamic religious tradition but there is evidence that his assertion has not been shared by other Muslims. The same can be said about the foregrounding of theology in any religious tradition.

Religious literacy restricted to religious traditions defined within terms set by the academic discipline of theology can lead to the conclusion that religion and religious literacy are primarily matters of private and sectarian interests, living in a hostile relationship to competitor education delivery systems, including public education. Perry Glanzer, writing about Christian post-secondary institutions in post-Communist Europe, describes "sectarian schools" as exhibiting "a more evangelical attitude." Their mission "is purposely centered on serving the church and not producing intellectuals or professionals for Romanian society."[24] George Marsden recognizes the same tendency, but suggests that "religiously based educational institutions, furthermore, can also be important contributors toward helping their supporting religious communities grow beyond narrowly sectarian, inward looking, and partisan interests."[25] Theological frameworks for religious literacy are logical but can be dismissed because of their narrow, sectarian reach and their exclusive truth claims about transcendent realities seen as harmful to personal self-realization and social cohesion.

---

23. See, for many examples, Alberta, *Kingdom*.
24. Glanzer, "Resurrecting," 175.
25. Marsden, "Renaissance," 276.

INTRODUCTION

The implications of both approaches include the marginalization of religion. The potential of religion as a public partner tends to be dissipated when religion takes on freight it cannot carry, either as a destructive anachronism or as the gatekeeper for truth. The reduction of religion to its sectarian forms has served to marginalize it in education and more broadly in society.

However, while in the secular age religion can be dismissed as a quaint sui generis category[26] with little to say in the modern world, José Mejia nuances that conclusion. Writing about "Christian Higher Education in Mexico," Mejia makes a distinction between Catholic institutions that, although they are "confessional in their history and philosophy, their emphasis tends to be in forming individual who would become effective participants in society." He contrasts that orientation with the tendency in "contemporary Protestant and evangelical institutions [that] tend to confine themselves to their denominations' more narrowly religious vocational interests."[27] While Mejia is more specifically arguing for Christian higher education, I expand his point to religion as an interpretive category that includes but is not exclusive to Christianity as a partner in generating public wisdom.

DEFINITION OF RELIGION IS KEY TO UNDERSTANDING RELIGIOUS LITERACY

My way forward is to place the idea of religious literacy in the context created by definitions of religion and literacy. What I am proposing is a model for religious literacy that draws students into understanding religion as one way to know the world and what it means in the sense that James Beckford suggests when he says that religion is "an interpretive category"[28] or, in Anthony Pinn's phrase, a "technology." Beckford argues that religion does not do anything. Rather, people do things with religion. In that sense, religion is a human capacity of knowing, like

26. Russell McCutcheon uses the term *sui generis* extensively in his extended argument rejecting religion as a legitimate theoretical knowledge category. He argues that religion has been "manufactured" as an "autonomous" category with unique, essentially mysterious characteristics that render it inaccessible to serious intellectual examination. *Manufacturing Religion*, 5. He is speaking to a way of thinking about religion exemplified by Rudolf Otto, who asserts that "the mental state is perfectly sui generis and irreducible to any other" that "cannot be strictly defined." *Idea*, 7.

27. Mejia, "Mexico," 199.

28. Beckford, *Social Theory*, 4.

science or the arts. People do things with religion, just as they do with science and art. Seeing religion as an interpretive category or a mode of human knowing creates conceptual space for students to get beyond a survey of beliefs and practices to which RE is often restricted. Anthony Pinn argues that religion, as "technology," is "a method of interrogation and exposure, with an archaeological quality to it"[29] and "a hermeneutic of sorts (a mode of interpretation or interrogation)."[30] As such, religion goes beyond *tolerance* of religious diversity, tolerance allowing us to take religion less seriously. Rather, religion lives alongside science, the arts, and other interpretive categories, modes of knowing as partners in generating public wisdom. Christopher Watkin says that "wisdom is about holding multiple perspectives together and knowing when to adopt each one."[31] Wisdom, the brass ring of education, includes the capacity to allow all interpretive categories to speak in their turn. A rainbow model of knowing truth, you might say.

Defining religion as an interpretive category or a technology begs the question of what kind of information, knowledge, and wisdom it foregrounds as a partner in interpreting the world. Beckford points us in a useful direction when he says that "religion is an interpretive category that human beings apply to a wide variety of phenomena, most of which have to do with notions of ultimate meaning or value."[32] His insight suggests that "religion" foregrounds consideration of the ways in which individuals, groups, and institutions conceptualize and operationalize their transcendent guiding principles. Pinn argues that religion as technology foregrounds "an approach, a particular framing of things."[33] Seen this way, religion and religious literacy can equip students to critically assess the ultimate values, concerns, and meaning narratives of institutions and social practices that we usually do not think of as "religious." Benjamin Berger, for example, draws our attention to "law's religion" in his examination of the dominant *aesthetic* of religion in Canadian constitutional law.[34] I am arguing that RE, delivering religious literacy, can equip us to

29. Pinn, *Interplay*, 1.
30. Pinn, *Interplay*, 3.
31. Watkin, *Biblical Critical Theory*, 335.
32. Beckford, *Social Theory*, 4.
33. Pinn, *Interplay*, 3.
34. Berger, *Law's Religion*, 41. In Berger, *aesthetic* refers to "the basic elements of sense or perception," drawing on Immanuel Kant's use of the term. When I use it in the way he does, I italicize it, using the spelling of *aesthetic* as Berger and others use it. In

see the everyday world as *problematic*[35] through the interpretive category that foregrounds ultimate values and meaning narratives. In addition, religion provides ways in which individuals construct their own personal journeys, imagining their lives as spirit quests.

This is where religion and education are inextricably intertwined, education being a more or less organized social practice designed to deliver the accumulated wisdom on which our worlds rest.[36] The "Why do we have to take this stuff" question expressed at the most inconvenient times is one that every teacher must engage. Teachers develop their own conversation stoppers, including "You have to take this stuff because I have a family to support," but we do have to get beyond that level of response. Students are asking a serious question that deserves serious consideration. The question is, What is the ultimate meaning of what we are doing here? or some other form of what Volf et al. call The Question.[37] Even if they sometimes are trying to derail your fascinating explanation of binomial theory, sooner or later teachers must face that question for their students and for themselves. Literacy includes thinking about our collective and individual lives in terms of what ultimately animates them. Building on Ben Berger's insights about Canadian law, I am arguing that literacy and the education practices designed to deliver literacy cannot avoid *education's religion*. Students are on a spirit quest, and we do them a disservice if we ignore their need to understand their own lives and the social practices and institutions in their world in terms of their ultimate values and meaning.

---

places I use "esthetic" where it is not so directly linked to a particular source.

35. I am borrowing *problematic* from Dorothy Smith, *Everyday World as Problematic*, whose feminist perspective encouraged us to see behind the normalization of male domination of sociology that backgrounded the voices of women. Ben Berger, *Law's Religion*, does something similar with religion in Canadian constitutional law that uses the language of "secular neutrality" to mask its own religious esthetic. I am calling for critical attention to the marginalization of religion in education and the esthetics in RE programs, the problematics of which are masked by the language of "religious neutrality" and "objectivity."

36. I am using *social practice* theorized by Norman Fairclough as "a more or less stabilized form of social activity." Fairclough, "Discourse of New Labour," 234.

37. Volf et al., *Life*, xv.

A CASE FOR RELIGIOUS LITERACY

While acknowledging the contributions of both civic skills and theological frameworks for education, I argue that we must get beyond them to develop a sustainable argument for religious literacy as a public good. I propose the purpose of RE is to deliver religious literacy as an essential contributor to public wisdom by providing students with the skills, sensitivities, and knowledge base to understand the ultimate concerns, values, and commitments that animate people, individually and collectively. It deserves consistent investment of public resources and space.

I am not advocating for RE as part of a process of conversion into a particular tradition nor am I foregrounding the role of RE in delivering civic skills and attitudes considered essential in the delivery of a model of social harmony. Those outcomes may be legitimate components of RE initiatives. However, they are not unique to RE, all education being transformative in the sense that educators take their students along a developmental path toward preferred skills, attitudes, and beliefs. At the same time, schools are not primarily institutions for the conversion of a captive audience but rather engage in "influence."[38] Education is more nuanced, providing a laboratory for people to take some distance from what they think and know to understand it more deeply.

Religious literacy should be (and in fact is, either explicitly or implicitly) on the table of all schools, because all education is animated by transcendent concerns, values, and commitments. All schools are *faith-based* or *confessional*. Therefore, I reject the distinction between religion and secular and between public and private as meaningful ways to think about education and the public legitimacy of education systems. Robert Jackson's definition of *confessional* quoted by Joachim Willems[39] is useful but does not go far enough, creating a distinction between two forms of education, the one "secular and non-confessional" sponsored by the state, the other "religious and confessional" sponsored by a "religious body." In education, as in life, the distinction cannot withstand scrutiny, all schools operating under the care of an organization energized by transcendent values and by strategies that nurture "faith" in the students in their care.

At the same time, all education is a public social practice, which must be held accountable because of its profound implications for society. There are multiple stakeholders who see education through the

---

38. Lewin, "After Religious Education."
39. Willems, "Fundamental Right," 27.

screen of their own perspectives. However, those perspectives must be held in partnership marked by creative tensions. Children are embedded in a network of relationships involving partners invested in the outcome of their nurture. Families are not private even though they are most intimate and foundational in the care and nurture of children. States and state actors have a legitimate role in the lives of children, including in the regulation of education that is one social practice characterized by a good deal of creative tension as partners find their respective roles. Colin Bloom's summary of attempts by the government in the UK to regulate homeschooling and education delivered in non-state settings gives us a glimpse into the complexities of developing systems of accountability through regulation and inspection that protect children while respecting the freedoms of educational choice for families. His comment that "it is a difficult subject" seems like an understatement.[40]

Despite the complexities inherent in its regulation, I argue that all education is faith based, and all education is public. I agree with Norberto Padilla when he describes as a "false dichotomy" the "opposition has been shown between free-of-charge, secular, and obligatory education on one side and a paid (privileged) and confessional one on the other." He argues that "education was defined as being always public; management might be different in public and private schools, but in principle all education is always of public interest."[41] At the same time, *public* does not mean *secular* and state-sponsored activity, while at best is fair in its treatment of religious diversity, is not *religiously neutral*. Education is animated by its own religious *aesthetic*.

ORGANIZATION AROUND THREE QUESTIONS

The first question is, What is religion?, the topic of chapter 2. Although common usage of the term refers to a transcendent reality usually associated with the gods or God, closer examination suggests that religion is more complex and less easily limited in the ways it is often defined. Because education and literacy are concerned with information, knowledge, and wisdom, RE and religious literacy are about the question, What kind of information, knowledge, and wisdom is generated by and within the interpretive category of religion? Another way to think about this is

---

40. Bloom, *Review*, 77.
41. Padillo, "Argentina," 17.

to ask, What aspect of human life and human knowing is foregrounded by religion? A further theme in this chapter is the social and political context in which religion is defined, and what purposes are served by definitions of religion. In subsequent chapters, the same question is applied to definitions of literacy and of religious literacy. I draw on James Beckford's definition of religion as "an interpretive category," which he develops as a sociologist with a focus on how people construct their religions. Another way to think about religion is that it is a kind of consciousness unique to humans, including a sense of time and the conundrums inherent in our consciousness of the passage of time.

Chapter 3 examines three objections to religion closely linked to definitions of religion that are particularly relevant to education. The first objection is to the *institutionalization* and *codification* of religion and spirituality that represents a threat to individual self-expression and agency. In education, religion is often linked to indoctrination and coercion, forms of pedagogical violence that have been called out in case law starting in the 1960s.

The second objection to religion is that it is essentially *irrational* and even *pathological* and therefore an impediment to the fully realized person. The New Atheist position on religion is on the extreme end of a continuum of assessments of religion and has been subjected to critical scrutiny but it continues to resonate in conversations about religion in a variety of ways.

The third objection, that religion is inherently *exclusive* and therefore a threat to social cohesion, finds its most clear expression in the state-sponsored interest in religious literacy.[42] The three objections to religion provide insight into RE programs that are, among other things, designed to address harm done by abuses of power narrated in the language of religion. However, objections to religion are also socially and historically situated and have themselves been subjected to critical scrutiny.[43]

There is no doubt that the term *religion* carries a great deal of cultural baggage that has inspired proposals for alternative terms and concepts, the subject of the concluding part of chapter 3. Alternatives include the ideas of the *spiritual but not religious* (SBNR), *lived religion, worldview, spirituality, cultural studies, values, shared narratives,* and

---

42. See, for example, ODIHR, *Toledo Guiding Principles*.

43. Rizzuto, *Birth*; Barnes, *Education, Religion and Diversity*; Van Arragon, "Contested Borders"; Gray, *Seven Types*; Wolterstorff, *Religion in the University*.

faith. Non-religion has emerged in the last decade as the subject of religious studies and the *church for people who don't like church* movement.[44]

However, objections to religion and the constructions of alternatives to religion are contextual, shaped by the logic inherent in secularism, accepted as normative in the secular age, and must be subjected to critical scrutiny of their underlying assumptions about religion but also about the nature and source of truth. Truth and truth claims in the language of religion are often linked to coercion, violence, and irrationality but, while those links deserve serious consideration, they also have their own religious esthetic.

Chapter 4, "Literacy," is organized around three questions, the first of which is, What is literacy? My argument is that competence in literacy includes the three *R*'s but does not end there. Rather, examination of definitions of literacy by UNESCO and selected Ministries of Education in Canadian jurisdictions adds *meaning* to understanding the personal and social implications of what is being heard, read, and seen. At the heart of literacy are questions of what it means *to know* something, which includes what it means to think well, to seek the truth or a true way of seeing the world. Literacy does not occur in the abstract. Rather, it and the story tellers delivering literacy are shaping a narrative about the world and the human journey in it in a context shaped by social and political networks designed to achieve an end.[45]

The search for truth in any meaningful sense involves appeals to *evidence*. Thinking well is the ability to base conclusions on evidence. This is obvious in the sciences where the scientific method is the widely accepted method of accepting evidence and rejecting anything that does not meet evidentiary standards or can be falsified. A different method of arriving at truth is at play in courts where legal matters are adjudicated to establish guilt or innocence. Neither method is foolproof, as we see in both science and in law, but the processes are well established. This is less so in religion where the contours of thinking well in terms of evidence are more contested and less clearly established. In any case, issues of thinking well based on evidence to arrive at something resembling truth is unique to each interpretive category. In addition, what is accepted as a legitimate way to establish truth in one historical, social, and political

44. Vaters, "11 Ways."

45. Social and political networks always involve "power," organized and operationalized in multiple ways, only some of which are formally organized, stable, and easily visible.

context or what is accepted as evidence are not universal. In other words, evidence and the methods to arrive at truth are socially constructed. The literate person is one who understands the methods of arriving at truth at play in particular situations and the cultural language around those methods.

The second question, engaging issues of power, is, What is the relationship between literacy and social order? Literacy lives at the intersection of freedom and social order. Definitions of literacy include *critical thought*, which is the *moral* aspect of literacy in the sense that literacy includes critical evaluation of what is true and untrue, right and wrong, good and evil. However, critical thought and literacy have unintended consequences because students will critically evaluate the literacy and education practices to which they are being subjected. Students will, to our dismay, bite the benevolent pedagogical hand that feeds them. Gregory Starrett's research in Egypt, Dale Eickelman's in Oman, and Albert Raboteau demonstrate the unintended consequences of education and literacy. The report of the Committee on Religious Instruction in the Public Schools of the Province of Ontario titled *Religious Information and Moral Development* (hereafter the *Mackay Report* or *Mackay*), tabled in 1969, recommended the adoption of *education about religion* to replace *religious instruction* in public schools. It advocated for student freedom of choice in education and, at the same time, reflected anxiety over the implications of students taking freedom of critical thought to some less desirable conclusions.[46] The point is that literacy and illiteracy are closely linked to social order and disruption or *civility* and *barbarity*.[47]

The third question is, What are the social networks within which literacy and illiteracy are linked to social order and disorder? Education as a social practice is designed to manage doubt and to adopt faith in a reliable platform for information, knowledge, and wisdom. Education and its preferred outcomes are conceptualized and operationalized by multiple actors, each with their own unique perspective on relevant information, meaningful knowledge, and wisdom. In principle, educators want students to be free and critical thinkers, but they are also anxious about the implications of the potential consequences of freedom and critical thought. Therefore, decisions about literacy are political, occurring in a

---

46. See Van Arragon, "We Educate," for a more detailed examination of *Mackay*.
47. Fitzgerald, *Discourse*.

INTRODUCTION

network of social relations designed to achieve a preferred graduate who will play a constructive role as an actor in a social context.

Chapter 5, titled "Religious Literacy: An Educational Paradox in Two Parts," addresses the overall question, What is religious literacy? by exploring the difference between religious literacy and illiteracy. The first paradox is inherent in religion, specifically that religion is the human capacity to reach for truths that are always elusive. The second paradox is inherent in literacy, living as it does at the nexus of doubt and faith. In religious literacy, we engage an interpretive category that takes us to truths we can never fully understand, to places of trust and dependability about which we want our students to think intelligently and critically without landing in a nihilistic intellectual and spiritual wasteland.

Chapter 5 is organized around three questions. The first question addresses the distinction between religious literacy and religious illiteracy, asking, What social, political, and intellectual work is done by the distinction between religious literacy and illiteracy? I argue that the distinction is contextual and that, among other things, it serves state purposes in the achievement of a preferred social order.

The second question is, What is the social context in which an oppositional relationship between religious literacy and religious illiteracy is constructed and in which it is given significance? The argument is that conversations about religious literacy occur in the context of anxiety about social cohesion, in which religious illiteracy is linked to social disruption to be addressed by religious literacy, however defined.

The third question is, What is the intellectual context in which the distinction between religious literacy and religious illiteracy is given its significance? The intellectual context is shaped by the elusive and malleable concept of *secularism*, operating with its own logic with implications for the ways in which religion and religious literacy are conceptualized and managed. Secularism has been the subject of increasing critical scrutiny by, among others, Charles Taylor and Hussein Ali Agrama, whose work, while not specifically about religious literacy, has implications for understanding a logic of secularism and the status of religion as a way of knowing and for religious literacy.

Ambiguities about religion and religious literacy in a social context of anxiety and an intellectual context of secularism have created a logic for the marginalization of religion and religious literacy in the world of education. I examine the marginalization of religion and religious literacy in three steps. The first is examination of the consensus that *religious literacy is preferable to religious illiteracy*. The second is analyzing *important differences within the consensus over the purpose and preferred outcomes of religious literacy*. The third is tracing the fact that *the consensus about the importance of religious literacy is not widely shared among educators except in faith schools*. There is evidence of frustration about the lack of commitment among educators to religious literacy and RE.[48] We hear disappointment in the ineffectiveness of religious literacy projects.[49] We see jurisdictions, having experimented with RE and religious literacy, moving away from a focus on RE and onto other projects to achieve their educational goals.[50] The question is, Why is religious illiteracy not widely accepted as a source of social harm and why are arguments for religious literacy not persuasive to most educators?

I argue that the logic of secularism includes the belief that religion is primarily a matter of private beliefs and practices. The logical outcome is the marginalization of religion and religious literacy as a matter of public interest that should not surprise anyone. However, I argue that the marginalization of religion and religious literacy leaves an important gap in the development of critical awareness and thinking, both in the ways students engage their spirit quests and in their ability to navigate their worlds. Therefore, a case for religious literacy depends on critical reassessment of the religious-secular binary and its logic, which takes us to chapter 6.

Chapter 6 addresses a fourth question about religious literacy in response to its marginalization in education. Question four is, What might an alternative to a social sciences or a theological framework for religious literacy look like that would support a case for religious literacy as a public good?

The chapter makes a case that religious literacy is a matter of public interest, delivering two gifts to the educational achievement of critical thought. I build on James Beckford's idea that religion is an *interpretive category* to argue that religion is a capacity inherent in human beings to imagine a transcendent (either vertical or horizontal) point of reference. A transcendent point of reference serves as a guiding star in a "hierarchical organization of directive, value, and sanctity" where we "note a

---

48. Dinham and Shaw, *RE for REal*; Moore, "Overcoming Religious Illiteracy"; Prothero, *Religious Literacy*; Clarke and Woodhead, *New Settlement* (2015).

49. Mwale et al., "Zambia"; Barnes, *Education, Religion and Diversity*; McCowan, "Bridges"; Wertheimer, *Faith Ed.*, ch. 7.

50. Zambia, Ontario, and Quebec, among others.

progression away from material or concrete regulatory values towards values which seem increasingly ideological."[51] Science, often considered the model for rational thinking, tells us how the world works but it cannot tell us why it does or why we are here.[52] The capacity to ask *why* questions of ultimate meaning and destiny and to formulate answers is religion or the religious aspect of human nature. I argue that sensitivity to and skills in navigating that most important aspect of their lives are essential to student flourishing.

In that sense, religious literacy is an essential element in critical thought. Its being defined in either theological or social sciences frameworks in a secular age has contributed to its being marginalized, an unfortunate development that deprives students of an important way of knowing the world and their place in it.

Chapter 7 looks at religious literacy from the perspective of the difference in status between universal questions and their socially constructed and historically situated answers. Confusion and ambiguity in the world of religious literacy and the marginalization of religion is due, in part at least, to insufficient attention given to the fact that questions of ultimate meaning and destiny and the capacity to ask and answer them are inherent in human nature. The logic of secularism is that ultimate questions and their socially constructed answers are essentially private matters that should not interfere with public interest in the smooth operation of the marketplace. However, in 2025 we are seeing evidence that the construction of boundaries between secular public and religious private spaces is less viable and more porous than we may have imagined. Universal questions have a way of demanding attention is all spaces and times around issues that may not seem to be related to religion. The distinction between universal questions and socially constructed answers is essential to making a case for religious literacy as a public good.

VOICE, AUDIENCE, AND LIMITATIONS

I am writing, in the first place, as an academic interested in theory enriched by my thirty-seven-year professional life in education, serving as teacher, school principal, and curriculum developer at both primary and secondary levels of schooling. As I reflect on religion and religious

---

51. Rappaport, *Ritual*, 425–26.
52. Gray, *Seven Types*; Greene, *Time*; Hossenfelder, *Existential Physics*.

literacy, I have in mind my students, what they need to know, and who they will become as fully realized human beings. I think in terms of a *graduate profile* as the inspiration for what we do as teachers and schools, or the end or ultimate purpose of education. Education is a dynamic practice in which students are expected to change over time, to become more of who they are meant to be or, perhaps more accurately, who we, their educators, think they are meant to be. Educators work with their students for a limited time after which they move on, but whether in kindergarten, in their final year of high school, or in university, educators work toward a preferred graduate profile.

I am sensitive to developmental issues and what may or may not be developmentally appropriate for students. However, I do not address pedagogical and developmental issues in this book. Rather, I am asking questions related to what we mean by the *religiously literate graduate* who we hope to see at the end of the educational process and the political and social contexts in which those questions are decided. The questions animating my reflections are theoretical ones about the intellectual, social, and political contexts in which questions about education are asked and resolved. Therefore, my primary audience is my academic friends and colleagues who have done so much to challenge my thinking but who I also want to challenge. I question their acceptance of distinctions between RE and religious education (or some iteration of the same binary), based on the idea that RE is more objective and neutral and therefore a more dependable platform for public discourse on religion. I invite them to see the problematics of a religious-secular intellectual and social model in which religion tends to be privatized. I invite them to question the emergence of state actors represented as religiously neutral and the role of state schools as religious actors in achieving a graduate profile preferred by states.

My secondary audience includes teachers, principals, program directors, and curriculum developers engaged in active service. I am interested in big picture educational issues that need to be front and center for all educators around the question of the ends or ultimate purposes of our efforts in education. However, classroom teachers are practitioners who tend not to lead with theoretical consideration of the nature of religion and literacy. Fascination with theoretical issues does not necessarily make better teachers, just as being an expert in political theory may not make one a successful politician. Teaching, like practical politics and health care, is essentially a pastoral practice (or, perhaps, a complex of practices) in the sense that its primary concern is the care of people at whatever stage of development teachers meet them. Nevertheless, teachers do need to be *reflective practitioners*, which involves thinking about their practice on multiple levels. What I am doing here is not designed to make my readers better teachers in a technical sense. The young teachers with whom I interact in a professional capacity are better trained and better at their craft than I was when I entered the profession back in 1973. Rather, what I offer here is consideration of literacy and religion that might add to their reflections about their professional practice. Academic and theoretical reflection is not the only key to more effective practice, but it is an important part of the conceptual scaffolding of which teachers need to be aware.

    I have worked in Ontario, Canada, in a privately funded Christian school system, which has given me an intimate and often conflicted awareness of the politics of religion and education in Ontario.[53] My doctoral research and thesis are a sociopolitical analysis of Ontario's regulation of religion and religious diversity in public education. The research for this book develops some of the broader implications of that work for religious literacy and its delivery.

---

53. Van Arragon, "We Educate"; "Epistemology"; "Conflicted Partnership."

2

Religion

DEFINING RELIGION

So, what is religion anyway? The question of religion is central to our thinking about religious literacy and the educational practices designed to deliver it. No educational endeavor can proceed without defining what it is that we are talking about and what we want our students to know about it. This book is about religious literacy and RE, so we must think about religion, entering the contested and risky world of definitions. In chapters 5 and 6 we put literacy and religion together to think about religious literacy and the social practice of RE designed to deliver it. But first, religion.

SOME PROBLEMS IN DEFINING RELIGION

A Confusion of Voices

The definition of religion seems straightforward in the sense that the term, like *science* and *art*, is ubiquitous in our world. We use the term and assume we know what it means. One example to get us started is Raymond VanArragon's telling us that, commonly understood, "religion is a phenomenon with which we're all familiar. It typically involves acknowledgement of a divine reality and the requirement of obedience to it; it includes rites and ceremonies that mark the human relation to this reality, and it has enormous impact on the way that its adherents see the world and their place in it."¹ Timothy Fitzgerald's rejection of religion as a distinct theoretical category relies on his identifying a "major assumption" that religion is universal, involving a "claim about human responses to the divine or the transcendent."² Jerry Coyne basically agrees with the common understanding described by VanArragon and Fitzgerald, drawing on the Oxford English Dictionary where he finds that religion is "action or conduct indicating belief in, obedience to, and reverence for a god, gods, or similar superhuman power; the performance of religious rites or observances."³ L. Philip Barnes bases his argument for the link between moral and religion education on the use of the term *religion* "in the context of belief in a transcendent or supernatural reality that is regarded as unconditionally and non-dependently real, and as such, should be regarded (in a stipulative sense), as 'divine.'" He goes on to say that religion includes "a distinctive account of the nature of the divine that is integrated into a wider form of life."⁴ In short, they agree that *religion* refers to beliefs and practices to honor some transcendent reality we might or might not call the *gods*.

Within the agreement about its definition there are differences in understanding the social and personal role of religion that have important implications for how we think about religious literacy and RE. Jerry Coyne disputes the legitimacy of religion as a source of knowledge and inspiration. For him, religion is a harmful anachronism that needs to be discarded in the modern world, an argument common among some high-profile New Atheists where he places himself.⁵ In another assessment of religion, Barnes links religion to morality to establish its legitimacy in education. Losing religion undermines the basis for a moral code, at least in Barnes's view. VanArragon assumes the validity of religion as an analytical category, his philosophical interest being in what is included in the term, its precise definition, and theological arguments based on

1. VanArragon, *Key Terms*, 1.
2. Fitzgerald, *Ideology*, 3.
3. Coyne, *Faith vs. Fact*, 41.
4. Barnes, *Education, Religion and Diversity*, 121.
5. The New Atheist voices, with their tendency to be extreme in their denunciations of religion, have been subjected to critical scrutiny from a variety of corners in the religious studies world, including others self-identifying as atheists. John Gray, *Seven Types*, for example, describes the New Atheism as a "nineteenth-century orthodoxy," rejecting it as a viable way to think about religion and atheism. However, I have found that New Atheist thinking, like extreme creationist voices, shows up in surprising ways in discussions about education and religion.

evidence. Fitzgerald's critical analysis directs our attention to the academic discipline of religious studies, objecting to the idea that religion is an analytical category with its own discrete place among other social sciences when he argues that "there is no coherent non-theological theoretical basis for the study of religion as a separate academic discipline." He also disputes the assumption that "religion is a universal phenomenon to be found in principle in all culture and all human experience."[6]

We have parallel conversations, one dismissing religion as a legitimate way of knowing in the modern world, the second arguing that religion and morality cannot be separated without violence to both, a third about religion defined in terms of its philosophical and theological boundaries, and a fourth conversation questioning religion as an analytical category and discrete academic discipline.

The differences in assessments have important implications for religious literacy programs, among them the question of why educators and academics should even be thinking about religious literacy in the first place. Why might we want our graduates to be religiously literate? The first conversation might well lead to the conclusion that religious literacy, if it has any value at all, should include skepticism about and rejection of religion in favor of science. The second argument assumes a particular answer to the *Can we be good without god?* question, the implication being that without religion, our students will become unmoored in a world of moral relativism. The third conversation might lead to a definition of religious literacy as familiarity with theological terms and arguments such as proofs of God, the doctrine of transubstantiation, and competing interpretations of the Qur'an. The fourth conversation will include the question of what we are talking about when we talk about religion and whether we need it at all as a distinct theoretical category.[7]

These conversations live in an uneasy relationship in most religious education programs. In other words, we cannot quite make up our minds about what we are trying to achieve with our religious education programs because we do not have agreement of what religion is, what social practices it includes, or about its role in a modern imaginary.[8]

---

6. Fitzgerald, *Ideology*, 3.

7. Robert Jackson provides a summary of the terminological complexity in *Signposts*, ch. 3.

8. I am using *imaginary* in the way proposed by Charles Taylor by which he means "something much broader and deeper than the intellectual schemes people may entertain when they think about social reality in a disengaged mode." *Modern Social*

Charles Clarke and Linda Woodhead suggest that "confusion about the whole purpose of the subject" is a factor in undermining a case for RE in UK schools.[9] Education being the social practice to achieve literacy, educators are left with the question of what kind of literacy is generated by or foregrounded in religion.

Timothy McCowan observes that the RE program in Melbourne Australia is rendered less attractive over the *So what* question, supporting his conclusions on interviews with teachers who expressed confusion over its overall purpose.[10] In short, we do not have a consensus about the enduring takeaways about religion for the graduates of an RE program, which undermines a coherent and persuasive case for the value of religion and religious literacy.

Ambiguity About Religion in Liberal Democracies

A complicating factor is that religion has an ambiguous role in liberal democracies because, on the one hand, religious freedom is seen as a marker distinguishing liberal from non-liberal regimes.[11] On the other hand, religion seems out of step with modernity in a secular age in three ways. The first is that modernity is linked to a consensus that public discourse must be *rational* in some way, based on evidence achieved through science and the rigorous testing by generally accepted methods. Religion, especially the forms resting on belief in a transcendent reality, seems irrational, or at least nonrational, and besides that, carries a complicated legacy of abuses of power. The second way religion seems anachronistic in a modern society is that it is associated with institutional authority that is offensive to the idea of the self-actualizing individual. This has salience in an environment in which the individual is seen as the ultimate source of truth and moral authority. The third source of ambiguity about religion is that religious truth claims are seen to be inherently exclusive and socially divisive, with potentially disruptive and even violent implications. Religious truth claims are seen to be what we do not need in a world already badly divided and at war over any number of issues. We

---

Imaginaries, 23. Timothy Stacey, *Saving Liberalism from Itself*, draws on Taylor's use of imaginary in his critical examination of liberalism.

9. Clarke and Woodhead, *New Settlement* (2015), 30.

10. McCowan, "Bridges," 207.

11. I further examine the ambiguities around religion in chapter 3, "Objections to Religion."

need unity and cohesion that true believers seem willing to sacrifice in favor of their own version of the truth.

There are ways of dealing with the ambiguities inherent in the role of religion in modern societies, one of which is to think of religion as a matter of private and individual choice so that it does not interfere with public discourse in common spaces. The other is to associate religion with an earlier time when tradition sustained through coercive indoctrination was accepted as normal. Modernity is narrated in a secular, progressive narrative of freedom and equality in which religion will give way to individualized spirituality. *Spirituality* fits more comfortably in a narrative of secular modernity and postmodernity because it can be seen as one way among many in which individuals can express their authentic selves, and it can live in privatized parallel spaces without transgressing into common or public spaces. One implication is that while all of us may be spiritual in some way, not all of us are religious.

However, religion is not going anywhere and, in fact, in the late twentieth and early twenty-first centuries we are seeing a resurgence of energized voices demanding a space for religion in public discourses and in the development of public policy.[12] Charles Taylor observes that, depending on how it is defined, there is evidence that, "if you cast your net even wider and think of someone's religion as the shape of their ultimate concern, then indeed, one can make a case that religion is as present as ever."[13] There is evidence that, although religion in a traditional sense may have been marginalized, religion seen outside the boundaries placed on it by common definitions has continued to be an important factor in human affairs. In fact, we cannot understand human affairs without reference to the ultimate values and concerns at play, even in those practices and products we usually do not think of as having anything to do with religion. We must talk about religion, and we will start with four observations about the common usage of the term.

Four Observations

Four observations about the common usage of religion complicate the picture in ways that have important implications for consideration of religious literacy and the RE projects designed to deliver it. The first three

12. Casanova, *Public Religions*; Dinham et al., "Towards a Theory"
13. Taylor, *Secular Age*, 427.

are specifically about the definition of religion, followed by questions related to the implications of those definitions for religious literacy.

A. An immediate challenge to the common usage is that there are forms of religion that do not include a transcendent divine, the most common among the *world religions* being Buddhism and some forms of Unitarianism. Even among religions that feature gods or God, there is a lot of variety about what that means. An example includes the Hindu gods who look quite different from the gods in other societies or God in the monotheistic Abrahamic traditions. The fact that much of what looks like religion does not include gods has contributed to confusion in the theoretical study of religion, narratives about it shifting from theology to several competing sciences and theoretical models. Timothy Fitzgerald observes, "A whole range of institutions that do not involve belief or God or even the supernatural are also called religions or at least religious."[14] The link between religion and the divine is not as predictable as we might have thought from the common usage of religion.

B. A related complication is that there are beliefs and practices that look and act like religion, but which are not exactly religious under the common usage definition. An example might be rituals involving transitions of power after an American election that are most obviously political, but include references to transcendent values, including references to God. In Canada, although we give the nod to God in our constitutional frameworks, what gets Canadians really exercised is any perception that our equality and inclusion principles are being violated in, for example, delivery of essential services such as education and health care. *Equality* and *inclusion* are transcendent values but are they religious? The intensity of reactions to hints of privilege and *two-tier* systems in Canadian public policy debates suggest that we are talking about transcendent values rather than pragmatic social and political arrangements for the delivery of services.[15] Benedict Anderson argues persuasively that nationalism is religious in all but name, saying the nation as

---

14. Fitzgerald, *Ideology*, 72.

15. In the Canadian federal election of 2021, the Trudeau Liberals were criticized for manipulating a video to suggest that Erin O'Toole, leader of the Conservative Party and prime ministerial hopeful, was going to undermine Canada's universal health care system by introducing for-profit health services. Equality of access is a key, transcendent Canadian value with considerable political traction. Yun, "Trudeau Defends."

an imagined community unified by transcendent values and rituals closely resemble churches and other collectives we more easily identify as religious.[16]

C. A third and related theoretical issue is the lack of clarity between what practices are considered religious and which ones are more appropriately considered social, political, ethical, or economic, to name just a few other theoretical categories. The point here is that once you define something, you must consider what can be included and what does not make the cut. Even a broad framework such as *family resemblance* raises questions of what part of the family is religious and what is not. Life cannot be so easily divided between what is religious, social, political, and just plain neighborly. The *gurdwara* in my Ottawa neighborhood is a social gathering place, a school, a food kitchen, and it provides transportation services for those who need them. Churches raise money to address world hunger, sponsor refugees, engage in advocacy for the homeless, support prison rehabilitation services, and participate in clean ups of local parks and streets. My devout Muslim neighbor tells me that, based on the Qur'an, his obligations to seven of his neighbors in any direction take precedence over his obligations to his brother in Lebanon. Many of these activities and values are accompanied by prayers, incorporated into religious rituals, and are narrated in religious language, but are they religious? Well, yes and no because the question cannot be answered in the way it is asked.

We can see another example of the ambiguous boundary around religion in the work of Philip Hadot who identifies *philosophy as a way of life*, examining the philosophical "spiritual exercises from Socrates to Foucault."[17] In theoretical physics, Stephen Hawking's work is, at times, difficult to distinguish from writings in religion. Is Hinduism a religion? Or Buddhism? What counts as religion depends on our definitions, which is more than an intellectual exercise. Definition provides a screen for what we can see and then it shapes our interpretation of what we see by foregrounding some things and backgrounding others. We gather data to tell a story but, as Timothy Fitzgerald says, "one cannot know how to interpret that

---

16. Anderson, *Imagined Communities*, 9–11.
17. The subtitle of his book *Philosophy as a Way of Life*.

data, or decide what is significant and what is trivial if one does not know how to place it in a wider context."[18]

Theology has been replaced by sociology, psychology, and anthropology as the leading academic disciplines in religious studies, foregrounding the social construction of religion and the roles it plays in society and in the life of an individual. However, Fitzgerald observes that even in religious studies there is little agreement about what religion is.[19] He questions Ninian Smart's reference to *dimensions* to nuance what we mean by religion, saying, "One problem with the dimensions is that the differences between, say, the ethical, the ritual and the experiential can seem rather arbitrary." With reference to practices exercised by Zen monks "setting out to tidy the grounds of the monastery," a "photo of a Zimbabwean exorcist," and a "photo of a Jewish family celebrating Passover," he says, "Surely they are all social and all ritual and all experiential."[20] While I agree with Fitzgerald's assessment of traditional definitions of religion, I part company with his conclusion that the category of religion as a way of knowing has nothing meaningful to offer. Rather, religion and religious literacy are unique ways of knowing that need to be cultivated in education.

The conclusion is that the definition of religion is not as straightforward as it seems from popular and academic usage of the term and that some of the definitions can lead some of us to reject religion as an analytical category altogether. In both our lived experience and in our theorizing about it, religion is a more elusive theoretical category than you might have expected. This takes us beyond the theoretical issues to their implication for education and literacy.

D. The fourth complicating question includes those related to what should be included in an RE program so that its graduates are religiously literate. In addition, we have questions about the role religions and religious modes of thought might or might not play in a fully realized citizen in a modern society. There are two issues at play here. The first is that schools and education endeavors have their hands, budgets, and timetables full of the challenges of getting students ready for successful entry into the modern world.

---

18. Fitzgerald, *Ideology*, 211.
19. Fitzgerald, *Ideology*, 6.
20. Fitzgerald, *Ideology*, 60.

You must be convinced that spending time and money on religion and religious literacy is a useful allocation of public resources in achieving that purpose. Just what kind of knowledge does religion generate that might be useful, essential even, to our graduates and their futures? Schools must make choices. Why should religion and religious literacy make the cut?

Even if we agree that RE has survived the hurdles of administrative choices, we are still left with the question of what should be included in the program. A world religions model offers astonishing possibilities because there are so many religions and variations on any one of them. How do you choose and who do you leave out? The choices we make in an RE program take us to a more fundamental issue in education, which is why we should concern ourselves with religion at all.

Good reasons to avoid precise definition of religion

I am not assuming that debating definitions of religion is high on the list of a teacher's priorities. In fact, there are some good reasons we would rather avoid the questions of precise definition, going where even the angels in our lives hesitate. In addition to theoretical ambiguities and identity confusion, we feel strongly about religion so avoiding it is a way to protect social harmony on any level. We disagree about religion in any number of ways, including which forms of religion are closer and which ones are further from truth and about whether we are all religious in some way. Putting religion on the table is risky, especially in state-sponsored public schools that are expected to serve a religiously diverse population.

In Christian schools (or at least some of them) there are good political reasons for not defining religion or the right form of it too precisely. The general identity category of Christian provides enough common ground that might be threatened by defining too closely the different theological forms of it among those making use of its services. The same thing could be said of public schools identifying themselves as *secular*, where controversies over the distribution of Gideon Bibles, clothing, prayer spaces, and smudging ceremonies tend to become animated. Jasmin Zine observed similar tensions in Islamic schools in Toronto that served students from a wide range of backgrounds and traditions, creating tensions over what constituted a true rendering of Islam. So, better to leave the definition of religion alone.

Political reasons aside, precisely defining religion is not something working teachers want to take on. Teachers want to get on with the job of teaching, caring for students who come into their classroom with a challenging and interesting array of social, psychological, and learning needs. This is especially true in religion that usually has ambiguous status in schools, particularly in academic programs and in our personal and collective lives. The descriptor *sensitive* shows up quite a lot in policy proposals about RE, giving us a hint of its potential as a catalyst for social disruption that we do not see in, say, mathematics or physics. The wrong approach can be career limiting, especially in a time of heightened tensions and decreased social resilience as teachers engage their students who come to their classrooms equipped with cell phones and cameras.[21] Timothy Fitzgerald suggests this when he says, "If we find the definitional problem too elusive, the fatal attitude is to yawn and say, 'I just want to get on with the job in hand and not get involved in pointless abstract definitional arguments that have no clear solution.'"[22]

However, a Case for Precise Definition

Nevertheless, a clear definition of religion is important for three reasons. The first is theoretical, specifically that the common usage of the term masks considerable confusion among religious studies scholars about what religion is, what should be included in the category, and what the enduring attitudinal takeaways should be in the graduate profile. In responding to students, schools decide, either explicitly or implicitly, on the space and time they will allow for the expression of religion, navigating sensitivities around religious freedom and its potentially disruptive exercise. Teachers guide students as they navigate their journeys from an appropriate loyalty to family and collective traditions to a more mature understanding of their religious selves. In educational settings, there are ongoing decisions about what forms of religion and religious freedom cross the line between those that can be celebrated and encouraged, those a school can tolerate, and those forms that are intolerable. Appeals

---

21. Breen, "Teachers' Approaches," 38.
22. Fitzgerald, *Ideology*, 53.

to common sense work only when there is a shared consensus about definitions, either implicit or explicitly supported by a theory.

Theory is a sophisticated way of telling a story or constructing narratives that shapes how we think about the world, including the textbooks we use for religious studies and the guidelines issued by the school authorities in whose jurisdictions we work. What we think of as common sense came from somewhere and, if you go back upstream from where you are living, you will probably end up in someone's study whose name you may never have heard writing books and papers you have never read. We need to know where ideas come from, including ideas about religion, that have become common sense.

The second reason why clarity is important is social and political. Theory and definition do interpenetrate and transform the social imaginary. Taylor's question is not *if* they do; rather, his question is what happens *when* they do.[23] Lack of clarity allows considerable latitude in the political uses for which the term and the boundaries around it can be deployed. *Religion, secular, culture,* and other commonsense terms are malleable, which reduces their transparency and accountability. Religion defined in some ways marginalizes it as a matter of private choice with an ambiguous role in the lives of modern people, some of us being religious while others have moved past religion to something else. Defined in other ways, religion can be deployed as a group identity marker to create boundaries of inclusion and exclusion. Either way, religion can become the basis for social fault lines reinforcing power relations that are inaccessible to public accountability. If we do not clearly identify what we are talking about, their use in the context of power relations remains opaque. Dorothy Smith's analysis of power relations in sociology shed light on the construction of religion in RE. Discussing *ruling* she says, "I am identifying a complex of organized practices, including government, law, business and financial management, professional organization, and education institutions as well as discourses in texts that interpenetrate the multiple sites of power."[24] Her insight is relevant to a discussion of the networks of power (or ruling) in RE and the uses of language to mask those networks.

Hussein Ali Agrama uses the term *precarious* to describe implications of lack of clarity in how things are defined in intellectual contexts

---

23. Taylor, *Secular Age*, 175.
24. Smith, *Everyday World*, 3.

identified as secular. He argues that appeals to secularism depends on precariousness and lack of clarity as courts in Egypt re-form the moral concept of *hisba* to fit into secular civil law in Egypt.[25] He adds that this is not unique to Egypt, saying that "it is also characteristic of many states considered to be paradigms of modern secularity, such as France, Germany and Britain."[26] What I hear Agrama saying is that confusion about the definition of key concepts or *indeterminacies* creates space for the exercise of power that is less easily accessible to critical scrutiny.

A third argument for clear definition is directly related to education, which is where the theoretical rubber hits the road of literacy in classrooms. A survey of RE programs indicates that the outcomes of religious literacy are defined in either of two ways. In one, identified as *RE* or *education about religion*, outcomes are expressed in terms of civic skills and attitudes, particularly tolerance of religious diversity and the skills of speaking of religion in terms that do not give offense. The social sciences, primarily sociology, provide the theoretical framework, accepting religion as a social fact on the ground that must be managed by education, persuading students to adopt ways of expressing their religious selves within social boundaries established in dominant discourses.

On the other hand, religious literacy in the context of theological definitions of religion is delivered by practices often identified as *religious education, religious indoctrination*, and *confessional education* or *training*. Religious literacy is expressed in terms of familiarity with and loyalty to the religious tradition in which it occurs. The point is that both have a role to play among the offerings under the RE banner and examination of policy proposals indicate an overlap between theology and sociology. However, educators need to be honest about the fact that education occurs in a network of social relations designed to serve an end, one of which is to produce a preferred understanding of religion. No education program is neutral or objective about religion nor should it pretend to be, the distinction between RE and religious education notwithstanding. All RE programs operate with a definition of religion that foregrounds some things and backgrounds others in service of a preferred end.

---

25. Agrama, *Questioning*, 19. "*Hisba* is defined within Islam as 'the commanding of the good when it is manifestly neglected, and the forbidding of the evil when its practice is manifest.'" The concept is moral and religious but also has implications for civil order that leave potential for ambiguities in state ruling.

26. Agrama, *Questioning*, 71.

Religion in the classroom (whether we like it or not)

Teachers encounter religion in their classrooms as a discrete subject and as a presence in any number of other disciplines. However, religious presence becomes messier and more immediate in the bodies of students and their families, so teachers can't avoid thinking about it. Schools have their preferred models of how to deal with religion and religious diversity and what is to be included in our RE programs. Part of a teacher's professional duty is to understand religion, how it can be defined and how it works so they can more effectively serve their students who encounter religion in the news and in their neighborhoods.

In addition, education professionals need to understand the boundaries of what is and what is not acceptable in their schools and the community they serve. Despite the marginal role religion plays in academic programs, students and teachers live in a religiously energized world with a confusion of voices deploying religion to support any number of political and social interests. Religion is going to show up in classrooms one way or the other and teachers do not stand apart from it, having their own prejudices, biases, and preconceptions about it. Lack of clarity, says Fitzgerald, "is fatal, because we are rendered impotent by our ignorance of the semantic and ideological bias of our own tools of analysis which means that we are not fully conscious about what we are doing."[27] Not only will lack of clarity limit a teacher's ability to serve students effectively but it can also be career limiting. So, I am going to encourage the reader to partner with me as we work our way through some ideas about religion. In fact, I argue that it is our moral duty to do so as teachers, which is risky, something I just said but worth repeating.

Religion and Religious Literacy as Categories of Knowing (Alongside Other Ways of Knowing)

I am arguing for a definition of religion that puts it at the center of the issue of religious literacy but does so in a way that affirms it as a source of public information, knowledge, and wisdom and as a way of knowing which students need access. Religion is not the queen of the sciences and the gatekeeper of universal truth, but neither is it a quaint, persistent anachronism in the modern world. Rather, it is a way of knowing the

---

27. Fitzgerald, *Ideology*, 53.

world, a unique kind of consciousness, one among several *nested stories*[28] that generates a particular kind of information, knowledge, and wisdom about the world and the human experience in and of the world. Living with and alongside other modes of human knowing, *interpretive categories*, or *technologies*, religion has its own logic and rationality that adds to our perceptual and interpretive bandwidth without which we see less. It is not a sui generis category of knowing living in a parallel knowledge universe inaccessible to public accountability.

As an educator, I am foregrounding epistemology as the theoretical screen and academic discipline rather than sociology or theology. The reason is that *knowing* is at the center of the social practice of education and the delivery of literacy. Knowing may not be all there is to be said about religion, but it is what I am foregrounding in thinking about religious literacy.

What does religious knowing lead us to know?

My working definition of religion foregrounds the issue of transcendence as an organizing principle in the construction of meaning. I understand James Beckford's definition to be getting at something similar although, as a sociologist, he is interested in what people do religiously and does not agree that everyone is religious.[29] However, his working definition recalls one that comes from Herman Dooyeweerd who does assume that religion is a universal human characteristic. Dooyeweerd, a Christian working as a philosopher (specifically a Calvinist in the Dutch Reformed Protestant tradition), is interested in precise definition of how knowing is structured. He distinguishes between the historically embedded social constructions and practices of religion that he calls *pistic* and the transcendent reality for which it is reaching.[30] The impulse and the capacity to reach for transcendence as a source of ultimate meaning and value is what Dooyeweerd calls *religion*.[31] Anthony Pinn agrees that religion is inherent in human nature, which he calls a *technology* that "pushes

---

28. Greene, *Time*, 70–72.

29. James Beckford, email to author, February 5, 2021.

30. "Of, relating to, or exhibiting faith; Late Latin *pisticus*, from Greek *pistikos*, from *pistis* faith + *-ikos* -ic; akin to Greek *peithesthai* to believe, be persuaded, obey." Merriam-Webster, "Pistic"; italics original.

31. Dooyeweerd, *New Critique*, 2:298–300. See also Basden, "Presentation of Dooyeweerd's Aspects."

underneath patterns of thinking and doing."³² According to Pinn, this is just what humans do because it is who we are, the key distinction for him being between *theistic* and *nontheistic* religion rather than between religion and non-religion.

Knowing in religion: Faith (in a meaning narrative)

The way people know the transcendent is through *faith*, by which Dooyeweerd did not mean that all people have faith in a vertically transcendent entity we might call God or the gods. What he meant was that human beings are driven by the need to make meaning of their lives in time and space and that they have faith in a fixed reference point from which to construct that meaning. People live by faith in that fixed reference point, which he called their "Archimedean point."³³ In that sense, *faith* is not restricted to the people we tend to identify as *religious*.

Ana-Maria Rizutto suggests something similar when she says, "Whosoever says he has religion must derive a faith from it, which is transmitted to infants in the form of basic trust; whosoever claims that he do not need religion must derive such basic faith from elsewhere."³⁴ *Basic trust* is going to come up again because it is central to both religion and literacy. Muhammad Iqbal agrees that faith is the central element in religion, saying, "Religion, in its more advanced forms, rises higher than poetry. It moves from individual to society" and it is "opposed to the limitations of man; it enlarges his claims and holds out the prospect of nothing less than a direct vision of Reality."³⁵

Dooyeweerd, Rizutto, and Iqbal do not reject rational processes in religious knowing. Rather, rational processes are preceded by faith in a reality or source of truth on which our rational processes rest. This is not, in the first place, a religious matter when religion is restricted to its common usages. Rather, it is fundamental to the ways in which people engage

---

32. Pinn, *Interplay*, 8.

33. Dooyeweerd, *New Critique*, 1:8. "The point from which we are able to form the idea of the totality of meaning."

34. Rizutto, *Birth*, 204.

35. Iqbal, *Reconstruction*, 1. I want to draw attention to the gender-specific language in this and many other references throughout the book. They come from sources that seem to assume that *man* is a universal category for humanity. However, this usage also indicates a gender hierarchy that triggers a critical alertness to gender caste issues. The critical analysis offered by Dorothy Smith about the field of sociology applies more generally to academic work.

the world. Timothy McCowan argues that faith is universal, describing it as "an orientation toward the whole of life," a "total response," a way in which people "compose a sense of the ultimate character of reality and then stake [their] lives on that sense of things."[36]

In their discussion about the astonishing evolution from the chaos of the big bang to the order that allowed life, including human life, Karl Giberson and Francis Collins ask, "Is the grand narrative of the origin of life a 'tale told by an idiot, full of sound and fury but signifying nothing'? Or is this a story of God's purposeful creation?"[37] If life is completely random, there really is no tale, or at least not one worth telling. There are stories, but while we may imagine a meta-story to tie them together in a framework of meaning, it remains a figment of our imaginations. Not real, in other words, in the sense that you can rely on it as a platform for truth in any meaningful way.

Giberson and Collins raise the issue of meaning that is central to RE and religious literacy. Miroslav Volf et al. see The Question[38] as the cornerstone to the quest for meaning in life. They tell us that "the Greek philosopher Chrysippus (279–206 BCE) once wrote a multivolume book called *On the Means of Livelihood*," an education book giving advice on how a wise person ought to make a living. But then, a complication arose in the form of an important question familiar to any teacher trying to persuade their students to do their homework: "Why make a living at all?"[39] The question Chrysippus is asking goes beyond survival (you have to make a living to pay the rent and your Netflix subscriptions). Survival is possible in all manner of ways, some of which might not involve rent and Netflix. However, humans have rarely been content to leave their lives at a survival stage, and even in extreme circumstances where survival is tenuous, those who survive are motivated by a sense that their lives have meaning and purpose.[40] You need a reason to overcome seemingly impossible circumstances. Sometimes impossible circumstances force you to think about what really matters.

Another way to put it is around the question of what it is to really live. Here's a questionable observation by Oscar Wilde, shared by Miroslav Volf: "To live is the rarest thing in the world. Most people exist, that

36. McCowan, "Bridges," 8, 26–27.
37. Giberson and Collins, *Language*, 198.
38. Volf et al., *Life*, xv.
39. Volf et al., *Life*, 110.
40. Frankl, *Man's Search*; Ten Boom, *Hiding Place*; Raboteau, *Slave Religion*.

is all." I am not sure that Wilde knew about most people, so his observation probably says more about his own life journey, but his follow up takes us to Volf's argument, when he says, "What man has sought for is, indeed, neither pain nor pleasure, but simply Life. Man has sought to live intensely, fully, perfectly."[41] Volf is arguing that the big questions of life's purposes are essential to a life lived intensely, fully, perfectly. Throughout this book, I argue that the question of a fully lived life is central to education and literacy. If there is a purposeful order and meaning in which we have faith, there is a tale that we tell about it in multiple nested stories. Nested stories include mathematics, microbiology, genetics, and physics that tell us how the world is ordered, but also art, literature, theology, and philosophy where we struggle to frame the meaning of origins, order, and destiny. It is our human burden and joy to ask questions about how we got here, but also why we did and what we are meant to do here in the immanent frame of our existence. In our darker moments we may conclude with Macbeth that it all comes down to sound and fury signifying nothing,[42] but our getting up in the mornings to go to work, visit art galleries, get our children to soccer practice, pay our taxes, and mow our lawns signify something quite different. We do, in fact, live tales we believe to be true on some level, giving our lives their meaning, transcending the ups and downs inherent in human life. We do have faith that our tales are true, which is the basis for hope. Those of us who really do lose faith that life has meaning will not survive either the deprivations of a death camp experience, according to Viktor Frankl, or stultifying prosperity as we see in the suicide rates among even our affluent friends. Loss of meaning in a transcendent story that will sustain us through the inevitable griefs and losses of life is pathological, something J. Edward Chamberlin tells us.[43]

Reliable sources of meaning on which our faith rests: Transcendence and immanence

Although all people live with a transcendent tale serving as a metaphorical polestar that guides their decisions and on which they build their lives, there is a difference in the way we understand its source and

---

41. Volf et al., *Life*, 251.
42. Shakespeare, *Macbeth*, 5.5.29–31.
43. Frankl, *Man's Search*; Chamberlin, *If This Is Your Land*.

location. Ursula Goodenough describes the differences between *vertical* and *horizontal transcendence* in her consideration of transcendence "from two perspectives: the traditional concept wherein the origination of the sacred is 'out there,' and the alternate concept wherein the sacred originates 'in here.'"[44] Charles Taylor argues something similar when he says that that "the debate in our society has to be understood as suspended between the extreme positions of orthodox religion and (in contemporary terms) materialist atheism." While he suggests that people find themselves somewhere between the two extremes in the way they live and interact, he says "these positions themselves are defined in a field in which the extreme ones, transcendental religion on one hand, and reductive materialism on the other, are crucial reference points."[45] About "exclusive humanism" he says that it "tends toward a rejection of the aspiration to transcendence; and yet it has trouble setting it aside altogether as the problematic attempt to define an internal transcendence."[46] One conclusion is that the idea of transcendence and the attempts to define it as a reliable source of knowledge in which we can have faith are not unique to frames of reference we normally think of as religious.

The two models of reality live as neighbors in any modern society. For many of us the transcendent is located within an immanent frame. For example, the Ontario Ministry of Education's character education program is based on *universal attributes* accessible to reasonable people without reference to a transcendent being or deity. While the Roman Catholic partners in the program agree that there are universal attributes and even agree on what those are, they identify their source in an ontologically real transcendent, holding what Robert Jackson identifies as "realist views of religious truth."[47] The Roman Catholic understanding of character attributes is embedded in Christian tradition with reference to God and the Bible as their sources.[48]

The idea of the transcendent is not all that controversial. Brian Greene accepts the role of religion that, for some of us, addresses questions the answers to which elude science, but, for him, the fundamental principles of transcendent cosmic order are rooted in the immanent laws of physics and mathematics. He follows the thinking of Erwin

---

44. Goodenough, "Transcendence," 1.
45. Taylor, *Secular Age*, 598.
46. Taylor, *Secular Age*, 656.
47. Jackson, *Rethinking*, 73.
48. York Catholic District School Board, "Communities."

Schrödinger who argued basically the same thing back in 1944 and in 1956. Goodenough accepts the idea of transcendence, but uses the concept of the esthetic, drawing from the Greek "*aiesthetes*, a person who perceives and to perceive, from the Latin *percipere*, is to take hold of, feel, comprehend.... Aesthetics is about order,... coherence,... beauty,... and purpose."[49]

Human life without an esthetic is unthinkable, but it is accessible to science only in part. John Gray says that "science can only be a tool the human animal has invented to deal with a world it cannot fully understand" and goes on to argue that, "above all, science cannot dispel religion by showing it to be an illusion." He says that "religion may involve the creation of illusions" but "there is nothing in science that says illusion may not be useful, even indispensable, in life."[50] The point is that human beings construct meaning, are driven to do so, that reaches beyond what we can know through science, even if we acknowledge that meaning to be illusory. Our faith may be tentative, but it still guides our lives.

Christopher Watkin, writing as an apologist for a critical theory based on the Bible, introduces the idea that the laws of nature, revealed by science, operate based on an "iron logic of necessity."[51] Life reduced to the iron logic of nature is inherently fatalistic. Religion (and his case, a Protestant Christian form of it) allows us to see that the world is, in the end, "unnecessary," to imagine and construct a view of the world that transcends the logic of science to include surprise or miracles that defy our categories.[52] Margaret Visser argues something similar, in her examination of Christianity's vision of grace and forgiveness being a way out of the logic inherent in honor cultures. She worries that "honor and shame are allowed to infiltrate our values more and more, and with them seeps back a belief in fate, with its concomitant hopelessness."[53]

I am not as persuaded as Watkin and Visser seem to be that sources of hope and relief from fate are to be found exclusively in Christianity. For one thing, Christianity is not a unified set of beliefs; it includes some forms (for example, hyper-Calvinism) that lead with interpretations of the theological doctrine of predestination, which are nothing if not fatalistic. In addition, the creative tension between freedom and necessity

---

49. Goodenough, "Transcendence," 4.
50. Gray, *Seven Types*, 13.
51. Watkin, *Biblical Critical Theory*, 420.
52. Watkin, *Biblical Critical Theory*, 59.
53. Visser, *Beyond Fate*, 42.

is not new or unique to European Christianity. However, I do agree with Gray and others that religion and a religious imagination open ways to consider transcendent sources of truth about the big questions of life beyond what is accessible to the sciences and rational processes. Whether those are found within a vertical or horizontal framework is another question.

However, the world is not so easily organized around binaries, including the one between vertical and horizontal transcendence. We can imagine and construct a transcendent reality that guides and anchors us in the ever-changing landscape of our lives we know in time and space. In fact, there's the problem. We construct, imagine, reach for realities that do not depend on our brief lives and limited perceptions. Paradoxically, our knowledge of the world depends on our bodies, is bodied. Our greatest commitments, our highest ideals are meaningless if they are not bodied and acted in time, space, and relationships. We are bodied animals with a special consciousness of the passage of time that inspires us, terrifies us, baffles us. Transcendence and immanence live in a partnership of creative tension.

Belief and unbelief: A transcendence-immanence binary with limitations

Some researchers equate horizontal transcendence with *unbelief* in contrast with vertical transcendence that is seen to rely on *belief*.[54] Charles Taylor seems to agree in his distinction between *believers* and *unbelievers*.[55] However, the construction of belief and unbelief as unique to religion (as commonly understood) masks the mystery at the heart of the human capacity to think about time and the problem of meaning of the limited time we have on this earth. In her examination of how people construct their images of God, Ana-Maria Rizzuto argues that, even "if the parents are not religious, the child must still deal with his having come into the world either as the result of his parents' wishes or as a biological accident."[56] The Humanist UK website tells us that "'nonbelievers' do, of course, have many beliefs, though not religious ones. . . .

---

54. Bullivant et al., *Understanding Unbelief*.
55. Taylor, *Secular Age*, 8.
56. Rizzuto, *Birth*, 183.

They typically hold that moral feelings are social in origin."[57] Like transcendence, a belief in belief is shared by people who identify as religious and by those who identify as nonreligious. The idea that some of us are believers in contrast with those of us who are unbelievers is questionable, nonbelievers acknowledging that they have their own beliefs. The beliefs of unbelievers is an oxymoron.

Charles Taylor's proposal that there is a no-man's-land between believers and nonbelievers is not entirely persuasive.[58] In his account of the change in the Western world, the shift from transcendence to immanence cannot be explained by discontent with Christianity. Rejecting what he calls a *subtraction theory*, he argues that intellectual elites began to construct paradigms within an immanent frame to replace the vertical transcendence that was common sense in an earlier time. I am arguing that we are not moving away from belief in a transcendent reality to unbelief in a more general sense. Unbelief is a category of subtraction that does not account for beliefs expressed by, among others, humanist organizations. Carl Becker makes a similar argument in examining the heavenly city of the eighteenth-century philosophers, including his description of Voltaire as an optimist and "a crusader pledged to recover the holy places of the true faith, the religion of humanity." Voltaire was "a man of faith, an apostle who fought the good fight, tireless to the end, writing seventy volumes to convey the truth that was to make us free."[59] Voltaire was a skeptic about religion, but he was also a believer, imagining a "heavenly city" within an immanent frame, according to Becker.

Justine Ellis invites her readers to go beyond a subtraction theory of secularism that has been described as the *not religious* to consider more recent theory that takes into account "the notion of secularity 'as something that is practiced, felt and experienced.'" She adds a teacher question: "Is there a secular student body?"[60] What I understand her to be saying (following Lois Lee) is that there is a "substantial secular" that "comes with its own positive life stances, norms, values, and social configurations."[61]

The distinction between believers and unbelievers is useful only when applied to specific claims. There are no unbelievers in a general

---

57. Humanists UK, "Non-Religious Beliefs," para. 2.
58. Taylor, *Secular Age*, 351.
59. Becker, *Heavenly*, 37.
60. Ellis, *Politics*, 13.
61. Ellis, *Politics*, 11.

sense. For example, I am an unbeliever in an argument for a flat earth, unlike the nice young man who trimmed my hair, but I am a believer in other things. In the same way, we are all believers in some forms of transcendence but unbelievers in others. Christopher Watkin argues that what we are seeing are "migrations of the holy in society and thereby understand how, in the language of Acts 17, we are still very religious despite ourselves."[62]

Timothy Fitzgerald engages the "serious hermeneutical problems" in Mark Jurgensmeyer's work by asking, "At what ontological level is the author using 'transcendent'?"[63] The confusion, in his view, is that the distinction between the religious and secular, and, I argue, between belief and unbelief, is never clear because its theoretical clarity is less important than the political context and purposes it serves. James Beckford points out similar ambiguities in Claus Offe who does not include religious sects in the category of new social movements. Beckford questions Offe, arguing that new social movements "have a religious quality in so far as they have to do with the values that are considered ultimately important for human life, and which transcend any particular social arrangement."[64]

That takes us back to definitions linking religion to beliefs and practices associated with vertical transcendence, which we usually call the gods or God. However, that way of constructing religion confuses the question of the human capacity to imagine, create, and rely on a transcendent reality to make sense of the world that frames life with its socially constructed embodied expressions. The ambiguities are evident in the question of whether "non-religion is the new religion."[65] Timothy Fitzgerald points out that Frank Whalen's "wide ranging assumption" that there is a "purposeful transcendent reality working through what he calls global history" does not explain "how a secular religion differs from a religious religion."[66] The distinction between the religious and the secular, and between religion and non-religion, is arbitrary in his view and central to his argument that we cannot understand the construction of

---

62. Watkin, *Biblical Critical Theory*, 521. Watkin attributes "migrations of the holy" to William Cavanaugh. Acts 17 includes the story of the apostle Paul's engagement with skeptical philosophers in Athens with whom he is establishing common ground by commenting on the many idols in the city, including one to "the unknown god." He tells them that they are also "very religious," recorded in verse 22.

63. Fitzgerald, *Ideology*, 111.

64. Beckford, *Industrial Society*, 156.

65. Zwilling, "Non-Religious"; Bullard, "World's Newest Religion."

66. Fitzgerald, *Ideology*, 48.

religion apart from its "ideological functions."[67] The clustered concepts of transcendence, beliefs, and ultimate meanings, among others, have traditionally been seen as religion, at least in the Western Christian world.

Commenting on Alan Touraine, James Beckford says, "The fact that Touraine tries to dissociate the kind of normative guidelines that are directly produced by society from 'God, Spirit or History' should not be allowed to conceal the close similarity between his project for *the* social movement and the general objective of many *religious* movements."[68] As a result, we have a language problem around religion originating in any number of historical and cultural sources, described by Timothy Fitzgerald as "extremely complex problems of contextual hermeneutics."[69] The colonization of the category *religion* by European Christianity has allowed us to think of religion as a unique set of practices and beliefs, which means that some of us are religious believers while others are not. It provides the basis for a bifurcated social and conceptual model we call religious-secular with lots of ink spilled over what and who belongs where in the model. The assumption is that some of us have religious experiences while others do not, and some of our institutions and practices are religious and some are not. Examinations of the distinctions between religion and that which is not religious leads to the complex problems to which Fitzgerald draws our attention. However, the distinction between belief and unbelief is not a useful way forward in locating the authoritative sources of transcendence.

Concluding thought about faith

One way to think about faith is that it bridges the imaginary gap between transcendence and immanence. Here's what I mean: we are gifted and burdened with a unique awareness of time, inspiring our reaching for points of permanence and meaning that transcend time, that give our lives a sense of continuity with generations that have preceded us and that will follow us after we die. However, anything we know is bodied, which means that our knowledge occurs within time, space, and relationships.[70] We don't really *know* anything outside our bodied selves.

---

67. Fitzgerald, *Ideology*, 53.
68. Beckford, *Industrial Society*, 160; italics original.
69. Fitzgerald, *Ideology*, 6.
70. I think of time, space, and relationships as the three media within which we

Our most lofty thoughts and complex consciousness are all stored in our bodies that will, at some point, return to the earth. So, what's left after that? We don't really know except by faith. Faith is a kind of knowing but it is ambiguous in ways that some other kinds of knowing are not. Faith lives in a more liminal space, between transcendence and immanence. Faith is not unique to what we usually think of as religion. It is basic to human life. That includes the social practice we call education. Not just RE: any and all education relies on faith.

Given the Hermeneutical and Theoretical Problems, Why Advocate for Religion?

I am not going to follow Timothy Fitzgerald and Russell McCutcheon in their rejection of religion as an analytical category. Without assuming that I am going to resolve the complexities inherent in the definition of religion, I am going to take a risk by proceeding with the term anyway, based on the distinction between what we typically identify as socially constructed, historically specific beliefs and practices and the human capacity to construct beliefs and practices. Our social constructions do political work, and they occur in astonishing diversity.

However, the critique of Robert Jackson's *interpretive approach* to RE identified by L. Philip Barnes as the "second chief weakness," is relevant to reconsidering the rejection of religion as an analytical category.[71] Barnes argues that Jackson confuses religion as a general category with its specific, socially constructed expressions. The diversity in any general category, including everything as mundane as a chair to something more mysterious such as love, does not cause us to reject either as meaningful. The point is that everything we do as humans is socially constructed but it is equally true that we work with what we are given in the raw material of the universe, including our human nature. Our language problem is inherent in the fact that what we see is socially constructed in a variety of adaptive behaviors and practices. However, while our social constructions are energized by their survival values, they are also embodiments of who we are as human beings, who we think we are, and who we want ourselves to be. Sometimes our social constructions jeopardize our survival,

---

live. A little like water for fish, we are immersed and can never really understand them. Unlike fish, however, we keep trying.

71. Barnes, *Education, Religion and Diversity*, 205.

but we still do them because our survival strategies are designed, not just to escape harm, but to escape it in particular ways to achieve a preferred end. Sometimes, for some of us under particular circumstances, that means we might be willing to die for our deeply held commitments.

There is something more going on here than survival in an individual, bodied sense. Johannes Fabian's insight about language can be applied to religion when he says, "Man does not need language; man, in the dialectical, transitive understanding of *to be*, *is* language (much like he does not need food, shelter, and so on, but *is* his food and house)" concluding that "Man *is* communication and society."[72] What I hear Fabian saying is that language did not arise out of a *need*, but rather language is a capacity that can be developed, embodied, and deployed in a wide variety of ways. We create language, language is socially constructed, but the capacity for language is inherent in who we are as humans, living as we do within an immanent frame but also opening up "contact with something higher and deeper (be in God or the depths of human nature, desired, the Will to Power or whatever) through language."[73] I am arguing the same thing about religion as the category referring to the human capacity to imagine a transcendent reference point serving as a guide for life reaching for "something higher and deeper." We *do* religion in a variety of ways because we *are* religion. Among a whole lot of other things, of course.

Definition as the Search for the Essence of Religion

Having argued for the rehabilitation of religion, I now turn our attention to the question of what religion is, or its *essence*. In this section I summarize some options that address the question of what religion is and what it does.

First, let's deal with the idea of an essence, which is controversial for two reasons. The first is that an essence suggests a kind of truth that will provide a key to unlock mysteries, accessible only to an authority or to true believers. The second reason is that an essence suggests a static kind of truth that, given the dynamic nature of the universe, is questionable. However, the quest for a definition of religion is a search for its essence. Religion is evident in all human cultures, or at least something like

---

72. Fabian, *Time*, 162.
73. Taylor, *Secular Age*, 758.

religion is, but it shows up in what seems like an infinite array of forms and iterations. The question of what constitutes their common element or characteristic that qualifies something or some behavior as religious as opposed to not religious accounts for a lot of energy in religious studies and other academic disciplines.

The search for an essence is not unique to religion. You can see a similar dynamic in the contests for pure science. For example, creationists engage in science, but can what they do in the name of science be considered a pure form of it? Is the work done by chemists a pure form of a pure form of it as they work in labs on new ways to produce yet another kind of dried cereal, or someone being paid by a sugar company to demonstrate that diabetes and sugar are only tangentially related? What about someone working in theoretical physics on something called string theory? In addition, definitions of science are historically situated. Can the sophisticated and disciplined observations of heavenly bodies by Chaldean astrologers, the search for fundamental elements by alchemists, or the knowledge of climate and weather by Aztecs be considered scientific? Christopher Watkin seems to agree with Rodney Stark who argues that "real science arose only once; in Europe," and while other cultures had "highly developed alchemy," it was only in Europe that alchemy transmuted into chemistry, and while many societies developed elaborate astrological systems, "only in Europe did astrology lead to astronomy."[74] In other words, if you want to find the essence of real science, this is where you should look, at least in Stark's (and Watkin's) analysis. But are they right or do they draw self-serving conclusions that should be questioned?

The question of the essence of a thing is related to its *value* in relationship to other things or in its role in the stories we tell about ourselves. In art galleries we see that the price of works of art or their protection in galleries depends on whether they are the real thing, at least in somebody's judgment. The acquisition of Barnett Newman's *Voice of Fire* by the National Gallery of Canada for 1.76 million dollars triggered lively debate about whether this piece was the real thing and worth the money. Apparently someone thinks so, its valuation in 2014 coming in at over 40 million dollars.[75] Baffling really, at least to me, but no less so than the astronomical value of the contracts signed by athletes and actors who

---

74. Watkin, *Biblical Critical Theory*, 39.
75. Simpson, "Newman's Revenge."

persuade the world that they are the real deal and worth it. And don't get me started on *influencers* who, by producing videos of their cats, make (a lot) more money than the staff who take care of the vulnerable at the nursing homes in my town. Value is elusive but is, in some way, connected to persuading someone (or a lot of someones) that their output is the essence of something valuable. In short, the quest for an essence is not unique to religion. However, like other modes of human knowing, conclusions about religion's essence and its value in society and even the debates about those conclusions are socially constructed in historical contexts.

The essence of religion and religion education

Questions about the essence of religion are important in the context of reflections on RE because any education endeavor is animated by a preferred graduate profile that includes ways of thinking about religion and religious diversity. Andrew Acquah argues that the idea of essence is central to the phenomenological approach to the study of religion, which he says "is in order to understand the essence and the manifestations of the religious phenomena of a particular religion."[76] Religious literacy is an important element in educational outcomes but any discussion about literacy in an educational context includes questions about what we want our student to really know, which is another way of talking about the essence of what we really value. Education is a persuasive social practice designed to draw students into a way of thinking about essentials for life. We seek to draw our students into a social imaginary and to reject modes of thought and practice that do not conform to the "kingdom of ends" envisioned by those in positions of political, social, and pedagogical power.[77]

What is true of education in general is also true of RE. Religion education is the persuasive social practice designed to draw students into a way of seeing and experiencing religion that fits into a social and intellectual context. The social practice of education draws us into questions of the essence of whatever we are teaching, including religion, whether we like it or not.

---

76. Acquah, "Phenomenologial Approach," 7.
77. Clark and VanArragon, *Evidence*, 171.

The problem of essence in time, space, and relationships

However, the search for an essence confronts us with a problem long ago identified by Heraclitus as the problem of change. Is the river in which I am standing the same one in which I stood five minutes ago even though I did not move even one step? The answer? Well, it depends. Is the river defined by its relatively unchanging banks and location or is the river the water that flows from high to low on its way to the sea? Is what I am looking at right now really religion? What about tomorrow? What if I am looking at what I think is the same thing in another location? Are the rituals practiced by people in Japan or the Amazon rainforest a form of religion or is that what I call it because they seem like my practices of going to church with others to offer prayers? What if my interviewees call it religion because they are translating something for me as an act of hospitality and kindness? Is my form of religion a deviation from a purer form practiced by my forebears, distracted as I am by worldly pleasures, or am I on a path to a purer form of it, on a path to greater enlightenment supported by advanced education? Take your pick.

The point is that our search for an essence of anything backgrounds the dynamic nature of that same something in the world accessible to our senses. We are bodied, swimming in time, space, and relationships that are always changing. One way forward is to propose a form of chaos theory that lands us on one side of the Heraclitus question. Timothy Fitzgerald tells us that "Arjun Appuradai, who stresses the dynamic situation of contemporary global trends, argues for the relevance of chaos theory for anthropology, emphasizing process, flow, and instability against stability and structure."[78] Chaos suggests that there is no such thing as *the river* in a static sense, because even its course, not just the water flowing along the course, changes over time. At the same time, we know that stability and continuity are built into the universe. Given the rapid replacement of cells in my body, I am not the same person as I was fifty years ago. And yet I am. My driver's license pictures have changed over time, but I am still me. The river flows but it is still the river.

The search for an essence is risky, tentative, but we still do it, trying to figure out and establish what is real, dependable, and true about something. Fitzgerald argues that "anthropology and sociology must include, if not be solely defined by, people's collective attempt to create a sense

---

78. Fitzgerald, *Ideology*, 240.

of order out of chaos, of permanence in flux."⁷⁹ Curiously, he does not apply the same principle to religious studies. He argues that "religion is only viable as a general category at the point where it becomes practically indistinguishable from culture."⁸⁰

However, I argue that religion, essentially, refers to the human capacity to imagine, construct, and have faith in a transcendent point of order, of permanence; it is a way of orienting our experience of our world and our bodies that are in a constant state of flux. Unlike Fitzgerald, who argues that the cases of *culture* or *society* are fundamentally different from the case of *religion*, I argue that setting the categories up in an oppositional relationship ignores a fundamental capacity inherent in human nature. That brings us to some of the ways in which people have tried to identify and describe that capacity in a search to establish what is really real or what is permanent about religion. You will also get my questions and cautions along the way through the options.

SOME OPTIONS IN THINKING ABOUT THE ESSENCE OF RELIGION

One question in the essence of religion discussion is about whether it really lives in the individual or in the collective, however that may be organized. Is religion essentially an individual or a collective matter?

Religion as Fundamentally Individual

One possibility is that religion is a matter of individual experience and testimony. Godfrey Museka argues that phenomenology is the most promising theoretical framework to define religion, providing space for intellectual detachment and empathy on the part of the teacher because it "seeks to historically understand and interpret religious phenomena from the believer's point of view."⁸¹ Further, he says that "there is no religious reality other than the faith of the believer."⁸²

William James tells us that "religion, therefore, as I now ask you arbitrarily to take it, shall mean for us *the feelings, acts, and experiences*

---

79. Fitzgerald, *Ideology*, 242.
80. Fitzgerald, *Ideology*, 244.
81. Museka, "Toward the Implementation," 134.
82. Museka, "Toward the Implementation," 135.

of individual men in their solitude, so far as they apprehend themselves to stand in relation to whatever they may consider the divine."[83] He goes on to distinguish between *morality* that, "pure and simple accepts the law of the whole which it finds reigning," is dependent on but different from religion: "But for religion, in its strong and fully developed manifestations, the service of the highest is never a yoke."[84]

Rudolph Otto agrees that religion is universal and innate, arguing that it is most highly developed in the moral codes of Western Christianity. Religion is essentially a matter of feelings, although for him feelings are akin to conscience or a consciousness of a universal moral code, of which Christianity is the most evolved expression.[85]

We find the same idea in the *Hope Commission Report*, an extensive review of education in Ontario, tabled in 1950:

> Christian love means kindness and consideration for others, which are mandatory by the Golden Rule. Honesty and love must be taught by precept and even more by example, as absolute rights or eternal verities, which everyone must accept, defend and strive to practise. To insist on their acceptance will do no violence to the conscience of any child or parent. No earnest Christian or Jew or sincere adherent of any other enduring faith or philosophy of intelligence and good will, could have conscientious scruples regarding these two virtues. They may be taught whole-heartedly and without reservation.[86]

I hear Otto and the authors of *Hope* saying that religion may have social consequences, but it is primarily a matter of individual belief. And that Christianity is its highest, universal expression, at least in their view.

Soteriology and Salvation

Soteriology is about individual salvation that tells us that religion as soteriology is a way of talking about it as a way of knowing how to be saved. Salvation may or may not include an afterlife and heaven, but it does mean that religion is a source of personal meaning that orients and anchors us in the inherently liminal nature of human life. Our soteriology

---

83. James, *Varieties*, 36; italics original.
84. James, *Varieties*, 48.
85. Otto, *Idea*, 1.
86. Hope, *Report of the Royal Commission*, 27–28.

may express itself by reducing our use of plastic and properly disposing of what we do use, or it can be embodied in our adhering to collective rituals of various kinds, but all of us have a belief system with a soteriological element with implications for salvation. Religion as soteriology is essentially personal and individual, at least in some definitions.

Religion: Are We All Religious Now?

Another conversation in the search for religion's essence is around the question of whether religion is inherent in human nature or an optional matter of choice. Either way, we are left with the question of what role it might play in human flourishing.

First the question, Is religion innate or is it an anthropological add-on we have adopted to manage our worlds? A provocative way of asking the question is, Are we all religious now? or, Do we all have a god-shaped hole we are seeking to fill? as Blaise Pascal argued we do back in 1670. The implication of Pascal's argument is that we are all religious in the sense that we are all on a human quest in which God is the ultimate destination and resolution.

Christopher Watkin identifies "the great contradiction at the heart of late modernity: its secularism is so thoroughly religious, its atheism so deeply theological, yet modernity itself is for the most part either unaware or unwilling to recognize it."[87] Does that mean that we are religious but are living with a kind of conceptual myopia? If so, what are the implications for religious literacy? Charles Taylor decides not to be distracted by the question from his project of tracing the emergence of the *buffered identity* in a secular age, saying, "What this common human religious capacity is; whether ontically it is to be placed with the psyches of human beings, or whether they must be seen as responding differently to some human-transcending spiritual reality, we can leave unresolved. Whether something like this is an inescapable dimension of human life, or whether humans can eventually quite put it behind them, we can also leave open." However, he adds in parentheses that "obviously the present writer has strong hunches on both these issues."[88] He observes that the search for *the one thing needful* is universal and becomes the guiding

---

87. Watkin, *Biblical Critical Theory*, 509–10.
88. Taylor, *Secular Age*, 147.

principle for a successful life, which can be found within in an immanent frame or in some form of vertical transcendence.[89]

William Cantwell Smith identifies religion as "that to which Ficino gives the name *religio*, on the other hand, is universal to man; it is, indeed the fundamental distinguishing human characteristic, innate natural and primary. It is the divinely provided instinct that makes man man, by which he perceives and worships God."[90] Smith is tracing the concept from its meaning as *ritual practice* and *obligation* through Christianity's systematized institutionalization to an internalized relationship with God as the essence that is at its heart, which, for him, was what characterized the Protestant Reformation. *False religion*, at least according to Zwingli, was the tendency "whereby men give their allegiance to religion rather than to God."[91]

However, because of the mystery of human inner life, Smith is cautious about the attempt to find and define a religious essence, arguing that "religions have a history" in contrast with essences that "do not have a history. Essences do not change."[92] His point is that definition can never fully capture the essence of something because the something we are seeking is dynamic, which Heraclitus also told us after thinking about rivers and riverbanks for a while. It is never stable in its embodied form, and its essence is always a mystery. We get hints of the essence through its embodied form but knowing the essence eludes definition because it is, in the end, a deeply interior matter. "Not to be ignored, however, is what we do not see; the Buddhist faith in the quiet corner of a man's inner heart."[93]

Smith's caution has not stopped the conversation, of course, and should probably not be restricted to religion as anyone who has tried to define love, or gender, or science, or gravity knows. Any definition triggers more debate, probably a good thing since it encourages us to hold our definitions with a light hand, which is Smith's point, or, at least, one of his points.

Émile Durkheim agrees that religion is universal but sees it as a social phenomenon more than an individual one, concluding that "thus we arrive at the following definition: *A religion is a unified system of beliefs*

---

89. Taylor, *Secular Age*, 310.
90. Smith, *Meaning and End*, 33.
91. Smith, *Meaning and End*, 35.
92. Smith, *Meaning and End*, 143.
93. Smith, *Meaning and End*, 147.

and practices relative to sacred things, that is to say, things set apart and forbidden—beliefs and practices which unite into one single moral community called a Church, all those who adhere to them." He adds that his definition "makes it clear that religion should be an eminently collective thing."[94] The implication is that religion is universal but is a response because every society needs it to maintain its coherence. Benedict Anderson's "imagined community" is about nationalism, but it comes down to roughly the same thing. In their formulation, religion is universal but an evolutionary add-on essential for social coherence.

Religion as an anthropological add-on can be explained within a Darwinian framework, some forms of which allow the possibility that it is both inherent in human nature and a behavior we have had to adopt for survival. Religion is unique to humans but added on over time (a long time) as our brains developed to incorporate consideration of our mortality and pesky questions about the meaning of life, something about which my dog never seems worried.[95] Do chimpanzees have religion? According to Brian Greene, even though they are close to us in the evolutionary family tree we don't think so, just as they don't have language in the way humans have it. Of course, we are not sure because getting into the mind of a chimpanzee is actually not that easy. Ernest Becker observes that one result of the evolutionary process was "the emergence of man as we know him; a hyperanxious animal who constantly invents reasons for anxiety even where there are none."[96] Darwin and his followers (or at least some of them) allow that religion is inherent in human nature but as an evolutionary coping strategy, constructing God or the gods within an immanent frame to deal with death.

Charles Taylor invites us to consider the human capacity to worry about ultimate questions as an anthropological matter, challenging models of religion as survival or as therapy. He refers to a Roman Catholic "view of a deeply divided being, 'a creature suspended between two infinities,' [which] replaced the orthodox scientific view of the human being as a mere 'organism in an environment.'"[97] Here religion is a matter

---

94. Durkheim, *Elementary*, 19.

95. There is a great line in Eccl 1:18 in which the teacher says, after his opening remarks about there being nothing new under the sun, "For as wisdom grows, vexation grows; to increase learning is to increase heartache" (NJPS). "Religion," the human capacity to think about our brief journey in time and space, does not necessarily make us happier. Smart person, the teacher.

96. Becker, *Denial*, 17.

97. Taylor, *Secular Age*, 731.

of innate anthropology, not an adaptive strategy to deal with terrifying things that we do not understand and that we might want to outgrow.

Karl Giberson and Francis Collins accept a Darwinian framework as the most convincing scientific theory to explain reality, including the idea that *Homo sapiens* emerged out of a long evolutionary process that can be traced through genetic research. That process included development of the neurological mechanisms allowing us to conceptualize God and reality in what we might identify as a religious imagination. They argue that God is not an imaginative construct we need for evolutionary survival, but rather we are the result of an evolutionary process that equipped us to reach for God. We might think of Giberson and Collins as Darwinian transcendence realists. Religion is an anthropological add-on as our brains developed to the point where we could grasp the ultimate reality of death and the meaning of our lives. Before we became fully developed humans in terms of brain development, we could not imagine God but that does not mean God is not real, more or less like certain colors are not accessible to people with the genetic anomaly resulting in color blindness; the idea of God is not accessible to chimpanzees and dolphins because they don't have the genetics and brain functions to get there, at least according to Giberson and Collins.

However, our ability to imagine God does not explain *why* we might need to do so. The idea that religion is an adaptive response rather than inherent in human nature leads to the question of why we might *need* it. This way of putting the question has implications for RE because religion becomes irrelevant if we can meet our needs in other ways.

WHY MIGHT WE NEED RELIGION? OR IS THE QUESTION OF *NEED* THE WRONG ONE? FOUR SUGGESTIONS

Why Might We Need Religion? Religion and the God Gap

The question of religion as an evolutionary necessity can be applied to the idea of human wellness or the healthy, integrated, and fully realized human person. Here the point is that some of us are religious to manage our fears and our unknowns. One implication is that those needs could just as well or more effectively be addressed by another mode of knowing such as science. Religion can be seen as a set of practices or beliefs allowing us to navigate a complex world with mysteries begging explanation in

Reflections on Religious Literacy

the absence of science. Thunder can be the voice of god, accompanied by lightning that can kill you if you are not careful or if you are unlucky, the gods being what they are. A flood can be the judgment of God if you follow the Ark Encounter[98] narrative or Dutch entrepreneurs feeling a tad guilty about their wealth acquisition in Simon Schama's telling.[99] On the other hand, it can be a sign of climate change that, depending on the lens you are using, might well be God's voice in creation calling us to account for our headlong rush to pursue a self-destructive form of prosperity. A flood can also be a lot of water where we don't want it, the result of spring flooding and extra heavy rainfall because of weather patterns that have nothing to do with the gods, which we now know thanks to advances in meteorological science.

One name for religious explanations in the absence of science is the *god gap*, a pejorative term placing religion among those of us who are simply not as smart or advanced as others who also see lightning but understand it as evidence of bursts of energy rather than the voice of some divine presence. Our brains developed to the point where we could imagine God but then some of us developed even further to see that God is a kind of wizard of Oz we no longer need, having pulled aside the curtain to reveal the wizard as an ordinary man or a figment of our anxious imaginations. Staying awake you find out that the presents under the tree are put there by your parents and not by Santa Claus, which you need to find out in order not to embarrass yourself in school where your friends figured this out three years before. But which also involves the loss of *enchantment*, the price we pay for growing up.[100]

---

98. You will get the backstory to my experience with the Ark Encounter further down. For now it is enough to say that the Ark Encounter is a huge reconstruction of Noah's ark, funded by Ken Ham, sitting just off I-75 in Williamstown, Kentucky. It is a graphic walk in a morality tale based on a strict-constructionist or literalist reading of the Bible and is a lot of fun to think with.

99. Schama, *Embarrassment of Riches*.

100. Gauchet, *Disenchantment*; Taylor, *Secular Age*. Some years back I spent time in Iceland where I heard quite a lot about *huldufólk*, roughly translated as elves or little people, who are part of the cultural landscape. My Dutch heritage similarly includes *kabouters*, and *witte wieven*, who did not, of course, show up in my more rigorous Calvinist intellectual framework but were present, nevertheless. There is something to be said for an imaginary that includes *huldufólk*, *kabouters*, and *witte wieven*.

Why Might We Need Religion? Religion as a Psychological Crutch (Another Kind of God Gap)

Religion as a psychological crutch is another way of seeing the god gap. To deal with the fear of death, we imagine heaven where we can live forever freed of our bodily limitations in the company of loved ones who have died before us. God takes the place of our absent fathers or our mothers who nurtured us or didn't, as the case may be. Religion is a crutch but less useful than some other, more rational explanation of noises in the night and practical safety procedures. We have become "self-sufficient agent[s who can] face down and set aside age-old human fears, of malevolent spirits, of not being chosen by God, of the blind, overwhelming forces of nature."[101] Making a different case, Zehavit Gross, describing "heritable religiosity" as one category in his typology of religion, says, "This type of religiosity is based primarily on extrinsic motivation, realized in devotion to pragmatic external ritual acts stemming from routine and habit that gratify the need for individual self-confidence, assuage existential human fear of the unknown, and nourish the desire to belong to the designated collective and social environment and maintain one's status therein."[102]

Seen in this way, religion may be a fact of life on the ground, but it is an option leading us to conclude that some of us are religious while others are not, having moved further in our understanding of our anxieties and existential questions. The mature modern adult has learned to live with the inescapable fact of the inexorable march of time ending in death with courage, not having to resort to a religious escape hatch. In fact, some variations on this theme include religion as evidence of intellectual immaturity and a *rationality deficit* or psychological pathology that we should discard on our way to a fully realized humanity.

God-gap thinking figures into the rejection of religion by Jerry Coyne and Sigmund Freud, but it does not take everyone to that conclusion. Francis Collins rejects creationism because of the god-gap explanations inherent in its questionable science but he does not reject religion, having adopted a Christian form of it. Ana-Maria Rizzuto agrees with Freud that we create object representations of God but rejects his conclusions that equate our representations of God with the reality of God. Rizzuto and Collins deal with god-gap reasoning by arguing, along with others, that science cannot answer the questions about why the world

---

101. Taylor, *Secular Age*, 262.
102. Gross, "Religious Education," 271.

exists in the first place and why we have the capacity to even think about the question at all. John Gray and Brian Greene argue that science can uncover how our bodies work (or don't) but we need religion to give the language of why they do and what it means when they don't.

Why Might We Need Religion? Religion and Morality, or Can We Be Good Without God?

A related issue in the question of why we might need religion occurs in the link between religion and morality. One way to frame the question is to ask, Can we be good without God? Kelly James Clark and Andrew Samuel make the link in considering the question "Why should we be moral?"[103] They present an argument like the one offered by Roy Rappaport, which is that religion is essential to counter the unique human ability to engage in deceit and deception by the creative use of language.[104] Religion and morality are linked moral codes deriving their legitimacy from a transcendent source that gives them their ultimate logic. James Beckford notes Talcott Parsons's linking morality with religion when he says that "the supernatural order thus gives cognitive meaning to the moral-evaluative sentiments and norms of an action system."[105] The argument is that religion gives us access to universal principles without which we are reduced to ongoing warfare, undermining achievement of harmonious social order. Religion allows us to transcend the animal origins from which we came and to live with hope and moral purpose, even if religious mythology is illusory. Beckford goes on to say, "In other words, the continuity and strength of value patterns were explained in terms of the overarching function of religion as the chief source of meaning in human life."[106]

Francis Schaeffer makes essentially the same argument within a Christian framework of reference in his warnings about secularization in Western societies with the rejection of Christianity as the basis for its organizing principles. Schaeffer finds the link between morality and religion in the Bible, of which a true reading is essential. Making a radical distinction between true Christianity and the rest of the human world,

---

103. Clark and Samuel, "Morality and Happiness."
104. Rappaport, *Ritual*, especially the introduction.
105. Beckford, *Industrial Society*, 58.
106. Beckford, *Industrial Society*, 59.

he took the idea of an *antithesis* between the kingdom of God and the kingdoms of this world seriously, imagining a fundamental spiritual conflict between them. His antithesis framework provided the basis for his condemnation of other forms of religion, including Roman Catholicism, which he accused of paganism. A bifurcated world constructed around an antithesis is pretty difficult to live out in real life when you get to know your neighbors, but it has provided a conceptual framework for culture wars in which morality plays a central role.

Schaeffer's view identified the moral task for true religion, which was to call a civilization that had lost its way back to the truth, at least the way he saw it. He stood in a long tradition of religious purity movements that came into its own in the early modern period when reformers of various kinds were engaged in the quest for ever more precise definitions of the truth. Religious reformers were motivated by the hope that the gaps between ideals and human reality could be reduced or even closed or, to improve on Saint Augustine of Hippo, to bring the *city of man* into closer conformity with the *city of God*.[107] That's the big moral task that cannot be imagined without religion, an idea that has long roots.

Zoran Matevski, Etem Aziri, and Goce Velichkovski argue that the link between religion and morality was key in the reintroduction of RE in post-communist Macedonia in a time of social and political crisis. They say that the arguments for RE "are supported by sociological research, which has led to the irrefutable conclusion that social ills have multiplied enormously," the fall of communism having left a "moral vacuum."[108] Confessional RE was seen as a key strategy in establishing a moral social order, based on the link between religion and morality.

However, the link between religion and morality is less predictable than it might seem to those who rely on history to support arguments that religion is a source of harm or that it is a source of social and personal morality. William Cavanaugh argues that the *wars of religion* is a misnomer, arguing that religious violence is a myth serving a secularization narrative. That tumultuous period of European history was shaped as much by changes in the way society was organized around emerging nation-states and the rise of capitalism, replacing medieval institutions. Lewis Spitz similarly tells the story of the Renaissance and Reformation in the context of massive social, economic, and political instability in

---

107. Taylor, *Secular Age*, 735.
108. See Matevski et al., "Macedonia," 143.

Europe in which religion was only one factor among others. Nicholas Terpstra agrees but reminds us that, while religion cannot be isolated from the political and social context in which it occurred in the early modern period, neither can it be ignored as a factor in the purgation movements executed in service of political control.

The moral goal of narrowing the gap between the city of God and the city of man was co-opted (and continues to be co-opted) by rulers representing themselves as God's instruments whose purpose it was (and is) to eliminate sin from their jurisdictions. They used religious purgation in their own projects of carving out regions under their control, unified by the religion of their choice. That weaponization of religion has provided evidence for the rejection of religion as a legitimate interpretive category. Taylor, among others, observes that the impulse to establish a preferred moral order was characteristic of colonial and imperial projects, interweaving models of morality with economic interests.[109]

Kristin Kobes-DuMez identifies the energy driving American evangelicalism that has adopted a form of muscular Christianity to rid America of moral impurities, particularly the sins of homosexuality and abortion, to return it to an imagined Christian past. Andrew Whitehead and Samuel Perry nuance the relationship between American evangelicalism and Christian nationalism, identifying key differences, but the two cannot easily be disentangled. The religious link between them is a shared suspicion and hatred of homosexuality and atheism, one outcome of which is religious and moral purification in making America even greater again.[110]

One outcome of the Protestant Reformation and the unraveling of the Holy Roman Empire was the emergence of nation-states unified by religious identity. Political unity and loyalty were linked to morality, which included strategies for rooting out forms of religion based on moral purity. Terpstra links religion and social and moral purity with the medical models of the day in which *purgation* of impurities was a common therapeutic response to illness. Purgation has had unhappy consequences for Jews, homosexuals, witches, and others identified as infections of the social body who had to be expelled. These groups continue to be targets of religiously inspired purgation efforts, along with

---

109. Taylor, *Secular Age*, 736.

110. Seven Mountain theology is interesting as a current formulation of an old idea in which religious and moral purgation play an important role. Got Questions, "Seven Mountain Mandate."

Muslims who have re-emerged to join them, at least in India, China, Myanmar, North America, and Europe. To be fair, some Muslim majority nations have also been enthusiastic religious and morality house cleaners in which not only non-Muslim citizens are under considerable pressure but also, and often primarily, forms of Islam identified as apostate. We see the same drive for religious and national purity in India, where an ever more energetic *Hindutva* is reducing safe political and social space of Muslim and other religious minorities. You can add your own examples since, in the twenty-first century, there are lots of others to choose. When you try to link religion with morality you land in some ironies, the obvious one being that religious purification efforts involve acts of astonishing immorality.

Religion may not have been the only inspiration for the wars of religion, but it is not wise to ignore its role in rationalizing violence against vulnerable groups. Of course, identifying religion itself as the source of moral infection has not been that great either. The French Revolution had its purgation impulse, something Ruth Scurr tells us, although it was narrated in the language of rational enlightenment rather than religious purification of the land to usher in its own nonreligious city of God. In his examination of the emergence of a modern social imaginary, Charles Taylor observes that purgation was given a "rational and moral basis; only those who really deserved to die were targeted according to the rational theory of virtue and purification. Second, the punishment itself was carried out in a rational, clean form, through a modern scientific instrument, the guillotine."[111] Purgation continues to be at play in French commitment to secular purity, targeting, among others, Muslim women whose clothing identifies them as infections of an ideological form of *laïcité*.[112] The same observation could be made of the Russian and Chinese Revolutions, energized by the idea that religion had to be put in its place, by rough methods as needed. The Cambodian killing fields were about class rather than religion, but that purification horror show looks a lot like the attacks on the Rohingya in Myanmar, the Uyghurs in China, and the bounty-hunting practices by Europeans clearing Tasmania of its aboriginal inhabitants. The lines between religion and other identity categories are not at all clear in understanding purgation activities by dominant groups.

---

111. Taylor, *Imaginaries*, 137; *Secular Age*, 687; Scurr, *Fatal Purity*.
112. Jamal, "French Government."

The policing of morality has taken on new forms in a social media world that acts as a public pillory of shame for transgressors. The historical reality is that human groups have tended to link diversity of any kind, including moral and religious diversity, with social disruption, especially in times and places where caste privilege and access to resources are perceived to be at risk. What is undeniably evident is that the link between religion and morality is contextual, serving political purposes of controlling diversity and challenges to power. It serves personal purposes as well. Being right and on the right side of history is quite energizing and often irresistible, especially when you get enough social support, and it serves to simplify a complex world.

The link between religion and morality is a complicated one, of course, because it takes us down a road we see in the Ark Encounter's depictions of the pure-hearted Noah, supported by his modestly dressed wife and daughters-in-law, in contrast with those questioning his great construction project who are drinking, carousing, and generally living morally questionable lives. Ken Ham may be convinced of the link, but others disagree that religion is essential to morality, based on evidence to the contrary.

There are links between religion and morality, but they are not straightforward. Charles Taylor avoids a direct link between traditional Christianity and morality, saying, "The realities of human life are messier than is dreamed of either by dogmatic rationalists, or in the Manichean rigidities of embattled orthodoxy."[113] He offers a balanced assessment of developments in religion saying, "It could and sometimes did inspire people to explore forms of faith other than those of the established synthesis," observing that the "father rebels against Victorian faith largely because it seems so much less humane than humanism." He goes on to add, "In the meantime, I want just to appreciate the importance of these new spaces for unbelief, whereby the reaction even against materialism (in the sense of the focus on purely material well-being) isn't driven to religious forms but can find atheist expression."[114] In Taylor's account of the emergence of the secular age there is loss, but the positive developments of new spaces and expressions indicate that the link between religion and morality is not straightforward.

---

113. Taylor, *Secular Age*, 387.
114. Taylor, *Secular Age*, 406–7.

He goes on to say "morality rationalizes" and allows us to "punish wrong-doers."[115] However, morality is based on the definitions of the good, the right, and human well-being, and identification of wrongdoers that reflect the highest values and concerns of those doing the defining and who have the power to do something to achieve the ends to which they are committed. Which means that morality is contextual, providing a rationale for astonishing acts of violence and equally astonishing acts of grace and healing. Harold Netland agrees, observing that "religion can be a force for enormous good in promoting human welfare, but it can also be a source of bigotry, abuse and horrifying violence."[116] A good word for the religious enthusiasts among us.

The link between religion and morality has implications for RE. L. Philip Barnes offers an apologetic for RE, arguing that the primary purpose of RE is its link to morality. His critical assessment of the shift from confessional RE to models based on the social sciences focuses on the delinking of religion from morality that he argues undermines RE. On the other hand, RE is also designed to counter forms of religion seen to be disruptive to individuals and society, including extremism, fundamentalism, and sources of ideas out of step with the moralities of secular modernity. Concerns about the moral implications of religion and religious diversity have triggered a great deal of investment in religious literacy projects around the world. Netland's observation echoes one offered earlier by Heinrich Schäfer's identifying the "Janus face of religion."[117] Much RE is, in fact, about morality—on the one hand, designed to manage the dark side of the Janus face and, on the other, to promote the beliefs, behaviors, and attitudes we want to see.

Jerry Coyne's and Christopher Hitchens's conclusion that religion is inherently poisonous provides a one-sided truth on a continuum of assessments that ask too much of religion, either positively or negatively. However, James Beckford's suggestion that religion is an interpretive category that does not actually do anything in and of itself provides a more balanced view. It also shifts the discussion away from the search for a religious essence imagined either as the glue essential for social order or as the virus that poisons the social body. Anthony Pinn suggests something similar when he says "religion is not a system as such but a technology

---

115. Taylor, *Secular Age*, 688.
116. Netland, *Christianity*, 46.
117. Schäfer, "Janus Face."

and, hence, does not invest things with deep meaning" that "provides no answers, just clarity, or what one might call deeper awareness regarding the connotations of our circumstances and naming-things in a world of other thing."[118] Their insights do not presuppose either Janus face but create room to consider both in thinking about the relationship between religion and morality.

Why Might We Need Religion? Religion as an Identity Marker

So, religion is located in either the individual or the group, either as a matter of choice or because it is the source of social morality, either because we need it for our survival or because we have a god-shaped hole we are trying to fill. Either way it can serve as an identity marker along with gender, race, tribe and clan, vocation, or avocation, among many other categories. Identity labels are a form of naming that is a capacity we share as human beings to create boundaries and common ground. However, our labels can also be about caste power and privilege. The gender-specific language used by William James and others alerts us to something else in the history of how religion has been defined, which is that a lot of it was written by men and, more specifically, by European white men. It is possible to believe that we are religion blind or secular when we think about how we think about religion but, like the myth of color blindness when we engage racism, it masks power relations. Isabel Wilkerson's examination of the ways caste is masked and maintained provides insight into how identity and religion are linked to support entrenched social hierarchies.

The silencing of voices and the marginalization of some identities are about power, something that must inform education and RE if it is going to approach its promise of delivering literacy. Feminist theology has provided a profound service in exposing the long histories of male theology just as liberation theology has done in exposing theological white supremacy and Christian colonialism.

Religion, Identity, and Moral Task

However, while identity labels can be about establishing power and privilege, they can also, often simultaneously, be windows on our relationships

---

118. Pinn, *Interplay*, 27, 29.

with others and provide a way of identifying moral task. We negotiate boundaries, identity, and moral task as we meet others in the world, and our lives are immeasurably enriched by friendships with people who identify in other ways. Sometimes our encounters with others include persuasion about what we see as truth about how to live well on this earth and about our ultimate destiny. This is not unique to religion. Jerry Coyne's frustration with the refusal of his audiences to be persuaded by his scientifically generated evidence sounds a lot like Ken Ham's Noah trying to persuade his recalcitrant listeners of impending doom. Coyne and Ham are both worried about the effects of resistance to conversion on people and society, which has given them their clear moral purposes.

Moral task as an expression of identity can lead to exercises of power in the construction and maintenance of social boundaries for individuals and for groups. Current forms include Christian *dominionism* and Indian *Hindutva*, but they are only two among many others. Religious identity provides the basis for which voices are included and which are excluded in social space with implications for access to resources. Collective and individual religious identity is fluid, but it is constructed within social and political contexts that are not always benign and never neutral, something to which Miroslav Volf alerts us in bringing to our attention the "excessive demand of loyalty."[119]

Based on his research in the Balkans, Heinrich Schäfer argues that religion is the key factor in the "re-culturing of politics." One outcome is "new wars" animated less by state interests and more by religious identity politics, "articulating nationalism through ethnic and religious identities."[120] He does refer to the context of political and economic disruption in the transition from Communism that has led to loss of confidence in national governing elites, replaced by religious and ethnic identities. Norman Cohn describes a similar pattern in the late Medieval and early modern period where political and economic insecurity gave rise to social movements leading with religion, creating opportunity for extreme behavior. Schäfer describes dreadful war crimes and, on the other hand, great acts of courage in protecting communities from the destructive outcomes of identity politics and war. The point is that religion cannot be isolated as the key factor in extreme behaviors, but neither can it be ignored in the construction of identities that emerge as

---

119. Volf, *Embrace*, 5.
120. Schäfer, "Janus Face," 411.

nonnegotiable places to stand. One conclusion is that we must be self-aware, self-critical even, about our identities, how we construct them, and the work they do for us in our relationship to others. Religious literacy includes understanding the ways in which religious identity is constructed and what that might mean both for individuals and in society.

Identity narrated in the language of religion can provide a place to stand, an organizing principle or an esthetic in an oft-confusing world. However, our differences do not have to negate the common ground we share about living well together. We can still agree to stop for red lights and go on green, which is one way we can take care of each other as we share our ways of engaging the poignant frailty of our lives. And the belief that *Black lives matter*, standing together to challenge social and political forces based on the idea that they don't. Or not as much.

Conclusion: Do We Need Religion or Are We All Religious (Whether We Need It or Not)?

So, here's a concluding question to take us into the next chapter where we engage some objections to religion: Are we all religious? Is religion inherent in human nature? Is it primarily a matter of individual spirituality or primarily a social matter? Well, yes and no. Yes, if you think of religion as that human capacity to construct meaning based on some point of transcendence. No, if you equate religion with a particular form in which that human capacity is constructed and embodied. Another way to ask the question is, Is religion a "meta-biological"[121] category of human knowing and experience, something irreducible in human nature that cannot be explained in terms of collective and individual well-being or survival? As you will have guessed, I am arguing that it is, just as other categories—for example, social, esthetic, scientific, and linguistic—are irreducible knowledge and experiential categories of human knowing.

Are we living in a less religious world? What we see and how we explain it depends on definition, and it depends on what we choose to foreground. Is what we are seeing a decline in religion or are we seeing "rather a kind of mutation"?[122] Taylor cites evidence suggesting a mutation, referring to the persistence of religious rituals, particularly at times of social stress. He rejects a traditional secularization thesis as

---

121. Taylor, *Secular Age*, 660.
122. Taylor, *Secular Age*, 522.

subtraction theory because it ignores the way "in which each stage of this process has involved new constructions of identity, social imaginary, institutions and practices." Despite the mutations, Taylor observes that "history is hard to deny," contextualizing the forms in which religion is socially constructed.[123] The responses in the United States to the attacks on September 11, 2001, or in Britain to the Hillsborough football tragedy in April 1989 expressed, in Christian terms, a collective reaching for transcendence in a time of trauma and grief. Like the English language, Christianity is deeply embedded in European imaginations, secularization notwithstanding.

I agree with Taylor when he says that "religious longing, the longing for and response to a more-than-immanent transformation perspective, what Chantal Milon-Delsol calls a 'désir d'éternité' remains a strong independent source of motivation in modernity."[124] In a later passage he reflects on the transformative implications of the Christian idea of the image of God, which, he says, "is the point of being a human animal and feeling this call to transformation, starting to be educated by God. There is now something higher in one's life, a dimension of something incomparably higher, which one can't turn one's back on totally, a dimension of longing and striving which one can't ignore."[125] This is more than nostalgia; rather, it is inherent in our awareness of the passage of time and of our engaging the meaning of our brief and often bumpy sojourn on earth.

However, there is no doubt that religion, in the ways we typically understand the term, is on the hot seat in the twenty-first century, even as it re-emerges as a voice demanding public attention often in ways that have been disruptive to the social order we have come to accept as normal and universal. Religious literacy includes understanding the objections to religion that will lead to chapter 5 on RE and religious literacy. The question there is, What does it mean to think well in religion?, but first we must think about what it means to *think badly* in religion. In summary, there are objections to religion about which we need to be honest in any RE program. You do not have to travel far to find them, expressed over coffee with your neighbor or family member, in political contests, and in both popular and academic literature.

123. Taylor, *Secular Age*, 520.
124. Taylor, *Secular Age*, 530.
125. Taylor, *Secular Age*, 668.

3

Objections to Religion

OBJECTIONS: INTRODUCTION

THIS CHAPTER ADDRESSES THREE objections to religion that are particularly relevant in religious literacy programs.[1] The three objections to religion are: first, that the institutionalization of religion is seen as a threat to individual spirituality, agency, and choice; second, that religion is irrational or, at best, nonrational and a questionable and even harmful source of information, knowledge, and wisdom; and third, that religion is inherently exclusive and therefore a threat to social cohesion and equality. All three have important implications for how religion is treated in RE programs and why religion and religious literacy are important matters of state interest in jurisdictions around the world.

There are good reasons to object to religion, and any discussion about religious literacy and RE must include them. Taking objections seriously is key to understanding the dynamic nature of religion and can lead to new forms of religion and revitalization of traditional ways of

---

1. Charles Taylor identifies two primary objections to Christianity, which I think could be applied to other, primarily Abrahamic, monotheistic forms of religion: first, religion invites us to "transcend" our humanity, one result of which is to engender hatred of our bodied existence. The second is religion's tendency to "bowdlerize" reality, creating a kind of escapist fantasy of the way our world really works. *Secular Age*, 623–36. He draws on Martha Nussbaum's work to develop the two objections. There is some intersection between his analysis and the three objections I summarize, so no argument there, but I am pursuing the ones more specifically related to issues in education.

doing things. There are forms of religion and religious practices that do harm and need to be called out and humbled.

Objections are based on an assessment of harm, in this case caused by religion or forms of it, with literacy being seen as, among other things, a therapeutic response to prevent harm. However, objections find traction in social, political, and historical contexts and also need to be subjected to critical scrutiny. Critical scrutiny does not make the objections go away, but it does contextualize them.

Honest reflection on objections to religion includes caution about overreach, including the impulse to reject religion as a legitimate way of knowing the world or that religion is inherently destructive to the world. Therefore, the summary of objections to religion below includes questions about the objections themselves.

Objections to religion fall into two broad categories. First, there are objections based on experiences of religious practice and abuses of power narrated and rationalized by the language of religion. An obvious example is the sexual abuse by clergy of people in their care. Others include religion used as a talisman during a COVID-19 pandemic or seeing prosperity-gospel religious snake-oil salespersons at work to sell their brand of magical thinking. *Christianity Today*'s account of the *Rise and Fall of Mars Hill* is a sobering reflection on power and religion, a cautionary tale for those of us who think we have unique access to the voice of God.[2] Uncritical acceptance of Mark Driscoll's celebrity status and charisma left a trail of damaged lives "thrown under the Mars Hill bus" (in Driscoll's words). Religion has also been mobilized to protect power relations, entrenching social hierarchies that are inherently unjust, based on assessments of human value rationalized as part of divinely inspired universal order.[3] Charles Taylor observes "running through much of the Enlightenment a motif of anger at, even hatred of orthodox Christianity."[4] The point is that there are good experiential reasons to object not only to orthodox Christianity but to religion as a general category and to reject it.

---

2. Driscoll was the charismatic co-founder of Mars Hill Church in Seattle, Washington, established in the late 1990s. He was accused by some of his parishioners of abuse of power and was forced to resign in 2014, after which, in 2016, he re-emerged as founder of Trinity Church in Scottsdale, Arizona. Cosper, *Rise and Fall*.

3. Ambedkar, *Annihilation*; Raboteau, *Slave Religion*; Pinn, *Interplay*; Wilkerson, *Caste*.

4. Taylor, *Secular Age*, 262.

The second category includes more philosophical objections to religion in principle. These are not as much about personal experiences of religious abuse and practice, but rather a negative assessment of religion as source of information, knowledge, and wisdom. More positively, philosophical assessments of religion tend to propose alternative sources of information, knowledge, and wisdom.

Changes in paradigms, imaginaries, or migrations of the holy occur in the dynamic interplay of the two categories of objections. In the early twenty-first century, we are seeing a reimagining of the role of religion in society, energized by both the experiences of abuses of power narrated by religion and by philosophical assessments of religion as a way of knowing the world.

Our objections to religion do not have to be based on personal experience. Rather, we remember and do not remember collectively, telling stories about the past, including stories about religion. Mircea Eliade suggests forgetting is part of a cultural shift that backgrounds religion.[5] What we choose to remember and what to forget can feed our philosophical objections to religion, providing evidence that might need to be balanced, most usefully through the memories of others who might remember differently. The wisdom that no one grows up in the same family applies more widely. Management of memory in stories of history has a political dimension and can serve to privilege some memories and marginalize others.

One response to objections to religion includes proposals for alternatives to religion. They include, among others, worldview, faith, and spirituality. While proposals for alternatives to religion add to our understanding of the role of religion in our collective imaginaries, they also need critical assessment, the topic of the concluding section of the chapter.

The challenge of telling truthful stories includes honoring evidence, memories we do not share, and the stories of those with whom we disagree and make us uncomfortable. Then we decide what to do with those memories, the challenge being to repent, break cycles of violence, and forgive abuses of power, allowing the pain of our pasts to become sources of wisdom as we move into a better and more just future together.[6] Religion education includes careful listening to objections to religion and to

---

5. Eliade, *Sacred and Profane*, 213.
6. Volf, *Embrace*, ch. 4; Bick and Schuurman, *Blessed*.

proposals for alternatives, both for what they tell us about religion and what they tell us about the objections and alternatives themselves.

OBJECTION ONE: INSTITUTIONALIZATION AND CODIFICATION OF RELIGION

The first objection to religion is to its institutionalization and formal codification, which includes philosophical issues relating to how the essence of religion is defined. If the essence of religion is defined as individual, inner spirituality and subjective experience, its institutionalization is a kind of pollution or dilution by people in positions of power. In some ways this is one form of the creative tension between the individual and the group, but it has taken a new language and respectability in the form of the *spiritual-but-not-religious* trend. The second source of objections is experiential, based on evidence that institutionalization and codification of religion have been sources of abuses of power that have been perpetrated by organizations and rationalized by codification.

Liam Gearon observes that Immanuel Kant considered institutionalization an evil deviation from what religion should be. Kant argued that perceptions guiding our moral sense are inaccessible to reason and beyond the reach of institutional regulation, saying "this sense of God and this morality do not need religion or its institutions. Rather, self-perpetuating ecclesiastical institutions are a social and moral evil."[7] Friedrich Schleiermacher went further, distinguishing between belief and "a mixture of opinions about God" and describing priests as "the most hated among men." Schleiermacher was not disputing the importance of religion, seeing it as integral to human nature. What he objected to was "the confusion between religion and that knowledge that belongs to theology. Knowledge whatever its value is to be always distinguished from religion."[8] In other words, knowledge in religion is codification, which is equivalent to killing the butterfly of the spirit and pinning it to an institutional display board to study it and control it (my metaphor, not his). Charles Taylor tells us that Ivan Illich "saw the actual development of the Christian churches and of Christian civilization (what we used to call 'Christendom') as a 'corruption' of Christianity."[9] In short, objections

---

7. Gearon, *Holy Ground*, 24.
8. Gearon, *Holy Ground*, 32.
9. Taylor, *Secular Age*, 737.

to the institutionalization of religion are not new and have quite a lot of support.

William James draws a distinction between individual experience of religion and the institutions where it occurs, saying about institutional forms of religion, "Were we to limit our view to it, we should have to define religion as an external art, the art of winning the favor of the gods."[10] He argues for a definition of religion and spirituality that privileges individual experience. The shift from external, institutionalized structures to individual religious authority takes several forms, including *lived religion* and *eclectic spirituality* to *non-religion*. Another form of it shows up in religious movements involved in a kind of *de-churching movement* (a nod to *de-schooling* proposed by Ivan Illich, 1970). Churches for people disaffected with church and who identify as SBNR are part of the church-planting movement.[11] This is not new, of course; reform movements in response to perceived deficits in religious institutions having been integral to new religious movements in religious traditions throughout history. The Anabaptist left wing of the Protestant Reformation, notable for its suspicion of institutionalization and codification of religion, started out as a de-churching movement although it did not take long for churches with their own hierarchies to emerge.

Philosophical objections to the institutionalization of religion do not occur in isolation from the social and political contexts in which they occur. Rather, they are energized and supported by evidence of abuses of power that have been a part of institutional life ever since institutions were invented (a long time, in other words). However, they have regained considerable traction in the latter part of the twentieth and into the twenty-first centuries. Institutional skeptics are not new, but they have moved into the mainstream, energized by stories of abuse by religious authorities who have been protected by institutions providing cover for the damage they have done.

One way to see the relationship between the philosophical objections to the institutionalization of religion and abuses of power is by thinking of a conceptual pendulum swing between the individual and the collective. Conceptual swings are corrective reactions so, in the second half of the twentieth and into the twenty-first centuries, there have been revisions of history suggesting a past dominated by coercive

---

10. James, *Varieties*, 34.

11. Barna Group, "Meet Those Who Love Jesus but Not the Church," provides survey data on this trend in American Christianity.

institutions being reformed by a swing to individual freedom. The shift from institutional authority to individual choice and agency has been an important corrective, given the control of institutions, including those self-identifying as religious, by people, usually men, in positions of power and privilege. Clarke and Woodhead identify the tension, arguing that "the influence of traditional religious authorities is likely to continue to diminish, and the authority of personal choice and new, more disorganized forms of authority is likely to grow." At the same time, however, "the influence of more conservative and 'fundamentalist' elements of religion relative to less activist liberal or 'moderate' majorities is also likely to increase."[12] There is evidence for their assessment at the time of this writing, both in the success of more conservative religious organizations that have engaged in formal and informal *concordats*[13] with state actors adopting the role of religious authorities in nationalisms narrated in the language of religion. What is clear is that religion is not immune from the creative tension between the individual and the group inherent in any society.

What is also true is that the institutionalization of religious authority has marginalized individual voices, particularly dissonant voices who call out religious authorities and hold them accountable for their abuses of power. Kristin Kobes-DuMez is one of many voices pulling the cover off evangelical high rollers who have been given institutional protection from the consequences of their behavior. Most of us cannot be bothered to do the work she puts into her research, preferring to vote with our feet (a nod to Vladimir Lenin) by switching our loyalties or leaving traditional forms of religion behind altogether. People in increasing numbers, particularly in Europe and in European settler jurisdictions, are leaving traditional, institutionalized forms of Christianity for a variety of reasons, one effect of which has been the emergence of *non-religion* as a demographic category.[14]

---

12. Clarke and Woodhead, *New Settlement*, 16 (2015); 53 (2018 revision).

13. The term *concordat* usually refers to arrangements between the Roman Catholic Church and state actors, starting with the French Revolution in the late eighteenth century, as a way of protecting their interests. However, the idea can be applied more widely to the relationship between state actors and religious organizations to describe the relationships between them.

14. At the same time, there is evidence of links or confluences between "nationalism" and tendencies to authoritarianism in politics and in religion. Jenkins, "New Survey." See also Taylor, *Secular Age*, 518, on "a polarity between spiritualities of quest and of peremptory authority"; Purpel, *Crisis*, xiv, on the rise of authoritarianism in

Martin Buber does not reject the codification of religion, but he alerts us to its dangers saying, "Principle there, dogma here, I appreciate the 'objective' compactness of religion dogma, but behind both there lies in wait the—profane or holy-war against the situation's power of dialogue, there lies in way the 'once-for-all' which resists the unforeseeable moment."[15] In other words, codification of religion in *dogma* always has the potential to shut down dialogue and dissident voices.

However, the emphasis on individual choice-based understandings of religion can marginalize people whose religious experience finds its inspiration in more institutional and traditional settings, including those in non-Western societies. It can also render less effective the voices of resistance to other institutionalized forms of power, including state actors focused on social order and corporations with their own interests in maximizing profits. Religious organizations provide stable platforms for resistance, examples being civil rights movements and refugee resettlement in the face of social tension over immigration. Margarita Mooney's research among Haitian diaspora communities demonstrates that strong institutions protect people and facilitate their adjustment to new environments.[16] In other words, traditional, institutionalized religion has allowed abuses of power, but it has also provided stability, platforms for resistance to market forces and state power, and for collective memory.

There is plenty of evidence to support the critical assessment of religious authorities and to imagine the state as the institution (or network of institutions) standing above and apart from sectarian divisiveness. The language of secularism and individual freedom suggests religious neutrality with protection of individual rights and agency often being the narrative linking deinstitutionalization to social progress. However, it is worthwhile to pay attention to Robert Nisbet's observations that the freedom seen in the shift to individual choice as the primary criterion for religious legitimacy is an illusion. His argument is that the shift does not really represent greater freedom but rather that it represents a shift in religious authority to state actors who are moving into the vacuum created by the declining confidence in institutional stability.[17] The construction of the autonomous individual can facilitate exploitation by state actors

---

reaction to the relativism inherent in postmodern critical theory; and Hedges, *American Fascists*, on "American Fascism."

15. Buber, *Between*, 18.
16. Mooney, *Faith Make Us Live*.
17. Nisbet, *Quest*.

who normalize global capitalism as the preferred social order and model of prosperity.

Danièle Hervieu-Léger alerts us to the loss of memory as one consequence of our suspicion of tradition and the shift to the individual as the source of religious authority. She is not talking only about memory in a technical sense but as a way of being in the world, providing continuity in time. Religion, in that sense, is more than belief; it captures a way of being in relationship to the cosmos, incarnate, "the notion that the spiritual is always incarnate, and that in chains which cut across time."[18] Loss of religion, then, is a loss of a way of seeing, of being. Institutions have dark tendencies, but they also protect, among other things, memory.

A final word from Charles Taylor, drawing on Ivan Illich who draws our attention to the dark tendencies inherent in institutionalization. Illich is critically examining and calling out the fetishization of codes of conduct and institutionalization in modern societies that prevents us from seeing each other as fully human. Taylor accepts Illich's deeply spiritual resistance and the creative tension inherent in human life, saying,

> We can't live without codes, legal ones, which are essential to the rule of law, moral ones which we have to inculcate in each new generation. But even if we can't fully escape the nomocratic-judicialized-objectified world, it is terribly important to see that that is not all there is, that it is in many ways dehumanizing, alienating; that it often generates dilemmas that it cannot see, and in driving forward, acts with great ruthlessness and cruelty. The various modes of political correctness, from Left and Right, illustrate this every day.[19]

You can hear Taylor struggling with secularization and with his Roman Catholicism, living with its genius and its "code fixation."[20] Those of us with deep religious attachments can identify and some of us choose to walk away without ever being able to fully leave. But that could be because the tension is inherent in human life. Our histories are written in our bodies and in the land we inhabit.

The potential for abuse of power in institutionalized religion cannot be denied or ignored but also cannot be said to be unique to religion or to institutions. Perhaps the problem is not institutionalization itself, but

---

18. Taylor, *Secular Age*, 751.
19. Taylor, *Secular Age*, 743.
20. Taylor, *Secular Age*, 750.

rather the human tendency to abuse power in any situation, including in any interpretive category. James Beckford's reference to Talcott Parson's "paradox of institutionalization" is not unique to religion.[21] Hockey and gymnastics are wonderful sports, but we have seen that the evidence of athletes who have been abused by coaches and medical practitioners, their abuse protected by, among other things, a code of silence to protect the institutionalized system in which sports are organized. Science and scientific thinking have delivered enormous benefits but there is plenty of evidence of abuse when science is institutionalized in labs owned and operated by an exploitive food industry, states, or any other social actor with a long reach and deep pockets. We might like to think of religion as immune from those tendencies or more prone to them than other forms of knowing but neither is true. Religion has its unique role in the generation of information, knowledge, and wisdom but it shares with other forms of knowing tendencies to institutionalized abuse that must be addressed by measures to ensure public accountability.

OBJECTION TWO: RELIGION IS IRRATIONAL AND EVEN PATHOLOGICAL

The science-versus-religion debate is one battle in the war between rationality and irrationality.

—JERRY COYNE, *FAITH VS. FACT*

Religion is comparable to a childhood neurosis.

—SIGMUND FREUD, *FUTURE OF AN ILLUSION*

Coherence between a set of propositions is typically regarded as a precondition of their collective truth, and for this reason is regarded as a principle of rationality.

—PHILIP BARNES, *EDUCATION, RELIGION AND DIVERSITY*

---

21. Beckford, *Industrial Society*, 59.

Thus, by a variety of routes, one could end up rejecting Christianity, because in calling for something more than human flourishing, it was the implacable enemy of the human good, and at the same time a denial of the dignity of the self-sufficient buffered identity.

—Charles Taylor, *A Secular Age*

A second objection is the epistemological assessment of religion as basically irrational and even pathological. To start with, there is no doubt that some claims made in the name of religion stretch the limits of credulity and have been the inspiration for evil attitudes and practices. There is lots of evidence to support the claim that religion is inherently irrational and pathological. However, this objection is hard to sustain for three reasons. One is that religion is a persistent presence in the human family, having provided language for personal and collective meaning in many contexts for a wide variety of people groups. The suggestion that most of the human family is irrational or motivated by pathological impulses deserves cautious reconsideration. The second is that religion has inspired literature, science, philosophy, art, architecture, and the delivery of social services among many other human achievements that have included sophisticated rational thought. Third, we know there are people at all levels of society whose scholarship, acts of kindness, professional integrity, and loyal citizenship are inspired by a religious imagination. My argument is that, although there is irrationality and pathology narrated by religion, the idea that religion is inherently irrational or pathological cannot be sustained.

This is an important issue because the assertion that religion is irrational has implications for how it is treated in RE programs. In addition, claims about religion as pathological and irrational create social fault lines between those who are imagined to be further along the trajectory of rationality and mental maturity and those who are less developed. Charles Taylor comments that, "From this standpoint, a faith in a personal God belongs to a less mature standpoint."[22] We have seen similar marginalization based on gender, race, language, and nationality, to name a few. One effect is that we are deprived of the wisdom that can be generated by modes of thought and experience we do not share—in this case, religion.

---

22. Taylor, *Secular Age*, 363.

The assessment of religion as irrational or nonrational works in two ways, one of which is to protect religion, the other to marginalize it. The first puts religion in a sui generis category inaccessible to public scrutiny and accountability. It becomes the sacralized gatekeeper of knowledge and truth and creates a self-serving knowledge priesthood.

The second result, opposite of the first, is that religion can do what it wants, off in its own irrational bubble, but its irrationality means that it does not have a legitimate role in public discourse. Liam Gearon recounts Charles Darwin's rejection of Christianity because he could not align the story of the Tower of Babel with his findings based on scientific observation.[23] His conclusion, in various forms, means that in liberal societies, religious freedom legislation protects religious people to do and believe what they want in their places of worship and other spaces identified as private if they stay within the bubble created by the language of rational and modern secularism. Either way, the insights generated in a religious imagination are privatized and religion's potential as a public partner is diminished.

We do not have to accept the rationality-irrationality problem that protects religion, on the one hand, and dismisses it, on the other. However, to reframe it we need to think about religion in a different way, and we will do so by thinking about what kind of information, knowledge, and wisdom it generates and on the kinds of questions foregrounded in the interpretive category of religion. To get us started, let's go back to Schleiermacher, who was not disputing the importance of religion, seeing it as integral to human nature. What he objected to was "the confusion between religion and that knowledge that belongs to theology. Knowledge whatever its value—is to be always distinguished from religion."[24] Among other things, *knowledge* in this context is seen primarily as the outcome of a rational process that can be codified in terms of falsifiable propositions.

Although he is arguing a different point about religious literacy, Stephen Prothero seems to suggest something similar when he links the "decline of religious literacy" to the "rise of public power in the early nineteenth century of a new form of Protestantism called evangelicalism. By the end of that century a lack of elementary knowledge of Christianity would constitute evidence of authentic faith." His concern is that "what

---

23. Gearon, *Holy Ground*, 3.
24. Gearon, *Holy Ground*, 32.

for generations had been shameful—religious illiteracy—would become a badge of honor in a nation besotted with the self-made man and the spirit-filled preacher."[25] However, while Justine Ellis is also committed to religious literacy, she challenges Prothero's limiting religious literacy to its rational and textual components, noting that the emerging interface between affect theory and religious studies invites a more nuanced and diverse way of understanding knowledge in religious literacy.[26]

One conclusion to the distinction between religion and knowledge is that religion is a mode of human knowing and experience separate from anything resembling rational thought. However, that way of thinking about it presupposes that the most important thing about knowledge is that its legitimacy rests on propositions that can be verified or falsified. Knowledge, in a propositional sense as Schleiermacher understood it, is not what is most important about the wisdom generated in any knowledge category, including religion. Although his formulation is problematic, he was thinking about knowledge and religion in ways that alert us to think beyond a rationality-irrationality continuum. The point is that rationality in the sense defined in the European Enlightenment tradition that foregrounds falsifiable propositions is one element in knowledge but may not be the only one or even the most important one in knowledge and wisdom. Rationality in the form of propositional knowledge in religion may be getting at something else, not in competition with other forms of religious knowing, but in partnership with them.

Assessing Religion: Science Versus Religion

A good place to think about the irrationality of religion is to place it on a rationality scale with science. To a certain extent, the choice to set religion alongside science is arbitrary but not entirely. I am choosing science because it is most often chosen as the talking point, either to protect a role for religion by pointing out the limitations of science and scientific knowing, or to demonstrate that religion is, at best, an anachronism in the modern world or, at worst, a harmful impediment to social and personal progress based on scientific reasoning.

However, aside from some extreme voices, the opposition to religion as a way of knowing the world is usually not against religion itself

---

25. Prothero, *Religious Literacy*, 111.
26. Ellis, *Politics*, 86.

but against forms of religion that stray into areas of public discourse where they are seen as transgressive. In somewhat the same way, opposition to science is usually not against science as such but is framed as *scientism*, to indicate the elevation of science to a status that exceeds what it can rightly deliver. Commenting on the "confusion of myths with theories" John Gray says that theists, "peddling an Argument from Design," have "tried to develop theories that explain the origins of the universe and humankind better than prevailing scientific accounts. In doing so they are conceding to science an unwarranted authority over other ways of thinking."[27] The opposition between religion and science, faith and reason, and religion and secular are the most commonly coded ways of summarizing a conflicted and competitive relationship between the two, which I argue is misguided.

Consider this: *I am visiting the Ark Encounter in Williamstown, Kentucky, Ken Ham's robust retelling of the story of a catastrophic flood recorded in Genesis, the first book of the Bible. I am amazed by the sheer size and ingenuity of the project, entertained by the dioramas, informed by the research about how the challenges of air flow, water, animal care— including the management of manure—food storage and production, and living quarters might have been addressed. My visit in the winter of 2019 coincides with a steady rainfall, which seems appropriate given the story I am entering. I am struck, impressed even, by the boldness of this statement just off I-75, unapologetically asserting the primacy of Biblical revelation as the interpretive screen through which scientific evidence is legitimized as a way of supporting one Christian understanding of the relationship between religion and science. I am not persuaded to adopt a Creationist view of origins and age of the earth or its interpretation of Biblical narratives. I am also not comfortable with its positioning itself as a moral tale in the context of a kind of culture war that seems to energize so much religious activity. I squirm during the video presentation of the interviews between Noah and the skeptical journalist interviewing him about his project, she and her support crew made up and costumed to suggest moral turpitude and existential despair that, in this telling, were the triggers for divine wrath. I do not share the subtext of pleasure accompanying this morality tale, in which the righteous are spared to repopulate the earth, replacing the multitudes who could have avoided their fate by responding appropriately to the one-hundred-year sermon Noah delivered as he prepared for the judgment*

---

27. Gray, *Seven Types*, 12.

awaiting them. I come away with mixed feelings, glad that I live in a world in which such boldness is possible, while at the same time recognizing that, like all bold cultural products, it is made possible by money, power, and privilege and that its impact depends on timing, taking hold in a particular historical moment to serve a political purpose. It also succeeded in getting me thinking about the relationship between religion, science, and education, perhaps an unintended consequence.

Consider another visit to another site: *I am visiting the Museum of Nature in Ottawa where even a cursory viewing reveals a narrative assuming Darwinian evolution. From a creationist perspective, it tells a story supported by evidence made questionable by speculative gaps about the origins of the universe involving something called the big bang and an unquestioned reliance on blind, mechanistic natural selection with a survival-of-the-fittest story to explain life itself in all its diversity, without reference to divine intervention or moral purpose. Religion has no place here as a way of explaining origins or anything else relating to the world in which I live and breathe. There is room for mythical interpretation, but the real information is generated by science. I see children being subjected to dioramas that tell a story without being given a hint that this is only one way to see the world.*

These are competing versions of the world between two quite different ways of seeing. In one, there are few if any references to the cultural and historical moment in which Darwin's paradigm took hold nor the political and social uses it serves that helps to explain its success. In the other, there are few if any suggestions that placing dinosaurs on the ark might be questionable, with little doubt that deviations from a creationist narrative lead to moral confusion and short skirts with a bit too much leg exposure, tattoos, and other evidence accounting for a catastrophic global flood. There is no doubt in the Ark Encounter narrative that the Bible is the authoritative source of anything worth knowing, being a divinely written, ahistorical document delivering universal truth about, among other things, science. However, it seems unaware of the confusion of myths and theories, adopting and adapting scientific theory to support religious myth, demonstrating that theists are among those who demand more of science and religion than either can deliver.

What commentators do agree on is that religion and science are quite different modes of human knowing. However, while the differences between the Ark Encounter and the Museum of Nature seem like an unbridgeable fault line, there is significant common ground between them. Both are origin and destiny narratives, and both are morality tales calling for repentance. They part company on the nature of the sin from which we need to repent but both include impending doom as the result of non-repentance. The Ark Encounter calls on us to turn back to God's truth away from personal immorality, particularly in skepticism and sins of a sexual nature,[28] something that seems to occupy the imagination of some forms of Christianity to a curious degree. The Museum of Nature confronts us with the morality of our role in environmental degradation, one form of which is our careless use of plastic.[29] Both reach for and assume a form of universal truth about life and our human moral task on earth that set both in a larger meaning story. Thinking about the Museum of Nature and the Ark Encounter as the embodiments of two morality tales helps us think about not only the differences between science and religion but also about the common ground between them.

Here's a question: Is a rationality scale the most useful way to consider the differences between science and religion, placing science on the rationality side with religion on the irrationality side? I am not sure it is. Here's why.

Two points, the first being that science, like religion, is not one thing, but the second point is that religion has its own unique contribution to knowledge of the world. Claude Lévi-Strauss alerts us to the wisdom that our definitions are socially constructed, cautioning us against the tendency to see our knowing as the culmination of a progressive historiography in a process of enlightenment and liberation from, among others, religion. The European Enlightenment tradition, leading with rationalism and fascination with science, was an understandable corrective to religion's overreach that had dominated public space and discourse. However, faith in science comes with its own tendencies to overreach. In the twenty-first century we are seeing critical examination of science, based on evidence of the limitations of science and the scientific method in delivering the resolutions of our greatest challenges. Rationality can generate its own irrationality, it seems, as it has in religion when it is asked to do things beyond its legitimate scope.

Religion has had its own day in a progressive historiography, the idea being that, while all civilizations have something like religion, European Christians were the ones who got it right. The point of *comparative*

---

28. Ark Encounter, "Door."
29. Canadian Museum of Nature, "Water Gallery."

religions through much of its history has been to demonstrate the superiority of European Christianity and secularized versions of it over all other forms of religion, even when the people under the anthropological microscope did not have a term for it. Timothy Fitzgerald is one voice among many arguing that religion is a European Christian construct imposed on a wide variety of practices and forms for which there are no equivalent terms among the people groups being observed. His way forward is that we discard the concept of religion altogether, although his encouraging us to do so is uphill work.

Despite its complicated heritage, religion has been a remarkably ubiquitous presence in human societies. It did lose out to science in the competition for preeminent status as the source for and gatekeeper of a common language for rational public discourse. Religion is seen as optional in Western and other societies in which the language of secularism has been adopted as way to transcend ethnic and sectarian identities. Science is seen to provide a language for dependable public knowledge. Not everyone agrees, as our anti-vaxxer and flat-earth friends will tell us, but so far, their arguments are more on the fringes of our common spaces.[30] However, the role of science in Western imaginaries creates its own blind spots, one of which is that other modes of knowing are marginalized as equal partners. The assessment of religion as basically irrational is, among other things, a strategy to keep religion in its limited place and to mask the blind spots of the narrative that replaced it.

Rationality and Thinking Well

One of the things at play in assessments of religion as an interpretive category is what it means to think well, often coded in terms of rationality. In academic programs we are familiar with the distinction between the *hard* sciences and other fields of learning, the idea being that the sciences and mathematics represent the pinnacle of a conceptual hierarchy of rationality. This leaves art and English teachers somewhat on the

---

30. In 2025 as I am writing this, I am less sanguine about the trends rejecting science and am drawn to the idea that the reaction may be against the overreach and abuses of science and other forms of authority exercised in service of any number of powerful interests. Shifts in paradigms are unsettling and, at the same time, create space for new ways of thinking about the world, not all of them welcome, of course. I disagree with the Creationist narrative animating the Ark Encounter and the anger of the anti-vaxxer movements, but they are interesting from a historical perspective.

defensive because they teach *soft* subjects. History is somewhere in the middle because, while it involves gathering evidence it also strays into the murky world of interpretation, the extreme end of which is history as literature and even fiction. Physical education can be rationalized on the *healthy body, healthy mind* model, which means that physical fitness allows us to think more rationally. English as part of an academic program makes sense because it is the language of commerce while art is a kind of educational luxury and first on the cost chopping block.

So where does that leave religion? Well, in short, religion is far down on the rationality hierarchy, particularly when it is seen as basically a matter of personal belief distinct from and even hostile to knowledge in any respectable sense of the term. In this construction, religion and RE have so little to do with real life in the marketplace that it is pretty much consigned to the broom closet of education delivery systems. One concern expressed by researchers advocating for RE is that it is not taken very seriously in most schools, except *faith schools*.[31] There are some good reasons for this that we will engage in chapter 5. For now, let's just say that advocacy for RE is marked by angst and must justify itself in ways that technology education, mathematics, and driver training do not. Linking religion to fears of social disruption, including terrorism, has given RE and religious literacy a period of exposure and even a measure of cautious respect after 2000 but who knows how long that will last? Religion teachers have, since the Enlightenment, been aware of the dustbins of history because religion seems only tangentially related to thinking well in the modern world. There are proposals addressing the dustbin of educational history worries. Dinham and Shaw call for a national RE strategy in the UK, the content of which "should reflect the real religious landscape, as revealed by cutting edge theory and data in the study of contemporary religion and belief,"[32] their concern being that RE has been marginalized because it is based on ways of thinking that no longer speak to the modern world. However, what is less clear is what a persuasive theory might be and how the real religious landscape might be identified. Data generated by scientific research is useful perhaps, but can it resolve the key issues of credibility of and thinking well in religion?

---

31. Dinham and Shaw, *RE for REal*; Clarke and Woodhead, *New Settlement* (2015); CORE, *Religion and Worldviews*; McCowan, "Bridges." Here I am using *faith schools* as the authors use it, not the way I use it, my argument being that all schools are faith schools.

32. Dinham and Shaw, *RE for REal*, 1 (recommendation 5).

I am not sure it can, at least not entirely persuasively, in part because it leaves the possibility that thinking well in religion will be defined in terms not true to the way religion works in life, by imposing one way of knowing on another. Carol Smart, Lori Beaman, and Ben Berger demonstrate the ways law distils what is and what is not real in legal proceedings. J. Edward Chamberlin observes misunderstandings and marginalization of stories told by indigenous peoples that do not adapt well to the forms of rationality preferred in modern legal systems. Science and law are seen to provide a common language for secular, rational public reality that marginalizes voices speaking in other registers. Advocates for RE are trying to figure out how to translate the irrationality seen as inherent in religion into the rationality of science to save RE.

As a tactical move to save RE, the shifting of categories do not really address the objection to religion as irrational and pathological. Let's go back to the Ark Encounter. The Ark Encounter assumes and even exalts a way of knowing with foundations that are not rational. There clearly are rational processes at work in the project, but it does not start there. And that's a problem for some of us for whom rational processes are the foundations of legitimate ways of processing information and knowledge. According to Jerry Coyne, this represents a deeply offensive problem, and he insists that there is a war going on over the encroachment of religion in society at the expense of science. In this war, religion is represented as fundamentally and dangerously irrational, representing itself as beyond the reach of rational and public criticism. It is not falsifiable in the sense that, say, a science experiment is. You cannot prove or falsify my belief in God, the efforts to do either notwithstanding, which is especially important if God tells me not to get vaccinated or to fly an airplane into a tower. The Ark Encounter and the creationist view of science it embodies provides evidence to support the philosophical assessment of religion as basically irrational and bad thinking. It runs roughshod over scientific evidence about the age of the universe, origins of life, and biological diversity but does so in its war against religious untruth rationalized by scientism. At least, that is the way it represents itself, but in doing so, the creationist framework imposes the category of religion on science, resulting in similar challenges to its credibility in being assessed as irrational. Thinking well in religion calls for a look at how *evidence* might work in religion, assessing it, not in terms of science or law that have their own rules of evidence but something more true to religion as a way of knowing the world.

Evidence

The link between the philosophical and experiential objections to religion is evidence, the question being, *What is the evidence for claims made in the language of religion?* Evidence establishes common ground and is the basis for accountability in any kind of knowing. Debates over evidence occur between those who object to religion or forms of it but also within and between forms of religion. Debates over evidence are a normal part of human knowing but they occur within accepted rules of engagement within an interpretive category. For example, debates over scientific assertions occur within the rules established by the scientific method. Is there a link between diabetes and sugar consumption? Well, what's the evidence established by commonly accepted practices in science? That's how the question is settled, in principle at least. The practice is complicated by the fact that science occurs in a network of power relations, political and economic interests, and professional ambition that can muddy the outcomes of scientific investigation, but let's leave that for now.

Disagreement and debate are an essential part of the process by which science is seen to progress. Somebody comes up with the idea that vaccinations are linked to autism and publishes a paper that triggers a lively debate about method and conclusions. The processes governed by the scientific method had consequences for the career of Andrew Wakefield who briefly thought he was onto a good thing.[33] The same thing is true of interpreting dinosaur bones and fossils, which means that scientists must be open to revising their ideas, sometimes with career-altering outcomes. The age of the universe and its size, the management of a virus, and the nature of gender are other examples of debates in which careers and industries find their futures or not, for better or worse. The point is that for meaningful debate to occur, there must be an agreement about the rules of engagement. However, while the rules of evidence in science are well established as they are in law, the same cannot be said of religion.

One factor in the rules of meaningful engagement is that there must be agreement that what is being debated is legitimate. This is true in religion but equally so in the sciences. For example, it would be hard to launch a debate about the evidence generated by the science of phrenology or eugenics. Both were considered legitimate ways to categorize human beings in the eighteenth and nineteenth centuries and, in the case of eugenics, into the twenty-first century with some disturbing implications.

33. Matthews-King, "Who Is Andrew Wakefield."

Debates in science are deemed legitimate or not by standards established outside the boundaries of the scientific method. The issue in the class action lawsuit relating to the Tuskegee studies on the effects of syphilis in African Americans was not about adherence to the scientific method. Rather, the social context of scientific investigation had changed between the 1930s and the 1970s so that what was normal at one time is horrifying at another.[34]

Currently there are debates among scientists about the possibility of life on other planets or the idea that there could be life in a fourth or fifth dimension or the idea of *imaginary time*. These discussions leave me unmoved and only slightly interested, since I am fully occupied with life on this earth in this time dimension. However, those arcane reflections on the nature of time—for example, can it move backward?—do raise some interesting (and distracting) possibilities regarding the reality of angels, sightings of the Virgin Mary,[35] and the resurrection of Lazarus as recorded in the Gospel of John (ch. 11). Could they have happened? OK, that's a discussion for another time and place, maybe, but the question of time and how it works suggests that it does intersect with what might or might not be considered rational, not based on the scientific method, strictly speaking, but on a more basic *So what* question. In any case, you must accept the basic rules of engagement to consider evidence but also the legitimacy of what is being debated within those rules.

Consider this: *I am in a cathedral in Orvieto. The cathedral was built under the orders of Pope Urban IV back in the fourteenth century to honor a miracle proving the doctrine of transubstantiation. There is a reliquary that I see, housing the relic, a cloth with blood on it that I do not see.*[36] *Now, you can see this in several ways. If you don't believe in the doctrine in the first place, there is no point in arguing whether the cloth on display there is evidence. The whole idea is ridiculous. However, if you do believe in the doctrine, you might still argue about the evidence, debating whether this piece of cloth clinches the argument or is a hoax. In other words, you accept the parameters of the debate that transubstantiation may be real, but this evidence may or may not prove it. The political context of the fourteenth century is relevant in understanding the Orvieto Duomo, built at a time when popes were feeling insecure about their positions in a dynamic religious and political context and the fact that the European world was*

---

34. Centers for Disease Control, "Untreated."
35. Sullivan, *Miracle Detectives*.
36. Thoman, "Pilgrimage to Orvieto."

being devastated by a pandemic involving rats, fleas, and Yersinia pestis.[37] *Transubstantiation was more than a marginal theoretical idea; it was an important theological belief but, in addition, the authority of the Roman Church as the mediator between God and the rest of us was at stake in a world in flux. The point is that debates about theological ideas, like those in science and art, take their meaning and energy from the context in which they occur.*[38]

Like the possibility of life on other planets, proofs of God and the doctrine of transubstantiation are not my things. My point is that there must be agreement, both about the logic of the debate but also about the relevance or legitimacy of the topic being debated. In that sense, assessments of rationality and irrationality are contextual. Was the medical research in the Tuskegee study rational? Well, it probably was when seen in terms of the internal logic of the scientific method. However, it was based on assumptions about the humanity of its subjects that we now consider deeply offensive, or at least they are to some of us. Not all of us, white supremacy still being a thing, as you may have noticed. The idea that African and Indigenous Americans are less human continues to be a powerful cultural basis for white supremacy but its overt expression in the 1930s is a shocking, although perhaps not such a surprising revelation, not of scientific incompetence, but of institutionalized moral evil. The Tuskegee story revealed truths unintended at that time, one of which is that science is embedded in social and cultural contexts in which it can be weaponized to entrench a social and political order.

Evil does not have to be perpetrated by people we think of as evil. Hannah Arendt, writing about the trial of Alfred Eichmann, used the term *banality* to describe this inoffensive civil servant's obsession with logistics, made efficient by highly rational principles, serving a regime that used science at a sophisticated level. Johannes Fabian, in his critical examination

37. Tuchman, *Distant Mirror*; Terpstra, *Religious Refugees*.
38. The reader might also be interested in Ginzburg's *The Cheese and the Worms: The Cosmos of a Sixteenth Century Miller*, the story of Mennochio, whose ideas about the cosmos got him into trouble with church authorities. They used the power of the Inquisition to try him, not just because of his unorthodox ideas, but because he was questioning the authority of the church to tell him what and how to think. And he would not stop talking about it. Very entertaining for us, although, in the end, more serious for him. In a story with more cultural traction, what got Socrates into trouble was his persistent questions. If he had stopped talking, he would likely not have gotten himself into trouble with Athenian authorities; Tillson, "Rival Conceptions." Critical and unorthodox (not necessarily the same things) thinking is a problem for those governing the world, especially in times of insecurity.

of the science of anthropology, draws on Thomas Kuhn and Paul Feyerabend to state "the obvious fact that all sciences, including the most abstract and mathematized disciplines, are social endeavors which must be carried out through the channels and means, and according to the rules, of communication available to the community of practitioners and to the wider society of which they are a part."[39] One conclusion is that rationality can deliver some kinds of truth but not the whole truth of anything and, in fact, sometimes can be an instrument of sophisticated evil.

Was the building of the Duomo in Orvieto rational? Well, we live in a different time and so it seems strange to us in twenty-first-century Canada, but a tour of the building and the context in which it was conceived and built, and the purpose it served, indicate rational processes. The fact that it has stayed upright for all this time provides evidence that the builders knew what they were doing. It is rational in the same way as the Ark Encounter and the World Trade Center. After 2001, the World Trade Center was rebuilt, a monument to a mythology of an indomitable American spirit after a shocking breach of the walls by some outsiders armed with box cutters and a rudimentary understanding of how to fly jetliners.[40] But was it rational? Like the Orvieto Duomo, the rebuilding of the World Trade Center is designed to provide evidence of certainty to mask the uncertainty that animates much social and political life. A faith-based project, in other words.

That's not unique to America, of course. My engagement in the global marketplace is based on faith. I use electronic media of exchange designed by shadowy, all-seeing, mega-organizations that deliver books I buy from people I never meet, delivered by people who I do not know, working for actors who operate pretty much like the church in the fourteenth century. They deliver me a good life defined in particular ways, but the whole thing depends on processes that I barely understand and that make me nervous when I think about their fragile hope based on faith. The evidence for my faith is the books that arrive on my doorstep but the mechanisms by which it happens are pretty murky. Rational? Well, yes, but our systems do not really start and end with rational, which introduces a considerable level of uncertainty about which I prefer not to think. The issues of faith, evidence, and rationality and irrationality are not unique to religion.

---

39. Fabian, *Time*, 109.
40. www.explorewtc.com.

Uncertainty and Rationality

Scientists (even the hard, rational ones) work in a world of uncertainty in which our rational processes are less secure than we might like. In 1926, Werner Heisenberg took Max Planck's quantum theory and Albert Einstein's theory of relativity to the next level by adding the uncertainty principle to the dynamic world of physics. If you go back further, you can trace a story that takes us from a conceptual universe with certainties into one of uncertainties.[41]

The twentieth century was a time of uncertainty in other interpretive categories as well, which continues into the twenty-first century. If you are interested, you can listen in on intense debates between modernist and postmodern historians over the nature of facts in the study of history and the role of interpretation of evidence. The science of knowing has shifted from a clear distinction between subject and object to a much more blurry, dynamic picture, one extreme of which is that there is no such thing as objective truth that can provide a reliable basis for rational discussion. It's all *interpretation*, as Roger Lundin tells us,[42] to be subjected to critical theorizing based on the idea that words are instrumental in constructing a fundamentally chaotic world, according to Terry Eagleton,[43] or *fake news*, a politically useful extension of the same idea.[44] Interpretation and knowledge, Michel Foucault argues,[45] serve political purposes, so not only do we have to understand interpretations but we also must think critically to understand the power positions of the interpreters and their political agendas.

---

41. I am not a physicist. I am unable to grasp the mathematics and the details of the principles of physics and am humbled by those who can do so. However, I began reading some math and physics people because of an interview between Steve Paikin and Brian Greene on TVO in which Greene talked about the problem of meaning in physics; see Paikin, "Brian Greene." As in, the implications of quantum physics for our humanity, evolution and entropy and the uncertainty principle for our humanity and our quest for certainty. That took me to reading Erwin Schrödinger, Stephen Hawking, Brian Greene, and Sabine Hossenfelder, among others who move into those bigger questions.

42. Lundin, *Culture of Interpretation*.

43. Eagleton, *After Theory*.

44. Artificial intelligence and information technologies are taking the issues of evidence and truth and the reliability of "facts" to a whole new level, similar to another technology we now take for granted: the printing press, which introduced new levels of social confusion back in the fifteenth century.

45. Foucault, *Archaeology of Knowledge*.

Sigmund Freud theorized human nature in a three-level psychological version of the underworld, the middle earth, and the spiritual upper story, calling it the *id, ego,* and *super ego*. One of the implications is that our motivations are buried somewhere in unconscious processes that, if you are sufficiently motivated, you can pay an analyst to unearth, including my belief in God who, it turns out, is the superego stand-in for my father. Not real at all, at least not in a real sense. In ethics, our moral universe has shifted from a firm belief that morality is God-ordained to something that is more tentative, trying to balance individual freedom to choose behaviors without fear of judgment of some outside authority and the potential anarchy resulting from taking that principle too far. Ursula Goodenough says that the "bio-centred life orientation locates its center of value, meaning and purpose squarely within the realm of the contingent" one result being "the very kind of irredeemable contingency identified with meaninglessness and absurdity."[46] We live in a world of uncertainty and contingency, heightened by social media that have detached information and knowledge from recognizable authorities. The authorities are there, but they are hidden by a variety of twenty-first century masks.

However, this is not as new as we might think. It took physicists until 1926 to formulate a truth that the writers of sacred texts have known for a long time, which is that most of what we know about how the universe works is tentative. Sigmund Freud was restating something you can find in the wisdom literature and poetry preserved in the Bible. There is a whole lot about reality and about ourselves that we simply do not know, including our motivations, which come from opaque places. Karl Marx's critical analysis of class structure and the manipulation of our consciousness can be seen in the Old Testament prophets calling out those in positions of power who used religious language to cover their self-serving privileges. Christopher Watkin observes that "however much they may wish to position themselves against Christianity, Nietzsche, Marx and Freud are echoing the Christian bent to suspect apparent motives; we might even impishly suggest that this complicity with the biblical gesture of suppressing the truth is part of the truth that they, in turn, are suppressing."[47]

Accepting uncertainty has not stopped us from drilling down through the shifting sands of our conceptual models to what we hope is

---

46. Goodenough, "Transcendence," 7.
47. Watkin, *Biblical Critical Theory*, 122.

the bedrock of certainty. Some of us have given up the search, agreeing that history is essentially meaningless, a conclusion proposed by Paul Conkin and Roland Stromberg.[48] One of the problems they identify for moderns is the essential tragedy of the human story[49] and the *terror of history*,[50] but that may be the price we have to pay for being, well, modern.

Nicholas Wolterstorff says about Max Weber that his "academic melancholy was a component of his far more pervasive 'melancholy of modernity,'" a consequence of Weber's theory of differentiation that rejects the possibility of a comprehensive meaning narrative.[51] His observation echoes one made by Charles Taylor who refers to a "generalized sense in our culture that with the eclipse of the transcendent, something may have been lost." Taylor adds, "The critics of nostalgia, nevertheless, accept that this loss is inevitable; it is the price we pay for modernity and rationality, but we must courageously accept this bargain, and lucidly opt for what we have inevitably become. One of the most influential proponents of this latter position was Max Weber."[52]

Taylor distinguishes two kinds of melancholy, one associated with *acedia* identified in earlier epochs as *sin*, the antidote to which was repentance.[53] The other is melancholy of the post-Axial age where it is seen as normal and inevitable, one consequence of which is a cultural "malaise."[54] Reflecting on the post–World War I "sense of living in a shattered order" he observes that "contemporaries are ambivalent about this earlier age, or at least their reactions are complex. We feel wider, less naïve, and somewhat patronizing toward our patriotic forebears, but also somewhat envious of their certainties."[55] However, in a later passage, Taylor draws on another tradition of understanding malaise, proposing the *dignity of sin* by which he means that the concept of sin includes the possibility of choice to make changes, to repent. We are not fated to melancholy, even when facing a world in which suffering and evil seem endemic, because there is a normative reality to which we can return, if

---

48. Conkin and Stromberg, *Heritage*, 102.
49. Conkin and Stromberg, *Heritage*, 235.
50. Eliade, *Myth*, ch. 4; *Sacred and Profane*, 113.
51. Wolterstorff, *Religion in the University*, 11.
52. Taylor, *Secular Age*, 307.
53. Kathleen Norris, in her book *Acedia & Me*, examines acedia as a spiritual matter that, in her view, is the source of melancholy that eludes therapy.
54. Taylor, *Malaise*; *Secular Age*, 308.
55. Taylor, *Secular Age*, 410.

we choose to do so. We may struggle with what normative reality is for us, but we can rest in the certainty that it exists. Or we can choose not to believe it, in which case our quest for certainty may well be meaningless. Therapy, while useful, cannot address the fundamental problem of meaning and purpose, but that may be all we have left, having rejected religion as a way of navigating an uncertain world. Taylor says, "The denial of much traditionally understood spiritual reality has been a crucial factor in the therapeutic turn."[56]

Of course, history may be just one damned thing after another, or one damned thing over and over again, but that ultimately unsatisfying quip has not stopped people in different fields from trying to formulate a coherent picture to make sense of life in all its multilayered uncertainty. Stephen Hawking tells us that "most physicists hope to find a unified theory that will explain all four forces as different aspects of a single force. Indeed, many would say this is the prime goal of physics today."[57] The science of physics has been driven by the question, "What are the truly elementary particles, the basic building blocks from which everything is made?"[58] What's really real, in other words or what's *the one thing needful*, "some higher goal which transcends, or gives sense to all the lower ones."[59] In a secular society we may imagine ourselves to have outgrown religion and accepted unbelief as the mark of a modern rational thinker. However, unbelief is a subtraction category that cannot account for the search for alternative sources of certainty and meaning. What makes our routines "really worthwhile, lies in [a] bigger picture, which extends across space but also across time."[60] Where we land in our quest for a bigger picture to anchor us in time and space and which bigger picture is the true one or the one that most closely approximates truth is a topic for another day. My point is that belief in something or someone is inherent in human nature, which does not mean

---

56. Taylor, *Secular Age*, 621.

57. Hawking, *Brief History*, 69. The three forces under consideration in a "grand unifying theory" are electromagnetic and strong and weak nuclear forces. The search for a "complete unifying theory that would cover everything" incorporates gravity but understanding "why it is that we and the universe exist" is another matter entirely. Hawking, *Brief History*, 74, 153, 175.

58. Hawking, *Brief History*, 65.

59. Taylor, *Secular Age*, 308. Roy Rappaport argues something similar although he does not draw the same conclusions about melancholy resulting from the loss of meaning in a secular age, which is where Taylor and Wolterstorff land in their conclusions.

60. Taylor, *Secular Age*, 716. Matthew Crawford talks about "jigs" as a key to successful living but, unlike Taylor and Miroslav Volf, does not refer to the bigger issues of ultimate meaning and purpose.

that belief removes all uncertainty. Belief and uncertainty are companions, dancing partners in life.

Uncertainty Is Inherent in Religion (And in Any Other Interpretive Category)

Religion has a built-in uncertainty principle in two ways. The first is the theoretical uncertainty about what religion is but second, there is uncertainty about truth in religion. We have seen many definitions of religion about which there are lively debates. In addition, however, there is uncertainty in what used to be considered eternal verities and how we get to them. There may be eternal verities but mostly they seem out of reach.

The point is that we seem to worry about our certainties and work hard to shore them up through a variety of means. However, the sacred text providing the basis of Christianity and other literature emerging out of that tradition are more cautious. In fact, the Bible is a collection of stories of uncertainty, recognizing that "we see through a glass darkly." That's according to the apostle Paul, eloquently rendered in the King James Version of the Bible,[61] recalling Plato whose cave model of what we know has been another source of wisdom about human limitations. Many of the psalms are cries of fear and pain written by people in mortal danger, expressing grief, anger, confusion, and despair. The writer of Ecclesiastes, identified as the teacher, gives us sobering advice when he says, "Do not be overrighteous, neither be overwise," to which he adds weight by his rhetorical question, "Why destroy yourself?"[62] His conclusion is that most of our best and sophisticated thinking, building, and striving amount to vanity, by which he means that, in the end, we have to give it all up anyway.

The great human dilemma (among others) is to meet "maximal demand," which is "how to define our highest spiritual or moral aspirations for human beings, while showing a path to the transformation involved that does not crush, mutilate or deny what is essential to our humanity."[63] Although there is competition among religious groups about who owns

---

61. A phrase used by the apostle Paul in 1 Cor 13:12 to describe our bodily limitations. He looks ahead in hope of seeing and knowing clearly in a life after death. The verse reads, "For now we see through a glass, darkly; but then face to face: now I know in part; but then shall I know even as also I am known" (KJV).

62. Eccl 7:16, NIV.

63. Taylor, *Secular Age*, 639–40.

the best way to reach maximal demand, Taylor is more cautious, saying, "Christians don't really have the solution to the dilemma. At best, Christians can only point to the exemplary lives of certain trail-blazing people and communities."[64] So, no final answer, at least not within the immanent frame in which we live. Final solutions have their own implications, among them that they "crush, mutilate or deny what is essential to our humanity."

Hope and Certainty in Our Lived Uncertainty: A Paradox

The teacher in Ecclesiastes reminds his son to enjoy what he has (the wife of your youth, your good teeth) while you have them because in the end, you are going to age (if you are lucky) and die (which you will, lucky or not). Curiously, this sets you free to hold life with a light hand, not to sweat the small stuff, to live fully while you can without taking yourself too seriously. The apostle Paul, well versed in Jewish wisdom, reflects on the implications of the death and resurrection of Jesus Christ, taking his readers from the contingencies inherent in human life to a place of hope. He is seen as the inventor of Christianity, taking religion from *law* to *grace* as a fundamental tenet of this Jewish subcult, which opened new possibilities of certainty proposed in a new paradigm. Much of that wisdom has been marginalized in Christian tradition, spiritualized as a way of mitigating its impact on the way we want to live. However, Christopher Watkin argues that contingency is built into religious wisdom because, in the end, we and the world are not necessary and are not eternal. He refers to the "higher principle of gratuity" that acknowledges the "pathos of contingency" leading not to despair but to a freedom to explore the cosmos and life in it as a gift.[65]

Francis Collins, who headed the Human Genome Project, reminds us that St. Augustine of Hippo was cautious about achieving certainty based on sacred texts.[66] The full range of human life lived on the razor's edge of hope and despair is often masked by the Disney-like representation of Christianity promoted by the prosperity gospel or other ways of doing religion designed to avoid ambiguity and guarantee health and

---

64. Taylor, *Secular Age*, 643.
65. Watkin, *Biblical Critical Theory*, 60–61.
66. Collins, *Language*, 83.

happiness if you push the right divine buttons. But sacred texts present a more cautious picture of the human condition.

Those of us who have been knocked around by life a bit find that certainties are elusive and nuanced, and that our hope cannot depend on our bodied experience. William Cowper wrote his poetry, including "God Moves in a Mysterious Way," while struggling with mental illness, and Horatio Spafford wrote the lyrics to the famous "It Is Well with My Soul" while traveling to meet his wife who had survived the shipwreck that killed his four daughters. On my desk I have a memento mori, in the form of a skull, in the tradition of monks who kept them on their desks as a reminder that life is fleeting. OK, mine is a plastic one acquired one Halloween at a dollar store, not the real thing donated by one of my brothers who had shuffled off this mortal coil[67] and did not need his anymore. It sits just above eye level, looking down at me as I write this, reminding me that I will follow friends and family members who have gone before me into the earth but also that life is sweet and pretty funny a lot of the time. The teacher whose wisdom is summarized in Ecclesiastes told us that a long time ago. Uncertainty is nothing new in religious traditions, and much of the tension within them is about where certainty lies and how we know what it is. The politics of nostalgia is alive and well in religious traditions who imagine a past when we knew truth as God revealed it to us, but nostalgia can serve to mask realities and truths we may not want to hear. Even a cursory survey of any religious tradition reveals that there never was a time when truth and certainty were uncontested verities, let alone eternal ones. It doesn't mean there are no certainties. It just means that no one owns them.

Faith and the Uncertainty Principle

The representation of religion as a mode of knowing relying on faith that is impervious to historical context and change works both for those of us who want to give religion a place of privilege and those of us who want to marginalize it. However, the same thing can be said about other ways of knowing. Sabine Hossenfelder, theoretical physicist and self-identified atheist, tells her readers that "if you want to believe that the past exists because it's math and all of math exists, that is up to you." She is more

---

67. The reader will recognize this from Hamlet's soliloquy "To be or not to be." Shakespeare, *Hamlet*, 3.1.75.

cautious, telling us that the assertions "implicitly assume that mathematics itself is timeless, that mathematical truth is eternal, and that logic doesn't change." She adds, however, "This is an assumption that cannot be proved because what would you prove it true with? It's one of the usually unstated articles of faith that our scientific inquiry is based on."[68] Faith, Hossenfelder argues, is inherent in science. We believe in a model of the world and build our lives on our beliefs. But we also know that our models are contingent, time bound, and socially constructed.

Our understanding of science is different from the way it was understood in the seventeenth century or the role it played in Aztec or Chaldean societies. No one is surprised by developments in scientific or esthetic knowing but it would be difficult to sustain an argument suggesting that science or art should be discarded as one ages or as society changes. While the quest for meaning and coherence is what makes us human, how we construct our narratives about their sources of legitimacy is dynamic and ever changing. As with so many questions around religion, the charge that religion is impervious to change and irrational because it is based on faith gets at a kind of truth but also misses some things.

Ana-Maria Rizzuto, saying that "belief in God or absence of belief are no indicators of any type of pathology," also argues that our representations of God do change in response to life stages and events.[69] While we may believe that God never changes, what is also true is that our representations of God or what we believe about God do change. In a world of contingency and uncertainty, we live with platforms of *basic trust* that Erik Erikson linked with religion.[70] The absence of basic trust is pathological but those platforms of belief, forming a silent presence in our lives, do evolve, are re-evaluated as we change. Our scientists know that, of course, and have for a long time, living their own uncertainties every time they publish a paper. Religion and science are different but, in some ways, not so much, especially in their shared search for certainty we will never quite achieve through a process of thinking hard and well. Certainty lies elsewhere.

Hossenfelder wants to "convey that some spiritual ideas are perfectly compatible with modern physics, and others are, indeed, supported by it. And why not? That physics has something to say about our connection to the universe is not so surprising. Science and religion have the same

68. Hossenfelder, *Existential Physics*, 22.
69. Rizzuto, *Birth*, 202.
70. Rizzuto, *Birth*, 203.

roots, and still today they tackle some of the same questions: Where do we come from? Where do we go to? How much can we know?"[71] The answers, however tentative, take us to a place of transcendence, our ultimate point of reference and coherence.

Transcendence, Certainty, and Uncertainty

Here's a question about transcendence coming to us from Plato, speaking through Socrates in discussion with Euthyphro: "Do the gods love piety because it is pious or is it pious because the gods love it?"[72] Or, if you are a monotheist, Is an action right because God commands it, or does God command it because it is right? In other words, what's the transcendent source of our hierarchy of values?[73] The point is that humans, being blessed and burdened with the consciousness of the passage of time, ask, How then shall we live, or by what principles shall we do so? And what is the source of those principles? Something Plato and the apostle Paul thought about quite a lot. We age, our children think differently from us, and sometimes catastrophes unhinge us. Does anything last? Although our answers do change, the question seems universal.

This brings us to the idea of transcendence and the human need to have faith in a fixed point of reference in a universe governed by uncertainty principles, or a grand unifying theory that Hawking acknowledges is elusive and may not happen any time soon. Living with uncertainty is destabilizing so we keep looking for the key to unlock all mysteries. Even in science, which we once hoped was a platform on which we could build secure structures of information, knowledge, and wisdom, we keep unsettling ourselves with new things, including new ways to think about science, triggering *paradigm crises*, theorized by Thomas Kuhn. We can live with a certain amount of uncertainty but wandering in the woods without a compass and a map to keep us oriented is terrifying, especially when the sun starts to go down, so we live in the hope of elusive certainties.

That does not necessarily lead to the conclusion that there is no such thing as a transcendent reality. It's just that we cannot know it finally.

---

71. Hossenfelder, *Existential Physics*, xv.
72. Westacott, "Summary," sec. "Euthyphro's 5 Definitions," para. 7.
73. See also VanArragon, *Key Terms*, 30–34, for a summary of the Euthyphro problem.

Here's some wisdom from Stephen Hawking about the implications of the uncertainty principle: "Since the structure of molecules and their reactions with each other underlie all of chemistry and biology, quantum mechanics allows us in principle to predict nearly everything we see around us, within the limits set by the uncertainty principle." And then he adds, in parentheses, "In practice, however, the calculations required for systems containing more than a few electrons are so complicated that we cannot do them."[74] In other words, it's out there but we cannot find it. Yet. And maybe never, at least not in this life, recalling Paul's reference to what we see and can't see through the dark glass of our bodied existence.

It's worthwhile to stay here for a bit. What Hawking is not saying is that there is no possibility of a grand, complete unifying theory[75] or transcendent idea that brings together all that we know into a coherent picture. Rather, we can't make the calculations to arrive at one. Some of the theories proposing a GUT look pretty funny in hindsight. Alchemists and the debates among them look out of place in the modern world although they were also looking for the basic building blocks of the universe. But the search for certainty goes on, taking us from physics (and other sciences, including theology) into metaphysics and the mysteries inherent in human life. And along the way, we find some amazing things, treasures, gifts, something we can learn from those alchemists of an earlier time. Some of them were motivated by the idea that you could turn lead into gold, at least in some accounts, reminding us that our great ideas and breakthroughs come out of complicated, base motivations, a kind of turning base conceptual metals into something resembling gold. The final answer is that there is no final answer, at least not accessible to any of the sciences, including theology, acting as truth gatekeepers. However, the quest is what makes us human.

In Christian tradition we hear Jesus telling Nicodemus that the Spirit is like the wind which blows wherever it wants to.[76] Nicodemus, like most of us, wants the final answer to the mysteries of life, but the wisdom of the Bible, like the sacred texts in other traditions, leans toward the humility that comes with recognizing our human limitations. This is not what most of us want to hear, although religious wisdom is echoed in science where we do hear about new knowledge that upsets our paradigms and

74. Hawking, *Brief History*, 60.
75. "Grand" or "complete" unifying theory are used interchangeably throughout the book as GUT or CUT.
76. John 3:8.

invites us to rethink what we had come to accept as normal. Miroslav Volf follows the insight to a place where he proposes that truth can be found, not through detached scientific knowing, but rather through messy life and relationship processes he identifies as *embrace*. Martin Buber gets at something similar through what he calls *dialogue*. However, embrace and dialogue create spaces of vulnerability where community, at its most meaningful, calls us to change, to repent, to truly hear. Meaning-filled knowing emerges in relationship, in community.

Histories of religious thought and practice have a similar dynamic as science, in which ideas and beliefs are proposed, practiced, challenged. Just one example: feminist theology has emerged as a significant challenge to theologies in which male supremacy was taken as a given. About time, too. While some, Jerry Coyne among them, see those struggles as evidence of religion's unreliability and irrationality, others see them as inherent in any interpretive category.

Transcendence (Again)

There is widespread, although certainly not universal, agreement that there is a legitimate social role for religion. Brian Greene, self-described atheist, accepts religion as an evolutionary necessity. So do Roy Rappaport, Jeff Spinner-Halev, John Gray, and Anthony Pinn, to mention just a few. Their self-identifying as nonreligious or atheist has little to do with their acceptance of religion as a social phenomenon and a legitimate way of knowing. Legislation, human rights codes, and constitutional provisions protecting religious freedoms do not depend on religious belief. There are constant negotiations of religious difference, most of which, thankfully, never reach the threshold of public attention and debate, something of which Lori Beaman reminds us.[77]

However, religion is not just one thing. Rather, it comes in different forms, some of which do attract scrutiny and can become fault lines that are hard to bridge. Transcendence in religion is one of those things. Transcendence can be seen in a couple of ways. To start with, all of us have a framework based on transcendence in one form or other. We have fundamental principles that are nonnegotiable on which we base our life decisions. We use different terms for our transcendent principles, among them *universal* as it used by the Ontario Ministry of Education

---

77. Beaman, *Deep Equality*.

OBJECTIONS TO RELIGION

to describe the character attributes in the preferred graduate profile.[78] Another one is some form of a *GUT* if you follow Stephen Hawking's quest for a transcendent organizing principle in physics.

One way to think about transcendence is that it occurs within an immanent frame, which is where Hawking landed, concluding that there is no God,[79] going further down the road of uncertainty than Albert Einstein was willing to go. Einstein believed in God "who reveals Himself in the orderly harmony of what exists"[80] and who does not "roll dice."[81] Groups accept a configuration of common or universal principles as essential to a kind of social contract or covenant that protects social order. For those among us for whom transcendent nonnegotiables are seen as human constructions accessible to anyone who thinks well, the gods are imaginative constructions. Not all of us think well and we may need to help our children navigate their lives as they find their way to rational, socialized adulthood. Societies need a prevailing principle transcending sectarian loyalties to establish a common sense of what is normal. We know what is good and do not need the gods to tell us. What we need is education. The idea of gods who are ontologically real is, well, irrational. For some of us, our Euthyphro answer is that the gods command something because it is good and, by extension, the gods are optional for us to know what it is.

We can see another formulation of transcendence in Sigmund Freud, whose interest was the psychological mechanism by which people come to believe in God and the role the *God object* plays in their psychological lives. He had confidence in scientific thought to get him to transcendent principles within an immanent frame that took him to a place of skepticism about God. However, Ana-Maria Rizzuto raises questions about the link between representations of God and the reality for which those representations are reaching.

Here's a question: What if our representations of God are like representations of trees in, say, paintings of trees?[82] The painting of a tree

---

78. Ontario Ministry of Education, *Finding Common Ground*, 3.
79. Spektor, "Stephen Hawking."
80. Spencer, "Albert Einstein," para. 6.
81. Baggott, "What Einstein Meant." There are lots of debates about what Einstein actually meant by his references to God. My point here is not to engage that more theological question. Rather, it is to demonstrate the unfolding of the uncertainty principle.

82. We are brushing up against the science of semiotics, not my area of study and not the focus here.

is not a tree, obviously. In the same way, what if our representations of God are not the same as God? Is God the ultimate imaginary companion who has acquired "a special and superior status on account of multiple sociocultural, religious, ritualistic, familiar and—not least—epigenetic phenomena"?[83] Or is God *real*? Did Freud make the mistake of equating our representations with the reality for which they are reaching, leading to his conclusion that a normal mature adult would outgrow the need for God? He argued that we need representations of God at immature stages of development when we had not yet developed the adult capacity to know how to behave well in public or when we tremble at unidentified sounds in the night. But as we grow up, we absorb a moral code, making it our own, our egos having matured in ways that allow us to make non-pathological behavior choices. We come to accept noises in the night as simply part of the human experience. Continuing to believe in God as an adult is pathological, at least in Freud's framework of psychological and social development.

Freud was writing in a period of European history when metanarratives included the idea that Europeans were the mature culmination of a progressive historical trajectory, having outgrown the need for God and religion (sort of like teddy bears), being replaced by science. He was writing and theorizing in the context of others who were saying roughly the same thing in other disciplines, including the study of religion, which seems to place Europeans ahead other human groups in a self-serving historiographical trajectory. In that story, the secular mature modern thinks about religion, observes its representations, but does not need it, strictly speaking, because the objects of religion do not actually exist except in the minds of those who still need them.

Secular thinking is not, in the first place, against religion or the idea of transcendence. It is a way of thinking about religion and transcendence within an immanent frame. Part of our resistance to religion is that we see vertical transcendence as a threat, a backsliding into a less enlightened way of thinking about ourselves in the world. Charles Taylor says, "What emerges from all this is that we can see the transcendent as a threat, a dangerous temptation, a distraction, or an obstacle to our greatest good. Or we can read it as answering to our deepest craving, need, fulfillment of the good."[84] The modern heroic stance is one that resists the temptation,

---

83. Rizzuto, *Birth*, 194.
84. Taylor, *Secular Age*, 548.

accepting the implications of a commitment to transcendence within an immanent frame. However, the longing for a source of meaning and hope in a transcendent source is pervasive, and it is embarrassing. ET is a kid's movie that we adults need an excuse to watch.[85]

Transcendence Realism—A Problem in Modernity

Not everyone is embarrassed, of course, nor does everyone accept the idea that vertical transcendence is out of step with modernity. For some, vertical transcendence provides a platform from which to critique the idea that secularism is an inevitable outcome of modernity, providing a conceptual model to manage religious diversity. Hussein Ali Agrama observes that "the social theory literature that explores and questions the modern is often premised on an attempt to escape foundations of any kind, and especially transcendent ones. It is precisely a suspicion and an anxiety about such foundations that motivate critical theorists to try to dispense with them."[86] Agrama argues that *transcendent foundations* provide a theoretical basis for critical engagement with modernity, rather than being out of step with it.

Rizzuto, parting company with Freud, tells us that "belief in God or absence of belief are no indicators of any type of pathology. They are indicators only of the particular private balance each individual has achieved at a given moment in his relations with primary objects."[87] In other words, although people process and reprocess their representations of God as they go through stages of development, it is a mistake to assume that we will all arrive at horizontal transcendence constructed within an immanent frame. For some of us, our representations of God find their origin and meaning in a reality that transcends time and space, the evidence being the very order of reality on which science depends and which the arts are imagining. We can call it God, the gods, or whatever, but it is essentially inaccessible to the five senses, living beyond the horizons of time and space.

The difference between the gods and humans according to the Greeks[88] was that the gods are immortal and we are not. They live beyond

---

85. Spielberg, *E.T.*
86. Agrama, *Questioning*, 16.
87. Rizzuto, *Birth*, 202.
88. "The Greeks" is an oversimplification, of course. There is development in Greek

the horizons that limit mortals. We may not fully understand the gods and what they want, and we may not live consistently by what they command as good. We are not gods, our five senses and our abilities to think well having been compromised by sin, by our passions, our being bodied and mortal, our short-term perception of harm, our race, our gender, or whatever else might cloud the glass and distract us from the straight path or the narrow way.

For transcendence realists, the idea that a universal good can emerge out of such human frailty is misguided, the evidence for human frailty being persuasive. They tend not to "incorporate the confidence that we can actually re-order and reshape our lives" or that we can generate "the motivation to carry this out for the benefit of all."[89] Belief in God provides the basis for a CUT for how the world works and how we should live in it, which transcends the vagaries of intellectual fashion, developmental stages, and the dynamics of history. Christopher Watkin offers an interpretation of the fateful encounter between Eve and the serpent recorded in Genesis chapter 3 that suggests something similar. He argues that to "know the distinction between good and evil" takes on additional significance when "in Hebrew, 'to know' can signify 'to choose.'"[90] His point is that when the distinction between good and evil is constructed without reference to God as a transcendent authority, it is all too easily defined in self-serving ways, avoiding the implications for one's own limited and flawed view of the world.

Agreement that the transcendent is ontologically real does not end the debates among those on that side of the transcendence-immanence fault line. There are intense debates and conflict, battles even, among those who share a belief in God but who part company over what that means or who owns the true God, something Karen Armstrong describes in her examination of religious history and of fundamentalism. What transcendence realists do not argue about is the reality of a transcendent being who is a source of order and meaning. Rather, the fights are about who is closest to and has ownership of transcendent truth or Truth. Transcendence, like anything else, can be weaponized to energize self-serving interests generating lots of evidence for objections to transcendence as

---

thought, including skepticism about the reality of the gods, which is one of the reasons "the Greeks" form an important part of the imagined heritage on which Enlightenment rationalism draws. But "the gods" are actors in the great Homeric stories, among others.

89. Taylor, *Secular Age*, 245.
90. Watkin, *Biblical Critical Theory*, 112.

irrational and harmful. One result is sweeping generalizations and interpretation of evidence to support predetermined conclusions about transcendence and people who think differently about the world, its meaning, and its destiny. Another is Jerry Coyne's *a plague on all your transcendence houses* (his sentiment, not his words), an understandable New Atheist response with, however, its own contradictions. Killing for ownership of God is crazy, irrational, unless you step into the logic of culture wars.

Transcendence as a Problem of Evidence

However, I want to take us into another implication of the transcendence fault line, which is where it places us in a progressive historiography based on rational thought and evidence. I am foregrounding the possibility that transcendence as an ontological reality is a key difference between the ways in which modern and traditional modes of thought are represented. Rational thought is seen as a marker of the boundary between modern rationality and traditional irrationality because the former is justified by appeals to evidence generated by rational thought while the latter is seen to rely on faith that is inherently inaccessible to reason and therefore non-falsifiable. The issue of evidence in arguments about the nature of transcendence is an important element in the boundary constructed between modernity and tradition.

Modernity is linked to the ability to think critically about religion as a mode of thought and experience, including the ability to approach religion with skepticism and intellectual mobility. In modern societies, vertical transcendence plays an ambiguous role protected by a kind of tongue-in-cheek tolerance of the idea that transcendence could be an ontological reality. Tradition is seen as characteristic of a past we have left behind, associated with closed communities who do not move, either geographically or intellectually. Forward-looking modernity is legitimized by evidence detached from entanglements while backward-looking tradition is embedded in history and geography. Timothy Stacey comments on the distinction between people characterized as "anywheres" and "somewheres" who are "less mobile, less educated, tied to particular places and people, and concerned with maintaining their cultural heritage."[91] The argument that something should be done

---

91. Stacey, *Saving*, 8.

because of tradition is not a preferred decision-making model among moderns. Appeals to God or the ancestors might have had traction in an earlier stage of human history, but not in a modern society. The answer "The Bible tells me so" to the question "How do I know?" is a kid's song, not an adult one, at least not modern adults. In the modern world we must have evidence based on science or a process of rational thought that is prepared to discard our practices and ideas that do not meet an evidentiary standard or serve an immediate purpose in achieving a defined end, resulting in personal decisions that can withstand rational argument. Agrama says that within liberal thought, "religion ought to be largely kept out of the public domain" because "religion lends itself to arbitrary decision making, and for that reason is not seen as capable of promoting the considered, authoritative determinations needed for a genuinely effective public policy." Therefore, in liberal thought, following what I have been calling the logic of secularism, "Religion's proper place—that is, the private domain—is therefore linked to its status as nonknowledge."[92]

This puts God and any other claims made in the language of religion on the evidentiary hot seat, of course where "God is set up to flunk the atheist exam, as surely as He was set up to pass that of Providential Deism with flying colors."[93] To argue that proofs for God are convincing only to the people who believed in God in the first place may be overstating the case, but it does call on us to be modest about the overall effectiveness of logical processes in resolving questions about transcendence. However, modesty does not suggest that there is no persuasive evidence for an authoritative transcendent reality. Francis Collins tells us that he drew his conclusions after reading C. S. Lewis, the great twentieth-century writer whose apologies for Christianity rested on his belief that *the moral law* or the *Tao* pointed to its divine origins.[94] In their view, the moral, physical, and biological order on which we depend cannot be imagined without reference to God.

In technical terms this takes us into the territory of *evidentialism*, related to *natural theology*, which is based on the idea that there is a common basis of evidence to which all rational persons have access.[95] James Ross questions evidentialism, which he says "fails to describe prerequisites for rational belief, and *a fortiori* for knowledge, first, because the

92. Agrama, *Questioning*, 75.
93. Taylor, *Secular Age*, 389.
94. Lewis, *Abolition*, 18, 83–101, appendix.
95. VanArragon, *Key Terms*, 34, 76.

principle is itself not evidentially justifiable."[96] In short, not all of us land in the same place after rational consideration of the same evidence and Giberson and Collins encourage us to be modest about evidentialism and proof-of-God thinking. They prefer the idea that the fine-tuning of the universe points toward the plausibility of God rather than proofs of God's existence, saying, "Fine-tuning looks like a point to a Creator—not a proof, to be sure, but a suggestive state of affairs."[97] Lee Strobel suggests something similar, asking his readers to reach a verdict in *The Case for Christ* by recalling his experience as a crime reporter. He says, "Ultimately, it's the responsibility to jurors to reach a verdict. That doesn't mean they have 100 percent certainty, because we can't have absolute proof about anything in life. In a trial, jurors are asked to weigh the evidence and come to the best possible conclusion. In other words, which scenario fits the facts most snugly?"[98]

There are good reasons to be cautious about evidence for vertical transcendence, an idea that is problematic for several reasons. One is the offensiveness of the very idea that we need an outside source to know the good, which takes us back to Euthyphro. Within an immanent frame, you can at least establish commonsense common ground, such as universal values or traits. We do not need a god to tell us what is good. The good is accessible to anyone who thinks well and has minimal social perception and intelligence. Do you really need God to tell you not to run a red light or not to abuse children? Surely we can agree on the fundamental principles and practices that allow my kids to get to school and learn safely, can't we? Or not clog our oceans with plastic? You might argue the details, but you at least know the rules of rationality guiding the argument. Calling God down to end the argument is an unfair and irrational power play or, at best, unnecessary. Aren't we smarter than this by now in the twenty-first century?

Another troublesome issue is just how we know the good if it arises out of a transcendent, authoritative deity. How do you know something is true if you can't defend it in an argument or if is not falsifiable?

---

96. Ross, "Willing Belief," 18.
97. Giberson and Collins, *Language*, 178.
98. Strobel, *Case*, 15.

Reflections on Religious Literacy

Rationality and Irrationality in the Construction of a Culture War

However, there is evidence that we are not smarter than previous generations, baffled as we are by high levels of anxiety among our young people, poverty, and any number of other things you can name. Human trafficking and slavery continue to generate lots of money for lots of people. However, do we experience evil because we no longer believe in God or is it because we need more and better education, so we think better? A conundrum of modernity is that, despite scientific and social advancement, we still have a few apparently intractable problems. You may have heard of climate change, for example, in which there is quite a lot of writing on the wall,[99] the meaning of which we continue to debate and resolutions to which continue to elude us. We are smart but is being smart overrated when it comes to living well and wisely?

I argue that we need each other, that it's all hands, minds, and interpretive categories on deck in the twenty-first century. The construction of an oppositional relationship between religion and science is counterproductive. The idea that knowledge generated by science is based on objective evidence tested by rational, autonomous, self-directed scientists in contrast with religion working on irrational faith is problematic. The construction of the autonomous individual freely choosing their own life path based on evidence achieved through a process of freely exercised rational thought is just that, a construction. Talal Asad has provided a valuable service in identifying the political and social contexts in which the idea of the autonomous individual occurs and the purposes it has served to establish a narrative of Western cultural superiority.[100] The culture war in which rationality becomes a weapon is a construction in which we do not have to be participants.

Rationality is contextual. It would be irrational to ignore the traditional wisdom of indigenous peoples in Canada's north about how to

---

99. Reference to Daniel chapter 5 in which, during a big party thrown by Belshazzar, a mysterious handwriting appeared on the wall close to where the king was sitting. Daniel is called in to interpret the script that conveyed the message that "God has numbered the days of your kingdom and brought it to an end; . . . you have been weighed in the balance and found wanting; . . . your kingdom is divided and given to the Medes and Persians" (vv. 26–28 ESV). The king breathes a sigh of relief, not at the grim implications of the interpretation, but because he can now file it and ignore it. He rewards Daniel for his work and goes back to partying. And then the story ends with, "That very night, Belshazzar the Chaldean king was killed, and Darius the Mede received the kingdom" (v. 30 ESV). Jewish wisdom literature leaves us with a lot to ponder.

100. See Asad, *Formations*, and *Genealogies*.

survive in extreme climatic conditions and unfamiliar terrain inhabited by predators who see me as their next meal. I do not need to test the risks inherent in that situation by a scientific method, arriving at my own conclusions by experimenting with some options. The fact that I accept the advice of those with superior knowledge does not mean that I am irrational. In fact, my refusal to accept the wisdom passed down for many generations would be irrational. Sir John Franklin's ill-fated arctic adventure is a cautionary tale on the limits of European rationality that, among other things, was animated by racism and ideological myopia that did not end so well. There is a lot of wisdom in traditional wisdom, some of it coded in riddles we find in ancient religious texts. We may not understand them on first reading but that may say more about our esthetic and imaginative limitations than it does about their rationality, which Mary Douglas argues.[101] The fact that some of my grade nine students would identify William Shakespeare as stupid said more about their encountering something that exceeded their grasp than it did about the great man and his literary genius. The same thing is true of religion. And science. And anything other mode of human knowing.

Carl Becker imaginatively reconstructs a conversation with Thomas Aquinas and Dante about the idea of natural law and the League of Nations, concluding that the misunderstandings between Medieval and modern thinkers cannot be explained away by privileging modern modes of thought in a hierarchy of rationality. He says, "What troubles me is that I cannot dismiss Dante or St. Thomas as unintelligent men," and that "if their arguments are unintelligible to us that fact cannot be attributed to lack of intelligence in them. They were at least as intelligent as many who in our time have argued for or against the League of Nations." He goes on to refer to Professor Whitehead's restoration of "climate of opinion," "a seventeenth-century phrase" that Becker argues is "much needed," saying that "whether arguments command assent or not depends less upon the logic that conveys them than upon the climate of opinion in which they are sustained."[102] What I hear Becker saying is that there is no universal standard for rationality. Rather, rationality is contextual, finding traction in climates of opinion.

---

101. See Douglas, *Leviticus*, and *Purity*.
102. Becker, *Heavenly*, 5.

Religion, Public and Private Space, and the Politics of Rationality

One way in which some kinds of knowledge are privileged while others are marginalized based on an assessment of rationality is how public and private spaces are defined. In the climate of opinion in which I am writing, science has been seen as the language of public discourse in a modern society while religion is seen as private. At one time, religion enjoyed dominant status in public space, and in some societies and among some groups it still does. Not so much in the society in which I live where science is seen as the reliable source of public information and knowledge.

Jerry Coyne argues that public language is provided by science, all other languages being private. He says, "Knowledge isn't knowledge unless it is factual, so 'private knowledge' that comes through revelation or intuition isn't really knowledge, for it's missing the crucial ingredients of verification and consensus."[103] In his view, nonscientific modes of knowing are, in the end, "useless" even in extreme situations.[104] However, on the other extreme where religion is the gatekeeper for public language, scientific findings are not considered valid if they have not been vetted by religious authorities deriving their authority from sacred texts and religious tradition.

Christopher Watkin, critically commenting on the privileging of science, says that, in our modern, secular world, "Reason, expressed supremely in the sciences, gives us direct access to knowledge, the whole of knowledge, and nothing but knowledge. Other modes of engaging with the world (including narrative, love, and religious knowledge attained through revelation) are not really knowledge at all, or else they are distinctly inferior to the scientific reason detached from all faith that gives us the truly true, the really real."[105] Watkin is identifying a statement of faith about where we place our confidence in the modern world.

---

103. Coyne, *Faith vs. Fact*, 186.

104. Coyne, *Faith vs. Fact*, 262.

105. Watkin, *Biblical Critical Theory*, 239. Although I agree that the Bible, like any sacred text, can provide a basis for critical theory, I part company with Watkin over his stark distinction between Christianity and other forms of religion and their consequences for individuals and society. His use of the concept of the antithesis between good and evil is too simplistically applied to the complex realities of society and the way people actually live. He offers a sweeping analysis of history based on his reading of the Bible, and in doing so makes many interesting and provocative observations. However, his is an example of starting with a conceptual framework and applying it to evidence rather than letting evidence speak, thus making statements and judgments about the world that are often questionable. Watkin has attracted critical reviews, among them

This raises questions about the basis on which rationality is assessed and further, which rationality has public traction and which ones are marginalized. Jerry Coyne is pretty sure he knows the answer, but he and the New Atheists are not the first to have claimed that they are further along in the journey to true enlightenment than the rest of humanity. Ken Ham, like Watkin, claims the same thing for himself and those whose interpretation of sacred texts align with his. However, what does rationality even mean? Are men more rational than women because of the way they think? Which men are we talking about? Who decided on the science that concluded that race or gender were important for a variety of reasons, one of which was that it was a determiner of rationality?

Richard Osmer and Friedrich Schweitzer observe the challenges to "classical and modern models of rationality that conceptualize knowledge as secured by following universal rules that can be transported from one disciplinary context to another, the rules of good research or logic." They observe three important implications: "rationality is conceptualized as a special form of communicative action and as inherently social"; "rationality is broadened to include the rhetorical norms that differ from field to field and from one audience to another"; and "rationality is viewed as informed by the epistemic values held by a particular argument field."[106] The politics of rationality include contests about who owns the universal rules and the argument field in which those rules are considered normative. The politics of rationality and irrationality are about establishing and policing the boundaries between barbarity and civility with important implications for religion and religious literacy. A *disciplinary society* works on several levels, starting with who sets and polices the rules for public discourse.[107]

The idea that there is no one gold standard for rationality delivered by one interpretive category, race, or gender means that no one group can claim exclusive ownership of rationality. Religion cannot claim exclusive access to universal truth, but neither can it be marginalized as inherently irrational. There are different kinds of reasoning in different modes of knowing and there is an element of faith in accepting the validity of any one mode as the basis navigating the world. William Wainwright comes at the problem of faith in an essay that "focuses on an objection to religious belief which claims that agnosticism is more admirable than

---

Carl Trueman's "Robust Biblical Theory Runs Along Diagonal Lines."
    106. Osmer and Schweitzer, *Between Modernization*, 273–74.
    107. Taylor, *Secular Age*, ch. 2; Foucault, *Discipline*.

the faith of a Christian whose strength of conviction exceeds what the evidence warrants since the latter sins against reason while the former does not." He argues that "this objection is mistaken because it assumes a faulty conception of the proper role of reason in religion."[108] One implication is that reason and rationality are situational rather than ahistorical, designed to serve a greater purpose.

Faith and Rationality in the Context of the Kingdom of Ends It Is Designed to Serve

A way to address the question of how rationality is decided is to see it in terms of the *kingdom of ends* it serves and the faith on which paradigms are based. Rationality is the systematic thinking process unique to the interpretive category within which it occurs, but it has political implications in the creation of an imagined ideal world. Ken Ham's project depicts an ideal world and the threats to it. When you step into the ark, clear thinking, planning, and engineering are obvious, astonishing really, if you can suspend your critical skepticism for a bit. In the same way, the pro-life movement has not been conceptualized and organized by people who think badly. Gun lobbies engage in political advocacy using a logic based on the idea of the free, manly individual having to self-protect in a fundamentally chaotic world. To an outsider, these are lunatic fringes and, don't get me wrong, most movements include voices that make you question the idea of the universal franchise. But it is too easy to bypass the logic in a movement by concentrating on extreme voices, and we can see struggles within movements around managing the extreme fringes who transgress the boundaries of its logic.

Jerry Coyne describes a world organized based on rationality without religion that echoes B. F. Skinner's *Walden Two*, written in 1948, and other imagined utopias. However, utopian projects always present themselves as rational and they always involve some form of purgation of conceptual infections in the body. Sometimes the purification efforts involved in the creation of a utopia can become extreme, our demonized iconic one being Nazi Germany. Demonized icons can serve as a distraction from the fact that the logic of eugenics and the enthusiastic, systematic subjugation and genocide in Nazi Germany were widely shared among Europeans. Hitler's problem was that he started doing to

---

108. Wainwright, "Theistic Proofs," 77.

Europeans what European Christian nations had been doing around the world for a long time, and they did not like it. He was not a gentleman who played by the rational European rules of colonialism and imperialism. He may be considered a fringe lunatic, but that assessment can be self-serving if it distracts attention from the logic of white supremacy shared in a European gentlemanly consensus.

The destruction of buffalo herds in the American land grab as the empire expanded and the design of residential schools in Canada were conceptualized by rational people who wanted to achieve a particular society that did not include indigenous modes of thought and practice. American policy in Vietnam was organized by the best and brightest rational thinkers whose hubristic brilliance defied common sense that did not work out so well for anyone, except maybe the global industrial producers of napalm.[109] Barbara Tuchman asks, "Why do holders of high office so often act contrary to the way reason points and enlightened self-interest suggests? Why does intelligent mental process seem so often not to function?"[110] The decisions and policies described by Halberstam and Tuchman did not arise out the imaginations of deranged minds. There are deranged minds, but the plan itself is rational when placed in the context of faith in the kingdom of ends it is designed to serve. Isabel Wilkerson argues that the perpetuation of caste systems includes inherent and enormous costs but they persist because of a transcendent faith in a kingdom of ends that normalizes a hierarchy of human value.

However rational the plan may be, it is based on a faith that it will create a preferred kingdom of ends. Jerry Coyne's description of a scientific utopia purged of faith comes close to a statement of faith in an imagined future. B. F. Skinner was a very bright guy, a scientist, working on the basis of a faith. He had a dream, an imaginary if you will, and for him the principles and practices of what came to be called *behaviorism* were the way to get to his version of a new heaven on a new earth, imaginatively narrated in *Walden Two*. In a similar way, arguments about the rationality and irrationality of religion cannot be seen apart from the political context in which they occur, and the political ends served by a preferred form of religion. This leads to several conclusions about rational thought.

First, all modes of knowing or interpretive categories include processes of rational thought, which is systematic thinking with its own

---

109. Halberstam, *Best and Brightest*.
110. Tuchman, *Folly*, 4.

internal logic. Roy Rappaport tells us that our thinking works within a hierarchy of values, based on commitments and assumptions that are not accessible to rational argument. We think in different registers, among them science and religion, each of which has its own rules for what constitutes rational thought.

Rational thought is code for thinking well. What it means to think well is an important educational issue, including in RE. There is a lot of awful religious thinking out there but the same could be said about any other mode of thought. The Ark Encounter takes some leaps in logic, doing some funny things with scientific evidence to achieve a particular social outcome, but is it irrational? Well, there is an internal logic at work, but you must step into the thing (literally in the case of my walk through) to see how it works. The same thing is true of the Museum of Nature. The problem of rationality or the lack of it must be seen considering the fundamental principles on which rationalities are based and what ends they are designed to serve. The distinction between rationality and irrationality cannot be sustained by linking either to a particular interpretive category, including religion. We must look elsewhere for the boundary between rationality and irrationality. However, there is one more objection to religion we must address, which is that religion is inherently *exclusive*.

OBJECTION THREE: RELIGION IS INHERENTLY EXCLUSIVE AND THEREFORE SOCIALLY DISRUPTIVE

Jesus answered, "I am the way and the truth and the life. No one comes to the Father except through me."

—JOHN 14:6, NIV

"(Ontarians) do not want to see our society divided. They do not want to see kids segregated from one another," Wynne said. "We need an inclusive system in this province that allows kids to learn together, be together and understand each other."

—KATHLEEN WYNNE, IN THE *TORONTO STAR*

OBJECTIONS TO RELIGION

What made Christianity particularly repulsive to the Enlightenment mind were two doctrines. The first was the belief that only a few are saved. The second was the doctrine of predestination.

—CHARLES TAYLOR, *A SECULAR AGE*

A third objection to religion is linked to the concept of *exclusion*, which includes claims of unique access to normativity and truth. The philosophical objections to religion as exclusive are based on the idea that religious truth claims rest on sources of information, knowledge, and wisdom that elude commonly understood rational processes, are accessible only to believers, are not scientifically falsifiable, and are therefore inherently exclusive. The experiential objections are the use of religion to create exclusionary boundaries protecting hegemonic power and privilege that marginalize people outside the boundaries.

Two clusters of questions animate this section. The first is, Is exclusion inherent in and unique to religion? The second is, What are the social and political implications of exclusivity?

Exclusion Is Inherent in Religion

I am going to start this section with a joke. Not a very good joke maybe, and it has been around for a while, but here goes anyway. Or stop me if you have heard this one before. A Pentecostal Christian gets to the pearly gates and meets St. Peter at the intake desk, is accepted and ushered into heaven (being Protestant, no Roman Catholic purgatorial purification process necessary of course) where she sees a hall with a lot of doors. From behind one she hears a speaker giving a lecture and she asks, what's going on in there? To which St. Peter says, that's where the Calvinists go when they get here but keep it down, they think they are the only ones here.

As I say, not a very good joke, but one that illustrates two themes in exclusivity and religion. The first theme includes the philosophical objections to truth claims made in the name of religion that are inherently exclusive. The second theme includes the experiential political and social consequences of truth claims with implications for access to space, resources, social status, and a preferred eternal life, among others.

Here are two examples of competing truth claims with built-in boundaries of exclusion.

> Throughout the Ark, you are also provided Answers to the many questions that both Christians and unbelievers have alike. Of course, if you are an unbeliever, God must first do the work of your conversion, but if you are a Christian, then this Encounter will truly strengthen your faith.[111]

> —truth is simply what *is*: what exists in reality and can be verified by independent observers. It is truth that DNA is a double helix, that the continents move, and that the Earth revolves around the Sun. It is not true, at least in the dictionary sense, that somebody had a revelation from God. The scientific claims can be corroborated by anyone with the right tools, while a revelation, though perhaps reflecting someone's real *perception*, says nothing about reality.[112]

Philosophically, the primary objection to the exclusivity of religion is that religion includes truth claims about matters of ultimate value that are accessible only to believers and, as a result, are not falsifiable. That can be seen as offensive on several levels, but the one I want to foreground is the idea that believers are part of an exclusive club with unique access to authoritative truth. There is an *in-and-out-group* feel to religious truth claims that violates social norms of inclusivity, particularly in Canada, where *equality* and *inclusion* are fundamental values. In addressing this objection, I argue that inclusion and exclusion are inherent in religion, but they are not unique to religion. Inclusion and exclusion are inherent in all aspects of social life. In addition, the link between exclusion and intolerance as a moral matter is tenuous.

L. Philip Barnes, in his "deconstruction of John Hull's religionism" argues that "intolerance—is a more general phenomenon. It is not something confined to religious contexts and religious individuals."[113] Hull, he says, "equates religionism both with the view that one's religion is right and others' wrong and with the adverse social consequences which he believes accompany this equation."[114] Hull's use of religionism is the basis for his proposal for religious literacy that addresses social and political outcomes. Key to Hull's argument is the idea that "different religions are complementary," downplaying their differences in the hope of achieving

---

111. PhilJ925, "Strengthen," para. 6.
112. Coyne, *Faith vs. Fact*, 29.
113. Barnes, *Education, Religion and Diversity*, 148.
114. Barnes, *Education, Religion and Diversity*, 150.

social harmony.[115] Barnes rejects the premise that religions are basically all the same and he questions Hull's hope. The question of inclusion and exclusion have important implications for RE and religious literacy, starting with the preferred outcomes of RE programs.

Inclusion and exclusion are inherent in religion in the sense that you believe something and not something else, which creates a bond with fellow believers and excludes nonbelievers. Traditionally Christians have taken the John 14 passage literally, which has meant that through Jesus, they have unique access to the Father who is God. In other words, God is their Father in a way that he is not the Father of those who do not believe in Jesus. You might want to join the family of God for a variety of reasons, but you must believe in Jesus to do so. What you have is a religious gated community and what is even more offensive, your being outside it is due to your choice to be an unbeliever.

The Ark Encounter takes theological difference one step further, telling us that we cannot even understand the truth embodied in this walk-in graphic novel unless we experience a religious conversion. You must join an in-group to even understand this project. Consequently, commentary by skeptical outsiders is marginalized on the basis that they simply do not understand because they are outsiders. And, of course, insiders do not have to take skeptical outsiders seriously because, well, they are outsiders and cannot understand, not really. Christopher Watkin's *Biblical Critical Theory* comes close to the same conclusion of a world fundamentally divided between people over differences in theology.

Not all forms of religion and of Christianity are constructed along stark lines of inclusivity and exclusivity and there are different interpretations of John 14 and other passages. However, there is something inherently exclusive about any ultimate truth claims, including those we more commonly identify as religious. On most matters we can compromise, negotiating differences in the interests of social harmony, out of respect for the opinions and life decisions of others. However, if you engage in a conversation with anyone about those life decisions, sooner or later you will get to a place where they stand and will go no further.

Here's a thought experiment: *Try out the idea that men and women were created in complementary completion of the image of God. In other words, men and women each have their own divinely ordained roles to play in the great picture of the world. Which in some religious traditions*

---

115. Barnes, *Education, Religion and Diversity*, 146.

has meant that women cannot exercise authority over men except maybe in the kitchens where church suppers are organized. Another conversation starter (or more likely stopper) is the idea that a divinely created separate but equal model is simply evident in understanding racial difference. Or that the universe came about through divine action within six twenty-four-hour days some six thousand years ago. Or that there are two genders (God made Adam and Eve, not Adam and Steve), and that the introduction of gender fluidity is an indication of liberal slippery-slope relativism that ends us in moral chaos. Claims like these tend to reveal unbridgeable fault lines, even among close friends and family members. Fault lines are often identified around competing interpretation of sacred texts, but thinking of sacred texts as road maps or codified understandings of the natural order of things adds depth to fault lines. Imaginaries of gender, race, origins, and the age of the earth indicate what is embraced as normal or universal, creating a ground for identity and moral task.

Religion seems to lend itself to exclusive claims for a couple of reasons. Recall James Beckford's definition of religion as an interpretive category that foregrounds matters of ultimate value and meaning. His including the descriptor *ultimate* is significant in a discussion of exclusivity, recalling Roy Rappaport's argument that someone's *ideology* is less accessible to debate. Our ultimate values are where we stand, our firm place from which to interpret the world, guiding and anchoring us through the complexities of any number of moral questions we face. For some of us, the slaughter of pigs and turning them into cuts of meat to be cooked and eaten is an unconscionable violation of what it means to be truly human living in harmony with all other living creatures with whom we share the earth. In fact, some of us put our lives on the line to defend the right of pigs to humane treatment.[116] For others of us, the truth claim that life begins at conception leads to the conclusion that abortion is murder and that, given the statistics, there is officially sanctioned mass slaughter of unborn children going on around the world. There is little room for compromise on this important issue, which has led to some extreme action.[117] Martin Luther's famous *Here I stand, I can do no other* may be apocryphal, but it does illustrate an important point. The fact is that we all of us have our limits in watershed issues beyond which we

---

116. Burlington Post, "March." Olga Tokarczuk's novel *Drive Your Plow Over the Bones of the Dead* is a journey into an imagined war between enchanted and disenchanted worlds. Beautifully written, disturbing, great read.

117. Stack, "Brief History."

cannot be pushed and that indicate our ultimate values. In fact, not to have limits or some basic principles relatively impervious to compromise indicates serious personality deficits.

But Exclusion Is Not Unique to Religion

The philosophical observations about religion as exclusive are accurate. However, this is not unique to religion, as a few examples will illustrate. Think about the Olympics and the idea that I could register to compete against Usain Bolt in the hundred-meter dash or Simone Biles in gymnastics. OK, no more need be said. I may feel hurt that I am excluded from the elite club to which they have earned access, but that's my problem, not Usain's and Simone's. High-end athletics should not be reorganized around my needs or wants and, in fact, are not.

Here's another one in which I come out looking better: to enter a PhD program at the University of Ottawa I had to go through a screening process that included the crucial role of Dr. Lori Beaman taking the risk of adopting me as her student. To complete the program, I had to go through a six-year process that included wonderful, energizing excitement, head-banging anxiety when my excitement proved to be ill founded, irritation with Lori (true confessions here) who kept pushing me to be dissatisfied with my work, and hand-holding by dear friends who were going through or had gone through a similar intellectual crucible. I experienced neck and back pain and the anxiety-producing scrutiny by an examining committee who took my intellectual baby apart for my benefit and improvement (although they were nicer than they needed to be).

It all culminated in my brief moment of glory when I got to sit on the stage with about a dozen other PhD candidates who had also successfully completed their programs. We watched from our place of privilege up there on the stage, all dressed up in our robes and recently donned academic hoods, along with faculty and dignitaries as the undergraduates and MAs came up and returned to their seats down below. A friend who also aspired to complete a degree but was unsuccessful in doing so felt bad about it, feeling excluded. This was my Usain Bolt moment of carnal pleasure that I have not confessed to anyone else. I am back to doing laundry with the rest of humanity, but I still savor the memory. The point is that exclusivity is not unique to religion and our feeling bad about being excluded may not be fundamental to an analysis of its legitimacy as a social phenomenon or as a source in information, knowledge, and wisdom.

However, let's look at the experiential consequences of religion's exclusivity, which is that there are real-life consequences of exclusion. Being excluded from full access to citizenship because of one's religious (or nonreligious) beliefs and practices is one such consequence, but also the macro- and micro-aggressions reminding those on the receiving end that they are religious transgressors. But here's a question: Which forms of inclusion and exclusion are acceptable and which are unacceptable, and further, how do we know the boundary between them?

One way in which we know the boundary between inclusion and exclusion is by the testimony of people who experience exclusion. Much of the testimony is based on feelings of exclusion but there are questions about the status of feelings as evidence that something actionable has taken place.

Consider this: *Redeemer University is a privately funded, Christian, post-secondary school that attracted public scrutiny in August 2020 for its code of conduct regarding sexual behavior. Reports included the testimony of one student noting "a school policy that says students will be disciplined for any sexual behavior that occurs outside a heterosexual marriage, based on what Redeemer calls 'biblical intentions,' which made her feel like an outsider."*[118]

The questions for institutions, for human rights tribunals, for courts, are, What is the role of feelings in assessing the legitimacy of exclusion? What is the status of feelings in determining public policy? The student in the interview was not arguing about the quality of the education delivered at Redeemer, which is ostensibly why they were there in the first place. Besides, students feel all kinds of things that raises the question of why feelings in this case became a story while others did not.

Consider this: *I am riding a bus heading home after one of my university classes. I am reading a book on caste and casteism by an Indian scholar in preparation for duties at an academic conference I will be attending in Delhi. The woman sitting beside me asks me about the book. She tells me that caste is a divinely ordained order that must be maintained to avoid social breakdown. I ask her what caste she is, and she tells me that she is Brahmin. I ask her about the experience of Dalits who have been agitating for entry into temples and other places from which they have been excluded*

---

118. Hristova, "Private Christian University," para. 3.

and other ways in which state and social strategies have caused great suffering. She dismisses my question, saying that they are motivated and stirred up by agitators who hate India. She feels strongly about the threats to the social order and, in the current climate in India, her feelings have considerable political traction. The feelings of Dalits do not register in her thinking, nor do they count for much in the ascendency of Hindu nationalism. She questions Ontario's emphasis on inclusivity. She likes Ontario, she says, but its social world seems chaotic to her, making her feel uneasy, the markers of social status and order seeming opaque. She feels like an outsider here even though Ontario prides itself on inclusivity. We agree that emigration and immigration are disruptive that way, something I understand, having grown up in an immigrant family. I do not share her defense of Indian social organization, not having benefitted from its caste system. I have benefitted from Ontario's social system, which, although operating on different principles, produces its own hierarchical structures that I mostly don't notice. Our conversation is cut short by my having arrived at my bus stop.

However, I have thought about that brief conversation ever since, including the question of feelings and at what point feelings of exclusion gain political traction. Feelings of exclusion matter but what is their social, political, and legal status? Further, what is their status in assessing the truth in any situation? More specifically, whose feelings are considered important and under what circumstances?

Let's go back to the statement by Kathleen Wynne quoted at the beginning of this section. The context in which she made it was a provincial election in Ontario in 2007 in which funding for non-Catholic faith-based schools became an intensely debated wedge issue. The argument against expansion of state funding to include non-Catholic faith-based schools was never about the quality of education delivered in privately funded and independent schools. Rather, it was driven by the idea that state-funded public schools are uniquely placed to deliver citizens committed to an idea of Ontario as an imagined community delivered by the state-sponsored public school system. *Togetherness* and its protection against the forces of division and exclusion represented by some forms of religion emerged as a powerful and effective theme. Disruptive forms of religion are embodied in privately funded faith-based schools, at least in Ontario public policy. Arguments that other jurisdictions have successfully incorporated a variety of education delivery mechanisms have little political traction to counter fears of threats to togetherness in Ontario.[119]

In Ontario public education, togetherness is seen in two ways. First is social togetherness, delivered by public schools by bringing together children of different backgrounds into shared space so they develop, at the very least, tolerance for diversity and, at best, respect for it. The second way in which togetherness is conceptualized is in the development of a consensus about common and universal values. In 2007, threats to common modes of thought and values focused on primarily two issues, the first of these being gender and the second being the relationship between science and religion, the intolerable interpretation of which is epitomized in *creationism*. Privately funded faith-based schools were represented as exclusive, elitist, sectarian places where students were isolated from mainstream society to be taught ideas and values in conflict with the universal values, modes of thought, and behaviors appropriate in a modern society. Interviews with Ontario citizens reported in various media made a clear link between certain forms of religion, social exclusion, and intolerable modes of thought, including questioning the citizenship loyalties of those who used the educational services offered in privately funded schools.

However, here's a reaction by Rabbi Bulka who, along with others, was bruised by his citizenship having been questioned:

> I am stunned to hear this coming from the Premier. Most troubling is the suggestion that funding my faith-based school could lead to problems with social cohesion. The Premier that I know cannot argue that children who attend publicly funded Catholic schools contribute to social unrest. So why does he argue that other faith communities, who have thus far been denied the opportunity to participate in the public system would be any less able to contribute to the peace and security, happiness and

---

119. Another factor was the role of the Ontario Teachers Federation who explicitly linked jobs to the loftier themes of *togetherness*, inclusion, and exclusion. The Federation argued that funding for non-Catholic faith-based schools would threaten jobs in an example of the confluence of interests in practical politics. Another example of such a confluence is the link between freedom and the interests of powerful health care and gun manufacturers in the United States. The politics of *religious literacy* occurs in forms of these confluences around the world.

prosperity, justice and freedom that abide in Ontario, especially when their tax dollars help pay for the current system?[120]

The Ontario election of 2007 amounted to a referendum on, among other things, the issue of funding for non-Catholic faith-based schools, but it was also a referendum of the social status of some forms of religion. The answer in Ontario was clearly to reject funding, but it was also a statement about which forms of religion were welcome in public spaces and which were not. Rabbi Bulka's feelings that he and others like him had been marginalized did not have effective political traction in offering other ways to address religious diversity and inclusivity.

In another case, the testimony of feelings of exclusion of LGBTQ+ students at Trinity Western University were part of the process by which the Law Society of British Columbia made its claims before the courts regarding TWU's attempt to establish a law school.[121] In yet another Canadian example, this one in Ontario, feelings of coercion expressed by students under the tutelage of religious instructors were central to the ruling in 1990 that religious instruction is a violation of the charter rights of students. However, in 1997 the feelings of parents and students trying to access government funding for their disabled children enrolled in privately funded faith-based schools were acknowledged by the courts but were considered less important than protection of public schools as a key mechanism to deliver universal values and behaviors.[122] In other jurisdictions, the feelings of Christians that they are an endangered minority competes for the feelings of LGBTQ+ trying to access public and private services.[123] In Italy, the feelings of Soile Lautsi about the crucifix in the classroom in which her child was being educated were considered less important than the interests of Roman Catholic identity of Italy.[124] In other words, feelings of inclusion and exclusion may or may not be viewed as important, depending on the social and political contexts in which they occur and narratives they serve.

---

120. Bulka, "Matter of Fairness," para. 15.

121. Harris, "Trinity Western."

122. Corporation of the Canadian Civil Liberties Association et al. v. Ontario (Minister of Education) and Board of Education of Elgin County, [1990] 37 O.A.C. 93 (CA); Adler et al. v. Ontario et al., [1994] 73 O.A.C. 81 (CA); Adler v. Ontario, [1996] 3 S.C.R. 609.

123. Reuters, "Kentucky Clerk"; PRRI Staff, "Wedding Cakes."

124. Interights, "Lautsi v Italy."

Inclusion and Exclusion in Religion and Citizenship

Inclusion and exclusion at the intersection of citizenship and religion is ambiguous in the sense that sometimes it is important and sometimes it is not. Religion might enter as an important consideration in the assessment of my citizenship if my religious practices lead me to violate Canadian law. If, for example, my religion involves the practice of human sacrifice, the officials handling my file might do well to ask a few questions. That's an extreme example, but what about, say, plural marriage? This became a legal and constitutional matter in Canada, the argument of the defendants in the case arguing that the criminalization of plural marriage violated their religious freedom rights.[125]

In a case involving the use of photographs on drivers' licenses, members of Wilson Colony, a Hutterite community argued that their refusal to allow the practice was a matter of religious freedom.[126] Their failure to convince the Supreme Court of Canada didn't get them excluded as Canadian citizens but it did have consequences for how they could participate in the economy. You can keep going to include First Nations practices and other groups whose religious practices have had to adapt to the model of what it is to be a fully included Canadian citizen. These are areas of contestation over inclusivity and exclusion that involve religion but not exclusively. Religion can rarely be lifted out of any issue as the one key factor in conflict, but neither can it be ignored.

When it comes to criminal code matters, it is obvious that human sacrifice is well outside the boundaries of good citizenship behavior, at least not in the ways we usually think of it. The pro-life movement might argue that abortion is a form of human sacrifice on the altar of individual choice. An environmental activist might argue that our inattention to environmental degradation is a form of sacrifice of our descendants and other living creatures we are willing to make to achieve a kind of prosperity. But to frame it in those terms might be seen as unnecessarily provocative so let's agree, for the purposes of this discussion at least, that human sacrifice is not a marker of good religious citizenship in Canada. However, the representation of religion as exclusive usually does not depend on extreme examples.

---

125. Postmedia News, "Canada's Polygamy Law."

126. Alberta v. Hutterian Brethren of Wilson Colony, 2009 S.C.C. 37, [2009] 2 S.C.R. 567 (Can.).

As I argued earlier, inclusion and exclusion are not unique to religion. In science, teachers take students into the boundary between good and bad thinking in science, as do teachers in any field of study. However, what also needs to be included are the implications of establishing those boundaries. For example, it seemed obvious, based on my mediocre performance in the maths and sciences, that I should be excluded from pursuing those fields in any professional capacity. However, should my identity as a Christian enter those considerations? What if I am a Christian or Muslim science teacher whose view of science includes some form of *intelligent design*? Should that language be allowed in a state-sponsored public school or should it be excluded?[127]

Women are asking questions about inclusion and exclusion all the time, the issue being the role of gender in establishing glass ceilings in a variety of professions and social and political roles. The construction of *race* as the basis for *caste* boundaries of inclusion and exclusion are being contested by the Black Lives Matter movement with violent reactions by those who resist social change that might threaten power and privilege.

Ultimate values are not always benign and are embedded in practices and beliefs that, on their surface, may have little to do with religion. Consideration of their implications is not straightforward. Let's take some examples. Among some religious groups, the conviction that non-Christians will go to hell provides the basis for an urgent moral task in the form of evangelism. Without evangelism, believers are morally culpable in the eternal damnation of many of their fellow human beings. God may be a God of love but there are limits to divine patience, which is an animating theme in the Ark Encounter. The point here is that hell is the ultimate metaphor (or ontological reality depending on where you sit on the matter) of exclusion. Eternal exclusion, with a lot of pain in some of the more dramatic models, that is. Lots of people believe this although maybe fewer than at one time. In any case, hell as the lower level of a three-level cosmology is an example of an exclusionary epistemology. It is other things, too, but let's just stay with my main point, which is about the link between epistemology, exclusion, and inclusion. The way to be included in redemption and avoid being condemned to hell is to listen to Noah and his current spokespersons and repent and convert. The possibility of conversion makes hell a matter of self-exclusion, resulting from your unwillingness to convert.

127. Van Arragon, "Conflicted Partnership," 85.

Citizenship, Assessment of Harm, and the Management of Competing Truth Claims

So, what's the problem with that way of thinking, particularly in a society that encourages competition of ideas in open and free expression? Is a belief that religious nones or Muslims or Jews are hell bound a sign of bad citizenship? On the other hand, what might be right with it? Christina Easton, in her review of Philip Kitcher's *The Main Enterprise of the World*, examines the distinction, important to his argument, between *epistemic* and *moral* assessments of forms of religion.[128] *Epistemic* assessments are of the rational validity of claims made in the language of religion while *moral* assessments address the social and emotional harm of religions.

The distinction is not unique to religion. Some of my friends felt offended and excluded by vaccination and masking requirements during the COVID-19 pandemic, but their feelings did not mean that the requirements were wrong. For those who believe the warnings in sacred texts that those who persist in false beliefs will be thrown into the eternal fire the real harm is not in the fact that it may be offensive. Rather, the harm is in not raising the alarm for people who may be headed for eternal damnation, not unlike the moral responsibility of health experts raising the alarm about the consequences of vaccine resistance. But should public space be protected from this and other beliefs that might offend? We may not all agree but in a democratic society ideas need to be tested and held accountable, including those we might find objectionable.

Besides, strongly held beliefs about eternal salvation indicate deep commitment to the idea that people and their choices matter. They energize urgent moral task expressed in altruistic acts including the idea that people can make positive choices that will make their lives better. For example, there is evidence that religiously based prison ministry has had positive effects on recidivism rates in the United States.[129] Some people in my town might hold strong exclusionary religious views but are generous with their time, their resources, their energy, and matter of fact about outcomes, one of which is that the people with whom they partner may not convert. They vote, pay their taxes, stay out of trouble with the law, organize, fund, and staff street-level drop-in centers and housing for vulnerable women, run the food bank, and are in many ways ideal citizens.

---

128. Easton, *Religion and Religious Education*.

129. Prison Fellowship, "What We Do"; Johnson, "Faith-Based Prison." See also Sullivan, *Prison Religion*; Walters-Sleyon, "Religion and Recidivism."

In fact, there are studies suggesting that a religiously based education has higher levels of positive social outcomes than some others.[130]

Some of the impulse animating evangelism is motivated by concern about hell as a future and eternal outcome, but, equally, that conversion will lead to better life decisions. The fact is that some of our friends live badly, addicted to various mind-altering substances, making poor financial and relationship choices that get them into trouble with the law, and that are written into their bodies. Going beyond thinking about the moral task of evangelism as an individual matter of future personal salvation is the idea that people can make changes to communal practices and structurally embedded injustices. Some of the community involvement by religious people includes political engagement to address housing and economic insecurity created by systems that deliver social and economic refugees, not only globally, but also in my small town.[131] There is deep, often not very dramatic, passion to see people change their lives based on the observation that, for some people, hell is not a post-death experience but one they live every day. Conversion is not so much about getting to heaven as it is embracing life in greater measure here on earth, which might well be framed in religious terms of, for example, repentance, forgiveness, and the restoration of a new, life-affirming identity.

In that sense, religion is not about some future, spiritual event but is an earthy, bodied matter based on ultimate truth claims about how to live well. Those truth claims may be exclusive, but they may not be inherently socially destructive and, in fact, may be evidence of deeply committed care so that vulnerable people can participate fully in society. People who experience conversion as a fundamental and radical change talk about their lives in a before-and-after conversion narrative, a move from darkness into light that can include giving up their destructive addictions and life choices. It may also mean giving up friendships that are part of the old life to which the convert does not want to return. Exclusion makes sense in those situations, which can lead to inclusion in supportive circles of care.[132]

Living with religious diversity is not straightforward because religion, like any other human mode of knowing and practice, is not

---

130. Glenn, *Ambiguous Embrace*; Glenn and De Groof, *Balancing*. Cardus has several good articles related to this topic; see, for example, Swaner et al., *School-Sector*.

131. St. John, "37 Frank Street."

132. Taylor, *Secular Age*, ch. 20, has some interesting things to say about "conversion" as radical individual and collective "paradigm shift."

straightforward. This is especially so when religion plays a comprehensive role in people's lives, providing truth claims that ground and orient them. Religious diversity is relatively easy to theorize, regulate, and practice when religion is defined as beliefs and worship practices that can be privatized. When they are privatized, exclusionary epistemologies may be offensive but irrelevant to public discourse. The privatization of the *spiritual* leads to its being depoliticized in the same way that *character* and *virtue* have been.

Privatized and spiritualized religion, like character and virtue, can be a conservative category that leaves untouched the issues of power embedded in social, economic, and political practices and institutions.[133] This is why, according to Berger and Zijderveld, religious diversity is less complicated to manage than moral diversity. When it comes to matters of morality or how we live together, things get a lot more complicated. Berger and Zijderveld remind us that "moral pluralization today creates sharper challenges than religious pluralization. What's more, at least some moral judgements depend on a measure of certainty that one need not have in matters of religion."[134]

However, their argument depends on a separation of morality from religion, which works if you define religion in a narrow sense, linking it to theological systems expressed in arcane propositions based on ancient texts and in personal and individual beliefs and practices. It works less well if you define religion more broadly as an interpretive category foregrounding our ultimate values based on a codification of a model of the natural order of things. In that case, morality is the embodied expression of our ultimate values resting on exclusive truth claims about the nature of life, the world we inhabit, and its meaning. Morality and religion are not so easily separated in real life and, when integrated, the gift of exclusive, robust competing truth claims can serve an important role in destabilizing destructive normality.

---

133. Robert Baden-Powell, in *Scouting for Boys*, used the metaphor of *bricks* to illustrate the preferred outcomes of Scouting as the *character factory*. One of his memorable sayings was "You should remember that being one fellow among many others, you are like one brick among many others in the wall of a house. If you are discontented with your place or your neighbors or if you are a rotten brick, you are no good to the wall. You are rather a danger. If the bricks get quarrelling among themselves the wall is liable to split and the whole house to fall." Rosenthal, *Character Factory*, 9.

134. Berger and Zijderveld, *Doubt*, 24.

Robust Truth Claims Are Not Unique to Religion

However, truth claims are not unique to religion defined in a traditional sense. Truth claims are essential to human life and competition between them is inevitable. To pretend that we do not have exclusive truth claims is disingenuous at best and even dishonest, according to Berger and Zijderveld. They describe the corrosive implications of relativism and its intellectual dishonesty but that does leave us with questions of *how* we arrive at truth and the implications of truth for how we live our lives. Our truth claims have implications for how we live our citizenship and how we interact with each other. The challenges for education include the delivery of citizens and, for RE, that challenge is more focused on the role of religion in citizenship.

This is important for education, but can you talk about truth in an inclusive way or is truth inherently exclusive? Jerry Coyne has little doubt that science and the scientific method are key to finding truth, but for him the scientific process of generating truth is exclusive to people who think the way he does. Truth is important to him and science, not religion, is the place to find it. His claim leaves him with some curious blind spots, one of which is that his argument rests on a kind of in-and-out-group thinking, dividing humanity between scientists and the rest of us. His blind spots do not allow room for traditional wisdom passed down through the generations, often in the language of religion. Coyne would happily exclude religion from his imagined future so that for religious people to participate in the sciences, they would have to figure out what to do about their religion. However, Alister McGrath, stating the obvious, says that "scientists are—and remain—human beings," which Ortega y Gasset suggested is why "many scientists find themselves experiencing a tension between their scientific calling and their basic humanity."[135]

Exclusion is inherent in religion because it is inherent in life. What we need is awareness of how the boundaries between exclusion and inclusion are constructed, in what context, and for what purpose. What we especially need is a stance of *agonistic respect*[136] as we listen to each other about the effects of those boundaries, being willing to give up boundaries that are self-serving to us and destructive to others. Richard Mouw uses the term *convicted civility* to imagine spaces for dialogue, robust

---

135. McGrath, *Surprised*, 40.
136. Connolly, *Pluralism*, 123–24.

engagement among differences.[137] Fear of difference diminishes the space for dialogue. Drawing on Robert Bellah's work he says, "This is why they insist that the recovery of particularized religious understandings of the issues of public life is necessary for a much-needed opening up of our communal 'spaces for reflection, participation, and the transformation of our institutions.'"[138] The link between theological difference, tolerance, and exclusion is more nuanced than the language often used in political and social competitions.

In conclusion, the three objections to religion most relevant to religious literacy are that religion is institutionalized spirituality, and thus a harm to individual agency; religion is fundamentally irrational and pathological, and thus harmful to individual self-actualization and to an agreed language of public discourse; and religion is basically and inherently exclusive and thus a threat to social cohesion. However, while objections to religion must be included in religious literacy projects, both the objections and the proposed alternatives to religion must also themselves be subjected to critical scrutiny. My argument is that they cannot sustain a rejection of religion as a legitimate category of knowing.

ALTERNATIVES TO RELIGION

The term *religion* carries a lot of historical and cultural baggage that has given rise to proposals for alternative categories. A way of thinking about the context in which the search for alternatives to religion occurs is that the interpretive category of religion has been colonized by, among others, Christianity. The proposals designed to address the colonization of religion go beyond a rejection of Christianity to include rejection of the entire category of religion to achieve more inclusive, common conceptual ground and civic harmony. However, Adam Dinham and Martha Shaw raise a caution about the risks of another kind of colonization of civic values and social cohesion that can obscure the value of religion itself. I will revisit this issue in chapter 5 where I examine the logic of the marginalization of religious literacy in academic programs.

A reading of the history of religion as a theoretical category suggests that religion has been colonized by theology and, in particular, European Christian theology with its history-shaping global reach. One conclusion

---

137. Mouw, *Civility*, 82.
138. Mouw, *Civility*, 83.

is that the emergence of *non-religion* and other alternatives is a process of decolonization of religion, in which religion is being detached from theology and its Christian forms. However, while I agree with decolonization efforts, I part company with those who reject religion as a theoretical category, arguing that the proposed alternatives have their own limitations and contradictions. In addition, the rejection of religion because of the legacy of Christianity still allows Christianity to set the terms of the discussions about religion.[139] I think a more productive way forward is to think of religion as a more fundamental human capacity, a unique kind of human consciousness that we can, in principle at least, detach from Christianity.[140]

The search for alternatives to religion creates liminal spaces that, although disorienting at times, create opportunity to assess what is considered normal. Liminal times and spaces are times of confusion and anxiety but also create opportunity to consider what can and should be discarded and to imagine something else. Transitions are marked by a kind of energy and hope that new things are possible. Taylor says, "The actual account of the transition as it has been lived, is often a story of great moral enthusiasm at a discovery, at a liberation from a narrower world of closer, claustrophobic relations, involving excessive control and invidious distinctions; and at the same time it has been lived as a liberation into broader space."[141] The process of decolonization of the category of religion by Christianity and theology is characteristic of the historical and cultural moment we are living. While disconcerting to some, it creates new and interesting possibilities, which, however, can themselves become colonizers, dominating the discourses around religion. I am not as persuaded as some that the category of religion itself needs to be replaced, and my cautions are included in the summaries below.

Here are some alternatives proposed to replace religion.

---

139. Ann Taves says something similar about non-religion as a category, which, while expanding "our focus beyond atheism and unbelief" creates other definitional problems because it defines "whatever it is in relation to religion," in "What is Nonreligion?" 1.

140. I think of this in somewhat the way we might think of the relationship between the study of linguistics and the English language. English is the current global lingua franca, but recognizing the dominance of English does not mean rejection of language as a category. In a similar way, Christianity is one form of religion, in the way English is one form of language, but rejection of Christianity does not mean we have to reject religion as a category.

141. Taylor, *Secular Age*, 575.

1. Worldview

One of these is *worldview*. Ann Taves links religion and non-religion to the construction of meaning systems under what she proposes is the more comprehensive idea of *worldview*. *Worldview* is another way of framing the human capacity for making meaning of experience, which Taves argues "provides a neutral starting point for analyzing worldviews that is not biased toward religion." Taves is looking for a category that encompasses both religion and non-religion that "relieves scholars of the obligation of defining religion and non-religion" to account for the human capacity to struggle with "big questions." In her argument, engagement with big questions is linked to "how individuals and groups characterize themselves."[142]

However, worldview is close to what Thomas Kuhn calls a *paradigm*, arguing that paradigms are anything but neutral, living in competition with and marginalizing others so that, among other things, they are political. There is more at play here than construction of a meaning system in an intellectual sense. We construct and adopt a worldview to serve as a metaphorical road map in our navigating the world, but our constructions are embodied expressions of something more fundamental and more baffling in our human nature.

2. Cultural Studies

Rejecting religion as an analytical category, Timothy Fitzgerald suggests "that religious studies be rethought and rerepresented as cultural studies, understood as the study of the institutions and the institutionalized values of specific societies, and the relation between those institutions and the institutionalized values and the legitimation of power."[143] His suggestion embeds religion in a social, political, and historical context, rejecting the sui generis construction of religion that places it in an ahistorical parallel universe. We can see the implications of that way of seeing religion in Rudolph Otto's theorizing the *holy* as the *mysterium tremendum et fascinans*, which places religion as an irreducible sui generis mode of knowing and experience, out of analytical reach and accountability. The idea of religion as a sui generis category has been subjected to critique,

---

142. Taves, "What Is Nonreligion," 1.
143. Fitzgerald, *Ideology*, 10.

leading Fitzgerald to reject it as analytically useful, proposing religion as one element in what he suggests is the more comprehensive category of *cultural studies*.

I agree that the embodiment of religion occurs in social and cultural contexts. Constructions of religion are not some imagined realities living outside culture. However, the definition of culture is also not uncomplicated, occurring as it does in ideological and political contexts, as Edward Said and Talal Asad point out. For example, about Fitzgerald's references to the culture of India and Japan we might ask if *culture* is a meaningful category, given the diversity of language, ritual practices, ethnicity, and class in both India and Japan. Given the fact that India and Japan are themselves social constructions with nationalist cultures depending on mythologies used to rationalize the deployment of power, Fitzgerald's resorting to *culture* raises its own questions of analytical usefulness.

In addition, Lori Beaman identifies the shift from religion to culture as a political strategy to protect privileged forms of religion, while for Liz Bucar the category shift from religion to culture is a strategy in "religious appropriation."[144] In her view, avoiding religion as a category does harm by marginalizing a deeply meaningful way of knowing the world that, in her study, allows religious practices to be exploited. In short, *culture* as a category carries complications like those in religion.

3. Values

Values are sometimes suggested as an alternative to religion as an analytical category. In his examination of B. R. Ambedkar's social reform initiatives, Fitzgerald argues that, although Ambedkar was seeking *true religion* as the basis for his critical analysis of caste, "for him [Ambedkar] the basis of religion is *values*" and "he came to see supernaturalism as irrational and irrelevant to true religion."[145] Fitzgerald follows up his conclusion by saying that "the concept of religion implied in this kind of analysis is not essentially about supernatural beings, transcendental worlds, or spiritual salvation in a life after death." In this context, Fitzgerald proposes *values* as an analytical and comprehensive category that incorporates religion.

---

144. Bucar, *Stealing*, 206.
145. Fitzgerald, *Ideology*, 125; italics added.

However, in making his case to reject religion as an analytical category, Fitzgerald comes close to a false consciousness argument when he says that Ambedkar "went beyond that concept, without ever quite realizing that he had done so. In fact, it was his ideas about religion that suggested to me why we could abandon the word without any real loss."[146]

Another reading of B. R. Ambedkar,[147] who Fitzgerald identifies as "highly educated and intellectually brilliant,"[148] suggests that he knew very well what he was doing when he identified *religion* as a key category that had to be addressed to understand the intractable nature of and commitment to caste. The quest for true religion was the basis for his argument with Mohandas Gandhi and led to his converting to a form of Buddhism, having concluded that the Brahmin Hinduism was inextricably linked to caste. Religion, you might say, is the basis for values rather than the other way around, at least in their arguments.

Fitzgerald's critical analysis, which leads to his rejecting religion as an analytical category, depends on a definition of religion that involves "supernatural beings, transcendental worlds, or spiritual salvation in a life after death." However, others, including Ambedkar, have a view of religion that takes us to the capacity of human beings to imagine transcendence as inherent in the ways we navigate time and space. Religion is not a sui generis category referring to a parallel universe that is fundamentally different from the ones we experience in our embodied lives. He says that Ambedkar "needed a religion that made a difference in this world, a religion that could change society and empower the backward classes."[149] But of course, that is what Gandhi, Ambedkar's sparring partner, wanted also. Gandhi and Ambedkar agreed that Hinduism was a religion deeply embedded in social order, and that social and indeed cosmic order was embodied in Hinduism. They fundamentally disagreed about what that agreement meant for social reform, but they shared the conviction that religion takes us to consideration of what is really real, the transcendent source of cosmic order and personal redemption.

---

146. Fitzgerald, *Ideology*, 123.
147. Ambedkar, *Annihilation*; Roy, *Doctor*.
148. Fitzgerald, *Ideology*, 123.
149. Fitzgerald, *Ideology*, 128.

4. Imaginary

Timothy Stacey, while appreciating the need to find language "for engagement with something beyond universalizing logics" to understand what draws people together around political action, takes distance from "political theatricality" and "drama." He worries that they imply "something inauthentic, artificial, and top down; assumes that actions always have an audience in mind; and risks constructing a 'fourth wall' between actors and their audience that then has to be theoretically overcome."[150] Stacey's quest is to identify what motivates people to engage in political and social action and to form communities that endure beyond the outcomes of that action.

He draws on Charles Taylor's use of *social imaginary*, "the ways in which people imagine their social existence, how they fit together with others, how things go on between them and their fellows, the expectations that are normally met and the deeper normative notions and images that underlie these expectations."[151] Stacey, examining the "place of shared narratives in making collective life meaningful," is "enamoured by the theory but frustrated by the lack of engagement with people's lived realities."[152] In his search for alternative atheist imaginaries that engage people's lived realities, including collective resistance to global capitalism, he asks, "How could such illusory images inspire such concrete action? More fascinating still was that many of the beholders of these dreams were aware of the flaws and did not deny them."[153]

5. Spirit

Stacey, not quite satisfied with *imaginary*, argues that s*pirit* is the human capacity to build communities of political participation around "everything that makes it [political participation] feel worthwhile beyond its immediate material impact."[154] He wants to avoid the adjective *spiritual* because of its having been colonized by Christian metaphysics, arguing rather that community action is *spirited*, something bigger than or transcending the individuals motivated by and unified around something he

---

150. Stacey, *Saving*, iv.
151. Taylor, *Imaginaries*, 23.
152. Stacey, *Saving*, iv.
153. Stacey, *Saving*, 2.
154. Stacey, *Saving*, 5.

calls *spirit*. What I hear Stacey saying is that "immediate material impact" cannot fully account for political or collective communal action and resistance.

A further comment about the use of *imaginary* is that the capacity to create an imaginary is evident in any interpretive category, referring to a reality not yet present in an embodied way. For example, the theory of black holes was imagined before evidence supporting it was available. We imagine community, a work of art, a marriage, before they actually exist. This begs the question of what a religious imagination imagines. What does it imaginatively create? The reference to dreams and illusory images includes community, but even more than that, Stacey refers to "shared narratives [that make] collective life meaningful."[155] He wants to avoid religion but, at the same time, is honest about the human capacity to seek a transcendent source of meaning and purpose.

6. Faith

Faith is another term deployed to replace religion. For example, in his examination of the Building Bridges Program (BBP) in Melbourne, Timothy McCowan, arguing that "faith is an activity rather than a thing" asserts that "it is human universal, something that all people have, even if they do not express a belief in or feel they belong to any religious tradition."[156] Colin Bloom refers to *faith* throughout *The Bloom Review* in which he examines the state of government interaction with *faith* groups in the UK. One of his recommendations is for *greater faith literacy*, given the rise of various less desirable forms of faith. The opening remarks in the *Review* include the statement that "whether people like it or not, faith plays a profound role in the life of the United Kingdom (UK). Life in our country would be markedly different without the historical legacy and the overwhelming contribution made by faith, people of faith and places of worship."[157]

However, the historical legacy was not *faith* in the abstract, but rather a particular form of Christianity that is still a powerful presence in the UK.[158] Bloom's use of *faith* reflects his desire to create a more inclu-

---

155. Stacey, *Saving*, iv.
156. McCowan, "Bridges," 27.
157. Bloom, *Review*, 10.
158. For example, the coronation of King Charles III was striking in its explicitly

sive and less offensive conceptual space, but it is also not without its own complications. For example, the use of the term *faith* begs the question, *Faith in what*? In other words, people do not have faith in the abstract. They have faith in something that will serve as their transcendent guiding principle.

James Beckford tells us that Niklas Luhmann, defining "modern social systems as self-referential," theorized that "the language for this self-reflection is that of *faith*."[159] Faith in this context is a way of describing religion as an essentially individual matter of the inner life, not linked in any obvious way to the external world or as a source of meaningful knowing the world.

However, *faith* is not unique to religion. People have faith in many things, including that their cars will start when they engage in the right sequence of steps. Some of us have faith that the vaccines injected into our arms will protect us from diseases. Some of us have faith in democratic processes to deliver relatively stable societies with orderly mechanisms to effect political succession. None of these faiths are uncontested and, given the nature of the universe, do not deliver the preferred results all the time. However, believers keep hoping that their faith will prevail, it being the closest approximation to truth, at least in their view. The point is that faith is active in any interpretive category indicating the search for some truth on which we can build and where we can rest. Often our faith is aspirational or, in the poetic language recorded for us in Heb 11:1 where we find this definition of faith, "Now faith is the assurance of things hoped for, the conviction of things not seen" (ESV). A good word for those of us hoping for a better world, and not one restricted to what we traditionally might think of as *religious*.

7. Spirituality

Another alternative to religion draws on the foregrounding of *spirituality* evident in the religion versus spirituality binary, one expression of which is *spiritual but not religious*. As with any bifurcated model, SBNR has some truth about how religion works as an interpretive category. In short, religion, or the construction of meaning and the adoption of ultimate values, involves individual choice and agency in service of some form

---

Christian themes and practices.

159. Beckford, *Industrial Society*, 84–85.

of salvation or redemption. There may be religious authorities in my life but there is always a process of negotiating what that means for me. Paul Heelas and Linda Woodhead analyze a religion-to-spiritual trend in a shift in spiritual authority from institutional hierarchies to individuals who adopt a variety of practices drawn from different sources. Meredith McGuire examines a similar trend in *lived religion*, analyzing the ways in which people make choices about their spiritual lives, most of them private, out of reach of religious authorities. Ana-Maria Rizzuto proposes that the (sometime slightly vengeful) God imagined by children may or may not be the official God of the child's religion, but as a personal companion he belongs to the "ineffably private" side of human experience where we are irremediably alone.[160] Muhammad Iqbal, writing in the 1930s, says, "Another important characteristic of the unity of the ego is its essential privacy which reveals the uniqueness of every ego."[161] He goes on to say, "My pleasures, pains, and desires are exclusively mine, forming a part and parcel of my private ego alone. My feelings, hates and loves, judgments and resolutions, are exclusively mine. God Himself cannot feel, judge, and choose for me when more than one course of action is open to me."[162] Albert Raboteau tells us that individual spirituality was important in slave religion because it created life space and expressions of religion that could not be regulated by the dominant classes of Christians to protect caste hierarchies in the institution of slavery. In short, *spirituality* has traction in our world as a way of avoiding some of the cultural baggage carried in the term religion, particularly in response to objection one above.

Limitations of Spirituality as an Alternative to Religion

The SNBR trend is often situated in the language of individual freedom and agency. However, Don Gillmor offers a caution in the reaction to institutionalization and the rejection of external authorities. Reflecting on the high incidence of suicide among baby boomers he says, "We tore down traditional structures—church attendance plummeted as did marriages" and "we toppled institutions that had sustained our parents and were seen by us as constraints. What we created in their place was an

---

160. Rizzuto, *Birth*, 204.
161. Iqbal, *Reconstruction*, 79.
162. Iqbal, *Reconstruction*, 80.

unprecedented freedom and the triumph of the individual. And this is fine as long as the individual is fine."[163] The vagaries of life, the fact that life is hard, the inevitable process of aging mean that we are not always fine. In fact, our moments of being fine are sweet, but fleeting. Gillmor suggests that life, in its beginning and its ending, is not a DIY project. We did not make ourselves and we are dependent on a vast, mostly invisible network of relationships to do life well.

Matthew B. Crawford, examining *distraction* as a cultural problem in the development of identity, observes that "there are so many enticements, but just as important, there is little in the way of authoritative guidance of the sort that was once supplied by tradition, religion or the kind of communities that make deep demands on us."[164] He argues that our illusions about freedom have made us more vulnerable to the "highly orchestrated" manipulation by "commercial forces [which] step into the void of cultural authority and assume a growing role in shaping our evaluative outlook on the world," one outcome of which is that "our mental lives converge in a great massification—ironically under the banner of individual choice."[165] One conclusion is that, while we may think we are choosing our form of spirituality, our identities and choices are being shaped by influencers masked in a variety of ways.

The Spirituality of Everyday Life

What the SBNR framework foregrounds is the individual response to religious authority but also the deeply personal nature of our spirit quests in time and space. However, what it less successfully accounts for are the ways in which institutions are also driven by ultimate values serving a *kingdom of ends* and the ways in which individual choice and agency occur in those institutional and communal settings. In that sense, organizations and institutions are also *spiritual*, adopting mission statements, codes of conduct, and other expressions that reflect an interpretation of a world order and a moral task.[166]

---

163. Gillmor, "Baby Boomer Generation," para. 19.
164. Crawford, *World*, 5.
165. Crawford, *World*, 6.
166. Here's something from McDonald's: "Our mission is to make delicious feel-good moments easy for everyone. This is how we uniquely feed and foster communities. We serve delicious food people feel good about eating, with convenient locations and hours and affordable prices, and by working hard to offer the speed, choice and

Reflections on Religious Literacy

One of Timothy Fitzgerald's critiques of John Hinnell's treatment of Hinduism in the *Dictionary of Religions* is that it foregrounded soteriology in Hinduism but largely ignored the institution of *caste* in India. The problem, in Fitzgerald's view, is not the soteriology inherent in Hinduism. Rather, it is the foregrounding of soteriology as the primary way to understand Hinduism. This misses the complexity of Hinduism that shapes Indian life through caste, including social relations, the organization of political power, distribution of resources, access to law, rituals, family, and community life. Soteriology is part of the mix but cannot account for the way Indian society works.[167]

Another example of the limitations of the SBNR emphasis is evident in how we might understand a statement on Remington's website. It says,

> *ABOUT US—THIS IS REMINGTON COUNTRY*
> For more than 200 years, Remington firearms have been forged from the untamed spirit that will always define our nation. The proud tradition that began with Eliphalet Remington's first hand-built rifle in 1816 continues to this day. Remington innovation is always ahead of its time, as evidenced by our rich history and long line of legendary firearms. The Model 700 and Model 870 have claimed their rightful places among the best-selling firearms of all time. Today, the Versa Max is quickly becoming the go-to firearm of choice for hardcore waterfowlers and the most demanding 3-gun competitors—an American icon on the rise. And Remington handguns like the Model 1911 R1 and the R51 are reinventing shootability and redefining performance. At our state-of-the-art R&D facility—the Rock—we're shattering convention and setting the performance standard all others must follow. As new generations inherit the American sporting heritage, we continue to expand—building new plants and acquiring new companies to meet the challenge of increased demand. Revolutionizing an industry. Building a nation. Remington Country is, was and always will be bigger than any one place—boundless as the American spirit.[168]

My caution about the SBNR emphasis is that it reflects a particular way of understanding religion that reduces its potential to critically

---

personalization our customers expect. At our best, we don't just serve food, we serve moments of feel-good, all with the lighthearted, unpretentious, welcoming, dependable personality consumers know and love." McDonald's, "Our Mission and Values," para. 1.

167. Fitzgerald, *Ideology*, 135–37.
168. Remington, "About Remington," first slide.

examine religious problematics of the everyday world. The Remington website places the company and its products in an American nationalist tradition. Its guns are narrated as instruments in building an *imagined community*, which has meant that any conversation about gun control is interpreted as an attack on the nation itself, at least by some people. What it masks is its functional value for making a lot of money based on a social Darwinist rugged manliness and what it avoids altogether is the effects of its products on the national health.

Religion seen as a unique interpretive category allows analysis of the difference between Remington's expressed and functional values, the way those values reflect American ultimate values, and the costs of both in terms of human health.[169] The Remington website indicates no critical awareness of the social, political, and spiritual climate of racism, fear, and hatred that makes gun ownership a badge of masculinity and an essential survival tool in a supposedly chaotic world. What I argue is that guns and the context in which they are fetishized are spiritual, in an individual sense but also in a collective, political, and economic sense. While it is true that individuals make their own choices about gun ownership, they do so in relationship to the social and institutional environment in which Remington finds its market niche. Choices about guns and about anything else are made within a meaning context that is bigger than the individual, accessible through the interpretive category of religion.

Religious Authorities Are Always with Us

A further caution about defining religion as primarily an individual matter comes from voices suggesting that the shift in religious authority is not from traditional religious organizations to the individual. Rather, the shift has been from traditional organizations to other authorities, among them state actors and the marketplace. For example, Kristin Kobes-DuMez places the support for Donald Trump among white evangelicals in the United States in a wider context of American religious nationalism and patriarchy that expresses itself in increasingly militaristic language. Her analysis draws attention to the foundational role of gender in American national identity, one result of which is that political and cultural

---

169. Gun ownership is a contentious issue with some voices identifying gun culture as a national health issue, particularly in the United States. However, there are no references to this debate in Remington's representation of its role in American society. See CDC, "Firearm Mortality."

leaders who have only tenuous relationships with religion have emerged as religious leaders and icons. Included in that gallery are John Wayne and Donald Trump whose rough masculine nationalism has been the basis for the confluence of interests and political alliances designed to achieve those interests. Evangelical Christianity is a social and political movement rationalized by religious language granting Donald Trump religious authority to make pronouncements on what is and what is not true American religion for a remarkably large number of Americans (and Canadians). Even those who reject his religious authority must deal with it.

Andrew Whitehead and Samuel Perry examine Christian nationalism in which religion is a key factor less accessible from an SBNR perspective. Religion is individual with a soteriological aspect but cannot be understood without its social, ideological, and collective character. The analyses offered by Whitehead and Perry and Kobes-DuMez recall the insights offered by Robert Nisbet who argued that the shift from religious authority to the individual is an illusion masking the emerging power of states in re-forming religion to suit state purposes. Among the many legacies left us by the ongoing Protestant reformations, coinciding with the rise of nation-states, is the role of state actors to take control of religion, a dynamic continuing in our world. The foregrounding of spirituality and religion as depoliticized individual matters has been important in that historical development. However, religion cannot be easily distinguished from matters of public interest. While the overt language in American religion follows the wider cultural foregrounding of individual choice freed from religious authorities, the functional values are shaped by the confluence of religion and nationalist interests with acceptance of political leaders as religious authorities.

Timothy McCowan's examination of the effectiveness of the BBP in Melbourne focuses on the pedagogical strategies designed to develop the preferred civic skills to allow individual students to be religious without disturbing harmonious diversity in a modern diverse society. However, what fades into the background in his analysis is the organizational, institutional, and political context in which the program lives. That context provides its own less visible RE, which is that religion, in a traditional sense, is unimportant. The BBP operates on principles like SBNR, which can do valuable work in encouraging students to be intentional about their own faith journeys. However, institutional priorities about scheduling, staffing, and resource allocation make the program less effective than it might be by creating a context in which diminished commitment by student and teacher is logical and understandable. The faith journeys of students are shaped by authorities who are de facto religious authorities by the fact that they are making decisions about religion and its role in the lives of students and the academic program.

In the same way, Benjamin Berger has given us ways to think about how law's religion has shaped the discourse about religion in Canada. Religion has been defined within social networks to fit the constitutional context within which individuals make their choices. In her "reappraisal of the secular and secularism," Winnifred Sullivan examines "the ways in which law regulates religion in the United States today," arguing that "religion [is] under the rule of law—as it is practiced in the United States." She says, "Nation-states since the early modern period have granted a certain measure of freedom to religious groups that agree to perform their assigned task of training moral and faithful citizens and that acknowledge the supremacy of nation and state. Religious groups that do not accept this task and acknowledge this supremacy are controlled in other ways."[170]

Hussein Ali Agrama examines the emergence of Egyptian state actors as religious authorities, which has led to ambiguities about Egypt's identity as a religious or a secular state. He analyzes the use of the language of secularism in courts and law that masks the role of the state in establishing boundaries around religion in a process designed to bring Islam into alignment with state interests. However, the use of the concept of *hisba*[171] by the courts in the case of Nasr Abu Zayd in 1995 "begs the question not only of Egypt's secularity or religiosity but also of secularity and religiosity more generally."[172] He concludes that "the Egyptian state is now bound to the responsibilities of maintaining the rights of God and acting in ways that conform to them.[173] The use of traditionally religious language (for example, rights of God) in Egyptian jurisprudence invites the conclusion that modernization in Egypt is incomplete in some way, a conclusion Agrama rejects. However, his insights have wider application,

---

170. Sullivan, "Religious Now," 1182.

171. Agrama defines *hisba* as "the commanding of the good when it is manifestly neglected, and the forbidding of the evil when its practice is manifest." *Questioning*, 18–19. *Hisba* is a moral concept in Islamic tradition so, on the face of it, a *religious* concept with rich meaning for individual and collective spirituality but one that has been widely used by the courts and other state actors to manage dissent.

172. Agrama, *Questioning*, 5.

173. Agrama, *Questioning*, 68.

which is that modern states have emerged as religious authorities, a key instrument being law and the regulation of religion, the language of secularism notwithstanding.

The *Bloom Review* of *faith literacy* in the UK and the *Routledge International Handbook of Religious Education* provide evidence that religion is more than individual, spiritual, and private, its regulation continuing to be a matter of public and state interests. While law is the coercive element in defining and maintaining public order, *education* is the persuasive strategy bridging the gap between public order and private faith.

In conclusion, the emphasis on individual spirituality contributes a great deal to our understanding of religion, creating space for the deeply personal nature of our spirit quests. At the same time, setting spirituality in an oppositional relationship to religion leans toward its decontextualization and can reduce its potential role in understanding and calling those who wield power to account. In addition, it allows us to imagine that we have outgrown religious authorities while, in fact, religious authorities are masked by the foregrounding of and faith in individual agency. Rather than representing progress in individual freedom, the SBNR trend dovetails with power structures by masking the network of power relations in the context in which it is defined.

Peter Berger identifies the tension between privatized spaces (including the family and religion) and the construction of public space linked with rationalized state power mobilized to facilitate capitalism, saying, "The aforementioned 'liberated territory' of secularized sectors of society is so centrally 'located' in and around the capitalistic-industrial economy, that any attempts to 'reconquer' it in the name of religio-political traditionalism endangers the continued functioning of this economy." He adds that "any attempts at traditionalistic *reconquista* thus threatens to dismantle the rational foundations of modern society."[174]

James Beckford notes development in Berger's thinking, saying that after 1967 he became more concerned about forms of socialism and millennialism, arguing that "the prospects for material well-being and political stability in the developed democracies are in part conditions by the course of modernization in the Third World and vice versa. The religious implications of this are, on the one hand, that voluntarism and the separation of religion and politics should be encouraged in developing countries and, on the other, that Western intellectuals should refrain

---

174. Berger, *Sacred Canopy*, 132.

from exporting socialistic and millennial Utopias to the Third World." Beckford argues that Berger, "almost stoically ambivalent towards the evolving character of modernity," opted for a form of the Lutheran "two kingdoms" model of society to resolve, however provisionally, the paradoxes in the role of religion in modern societies.[175]

The SBNR model of religion in society reflects a similar ambivalence, recalling a form of two kingdoms, one spiritual and private, the other rational and public. My point here is not to advocate for a return to some form of society dominated by traditional religious institutions. Rather, the point is to call for critical reconsideration of SBNR, embracing what it offers but, at the same time, to note its way of framing religious freedom of choice based on individual preference that fits into a sociopolitical context.

Some Conclusions: Religion as a Wild Card in Human Nature

Worldview, culture, values, imaginaries, faith, and spirituality offer useful ways to think about religion but what I am after here is a way to think about the more primitive, nonrational, and comprehensive place out of which our more intellectual formulations, worldviews, social constructions, values, cultural products, and imaginations arise. Stacey's engagement with and extension of imaginary gets at that deeper, wilder human characteristic, as does William James, referring to spirituality in Emerson when he says, "Religion, whatever it is, is a man's total reaction upon life, so why not say that any total reaction upon life is a religion?"[176] Stacey, wanting to avoid the problem of disembodied theory he sees in Taylor's use of imaginary, suggests that *spirit* provides a category "simultaneously grand enough to speak to what makes a human life feel worth living, humble enough not to alienate people, and authentic enough not to appear as something we do to manipulate people."[177] James K. A. Smith argues that we are what we love,[178] suggesting that the mainsprings of our lives are deeper, more volatile, and dynamic than intellectual constructions to which we give rational assent. Terry C. Muck says that "in Christian circles, confession has often meant the statement—written,

---

175. Beckford, *Industrial Society*, 99.
176. James, *Varieties*, 40.
177. Stacey, *Saving*, 5.
178. Smith, *You Are What You Love*.

spoken or implied—of what it is we believe." He adds that "when the act of confession is used in this sense, the Latin word *credo* is used in its stead, and *credo* is sometimes translated simply as 'I believe.'"[179] He goes on to cite examples of confessions as credo statements from other religions and cultures, including Confucius, Mahatma Gandhi, Al Ghazali, and Reinhold Niebuhr. A credo is a place on and in which we stand, by which we live and die.

Justine Ellis and Megan Watkins foreground the affective to think about religion as embodied in the way we live and move in the world. The focus on religion as intellectual propositions, foregrounding confessions of belief, can miss the wild-card bodied nature of religion to which they draw our attention. Volf et al. argue that "no matter how valuable it is to know what the good life is like, the real point is to live good lives," and that "the point is to act."[180] Quoting Rabbi Elazar ben Azarya (first century CE), they argue that "*Deeds* are the roots, *wisdom* the branches," rather than the other way around.[181] They refer to the *Spiritual Exercises of St. Ignatius of Loyola* to make the point that our beliefs are meaningless if they are not embodied in a disciplined life of service, doing good on this earth, in this life.[182] Martin Buber uses the metaphor of the circulatory system to get at something similar when he says, "Religion as risk, which is ready to give itself up, is the nourishing stream of the arteries; as system, possessing, assured and assuring, religion which believes in religion is the vein's blood which ceases to circulate."[183]

We are not brains on sticks or rational souls riding in and trying to control the fleshy, mortal vehicles to which we are condemned, or, as Ellis argues, "ambulatory embodied minds, who receive and assimilate information passively."[184] We are bodied, spirited animals, more specifically mammals, living in time and space and, through some mysterious processes, are gifted with the capacity to think about it and tell stories of our joys, sorrows, accomplishments, and losses. Being bodied means, among other things, that we live within the limitations of and draw life from time, space, and relationships. We live within timed and spatial horizons. We did not create ourselves and do not sustain ourselves in a vacuum,

179. Muck, *Why Study Religion*, 116.
180. Volf et al., *Life*, 230.
181. Volf et al., *Life*, 232.
182. Volf et al., *Life*, 266.
183. Buber, *Between*, 18.
184. Ellis, *Politics*, 104.

but rather we are here as the result of an act of bodied intimacy enacted by our parents and we depend for our lives on a vast network of relationships, most of which are beyond our conscious awareness and control. Our being bodied is expressed in any number of capacities that can be bodied in any number of ways. You can also say that we are (among other things) social, or esthetic and religious, although what that looks like is dynamic and astonishingly diverse. In addition, our bodied expressions arise out of a complex of bodied functions.

Justine Ellis argues that "framing religious literacy as an educative project of liberalism blinkers the endeavor from its inception because, in elevating the role of reason, it has the capacity to de-emphasize the role of emotions and bodies." She goes on to say that "although affect theory has only recently begun to interface with religious studies, its spotlighting of aspects of embodied life that emphasize the role of non-linguistic and non- or para-cognitive forces, has implications for the discussion around religious literacy."[185] Our stories take shape in and give shape to our world making capacities in a vast array of forms and expressions.[186]

Not only do we write *Hamlet*, but we also build the theaters in which *Hamlet* comes to life to tell us an old story on stages located in twenty-first-century cities of amazing complexity. Stonehenge was not built to occupy people who did not yet have the benefit of the internet to entertain them on a Saturday afternoon and the pyramids in Egypt were not just a make-work project to keep the peasants fed. We reshape the land and our bodies so that they tell a story of who we have been and what that meant to us. I am arguing that religion lives in that place of creative tension between our being bodied and mortal and our being able to imagine, struggle with meaning and purpose, to contemplate immortality, and to fall deeply in love with something that or someone who becomes our polestar.

In Defense of Religion

I am calling for a rehabilitation of the term *religion*, albeit cautiously. One reason for my caution is that I also agree with the alternative proposals to decolonize religion from both Christianity and theology. We live in an exciting historical moment in which it is possible to do so. However, we don't have a better theoretical category for a fundamental capacity

---

185. Ellis, *Politics*, 85.
186. Taves, "What is Nonreligion?" 2.

we share as a human family. I agree with Charles Taylor when he says that "we don't have to follow the masses in our use of this term, but we need some word and 'religion' is certainly the handiest one," although I disagree with him when he interjects that the term is useful "if we are to try to understand the significance of this decline."[187] Two things: first, I am cautious about the use of the term *decline* as a descriptor, and further reading suggests that he is using it to describe the process of *decline* of traditional forms of religion and religious authority and not as a more general social disintegration. Other authors seem to link changes in religion to social and moral decline, but Taylor is more nuanced in his assessment. Second, I think his accepting the common definitions of religion, citing Steve Bruce,[188] detracts from the implications of his suggestion that we could cast "our net even further to include the shape of (their) ultimate concern."[189]

In any case, there is, without a doubt, a lot of historical and cultural baggage associated with *religion* but the thing I am asking us to consider is a more enduring truth. The truth to which I refer is that human beings share a capacity for constructing organizing principles that serve as polestars as we navigate the paradoxes inherent at the intersection of our experience in time and our awareness of its limitations. In short, we all die at some point in time, and we are driven to figure out what that means.[190]

However, our stories are designed to secure our place in the world that brings us into conflict with competing stories, the results of which are not always pretty. I agree with Timothy Fitzgerald when he says that what is really important is the "cultural construction of identity and values and the legitimation of power."[191] What I understand Fitzgerald to be saying here is that the construction of religion as a sui generis category outside the more comprehensive category of culture is a modern, Western construction serving colonial and imperialist purposes. The distinctions between the religious and the secular, between religion and

---

187. Taylor, *Secular Age*, 430.
188. Taylor, *Secular Age*, 429.
189. Taylor, *Secular Age*, 427.

190. In a spirit of mischief, I have wondered if the attempts to avoid the term *religion* are a form of the "Don't Say Gay" movement in Florida and elsewhere; Lavietes, "Florida." Avoidance of religion in education is more pronounced in Canada than in some other jurisdictions; see Patrick et al., "Call." What is it about religion that makes us want to say "Don't say religion" in a modern, supposedly secular world?

191. Fitzgerald, *Ideology*, 10.

non-religion, are *cultural arbitraries* that do political work. Our cultural arbitraries, including our constructions about religion, have important implications for the role religion plays in our societies, including our definition and delivery of religious literacy. Our answers to the questions of religious literacy and RE reflect the role we expect it to play in our public discourses.[192]

Our shifting to worldview and our self-image as *secular* are among other constructions that marginalize *religion* to avoid an uncomfortable truth, which is that we can be rational, but we are fundamentally driven by loves and hates that elude rational domestication. To pretend otherwise is to render ourselves defenseless in the face of truly destructive forms of religion, dismissing them as some kind of mental deviation and psychological pathology that could be addressed by educational and psychological therapies. It also renders us impotent in the face of our cultural addictions, which are killing our planet. Religion as an analytical category resting on a narrow definition allows us to marginalize it or to place it out of critical reach and accountability. Definitions of religion restricted to beliefs and practices provides persuasive ground to reject religion as a legitimate analytic category, which is where Fitzgerald and others have landed.

However, I am more cautious than he is in concluding that "'religion' as an analytical category has no useful work to do" in understanding India and Japan.[193] The process of rehabilitation must include more precisely disentangling the human capacity to construct meaning from its many socially and historically unique expressions in a wide range of political contexts. Religion as an analytical category has been deployed in European colonial exploitation and, as a result, carries a lot of cultural baggage. No doubt about it. But so do gender, science, art, geography, the economy, culture, and any other analytical category we might want to include. Europeans do think about the world in socially constructed categories that have been deployed to serve political purposes. That does not mean the categories have no value or have nothing to contribute. They are not everything, but neither are they nothing. Other people groups have categories that do not easily translate into European analytical categories and one of our colonial abuses of power has been to marginalize their wisdom about the world because we cannot see what they see or love

---

192. Bourdieu and Passeron, *Reproduction*, book 1 outlines "cultural arbitrary" theory.

193. Fizgerald, *Ideology*, xi.

what they love. However, we do not have to reject the categories as part of our addressing historical abuses of power in a process of decolonization, however necessary decolonization is as part of our collective repentance.

Rather, I am going to follow Fitzgerald when he offers another possibility, saying, "In breaking free from an artificially restricted concept of religion, the problem is how to specify the core elements of the social order that are reproduced in the performance of the various rituals directed toward gods, ancestors, and the boss."[194] His acknowledgment that the concept of religion has been *artificially restricted* gives a promising hint in the rehabilitation of religion as a potential partner or one of the nested stories in how we might think about education as a social practice to deliver literacy and religious literacy.

Howard Thurman suggests something similar in drawing on the life of Jesus in his call for racial justice. He makes a distinction between Jesus and the Pauline tradition out of which Christianity arose, much of which has deliberately avoided the implications of Jesus having been born into poverty and social marginalization. Jesus, he argues, is one with humanity, especially those "who stand with their backs to the wall."[195] He asks, "Why is it that Christianity seems impotent to deal radically, and therefore effectively, with the issues of discrimination and injustice on the basis of race, religion and national origin?" And then he asks a question that comes close to what Fitzgerald is asking, although for different purposes: "Is this impotency due to a betrayal of the genius of the religion, or is it due to a basic weakness in the religion itself?"[196] His question about Christianity is one I am asking about religion as an interpretive category. I argue that the confusion between religion as an interpretive category and its embodiment in a vast variety of social constructions has opened the door to its marginalization or, in Thurman's words, "a betrayal of the genius of religion."

One last thing: religion does not make us better or nicer people. Our deepest passions and beliefs lead some of us to kill others or destroy what we identify as heretical contaminations and obstacles to our dreams for a better future. Charles Taylor observes that "religious faith can be dangerous. Opening to transcendence is fraught with peril,"[197] while William James points out that religion can lead people to become "exceptional

---

194. Fitzgerald, *Ideology*, 185.
195. Thurman, *Disinherited*, viii.
196. Thurman, *Disinherited*, xix.
197. Taylor, *Secular Age*, 769.

and eccentric."[198] The Bible, like all great sacred texts, is a collection of profound literature that takes us into considerable eccentricity and into the human heart of darkness. Religious literacy includes a gritty honesty about where our capacities can lead us when we allow our destructive passions to drive our powers.

However, religion also does not inherently lead us to become worse, less tolerant, more violent, or more stupid. Our deepest passions also lead us to give up our lives for each other, to fight for social justice and protection of the environment, create music and art that have inspired and expressed who we are as a human family. My argument for religious literacy includes awareness of the dangerous nature of religious faith, but I do not land in the conclusion that because it is fraught with peril that we should avoid it or domesticate it. Living dangerously can be productive but, like any human capacity, religion must be embraced and trained so that it can be directed toward its great potential as a partner in the healing of the world.

Moving Toward Religious Literacy

The distinction between religion as a human capacity and its vast, socially constructed manifestations has important implications for the ways we understand religious literacy and RE. One of these is that our students need some level of familiarity with the varieties of religious beliefs and practices in their environment. They need to develop some level of skill in distinguishing between harmful and constructive forms of religion. However, they also need to understand how religion works as a common human characteristic that is both our burden and our glory. We cannot understand Shakespeare without reference to religion. By that I mean his specific religious references but also his brilliant expression of the deepest loves and passions that sometimes drive us to extreme behaviors. We also cannot understand the nature of social hierarchy in Japan or caste in India without reference to their bases in a transcendent order embodied in social practices. We cannot understand the depth of racism in the United States and Canada without seeing its profound roots in transcendent values, including white supremacy. Debates over gun control and access to abortion services are divided over our deeply held beliefs over who is fully human and who is on the way to becoming fully human and

---

198. James, *Varieties*, 8.

who will likely never make it. In other words, our social constructions and embodied expressions of religion occur in *climates of opinion* that create their own normal, with its mixed legacies.

That does not mean that our climates of opinion cannot be reimagined. However, that reimagination cannot occur without recognizing the nature of religion and its role in normalizing and entrenching what we most value. That's the religious good, the bad, and the ugly of humanity. And, I argue, RE has a very important role in getting us to a place of recognizing our most deeply held beliefs about what is normal and universal and then reimagining them so that we can talk to each other about how best to raise our children and protect our earth.

4
Literacy

Man does not need language; man, in the dialectical, transitive understanding of to be, is language (much like he does not need food, shelter, and so on, but is his food and house)—man does not need language as a means of communication, or by extension, society as a means of survival. Man is communication and society.

—JOHANNES FABIAN, *TIME AND THE OTHER*

INTRODUCTION: DEFINITION OF LITERACY

HAVING DEFINED RELIGION AND considered three objections to religion, I now turn our attention to religious literacy. However, religious literacy is a subtopic under the more general topic of literacy, so we need to stop there for a while. We will keep this short since my claims and arguments here are not controversial. Or not very controversial.

On first thinking about it, literacy seems a straightforward matter of the three *R*'s. Literacy is the ability to read and (w)rite. In schools we add numeracy, of which a dictionary definition is "the ability to understand and work with numbers; the quality or state of being numerate,"[1] meaning that being literate in numbers and number systems gives us (a)rithmetic, our third *R*. As I say, straightforward.

---

1. Merriam-Webster, "Numeracy."

However, other definitions add layers of complexity to our common sense. Here are a couple to get us started. The first is from the Alberta Ministry of Education, which tells us,

> Literacy is critical in helping us make sense of our world. From the time we wake up to the time we go to sleep, we are constantly making meaning of the world around us.
>
> Literacy has traditionally been thought of as reading and writing. Although these are essential components of literacy, today our understanding of literacy encompasses much more. Alberta Education defines literacy as *the ability, confidence and willingness to engage with language to acquire, construct and communicate meaning in all aspects of daily living*. Language is explained as a socially and culturally constructed system of communication.[2]

The United Nations links literacy and access to *development* in its definition, saying that

> UNESCO has been working to realize the vision of literacy for all since 1946 in the belief that acquiring and improving literacy skills throughout life is an intrinsic part of the right to education and brings with it huge empowerment and benefits. But despite progress globally, 739 million adults (UIS, 2025) still cannot read and write. Literacy drives sustainable development, enables greater participation in the labour market, improves child and family health and nutrition, reduces poverty and expands life opportunities. UNESCO's approach to literacy continues to evolve as the definition of what it means to be literate changes in an increasingly digitalized world.[3]

These definitions suggest that *literacy* goes beyond the decoding skills of reading, writing, and arithmetic to include questions of *meaning* and *purpose* in the social and political contexts in which literacy is defined and delivered.

This chapter lifts two themes most relevant to the consideration of religious literacy out of the Alberta and UNESCO definitions for further examination. First, in the Alberta definition, literacy includes "helping us make sense of our world and making meaning of the world around us." In case you missed it the first time, the definition repeats the theme of *meaning* and adding some personal qualities or attributes saying, "Alberta

---

2. Alberta Education, "Literacy," paras. 1–2; italics original.
3. UNESCO, "Literacy," para. 1.

Education defines literacy as *the ability, confidence and willingness to engage with language to acquire, construct and communicate meaning in all aspects of daily living*." In other words, not only does literacy includes skills of decoding in a process of meaning-making, literacy also has implications for personal character and virtue development.

The UNESCO definition adds another theme directing our attention to the social and economic implications of literacy: by equipping students to fully engage in a modern society, they are rewarded with access its economic and social benefits. Reduction of poverty has benefits for individuals but also for the society of which they are members. The point is that increased literacy has implications for the literate individual but also for the society in which they find themselves and for the world by reducing poverty.

Although the Alberta and UNESCO definitions complicate a simpler three *R*'s model of literacy, they are not controversial. It seems obvious that anyone makes meaning out of what they read, write, and hear, and that increased levels of literacy and numeracy provide social and economic advantages. It seems equally obvious that anyone who is illiterate is at a disadvantage both socially and economically. In addition, in a modern society that values egalitarian access to resources, education is a social practice designed to deliver literacy that frees individuals from socially constructed constraints to reach their full potentials as human beings, a strategy to enhance social mobility. At least, that's the theory, for which there is some evidence.

Three Questions About Literacy Around Which This Chapter Is Organized

The definitions above invite some questions, three of which are relevant to religious literacy and around which the rest of the chapter is organized. The first question (or cluster of questions) is about the making of meaning, the question being, What does it mean to "make meaning"? Making meaning is closely linked to knowing. What does it mean to know something, and what does it mean to know when, under what circumstances, and in what context does something become meaningful? The point is that there is not a universal standard for meaning. Rather, knowing what is and what is not meaningful is established in social and political contexts that include networks of social relations. Further, the link between religion and meaning-making suggests overlap between *literacy* and *religion*. Another way of thinking about this is to suggest that the question of meaning takes us into consideration of the *spirituality of literacy* or *literacy's religion*.

A second question is about the link between literacy and social order. Both the Alberta and UNESCO definitions assume a future social order, the nature of which we see in UNESCO's approach to literacy, which "continues to evolve as the definition of what it means to be literate changes in an increasingly digitalized world." Success and the alleviation of poverty include adaptation to a particular kind of social and economic order. The question here is, What is the link between literacy and social order and between its opposite, illiteracy and social disorder? The point is that education is a social practice to deliver literacy, but any education program or enterprise is animated by a graduate profile preferred in a particular social context or social order.

A third question is about the politics and the networks of power relations in the social context in which literacy and illiteracy are conceptualized and enacted in policy and practice. Literacy is delivered in any number of ways, but the question here is, What are the networks of power in which the preferred social order and the preferred literate graduate profile are conceptualized and produced? The point here is that literacy and the mechanisms by which it is delivered are socially constructed in networks of power to produce a preferred graduate profile and a preferred model of society. I am not thinking of power as a negative thing. Power is inherent in all relationships. What I am foregrounding is the need to be critically aware of power in the social networks in which literacy and illiteracy are defined, given meaning, and operationalized.

The three questions are important in general discussions about education, but here they serve to set the stage for a discussion about RE and religious literacy. In chapter 5 we ask questions about meaningful religious knowledge, the distinction between religious literacy and illiteracy, social order and disorder, and about issues of power in which religious literacy is conceptualized and delivered.

In addition, I argue that the resolutions to the three questions about literacy are inherently *ambiguous*. The ambiguity at the heart of literacy and the education programs designed to deliver literacy is that, while we want our students to think critically and make meaning, their learning also makes us nervous. While this is not a new problem, our anxiety is deepened in the twenty-first century because our students have access to information and information influencers that we could hardly imagine in another time. We want our students to think critically but we worry about the implications of critical thought and what our students might do with the information they are acquiring while we are sleeping. Ambiguity is the theme humming away in the background, to which I do not pretend to have a final answer. In fact, there is not really a final answer in the sense that teachers, like parents, will never stop being hopeful and anxious about the outcomes of learning. However, while ambiguity is inherent in learning and growth, it is more like a travel companion than a destination. Eventually we hope our students will land in a secure place we might call *truth*, but we want them to land there knowing that there are other landing places, to live there with a fine balance between respect, humility, and critical engagement.

On to our three questions.

QUESTION ONE: LITERACY'S RELIGIOUS PROBLEM— WHAT DOES IT MEAN TO MAKE MEANING?

The Alberta and UNESCO definitions are based on the idea that literacy starts with the three *R*'s but does not end there. Rather, literacy includes understanding the meaning of what is being heard, read, and seen. Further, meaning is contextually conveyed in story. At the heart of literacy are questions of what it means to *know* something at three levels. The first is that knowing something means having control of *information* and basic skills of reading, writing, and numeracy. The second level is *knowledge*, which means that the basic information fits into an intellectual, social, political, and historical context. The third level is *wisdom*, which is the organization of information and knowledge into a meaning context, the question being, *What is the ultimate meaning or purpose of what we are learning here?* Wisdom includes appropriate and redemptive action so that the earth and our world experience healing. Wisdom is knowing how to live well in the world but is guided by and rooted in a sense of time that transcends our immediate experience.

The three levels of knowing live in a dynamic relationship with one another. New information changes our knowledge and our meaning stories. However, as our wisdom grows, we also revisit the information acquired at an earlier time so that it means something new. It is important to have your facts straight but sometimes information can be weaponized or miss the point of what needs to be said in a relationship. You can be very smart but not know how to live well, especially if you think you are smarter than everyone around you or that you do not have to pay attention to the messages you are getting from your body, your relationships, and from the earth.

Megan Watkins nicely captures this in her reference to William Blake's line, "To see a world in a grain of sand," as she reflects on the distinction between *chronos* and *kairos* time.[4] "To see a world in a grain of sand" and to allow "Each outcry of the hunted hare / A fibre from the Brain does tear"[5] is the brass ring of education and literacy. A commitment to lifelong learning means, not only that we are open to new information and knowledge, but also that our meaning stories develop to allow ourselves to wonder at the grain of sand and to be wounded by the wounds of the hunted hares of the world. We do not become wise if we do not allow ourselves to be overwhelmed by wonder and we do not become wise without having been wounded in some way.[6]

The Ontario Ministry of Education addresses the importance of big ideas that guide learning so that it becomes a transformative, life long process. In a document issued in 2013 it said,

> A common concern among educators new to inquiry is how to teach with an inquiry approach when there are so many curriculum expectations to address. By focusing on the "big ideas" rather than on the specific expectations alone, students' questions often lead to, and often exceed, overall curriculum expectations (*Natural Curiosity*, 2011). It is essential for educators to have a deep knowledge and understanding of the big ideas of the curriculum. This way, they are sensitive to the types of student cues that, if explored further, are likely to touch upon some of the overarching curriculum goals. Moreover, because ideas

---

4. Watkins, "Gauging," 77.
5. Blake, "Auguries of Innocence."
6. The reader will no doubt be aware of the origins of *kairos* and *chronos* time in Greek thought, their mythological rendering of the creative and paradoxical tension in human experience between "fate" and "freedom." The god *Kairos* (another spelling is *Caerus*) would show up but you had to be quick and alert to catch the opportunity or moment for action because he did not hang around very long. For the mythological source and definition of Kairos/Caerus, see, for example, Theoi Project, "Kairos." Watkin is getting at something that teachers know, which is that you have to be alert to "teachable moments" or opportunities when an important learning comes by. The terms have been adapted in Christian thought, the common theme being that those moments have divine origin.

play such an important role throughout the inquiry process, it is only natural that opportunities exist in which students see the need to gain access to ideas and to express them in a variety of ways. In this way, inquiry-based learning gives reason to value, use and develop skills, such as reading and writing, and does so in ways that blur the conventional boundaries between discrete subject areas. Educator inquiry into practice supports this kind of integrative and creative thinking about curriculum.[7]

The Ontario Ministry of Education's guidance for teachers is like that offered by the Alberta Ministry of Education and UNESCO. Literacy involves basic skills and information that are expected to serve a big picture of meaning that will have positive personal and social consequences. We want our students to know things but *knowing* is more than absorption of and regurgitation of information. We want our students to believe in something bigger than themselves so that they will have guiding principles and framing questions to sustain them as they navigate the details of the subjects under investigation. The Ontario Ministry acknowledges that students will have forgotten most of what they need to know to pass tests and exams but is committed to the idea that there are enduring takeaways that will serve them in their futures. Teachers must catch those moments, and good things can happen when they do.

The world of education has moved beyond the *banking model* of education challenged by Paulo Freire who argues that the banking model is essentially an educational strategy by those in positions of power to maintain a preferred social structure. We want our students to know information and acquire knowledge, but we really want them to really know the big ideas, and we want them to adopt *linking big ideas, wonder, and learning*. At least, that's the big idea animating Ontario public education.

Education's Religion: Education, Literacy, and the Making of a Better Person and a Better World

There is something more going on than just an intellectual construction of meaning in a personal sense to include its implications for making a better world. Paolo Freire is arguing for education and literacy as essential to social change and the achievement of social equality and

7. Ministry of Education, *Inquiry-Based Learning*, 3.

justice. The UNESCO definition does something similar by identifying the "multiplier effect of literacy," which then "empowers people, enables them to participate fully in society and contributes to improving livelihoods," describing it as a "driver for sustainable development."

In these definitions, the preferred graduate profile includes basic skills of literacy, but more than that it includes the ability to construct the meaning of that basic information, having acquired the skills and character traits mobilized in service of a preferred social end. The Alberta definition refers to skills and willingness to engage in the construction of meaning. Literacy and knowing include virtues, including commitments to creating a better world. There is hope for a better world and faith that literacy will get us there. A better world is based on or reflects an idea of what is *normative* or *right*.

Education in Canadian and other jurisdictions is animated by hope in a future world and that education will call that into being in the minds and imaginaries of their students. This is not a new idea. The ancient Jewish concept of *shalom* captures what it means to know something in any meaningful way. One explanation of the term is "the ancient Hebrew concept of peace, rooted in the word "shalom," meant wholeness, completeness, soundness, health, safety and prosperity, carrying with it the implication of permanence."[8] Another definition identifies *shalam* as the root word, saying that "in the translation of Exodus 21–22, *shalam* is translated as 'make it good,' 'shall surely pay,' 'make full restitution' or to 'restore.' The ancient Hebrew meaning of shalom was 'to make something whole.' Not just regarding practical restoration of things that were lost or stolen. But with an overall sense of fulness and completeness in mind, body, and estate."[9]

Charles Taylor, expanding on "our ethical predicament,"[10] refers to the human impulse to seek *fulfillment*. He argues that, in a secular age, the search for fulfillment has been complicated by the foregrounding of rationalism in the European Enlightenment. The triumph of rationalism, conceptualized within an immanent frame, has not resolved our search for fulfillment, but rather has left us with the dilemma of finding an ontological basis for it. He says, "The question arises here of what ontology can underpin our moral commitments, which for most of us constitute a crucial 'fulfillment,' in the sense I'm using here, that is, a mode of the

8. Perlman, "What Is Shalom," para. 1.
9. Hershey, "True Meaning of Shalom," para. 4.
10. Taylor, *Secular Age*, 604.

higher, of fullness which we are called on to realize."[11] I am arguing that education, designed to deliver literacy and knowledge, is the social practice of drawing students into an imagined model of the world based on normative principles of *wholeness* as a way of equipping them with the sensitivity and knowledge to enter a life marked by *fulfillment* in the deepest sense.

Education, Literacy, and Love: The Brass Ring

Another layer in the concept of shalom is that the work of teachers is animated by *love*. This is hard to remember sometimes, especially on a Friday afternoon at the end of a hard week with end-of-term evaluation reports looming over the weekend. It is also true that teachers do what they do to pay for groceries. However, they do, on some level, fall in love with their students, wanting them to fall in love with their role in a story that includes a better future, both for themselves and for the world. William Blake opens our eyes to another way of knowing deer, lambs, and anything else in the world, something that for students might well be a kairos moment:

> The wild deer, wand'ring here & there
> Keeps the Human Soul from Care
> The Lamb misus'd breeds Public Strife
> And yet forgives the Butchers knife[12]

Harro Van Brummelen, writing within a Christian frame of reference, argues that "truth leads to love with actions," rooted in God's love, which "demands that we walk in His truth; love and truth may never be separated." In other words, truth "is not just a correct statement but a correct deed."[13] Parker Palmer warns us that "curiosity is an amoral passion," "another word for power" with a "tendency toward corruption," which will "generate knowledge that eventually carries us not toward life but toward death." However, he says, "another kind of love is available to us, one that begins in a different passion and is drawn toward other ends. This knowledge can contain as much sound fact and theory as the knowledge we now possess, but because it springs from a truer passion it works toward truer ends. This is a knowledge that originates not in

11. Taylor, *Secular Age*, 607.
12. Blake, "Auguries of Innocence."
13. Van Brummelen, *Stepping Stones*, 77.

curiosity or control but in compassion, or love—a source celebrated not in our intellectual tradition but in our spiritual heritage."[14]

In his reflections on hate, Howard Thurman says that "it is a grievous blunder to assume that understanding is always sympathetic. Very often we use the phrase 'I understand' to mean something kindly, warm and gracious. But there is an understanding that is hard, cold, minute, and deadly. It is the kind of understanding that one gives to the enemy, or that is derived from an accurate knowledge of another's power to injure."[15] Facts and knowledge, detached from love, are weapons, which is not where we want our students to land.

Christopher Watkin, drawing on Esther Meek, places *knowing* in the context of *covenant*. He says, "Knowing is therefore 'situated'—as philosophers are fond of saying these days—not only bodily and culturally but also covenantally," adding, "the fundamental situation in which we find ourselves is, covenant epistemology."[16] In other words, knowing in any meaningful sense cannot be detached from relationships. He says, "One further important aspect of Meek's covenant epistemology is that knowledge is preceded by love; one cannot know what one does not care about. 'Great knowers need to be great lovers,' she argues. 'Rather than knowing in order to love, we love in order to know.'"[17] *Covenant* in the sense that Watkin is using it places learning in relationships of promise to love. Love is not a good feeling, in the first place. It is a lived promise to seek the welfare of our neighbor, whoever that might be. Teachers do not have to like the neighbor sitting in their classrooms, but they do have to seek and encourage their flourishing, even if that means steering them away from choices that may harm them.

Miroslav Volf adds a caution to the idea of *covenant*, arguing that "covenant has no sufficiently strong moral legs of its own but must rest on substantive values that come from elsewhere."[18] He adds that "covenant could become a useful political category because it was first a moral category and it became a moral category because it was at its core a theological category. Covenant may well serve as the bond of political community, but the political community will be no better than the values

---

14. Palmer, *To Know*, 8.
15. Thurman, *Disinherited*, 66–67.
16. Watkin, *Biblical Critical Theory*, 250.
17. Watkin, *Biblical Critical Theory*, 252.
18. Volf, *Embrace*, 154.

it espouses."[19] While his focus is not literacy and education, his proposals about *embrace* take us to some important implications for education, specifically about the network of relationships in which transformative education occurs. He argues that the idea of covenant must include the transformation of how we are in the world, not bound by external expectations of law and social relations to a redirection of our inner lives, something he calls a *new covenant*.

Here I am arguing that all education is transformative, in the sense that we want our students to have basic competencies but what we really want is for them to be better human beings. Volf says, "A key political task must be to nurture people whose very identity should be shaped by the covenant they have formed so that they do not betray and tyrannize one another." However, drawing on his Christian framework of reference, he says that "the new covenant raises the fundamental issue of how to take the covenantal promises from stone tablets and put them with the people and engrave them onto their hearts."[20] While I have some arguments with it, this is the best of Ontario's Character Development initiative. It recognizes that education is transformative, not just in terms of the facts and knowledge our students will acquire but, more profoundly, who they will be.

This is not a new insight, of course, Volf's metaphor coming from the Old Testament prophet Jeremiah (Jer 31:31–40). Jeremiah was referencing the story of the encoding of the Law summarized in the Ten Commandments, written, we are told, on tablets of stone by the great liberating leader Moses (Exod 20:2–17; Deut 5:6–21). Jeremiah calls for a *new covenant* calling out scrupulous attention to legal purity among his privileged fellow Israelites who were running roughshod over the poor and the marginalized among them. Teachers do not want to raise students whose legal literacy is motivated by their desire to escape its consequences, whose historical information is used to justify colonialism and its dreadful legacy, whose scientific interest in chemistry is to weaponize it.

Matthias Scharer, examining the implications of Vatican II (1962–1965) and the Wurzburg Synod (1971–1975) for RE in Germany, uses the metaphor of *holy ground*[21] to describe the purpose of RE, arguing that

19. Volf, *Embrace*, 155.
20. Volf, *Embrace*, 157.
21. See Exod 3 for the story of Moses meeting God at the burning bush for the source of this metaphor.

care for *the other* is central and that trampling on the other amounts to a *transgression*. He says that "immediate experience" of the "Other" is at the heart of "learning religion" in a way that is neither "catechesis" or "the mere teaching of religious facts."[22] Religious literacy occurs in relationships, in an environment of care and love.

Education as Holy Ground

I agree but argue that the idea of *holy ground* is more generally applicable to education, not confined just to RE. While *holy ground* might be seen as a religious concept because of its origins, all education is designed to draw students into a place of ultimate value and even reverence. Scharer goes on to say that "learning religion is not an additional strategy for the efficient spread of faith and religion, but a change of perspective on the world, life, and indeed on individual religious beliefs in general."[23] I agree and would add that this is *education's religion*, or the religious aspect of all education, not something confined to religion classes. *Holy ground* takes us from education as transactional contract or narrowly defined covenant to what Miroslav Volf calls *embrace* in covenant as a moral and theological category, transformative relationships that heal the earth and all who live here.

Jasmin Zine introduces her research with a reference to the *straight path* as the transcendent point animating the Islamic schools about which she is writing. She says, "The opening verse of the Holy Qur'an ... speak[s] to the practice of staying on the 'straight path,' *siratul mustaqeem* in the Arabic language—that is, on the path of righteous knowledge and behavior. This is often termed in Islamic discourse a 'middle path,' one of moderation, balance, peace, and justice."[24]

One conclusion is that meaningful knowing and love are inseparable. Meaningful knowing is not detached curiosity but engaged love and hope for a better world and for our students finding and walking a straight path in and toward that better world. Curiosity is probably where learning starts but curiosity can be satisfied by a trivial pursuit of information and knowledge serving instrumental ends. Robert Orsi recounts his conversation with Clara, member of the parish of St. Jude,

---

22. Scharer, "Learning," 41.
23. Scharer, "Learning," 42.
24. Zine, *Canadian Islamic Schools*, 3.

which he was studying. Clara asks him, "Have you ever prayed to Saint Jude" and, when he tells her he has not, asks, "Then how do you expect to understand what we're doing when we pray to Saint Jude?"[25] Information and knowledge are multilayered and become truly meaningful in relationships in which they serve to develop wisdom.

By *information* I mean having access to the facts of a matter (for example, John A. MacDonald was the first Prime Minister of Canada) and the reading, listening, and decoding skills necessary to acquire that information. By *knowledge* I mean understanding the context of that information (John A. MacDonald was the first Prime Minister of Canada, an important leader in the establishment of the new nation of Canada and the building of the Canadian Pacific Railway, among other things). By *wisdom* I mean understanding the meaning context of information and knowledge and, further, a commitment to understanding what the building of the railway as a nation-building strategy meant for, among others, Indigenous people whose lives were fundamentally altered by the establishment of the Canadian confederation. Teachers want their students to be moved by compassion for the people caught under the harrow of empire, inspired by an imagined future in which things are made right. Teachers want their students to be horrified by evil, not jaded by information detached from a meaning context.

However, teachers also want their students to be balanced in their assessments, to avoid simplistic judgments of Sir John as totally other whom we can dismiss, but rather see him as a fellow human with tendencies we share. He was a person of his time, with complex motives, responding to circumstances we may not completely understand, but his legacy lives on in us. Wisdom includes humility so that we do not turn our information and knowledge into self-serving weapons the purpose of which is to present ourselves as more righteous and advanced than our grandparents.[26] Education is animated by big, impossible ideas that make us and our world better than what we inherited, but it is also a process of expanding our hearts and equipping our bodies for the service of others, including those who cannot speak for themselves. And it is marked by the humility of knowing that our descendants will look at the mixed blessings of what we have left them.[27] I am not arguing that

---

25. Orsi, *Between*, 148.

26. Sandle and Van Arragon, *Re-Forming*, ch. 5; Sweet, *Inventing*, Introduction.

27. I recommend Claire Dederer's *Monsters: A Fan's Dilemma* for a readable exploration of the complex relationship we have with cultural giants. Dederer works

teachers should avoid judgment and assessment of evil, judgment being inherent in critical thinking. Rather, judgment deepened by wisdom and love avoids self-serving othering.

Literacy finds its meaning and purpose in wisdom, which includes a commitment to lifelong learning, repentance, and redemptive action toward creating a better world. This is a life of robust, engaged love, the brass ring of education. Educational systems are organized to deliver a better future, marked by wholeness, restitution for those who have been hurt, and a deep commitment to do better. However, that takes us to another question.

QUESTION TWO: WHAT IS THE LINK BETWEEN LITERACY AND SOCIAL ORDER? LITERACY AND THE PROBLEM OF UNINTENDED CONSEQUENCES

Literacy and Socialization

On to our second question about the link between literacy and social order. To start this section, let's agree that the link between literacy and social order is only one among multiple ways to think about literacy. For example, the neurosciences have provided much useful information about how information is processed, how letters on a page are decoded or not, and how memory works. Insights provided by studies in the psychology of learning have equipped educators to develop more emotionally safe spaces for learning, with practices that enhance a student's learning readiness. A legal perspective on literacy includes regulation of education and requirements for school attendance and for school programming. A theological perspective foregrounds literacy in belief systems, asking about what people believe and practice. However, in this section we focus our attention on the link between social order and literacy because social order is high on the list of topics and priorities in the literature on religious literacy.

---

in the arts with a background as a film critic, engaging the ambiguous moral dance with the great art produced by people who were also moral monsters. Her insights and questions are good for teachers, especially given the information available to students and our heightened sensitivities that can fuel self-righteous judgment that avoids the discomforts of self-awareness. There are monsters in history, but Dederer invites us to see that there are sleeping monsters in all of us. To be honest, I am not sure what to do with this as a teacher, so am just letting it sit there for a while on my inner bookshelf.

The Alberta and UNESCO definitions of literacy above assume a future social order but also, both implied and explicit, we see identification of disorder or harm. I am foregrounding the idea of a future social order that includes an assessment of our current reality and our likely future reality. The UNESCO reference to an "increasingly digital world" is just such an assessment, with implications for literacy in preparing students for that future, which is upon us for better or for worse. Success and the alleviation of poverty include adaptation to a particular kind of world order.

Literacy and Critical Thought

However, the Jewish concept of shalom invites us to imagine, not only an inevitable future as it is likely to be and to which we must adapt, but also the idea of a better world we can create by rising above adaptation to inevitable developments and acting as agents who resist those developments if they do harm. There will be a social order in our futures. That's a given. The question is whether it is the preferred one of our hopes and dreams or a dystopian one of our fears and nightmares. Or something between those two extremes, which is more likely. Education is the social practice designed to deliver literacy equipping students for adaptation to a preferred future. However, education includes critical thinking about and resistance to futures we do not want to see. Illiteracy, the opposite of literacy, is (among other things) whatever condition impedes either successful adaptation or effective resistance. Illiteracy can be skills deficits, misinformation, or knowledge deficits but it is also commitment to the wrong big ideas, however those are defined. Literacy and its dancing partner, illiteracy, are contextual, depending on each other for meaning.

Besides compliance with and adherence to a normative social order rooted in the *word of God*, the Old Testament includes the denunciations and exposure of abuses of power and privilege issued by prophets who, like journalists in our world, sometimes paid with their lives for their whistle blowing. Prophets were animated by a shalom social imaginary, a time when all would be made right. Jews were (and are) *people of the book*, highly literate, which meant that they knew the universal social order and the implications of violating it, but also had the skills of critical thought and resistance. And, to balance the stories of prophets in the Old Testament, we encounter false prophets whose utterances supported the power structures and practices of their day.[28] We see forms of false prophecy in our world also, among them prosperity gospel preachers much loved by capitalist power brokers and would-be presidents for life, religious leaders who bless the Russian invasion of Ukraine and the competing narratives of conflict in the Middle East.[29]

Literacy and Critical Thought as a Mixed Blessing

Literacy is a mixed blessing for social order. The definitions of literacy quoted above refer to students being empowered, developing confidence and abilities, all of which set them free to pursue a better life for themselves and for the world in which they find themselves. The Ontario definition refers to *critical thinking* as a component of literacy. However, empowerment, confidence, and critical thinking skills take us to the intersection of freedom and social order. Lori Beaman, examining the case of Bethany Hughes being adjudicated within the framework of Canadian constitutional law, writes that she wants to "stir debate and discussion about what it means to have a constitutional guarantee of religious freedom and, at the same time, a constitutional balancing of that freedom."[30] Literacy lives in the balance of freedom of thought and the management of its implications.

One implication is what Margaretta Patrick et al. identify as "difficult citizenship," defined as "critical, engaged citizen participation for social change toward justice," adding that "those who promote difficult citizenship view with concern education policy documents that reduce equity and diversity to individual skills and superficial celebrations."[31] Literacy, Patrick argues, goes deeper than the construction of meaning in a personal sense to include the capacity and skills of responsible and sometimes difficult citizenship.

---

28. There's a funny story of Micaiah and four hundred false prophets who landed on opposite sides of advising Kings Ahab and Jehoshaphat in their plans for war. Not so funny for Micaiah who ends up on the receiving end of some royal violence for accurately predicting the death of Ahab in the subsequent ill-conceived battle. And not funny for Ahab, of course, although you kind of get the impression from the writers that he got what was coming to him (1 Kgs 22).

29. I am writing this while the conflict between Hamas and the state of Israel has exploded once again into horrifying violence with conflicting narratives about what has happened and its meaning. Khouri, "Watching."

30. Beaman, *Harm*, x.

31. Patrick et al., "Call," 610.

Critical Thought: Literacy and Morality

One way to think about this is that *critical thought* is the morality aspect of literacy, by which I mean that literacy includes critical evaluation of what is true and untrue, right and wrong, good and evil. As a result, literacy and critical thought have inherent unintended consequences, because students will critically evaluate the literacy and education practices to which they are being subjected. Matthew Crawford argues that *our evaluative outlook* distinguishes humans from other animals who, although they "certainly have memory and the ability to learn, human beings are thought to be the only creatures who can deliberately recall something not cued by the environment."[32]

Our evaluative outlook and its unpredictability are based on a model of the world, a standard of truth that transcends our immediate circumstances. We operate with moral standards of measurement, "images of the moral order, [which] although they make sense of some of our actions, are by no means necessarily tilted towards the status quo. They may also underlie revolutionary practice."[33] This is not what rulers of the world want to hear.

Muhammad Iqbal says, "It is this sense of striving in the experience of purposive action and the success which I actually achieve in reaching my 'ends' that convinces me of my efficiency as a personal cause. The essential feature of a purposive act is its vision of a future situation which does not appear to admit any explanation in terms of Physiology."[34] Iqbal is examining the mystery of human consciousness, which, although bodied, includes the capacity to rise above the inevitability of necessity or fate. He links our critical faculties to a transcendent source, saying, "God reveals his signs in inner as well as outer experience, and it is the duty of man to judge the knowledge-yielding capacity of all aspects of experience."[35] For Iqbal, God's revelation is what inspires true critical thinking, anchoring our evaluative outlook and giving moral order an endurance that transcends our short horizons and limited positionality. While we may not all agree with his argument, it is a way of seeing what Justine Ellis suggests when she says, "This lack of predictability in learning challenges the notion that students will engage with learning

32. Crawford, *World*, 20.
33. Taylor, *Secular Age*, 175.
34. Iqbal, *Reconstruction*, 86.
35. Iqbal, *Reconstruction*, 101.

materials in purely autonomous and cognitive ways."[36] Critical thinking, which I argue is the morality of literacy, is animated by a transcendent framework of the world. We can argue about the nature of transcendence, but our students are not served well if we encourage them to think of their critical faculties in *purely autonomous and cognitive ways*.

Critical Thinking, Freedom, and the Problem of Difficult Citizenship

Critical thinking is an essential element in education and the development of literacy. However, it is also one of the wild cards in education in the sense that teachers and regulators do not control the outcomes of their efforts. One consequence is that our students will deliberately recall something not cued by our carefully constructed pedagogical environments. Their preferred world futures and their role in bringing it about may not be the ones for which we were aiming. This is where freedom intersects with social context and limitations.

Here's an example from Ontario education history: the creative tension built into education was evident in the *Mackay Report*, a supplement to the *Hall-Dennis Report* submitted in 1968, both of which were part of a reform initiative of public education along *progressivist* principles. Both called for a shift from what was seen as the existing *coercive indoctrination* to something more truly *educational* in which student choice and freedom played a central role. Behavior and morality were to be based on scientific principles articulated by the developmental theory of Lawrence Kohlberg, replacing the religious, specifically Christian, basis for moral education and *character*.

The assumptions and hopes were that students, given the right kind of information and set free to explore various moral choices, would come to conclusions and life choices preferred by the writers of the *Report* and the educational authorities who had commissioned it. The writers say, "We hope it will be through true education and not through any kind of indoctrination, that he will be encouraged to choose the religious and moral values that will hold as good for his time as those which we ourselves prize so highly have held good in ours." However, they are nervous about the implications of student choice and freedom, saying, "Nothing in what we have just said should be interpreted as our willful criticism of

---

36. Ellis, *Politics*, 108.

good behavior as such, as a plea for permissiveness or as our reluctance to commend virtuous conduct for its own sake wherever it can be found." They add that "it is true that a hedonistic philosophy is likely to lead to moral bankruptcy, but this is a conclusion that a morally mature person should be capable of reaching independently."[37] In short, while the authors argue for freedom of choice based on information, they recognize that someone introduced to a hedonistic philosophy might well like it and choose it even if they should not. In another expression of hope, the writers say, "We hope that he will be helped to arrive at personal judgments and to make personal decisions which are as mature, i.e., as just, as his progressing levels of moral development permit."[38]

The problem is that while information and critical thought may set us free, we are troubled by what freedom might mean in real life because ideas and literacy are embodied in action. The troublesome implications of freedom are evident in a shift in Ontario from 1969 to 2008 in the management of freedom and critical thought. To understand the shift, we will take a brief trip into a legal challenge that landed in the Ontario Court of Appeal in 1990.

The issue before the court in 1990 was the constitutional status of *religious instruction* in public schools delivered by, among others, local pastors and church-related volunteers. The court ruled that *religious instruction* was *coercive indoctrination* that violated the religious freedom rights of public school students. *Religious instruction* was to be replaced by *education about religion*, the court relying on a distinction between *education* and *indoctrination* established in the *Mackay Report*. It expanded on the distinction by saying:

- The school may sponsor the *study* of religion but may not sponsor the *practice* of religion.
- The school may *expose* students to all religious views but may not *impose* any particular view.
- The school's approach to religion is one of *instruction*, not one of *indoctrination*.
- The function of the school is to *educate* about all religions, not to *convert* to any one religion.
- The school's approach is *academic*, not *devotional*.
- The school should *study* what all people believe but should not teach a student *what* to believe.

37. Mackay et al., "*Religious Information*," 47.
38. Mackay et al., "*Religious Information*," 49.

- The school should strive for student *awareness* of all religions but should not press for student *acceptance* of any one religion.
- The school should seek to *inform* the student about various beliefs but should not seek to *conform* him or her to any one belief.[39]

The distinction between *study* and *practice, exposure* and *imposition*, and other binaries reflected confidence that students exposed to information about religion and morality would more or less naturally choose the outcomes preferred by the adults in their lives.

In fact, the court was more confident about the outcomes of free choice than the authors of *Mackay* had been. There are good reasons for this, among them that the *Mackay Report* was written by educators who, while as committed as the court to a progressive model of education, were less confident that students would find their way to what amounted to traditional morality if left on their own. Classroom experience has a way of exposing gaps between progressive optimism and human nature. The language of anxious hope and faith occurs throughout the 1969 *Mackay Report* despite its claims to be progressive, modern, and scientific.

That's not surprising, since education is based on hope and faith that is often tenuous. The fact is that literacy and critical thought have inherent unintended consequences because students will critically evaluate the literacy and education practices to which they are being subjected. In short, students can bite the pedagogical hand that feeds them and often do. Most teachers have scars. Beyond that, however, the (post) modern information world is less easily traced to its sources and literacy is less easily managed. That does not mean there are no information authorities, but they are likely to be ones we often do not think of as educational in a traditional sense. The two primary actors in the world of information management are nation-states and shadowy commercial enterprises that generate enormous profits for a new elite. However, they are not all-powerful and often their strategies have unintended consequences.

Gregory Starrett traces the introduction of mass education in Egypt designed to transform Egypt into a modern state. Islam provides

---

39. Corporation of the Canadian Civil Liberties Association et al. v. Ontario (Minister of Education) and Board of Education of Elgin County, [1990] 37 O.A.C. 93 (CA). The Ontario Court of Appeal drew on *Religion in the Public Schools*, a 1986 publication of the American Association of School Administrators, at p. 33, which, in turn, quoted from an earlier statement of the Public Education Religion Studies Center, Wright State University.

the language of public discourse in Egypt, but that discourse must be managed by the state and state actors lest it interferes with the project of modern nation building. This includes making distinctions between the right and wrong forms of Islam. However, he says, "An unintended consequence of making Islam a part of the curriculum is to make it a subject which must be 'explained' and 'understood.'" To make the right choices about Islam, students must be equipped to resist the wrong forms of it that show up in families, villages, local councils, and local religious authorities. Literacy, in this case about Islam, is a tool of "mass socialization" or compliance with the right forms of Islam, at least from the state's point of view.[40]

However, Starrett asks "why the political and educational strategies chosen by Egypt's ruling elites over the last century have resulted in the diminution rather than the augmentation of their ability to control the public discourse on Islam." The unintended consequence at the heart of Starrett's research is that the project of providing mass schooling "has resulted instead in new modes of political opposition, a renewed public attachment to religious values." One response has been the "forced resort to the tactics of the police state," including the story of the police raid in August 1998 with which Starrett begins his account.[41]

Saba Mahmood describes similar anxiety operationalized in coercive action by Egyptian state and religious authorities in response to the women in the mosque movement. Women gathering to study the Qur'an had several consequences, one of which was that the authority of the Qur'an and their ultimate allegiance to God began to take precedence over the authority of men and of the state and state actors. The point is that throughout history, literacy has been a source of anxiety because its consequences cannot easily be predicted or controlled. We hope for a particular outcome, and we have faith that our educational practices will deliver a preferred graduate profile, but we are never sure. Education, like religion, lives with a great deal of uncertainty.

In a similar way, B. R. Ambedkar, fighting an uphill battle for the abolition of caste in India, argues that literacy provides the tools and

40. Starrett, *Putting*, 9–10. Dale Eikelman, "Mass Education," 643, similarly examines "the objectification of the religious imagination" in mass education "by which three questions come to be foregrounded in the consciousness of large numbers of believers: What is my religion? Why is it important to my life? and, How do my beliefs guide my conduct?" Consideration of these questions has unintended consequences for the management of religion, which he demonstrates in contemporary Arab societies.

41. Starrett, *Putting*, 14–15.

furnishings essential to reflective thought, but also that withholding educational opportunities and literacy from Dalits in India is an important strategy to maintaining the caste system. Barriers to education and literacy in a society indicate recognition of the potentially disruptive consequences of literacy. Albert Raboteau describes the challenges for slave owners of managing literacy among their slaves, caught in the contradictions between their obligations of Christian evangelism and their language of freedom and the disruptive implications of literacy that might well lead slaves to come to some inconvenient logical conclusions about their own humanity and the state of slavery in which they were caught.

Our evaluative outlook can be a nuisance from a management point of view, something every teacher knows in keeping a class on track and focused on the wonders of *meiosis* and *mitosis* on a Friday afternoon in May. Students are always evaluating whether the activity in which they are expected to be actively engaged is worth their full attention and may consider alternative applications of the information and knowledge being delivered. Teachers include (or perhaps should if they don't) the advice "Kids don't try this at home" in their lessons about revolution and the explosive properties of certain chemical compounds. Some students (fortunately most of them, actually) adapt by accepting the need to comply, trusting that the process will yield positive results that they may not yet see clearly. Education is a matter of faith on so many levels.

However, schools, particularly high schools and universities, have also been sources of social disruption when students question the faith of their pedagogical fathers and mothers and express their doubt in disruptive action. Do we want them to think critically? Well, maybe; and then again, maybe not. Critical thought is essential to social reform and renewal that can, at the same time, be uncomfortable. This gets us to question three and the issue of the management of critical thought.

QUESTION THREE: WHO DEFINES LITERACY AND CONTROLS THE MECHANISMS BY WHICH IT IS DELIVERED?

The problem is that the evaluative capacities inherent in literacy have outcomes for individuals and societies. OK, that's not the real problem. The real problem is that some of the real-life outcomes are not included in the preferred graduate profile animating the education programs and practices designed to achieve it. A graduate profile is significant, not just for the individual graduate but also for society, being a picture of a preferred future of the world coming into being. Education, while it is formally organized in schools and school systems, is a social practice involving multiple partnerships held together by a consensus amounting to a social covenant[42] about a preferred literate graduate. The configurations of partnerships are unique to the social and political context in which they occur, but no society can tolerate deliveries of education that fall too far outside the consensus or that violate the social covenant providing a consensus for a preferred social order.

In addition, literacy is delivered within social networks in which one actor tends to emerge as the dominant one to shape the social covenant and educational programs, policies, and practices. The dominant partner polices the boundaries between what are and what are not tolerable literacy outcomes and who are and who are not legitimate partners in delivering it. Globally the contestants for dominance in education partnerships have been state and state actors and religious organizations. Since the nineteenth century, states and state actors have more or less successfully won the contest, claiming education as a matter of public interest of which states and state actors are the primary custodians. However, there are multiple other players competing for the attention of students, including the shadowy owners of social media platforms, working in dynamic partnership to deliver literacy.[43]

---

42. I am using *covenant* rather than social *contract* because it more adequately captures the intimate nature of social relationships. Contract is more narrowly focused, implying transactional relationships based on mutual benefit, while covenant implies relationships made meaningful in the context of transcendent values and promises about mutual care. Social contract theory foregrounds the exchange of benefits but that's not actually the way a healthy society works. An example is Canada's national health care system, which emerged in the 1960s inspired by Tommy Douglas's Christian vision of a covenant-based society, inviting us to be better than our self-interested selves. Christopher Watkin, *Biblical Critical Theory*, ch. 10, expands on the difference within a Christian framework, although I would argue that covenant is evident in other conceptual frameworks as well.

43. There is considerable variation in how the relationships between state and non-state actors play out. The issue of access to resources, including school funding, control of textbooks, and curriculum development, provides an entry point into this discussion. While it is true that since the nineteenth century, states and state actors have emerged as the primary stakeholders in education, there are ongoing and lively contests between state and non-state actors.

All Education Is Public, and All Education Is Faith Based

The social practice of education lives at the intersection of critical thought and social order. Another way to think about it is that education is a social practice designed to manage doubt and, at the same time, is also the elusive search for a reliable platform for information, knowledge, and wisdom in which we can have faith. We want our students to be free and critical thinkers, but we are also anxious about the implications of the potential consequences of freedom and critical thought. The search for a reliable platform for information, knowledge, and wisdom is not open ended. Rather, it is animated by faith that the process of education will deliver a fully realized human being committed to the consensus of the good society while doubting competing models.

Therefore, I argue that all education is *public* in two ways. First, all education, including homeschooling, has implications for the common good and public space and should be held accountable for its role in a public partnership. Second, however, in modern secular states, education is a site where we see what Agrama describes in law as the "continual entanglements between religion and politics."[44] While it is possible to distinguish between common space and practice from private ones, in modern secular states such disentanglement is not straightforward.

In addition, however, all education is *faith based* in three ways. Educators have faith that the graduate profile animating their efforts is the best way forward for their students and for society in achieving a preferred future. Educators also have faith that their educational practices and the institutions in which they practice are the best ways to achieve their preferred graduate. Further, educators have faith that they are directing their students toward a reliable platform for truth and wisdom in which they can put their trust, which will equip them to identify and resist untruth, and on which they can build their lives.[45]

In the modern world, states and state actors are the dominant stakeholders in education. There are non-state stakeholders in the delivery of education, but they operate within regulatory and legal frameworks that serve as state instruments to manage all aspects of education. Winnifred

---

44. Agrama, *Questioning*, 101.

45. This is not to imply that teachers have unquestioning faith, evident in the lively discussions in staff rooms, at staff parties, and in the burnout of teachers who lose faith that their efforts and their institutions are really able to deliver the outcomes presented in crafted public statements.

Sullivan's observation that religion in America is subject to law is evident in the regulation of education, which is the persuasive social practice of enculturation drawing students into a framework for truth, however defined.

Education, Literacy, and Identity in a World of Multiple Actors

However, in education, like almost anything else, nothing is simple. There is a creative tension between stakeholders in education, which means that education is the site of lively social interactions, competition, and conflict. In a social and cultural context, education is delivered on multiple sites in ever more sophisticated ways. Matthew B. Crawford starts his account of *attention as a cultural problem* by recounting his being subjected to commercial messages in the delay at an ATM between entering his PIN and the delivery of what he had requested. The colonization of our time and attention is ubiquitous, with commercial graffiti cluttering our highways, filling our fuel tanks and our wait times in airports. Christopher Watkin draws on Pierre Bourdieu who argues that "pedagogies of insignificance" are "small ways of habituating us to patterns and rhythms of understanding and acting [which] can instill a whole cosmology, thought injunctions as insignificant as sit up straight or don't hold your knife in your left hand." He adds that James Smith glosses Bourdieu's analysis by adding that "what appear to be micro practices have macro effects."[46]

Crawford's subtitle *On Becoming an Individual in an Age of Distraction* suggests that the ubiquitous virtual realities indicate a kind of social pathology interfering with healthy engagement with the world. Our children are expected to be literate in navigating this complex world but there is competition among influencers, each with their own interests in shaping their preferred literacy.

In her collection of essays titled *Trick Mirror*, Jia Tolentino examines "five intersecting problems" related to questions of identity in the internet age. They are: "first, how the internet is built to distend our sense of identity; second, how it encourages us to overvalue our opinions; third, how it maximizes our sense of opposition; fourth, how it cheapens our understanding of solidarity; and finally, how it destroys our sense of

---

46. Watkin, *Biblical Critical Theory*, 471.

scale."[47] Having grown up with the internet, she traces the trajectory of her early enthusiasm about the potential for free self-expression to her sense of being overwhelmed. She says, "Platforms that promised connection began inducing mass alienation. The freedom promised by the internet started to seem like something whose greatest potential lay in the realm of misuse."[48] The internet and the creation of virtual worlds, like so many other things, has a Janus face. Crawford and Tolentino identify the seemingly infinite sources of information and imagination, but they also see that the information and imaginations are managed by mostly invisible actors who have their own interests and preferred outcomes. Most are micro practices that are normalized to the point where they are virtually invisible but, cumulatively, they have macro effects on the way we live in the world and in our bodies.

Formal Schooling as a Social Practice: A Window on the Management of Literacy, Critical Thought, and Faith

Nevertheless, granting the complexity of multiple players competing for the attention of students, each with their own models of the social good or a kingdom of ends, I am going to limit consideration of question three to education delivered in formally organized programs and, within that, focusing on the concept of *public education*. I am concentrating on schools for three reasons. The first is pragmatic: I understand the world of schooling. The second is that schools provide students with a more controlled environment in which they can develop information, knowledge, and wisdom in a disciplined way guided by teachers. In short, I believe in the positive power of schools to protect and guide students, drawing them into imaginaries they can trust. I am aware of the shortcomings of schools, abuses of power, legitimate critiques and cautions about the institutionalization of learning but, like religion and its institutionalization, it has not shaken my faith in their potential and their good work. This continues to be true in the internet age of information, knowledge, and wisdom confusion, a fog created by manipulation of invisible actors. The third reason is that education is a persuasive social practice embodied in formal, visible programs and informal cultures designed to deliver what a society most values. Schooling is good to think with, because it

---

47. Tolentino, *Trick Mirror*, 12.
48. Tolentino, *Trick Mirror*, 8.

provides a window on the transcendent and competing visions in the social networks in which it occurs.[49]

The State and State Actors as Primary Stakeholders in Education, Literacy, Critical Thought, and Faith

During the nineteenth century, the state emerged as the dominant player in the social and political organization of nations, with implications for how citizenship and public space were imagined. Education became a matter of state interest and, while the dominant role of the state is contested by, among others, religious organizations and parent groups, public education is generally equated with education systems owned and operated by state actors.

The primary purpose of state-operated public education systems is the mass education of good citizens, equipping them to participate successfully in the society in which they find themselves. Besides skills for successful adaptation to the modern world, education is also designed to develop a common ethos transcending sectarian modes of thought and practice. Benedict Anderson's concept of an *imagined community* is relevant here, public education systems being designed to deliver citizens persuaded of the moral superiority and efficacy of the society in which they find themselves. James Beckford comments on Kenneth Thompson's definition of *ideology* when he says, "Thompson also insists that any part of culture could be considered ideological if it produced ideological effects, that is, if it persuaded people that their society is a particular kind of unitary place in which they have a particular kind of identity."[50] In Ontario public schools this is coded as *togetherness*. Beckford goes on to discuss Claus Offe who "regards socialization as now largely the preserve of the state. It is allegedly accomplished by mean of, inter alia, education, welfare agencies and the subsidized arts." Offe, Beckford says, "argues that the welfare state deliberately intervenes to preserve harmony between the economic, political, and cultural spheres. In other words, the

---

49. I acknowledge my debt to the late James Beckford's comment that prisons are good places to consider the management of religion in societies, being state-regulated spaces to discipline people into accepting the deeply held values of the societies in which they occur. Beckford's research interest was comparing the management of religion in British and French prison systems. The same idea applies to schooling.

50. Beckford, *Industrial Society*, 140.

state actively provides explanation of problems and motives for action."[51] The conceptualization and delivery of literacy delivered in schools is framed by what Thompson identifies as *ideology*.

States and state actors have their own interests in literacy and critical thought. They want their graduates to be critical thinkers about sectarian loyalties, modes of thought, and practices that compete with state priorities but are less likely to welcome critical thought that challenges loyalty to the nation. A similar creative tension lives in literacy projects sponsored by non-state actors. For example, religious organizations want their adherents to be critical of their competitors while remaining loyal to their own interests, goals, and beliefs. There is no such thing as neutral education delivered by objective practitioners.

One of the ways in which state control of education is normalized is through the relatively unquestioned acceptance of two things. The first is the conceptual opposition between *public* and *private space*, public or common space being linked to state and state actors while private space is inhabited by non-state actors. The second thing is the distinction between *education* and *indoctrination*. The idea is that the social practice delivered or controlled by state and state actors is represented as education while indoctrination is seen to be delivered by private or sectarian interests. The world is not that neatly organized but the distinctions serve an important role is establishing legitimacy of dominant actors while masking their power and the marginalization of other actors in the delivery of education.

The construction of religion as primarily a matter of private interest is significant in the distinction between public and private space and the link between religion and indoctrination. In his comments about Michel Foucault, James Beckford says that "the most provocative and disturbing of Foucault's thought is the implication that the very idea of privatized religion, far from being marginal to the operation of modern society, might actually be a pre-condition for the latter's success."[52] While I agree that Foucault's foregrounding of power relations in his critical theory has its own contradictions, his critique of the distinction between *secular/public* and *religious/private* educational spaces deserves our attention.

---

51. Beckford, *Industrial Society*, 154.
52. Beckford, *Industrial Society*, 127.

Ontario Public Education: Persuasion and Indoctrination in the Delivery of Character

The narration of Ontario's education history as a progression of secular education over religious indoctrination is a case study to illustrate what Foucault is telling us about the privatization of religion in pursuit of togetherness. The story of public education in Ontario reflects the growth of state power in delivering education and the management of the ambiguities inherent in literacy.

Here's a story that follows the 1990 court ruling recounted above: in 1990, the Ontario Court of Appeal concluded that religious instruction in state-sponsored public schools delivered by non-state actors violated the religious freedom and equality rights of students. The 1990 decision specifically addressed the question of religious instruction in state schools delivered by non-state actors, mainly churches and volunteers. However, the court went beyond the specific educational question to address its vision of the kind of society it wanted to encourage and protect. It did so by linking indoctrination and practice with religion contrasted with education delivered by secular state actors.[53] The court concluded that *indoctrination* and *practice* were linked and coercive, violating students' religious freedom of choice and equality rights and further, describing those as characteristic of a past we wanted to leave behind in favor of modern secularity.

Given the history of a common school system dominated by a form of Protestant Christianity, the 1990 decision was long overdue, addressing a long-standing irritant for and injustice to religious minorities. However, the specific issue of Christian domination of public education was expanded to include religion as an interpretive category. One effect was that the link between indoctrination and religion allowed the state to successfully marginalize religion and the non-state actors involved in delivering RE in public schools. What the focus on religion also did was mask the networks of power within which literacy and religious literacy were defined and operationalized under the guise of *secular neutrality*, replacing the earlier mask of a *common Christianity*.

The 1990 decision legally established the identity of the Ontario public school system as secular and religiously neutral. It relied for legitimacy on linking religious indoctrination with coercion, identifying

---

53. For a more in-depth analysis of the case law and politics of religion in Ontario public education see Van Arragon, "We Educate."

Ontario public education as secular and therefore, in the opinion of the court, inherently noncoercive. In 1994 the Ontario Court (General Division) rejected a legal challenge by several citizen groups to the 1990 decision and to subsequent Ministry of Education memoranda and RE initiatives. They had argued that secularism is an ideology with its own coercive impulses. However, the court said,

> In *Zylberberg* and *Elgin County* there was indirect coercion compelling those children who held different beliefs from the majority to be indoctrinated with the majoritarian views. The public school system is now secular. Its goal is to educate, not indoctrinate. This is very different from the goal in place at the time that *Zylberberg* and *Elgin County* were decided. *Secularism is not coercive, it is neutral.*[54]

There are several things to consider in this statement and in the ruling in which it occurs, affirmed by the Ontario Court of Appeal in 1997. I am arguing two points here. The first is that the plaintiffs in the case identified the networks of power within which education was defined, arguing that secularism is productive, not religiously neutral, with its own coercive impulses and that the state is not a religiously neutral social actor. The second is that the court accepted the masking of the coercive impulse inherent in the networks of power dominated by the state within which literacy and education are conceptualized and operationalized.

Freedom of Choice with Strings Attached: The Blurred Line Between Education and Indoctrination

Developments in Ontario public education after the 1990 decision demonstrate the creative tension inherent in education and the masking of power in the policies designed to address it. By 2008, the anxiety over the implications of freely exercised critical thought expressed in the *Mackay Report* is evident with the adoption of *character education*. The character development initiative issued in 2008 reflects a more robust program of indoctrination including instruction, modelling, practice, and reinforcement by the entire school community. I am not faulting the ministry for this shift in its adoption of character education. The *Mackay Report*,

---

54. Bal et al. v. Ontario (Attorney General), [1997] 34 O.R. (3d) 484; italics added. Ontario's education policy since 1997 does not reflect current critical reconsideration of the idea of the secular as religiously neutral.

while anxious, was more confident that access to the right information delivered without coercive indoctrination would lead to the preferred character. The optimism of the 1994 and 1997 court decisions uncritically relied on the 1969 *Mackay Report* whose own optimism, albeit tinged with anxiety, was not surprising given the time it was written in a cultural moment of progressive hope and faith.

In 2008 the distinction between education and indoctrination is less clear than its representation back in 1990. In fact, the issue of indoctrination is not considered in relationship to educational programs and practices by the Ministry of Education because the link between religion and indoctrination makes such consideration unnecessary. Its description of character development reveals a shift away from freedom to more carefully crafted control of education. However, the shift escaped critical scrutiny because character is represented as a nonreligious, nonpolitical, and ahistorical category. Indoctrination and practice are evident in its summary of character education, saying,

- Character development is about excellence in education, communities that are vibrant and caring, and students who will think critically, feel deeply, and act wisely.
- A quality education is about more than academic achievement—it is about the development of the whole person.
- Parents and families have the primary responsibility for the development of their children's character, with the support of their school and community.
- Student engagement is essential to all character development processes.
- Ontario teachers and all education workers play a pivotal role in the success of character development in our schools.
- Character development must be a whole-school effort. All members of the school community share the responsibility to model, teach, and expect demonstrations of the universal attributes in all school, classroom, and extracurricular activities.
- Respect for diversity must be at the heart of our policies, programs, practices, and interactions.
- Learning cultures and school communities must be respectful, caring, safe, and inclusive.
- Character development must be integrated into the curricular experiences of students and embedded into the culture of the school and classroom in an explicit and intentional manner.

- Character development is not a stand-alone initiative; it has linkages with learning and academic achievement, respect for diversity, citizenship development, and parent and community partnerships.[55]

I agree that *character formation* is inherent in any education enterprise. Character education has been the unifying theme of the Ontario public education system since its establishment in the second half of the nineteenth century. However, here I am foregrounding the ambiguous nature of education and literacy, including anxiety about unintended consequences evident in the shift in thinking in Ontario from 1969 to 2008.

This shift is not surprising and reflects widespread concerns about the management of religious and cultural diversity. After 2000, there was a great deal of investment in attempts to understand and manage the resurgence of energized voices, many of them religious, claiming space in public affairs. The European Union, the UK, Canada, and the United States were among other states mobilizing education to manage the confusion of voices threatening social orders while protecting freedom of religion and conscience. The framers of the 2008 Ontario character education initiative had come to see that, while belief is important, belief without bodied expression is meaningless and further, that bodied expression needs to be trained, modeled, practiced, and managed. Not all bodied expression is acceptable. All actors in education have a model of a good life and want students to land there. The question is how to get them to do so. There is less confidence in the twenty-first century that the preferred outcome can be achieved without indoctrination by whoever delivers it and whatever it is called. However, indoctrination presupposes a meta-narrative of a truth in which we have confidence, transcending our doubts. Therein lies a key problem for educators in the twenty-first century context of competing visions of truth, including the possibility that there is no such thing as truth in any meaningful and authoritative sense.

Context: Education and Literacy in Anxious Times

To focus on the rise of energized religious voices as the source of social disruption may miss another important cultural and intellectual development. Hussein Ali Agrama's argument that "the modern rule of law . . .

---

55. Ministry of Education, "Finding Common Ground," 4.

must also be understood as the emergence of a new form of organized suspicion that continues to suffuse social life"[56] deserves consideration for its implications for education. One way to think about the implications is that the mark of an educated, modern person is critical thinking as a stance of suspicion in relationship to meta-narratives. Here's the thing: if nothing is sacred, then any voice is, in principle, equally valid. Restrictions on any voice are, in principle at least, arbitrary exercises of power. Putting the burden of our anxiety on energized religious voices may mask deeper cultural implications of the idea that doubt and critical thought are the marks of the fully realized, modern person. Suspicion and doubt are no longer restricted to intellectuals questioning, among other things, the role of religion in society, or among lawyers questioning the testimony of witnesses in the confines of a courtroom. They are more widely evident throughout social life, which has had consequences for social consensus, including the demands of religious voices for recognition.

One of the consequences of the resurgence of religious voices demanding public recognition is that there has been increased competition for what had once been a relatively stable consensus about the nature of reliable public information, knowledge, and wisdom. Science and rational thought replaced religion as the basis for a social and intellectual consensus with its own consequences, among them postmodernism and suspicion as a normative stance. Science and authority that rely on scientific thought are now also under critical scrutiny. This has created space for energized religious voices, offering alternative platforms of truth, including those embodied in the "conservative and fundamentalist elements" identified by Clarke and Woodhead.[57] That is not new, competition for public recognition having yielded changes and reforms, including which voices should be given traction in shaping public education systems around the world. In Ontario, for example, advocacy for French language and Roman Catholic education throughout the twentieth century resulted in reforms creating legal and regulatory space for both under the public education tent.

However, after 2000, there has been greater urgency for state actors to address and manage competition for public legitimacy for several reasons, the most obvious of which is political violence narrated in the language of religion. Religious extremism and, more specifically, *jihadism*

---

56. Agrama, *Questioning*, 130.
57. Clarke and Woodhead, *New Settlement* (2015), 16.

when Muslims were involved, became part of the working vocabulary in both international and domestic politics. One response is the ironically named *war on terrorism*, particularly after the attacks on the United States in 2001 and the strategic uses of *social order* and *national security* by the emergency state as a way of managing dissident voices while, at the same time, allowing the growth of state power.

Less obvious sources of concern have been ideas and practices considered offensive and impolite violations of a consensus about the marginal social role for religion in a secular, modern society. The links between ideas and action are more explicit in the twenty-first century, with education playing a key persuasive role in the efforts to change hearts and minds. However, the distinction between coercion and persuasion often depends on where in the social network the distinction is made and the relative positions of the actors in power dynamics. This is evident in the actions of state and state actors in France designed to protect a particular way of understanding republican social order.[58] Examining the definition of blasphemy, Talal Asad asks, "So, how clear is the liberal distinction between coercion and reasoned choice that underlies the notion of free speech? There is, in fact, a large area between these two opposites in which everyday life is lived."[59] He challenges the idea that liberalism, as secularized Christianity, has a unique claim to free speech, having its own boundaries on free speech. The distinction between coercion and persuasion is useful as a strategy to mask a network of power but needs to be interrogated when it is used to support a self-serving myth.

Education plays an important role in enculturating students into a consensus about what to doubt and what to believe. The 2008 character development initiative in Ontario was only one such effort among many around the world, reflecting a doubt in a model of original *unspoiled human motivation* set free by education rather than indoctrination proposed by *Mackay*, drawing on Lawrence Kohlberg in 1969. There is wider acceptance of the idea that acquiring an "impartial view of things, or a sense of buried sympathy within, requires training or inculcated insight and frequently much work on ourselves." This project is never neutral, Taylor observes, continuing, "It is in this respect like being moved by other great moral sources in our tradition, be they the Idea of the Good, or God's agape, or the Tao, or human-heartedness."[60] However, in a time where

58. Suleiman, "France's Laïcité."
59. Asad et al., *Critique*, 31.
60. Taylor, *Secular Age*, 254–55.

doubt is normative, enculturation and indoctrination cannot escape the suspicion that they are exercises in arbitrary power.

Education, the Management of Literacy, and the Production of the Civilized Person: A Global Challenge

Education is the persuasive social practice to deliver literacy, which includes the establishment of a reliable platform of truth on which our students will successfully navigate their worlds. In the framework offered by Peter Berger and Anton Zijderveld, we want our students to doubt without becoming relativists. However, we also want them to have convictions without become fanatics. Finding the sweet spot between doubt and conviction, or knowing what to doubt and what to believe, is the mark of the civilized person. The profile of the civilized person is constructed within a social network of relations, which means that there is not a universal civilized person. In fact, what looks civilized in one society can look pretty strange in another. In addition, being civilized or well adjusted in a society may not be a predictor of its outcomes for the human family and the earth. Being civilized might not require a high degree of intelligence but it does depend on loyalty to a consensus of what it is to be civilized.

Charles Taylor comments on the critical reaction to loyalty as the ultimate social virtue in Britain, which "always astonished foreigners, but [which] expressed a powerful ethos for Englishmen," saying that "one can see right away how this kind of training was in danger of producing ultra-loyal hearties, with underdeveloped intelligence and imagination—not to speak of the 'underdeveloped hearts.' . . . It could easily generate philistinism, a contempt for or disinterest in outsiders, a calm assumption of English superiority, allied with blank ignorance of other societies."[61] The role of loyalty as an ultimate value may have astonished foreigners but in Britain it was normalized as a mark of the civilized person.

One purpose of education is to deliver the civilized person, who can think critically within boundaries defined and operationalized in and by social networks. Pierre Bourdieu and Jean-Claude Passeron examine the role of education in France to maintain social class, with a model of the "cultivated man" and the "accomplished man."[62] The profile of the literate

---

61. Taylor, *Secular Age*, 399.
62. Bourdieu and Passeron, *Reproduction*, 35.

person is opposed to the illiterate person, Bourdieu and Passeron saying, "Like the scale of dominant values, the scholastic hierarchy of abilities is organized in accordance with the oppositions between the 'brilliant' and the 'serious,' the 'elegant' and the 'laboured,' the distinguished' and the 'vulgar,' 'general culture' and 'pedantry.'"[63] They argue that the persistence of teaching Latin serves little use in the lives of students, saying that "only the functional relationship between the pedagogic conservatism of a system dominated by its obsession with its self-perpetuation and social conservatism can explain the constant support which the conservers of university order, for example the champions of Latin."[64]

While I think that teaching Latin, like teaching cursive writing,[65] can be defended on other grounds,[66] Bourdieu and Passeron are drawing our attention to the social context in which literacy occurs and the purposes it serves. Paulo Freire's critique of the banking model of education is about the model of society it was designed to reproduce as much as it is about a particular pedagogical system. Charles Taylor notes that to be civilized means to have internalized a demanding discipline, self-control, and high standards of behavior governed by ethics, manner, and other necessary conventions.[67] The conclusion is that literacy and the education programs designed to deliver it reflect not only a definition of literacy but also the graduate profile and civilized society they are designed to achieve. At the same time, definition of a graduate profile creates its opposite, the graduate we fear in whom the civilizing efforts did not take.

The Bloom Review reflects anxiety about civilized social order in the UK, drawing a clear distinction between forms of religion that are partners and those that represent threats to social harmony. However, Bloom links the distinction to literacy when he says, "Harming or exploiting others in the name of faith is not justified or condoned by genuine scholars and teachers within any mainstream religious tradition." This begs the question of who defines the *genuine scholar* and by what criteria and to what end. He argues for religion and faith as essential elements in

63. Bourdieu and Passeron, *Reproduction*, 201.

64. Bourdieu and Passeron, *Reproduction*, 198–99.

65. Cursive writing is being reintroduced in Ontario public schools: "The research has been very clear that cursive writing is a critical life skill in helping young people to express more substantively, to think more critically, and ultimately, to express more authentically," Stephen Lecce, education minister, said in an interview. Jones, "Cursive," para. 4.

66. The resurgence of "classical education" is interesting in this regard.

67. Taylor, *Secular Age*, 394.

social order and worries about the minority of people who "turn away from conventional peaceful religious teachings towards extremism and violence. Whether this is in superficial pursuit of power and money or reflects more deeply held beliefs, these individuals use faith as an unacceptable justification for anti-social aims."[68]

Bloom seems to assume a consensus about faith as an ahistorical force for good without critical attention to the question of the object of faith and its implications for social cohesion. He argues that genuine scholars of all faiths will adopt *British values*, suggesting that true faith is linked to a particular set of values embedded in a political, social, and historical narrative. In addition, there is evidence that there are forms of faith and religion with their own narratives and that genuine scholarship will not necessarily land where he thinks they should.

The problem in a liberal society that values free and critical thought is its management. The point here is not to minimize the fragility of any social order and, particularly, those orders where freedom has a high value. Education and literacy live at the intersection of freedom and order, which make them, among other things, matters of political interest and concern. Any education project serves a social and political end or purpose, something Biesta et al. observe when they conclude about literacy that "it is imperative to grasp that it is a deeply political concept."[69] The COVID-19 pandemic in the early 2020s saw an anxious social environment over the issue of vaccinations. There are deep fault lines between those who thought of vaccinations as the pathway to reestablishing a new normal while others resisted, withholding their consent for a variety of reasons. Both sides are literate and both sides doubt the other. Both sides think of their choices as right in contrast to those others who are wrong. Each side engages in critical thought, doubting the other, and both have accepted what they consider a reliable source of information and knowledge that equips them for what they consider wise decisions. A great deal of energy is invested in education around this and other issues, resolutions being elusive.

Therefore, on one level, the resolution to the conundrum inherent in literacy is political, occurring within networks of power relations. While states have achieved control of public education, non-state actors deliver literacy in the regulatory spaces allowed them. There are ongoing

---

68. Bloom, *Review*, 110.
69. Biesta et al. *Religious Literacy*, 5.

contests in those spaces over any number of issues but the common element among them is over who is competent to deliver literacy, however defined. At the heart of those contests is the definition of literacy and the achievement of the literate person and the good society, delivered within the limitations of school organization. Schiffauer et al. use the phrase *civil enculturation* to describe the education and resistance to it at the four European schools in their research project. They observe that schools "have but ten years or so to imbue any one cohort of children with the idea of the nation-state, and thus they often turn to rather more normative and disciplining notions of how civil society and civil exchanges should be structured and conventionalized."[70]

Two observations: first is that education does have a role in drawing students into conventions of "the skills of courteous behavior and civility" essential to harmonious diversity. We want our students to have "sociocultural competence"[71] that frees them to serve the society in which they find themselves. The precise nature of those conventions may vary from one society to another and there is a sense in which there is a kind of *cultural arbitrary*[72] rooted in *tradition* and other factors. Cultural arbitraries serve as *jigs*, which Matthew Crawford argues are essential to social and cultural expertise. The second observation is that competition about the nature of a good society, the literate person, and the cultural arbitraries designed to produce both is healthy in a democratic society, essential for social renewal and reform. Competition can be intense, but it does not have to become war in which we turn each other into enemies.

The Bible, the Qur'an, the *Toledo Guiding Principles*, the Ontario Ministry of Education's character development initiative, Dinham and Shaw's hopeful proposal about the outcomes of RE, and others should be subject to critical scrutiny. However, what is equally true is that they are inspired by a noble goal, which is to imagine a form of wise literacy that makes the world a better place in which students will commit themselves to a life of redemptive activity as people made better because we have walked with them for a little while.

A noble goal to which our students can commit themselves is key to avoiding *malaise*, loss of hope and moral purpose. I am not as persuaded as Charles Taylor seems to be of the direct link between horizontal transcendence and malaise, this book not being a work of prophetic

70. Schiffauer et al., *Civil Enculturation*, 6.
71. Fitzgerald, *Ideology*, 229.
72. Bourdieu and Passeron, *Reproduction*, 16.

social criticism. In addition, the modern age is not the first in history to experience significant shifts in social imaginaries, triggered by plague, changes in communications technologies, political upheaval, and other disruptions.[73] Taylor is tracing the development of malaise in modernity, which he makes clear in limiting his account to developments in Western Christianity. While every tectonic social change is unique, common to them is both hope and malaise. Psalm 137 speaks of the pain of social disruption, an eloquent expression of loss of hope and anger by religious and political refugees who had been forcibly relocated from their sacred promised land to Babylon.[74] Malaise, loss of a sense of meaning, is not new in human history.

However, each period of malaise does have unique features and Taylor echoes others commenting on cultural malaise in the modern period in Western Christianity. In his *Reconstruction of Religious Thought in Islam*, Muhammad Iqbal wants to prevent a similar development in the Islamic world. Commenting on the mixed heritage of the theory of evolution, he says, "The formulation of the same view of evolution with far greater precision in Europe has led to the belief that 'there now appears to be no scientific basis for the idea that the present rich complexity of human endowment will ever be materially exceeded.' That is how the modern man's secret despair hides itself behind the screen of scientific terminology."[75] Science and technology can open ways to more effective care for the earth and its inhabitants, but they cannot, in the end, tell us why we should lay down our lives and our self-interests in order to do so. The same thing can be observed about literacy, detached from a transcendent framework that gives it meaning.

---

73. Cohn, *Pursuit*; Tuchman, *Distant Mirror*; Roetzel, *Letters of Paul*; Terpstra, *Religious Refugees*.

74. The poignant opening verses of Ps 137 (NIV): "By the rivers of Babylon we sat and wept when we remembered Zion. There on the poplars we hung our harps, for there our captors asked us for songs, our tormentors demanded songs of joy; they said, 'Sing us one of the songs of Zion.'" And, the shocking closing verse: "Happy is the one who seizes your infants and dashes them against the rocks." I include that one to remind my reader of my comment above that religion does not make us better or nicer people. It is also worth noting that the Bible, like any sacred text, takes us through the full range of human emotion, including a desire for revenge to right the scales of power gone awry.

75. Iqbal, *Reconstruction*, 148.

Religion Education and Religious Literacy: Next Stop, Chapter 5

My interest is in education, my argument being that religion and religious literacy create space and deliver skills to ask questions about the religious problematics of everyday life, about the ultimate values and commitments animating the cultural and social practices of our lives. However, modernity, with its drift toward horizontal transcendence, has created an intellectual context in which religion itself is problematic and religious literacy finds itself on the margins of educational respectability. Chapter 5 examines the implications for religious literacy in a context in which religion and the advocacy for religious literacy find themselves in spaces of social and intellectual ambiguity.

5

Religious Literacy

An Educational Paradox in Two Parts

INTRODUCTION

CHAPTER 5 EXAMINES THE idea that RE is a social practice designed to deliver religious literacy. This seems obvious, of course, until we entertain the idea that the social practice of education takes us into a double paradox inherent in both religion and literacy. First, in religion we see a quest for a CUT like one we see in theoretical physics. In physics the search is for a CUT that brings the four great forces into one explanatory and coherent framework. In religion we see a similar quest, but in religion, the quest is for a CUT or transcendent point of reference for life, its meaning and its purpose. The paradox in religion is that transcendence is always beyond our reach. We can never really *know*, living as we do within the limitations of our humanity, lived as it is within an immanent frame. Our lived horizon is marked by contingencies we cannot control, let alone understand, but we are blessed and burdened by our search for some point that we can count on as truly true. Nevertheless, religion is a ubiquitous presence in all human societies with real-life consequences as people live out their ultimate values and commitments that they believe to be universally true. Life at the intersection of time and eternity has inherent ambiguities that we navigate guided by a simultaneously elusive and foundational faith.

The paradox in literacy is that we want our students to engage in critical thought but critical thought without boundaries has implications we would like to avoid. In other words, education is, among other things, the management of doubt and the search for an elusive and reliable platform for information, knowledge, and wisdom. In addition, any educational project to deliver literacy and the literate person has unintended consequences, which means that our students may not doubt what we think they should question, and they may land on platforms of truth that astonish and sometimes dismay us. Education is never a safe social practice, something any teacher knows. Education is the social practice in which we lead our students to engage big questions the answers to which will serve them as reliable anchors in a complex and dynamic world; paradoxically, we are also equipping them to engage those very questions with critical thinking skills that must be managed to protect them from destructive nihilism and despair. Paradoxes aside, we want our students to land in a place where they can engage in big questions of meaning and purpose with confidence and a sense of security.

In Religious Literacy We Live the Double Paradox of Religion and Literacy

Religion education, at its best and most meaningful, takes us into places of paradox and teaches us how to live well there, without being trapped in either extreme of relativism or fundamentalism.[1] Religious literacy lands us inescapably in the "cross-pressures" and the "ethical predicaments"[2] inherent in the secular age, at least if we are not going to turn it into an exercise of civic domestication or sectarian indoctrination.

Taylor describes the secular age as "schizophrenic, or better, deeply cross-pressured. People seem at a safe distance from religion; and yet they are very moved to know that there are dedicated believers, like Mother Teresa."[3]

Let me complicate this even more. Not only is religious literacy inherently paradoxical; education, at the best of times, has many stakeholders highly invested in the outcomes but it is even more freighted in religion where parents, communities, and regulators contest questions of its ultimate meaning and purpose. This is not new, as even a cursory survey of a history of controversies around religion indicates the political

---

1. Berger and Zijderveld, *Doubt*.
2. Taylor, *Secular Age*, 604.
3. Taylor, *Secular Age*, 727.

nature of religious literacy. What is worth a deeper dive is state interest in religious literacy, particularly in our secular age.

States and state actors have always been and continue to be important actors in defining and regulating religion and religious literacy, which can raise the stakes for educators working in state education enterprises. States have a unique role in managing social order, balancing order with individual and communal freedoms of expression, in a time when a consensus about the role of religion in society is being vigorously contested by parents organized around commitments and loyalties that can diverge from state interests and priorities.

States have a role to create safe space for competing religious voices, but they operate with their own religious *aesthetics* and *cultural arbitraries*. In any society not everything goes, and freedoms, including religious freedoms, are constructed by authorities and contested by social actors who feel that they are not getting the space and the resources to which they think they are entitled. Contests over religion are not theoretical but can show up in classrooms and school spaces over issues that may, at first glance, not seem related to religion at all. Put that way, it is no surprise that most educators do not want to touch RE, which is often described as *sensitive* by those in a position to know. Linda Wertheimer, commenting on the highly energized controversies about RE in the USA, says, "Religion will always be a volatile subject. There is no escaping that fact."[4] There are good reasons for the decision by educators to avoid religion as much as they can.

In this chapter we are going to touch on it anyway and, even more, dig into it, not to resolve the paradoxes, but to examine them to frame an argument supporting the idea that religious literacy is an essential element in any education endeavor. The chapter is organized around three questions and claims about religious literacy and RE in society, with a focus on the role of states and state actors. Throughout is our awareness of paradox, which leads us to hold our claims and arguments with a light hand. Here are the three questions for chapter 5 and a fourth question to introduce the topic of chapter 6.

---

4. Wertheimer, *Faith Ed.*, 196.

THE THREE QUESTIONS

The first question addresses the distinction between religious literacy and religious illiteracy. Here's the background: many RE projects are organized to deliver religious literacy to address the harm done by religious illiteracy.[5] However, examination of religious literacy projects and theoretical consideration of religious literacy suggests that the binary construction of religious literacy versus religious illiteracy is a distraction if we do not consider the contexts in which it is given its significance. The question is, What work is done by the religious literacy-illiteracy binary and why is it a distraction? My argument is that the focus on the harm of religious illiteracy avoids critical attention to the fact that the binary itself is productive of a preferred outcome. Definition of illiteracy presupposes literacy. In other words, we do not just want to prevent harm, in this case, of religious illiteracy. We want to produce a citizen who is religiously literate in a particular way.

The second question is, What is the social context in which an oppositional relationship between religious literacy and religious illiteracy is constructed and in which it is given significance? The background to question two is this: religious literacy and illiteracy are often linked to anxiety at the nexus of social cohesion and public order, on the one hand, and individual and group freedom to pursue their spirit quests and identities, on the other. I am writing this at a time of conflict over religion and literacy, which is straining social cohesion in societies around the world. Religion education and religious literacy projects cannot be seen apart from the context of tensions around social diversity in which religion plays an important role.

The third question is, What is the intellectual context in which the distinction between religious literacy versus religious illiteracy is given its significance? The intellectual context is shaped by the elusive and malleable concept of *secularism*. The logic common to all forms of ideological secularism is that religion is represented as a private and individual matter of beliefs and behaviors. Given the definition of religion as an interpretive category of knowing matters of ultimate concern and value, the logic of secularism means that the big questions of life and its

---

5. Prothero, *Religious Literacy*; Moore, "Overcoming Religious Illiteracy"; Dinham and Shaw, *RE for REal*; Clarke and Woodhead, *New Settlement* (2015; revised 2018); ODIHR, *Toledo Guiding Principles*.

meaning are seen as private and personal and then intrusive and transgressive when they are introduced into public discourse.

That leaves the question of why religious literacy should be a matter of public educational interest except as a civic and political problem of management and control, which can the achieved without reference to religion. As a result, RE lives on the margins of state-sponsored education endeavors, which leads to question four, the topic of chapter 6. However, here's a preview of the problem.

Question four is, What might an alternative to a social sciences or a theological framework for religious literacy look like that would support a case for religious literacy as a public good? Here's the background to question four: in the advocacy for religious literacy, in public policy proposals and commentary on religious literacy, we can identify a note of anxiety about the implications of religious illiteracy. However, we also hear frustration among advocates about the lack of commitment among educators to religious literacy and RE.[6] We hear disappointment in the ineffectiveness of state-sponsored religious literacy projects.[7] We see jurisdictions, having experimented with RE and religious literacy, moving away from a focus on RE and onto other projects to achieve their educational goals.[8] I argue that, based on the logic of secularism, which includes the construction of religion as primarily a matter of private beliefs and practices, the marginalization of religion and religious literacy as a matter of public interest should not surprise anyone.[9]

Nevertheless, I am making the case that religion and religious literacy are a public good and an essential component of any educational endeavor. However, making the case requires us to think about both religion and religious literacy in a different way. In chapter 2 I detached religion from any particular belief system, claiming that it is the universal human capacity to ask and answer questions about our ultimate meaning

---

6. Dinham and Shaw, *RE for REal*; Moore, "Overcoming Religious Illiteracy"; Prothero, *Religious Literacy*; Clarke and Woodhead, *New Settlement* (2015).

7. Mwale et al., "Zambia"; Barnes, *Education, Religion and Diversity*; McCowan, "Bridges"; Wertheimer, *Faith Ed.*, ch. 7.

8. Zambia, Ontario, Quebec, and others.

9. The logic of secularism is that matters of meaning, fundamental beliefs, and ultimate concern are essentially private. Later I argue that this has implications, not only for religion but also for the humanities and the liberal arts that are increasingly being marginalized in favor of technical subjects of investigation and learning. I reject the idea that the secular is religiously neutral, agreeing with the critical assessment of secularism as productive.

and purpose. In chapter 4 I argued that literacy is about thinking well in a search for truth within a meaning context. In chapter 5 I examine the marginalization of religious literacy and religion in the world of education. In chapter 6 I offer an alternative way of seeing religion and religious literacy to make the case that it should be included in any education endeavor, arguing that religious literacy is essential to critical thinking.

Here's why religious literacy is important and should be part of any education endeavor: religious literacy equips students to follow a straight path from the evidence of their everyday realities to the ultimate values and concerns embodied in the cultural practices and products in their world. It also equips them to think critically and honestly about their own spirit quests as they move into mature consideration of their moral tasks in the world. Detaching the science of theology from any one belief system, I argue that religious literacy equips our students to develop an articulate formulation of their own beliefs and about the ultimate values and commitments animating the societies in which they are more or less voluntary participants. All education systems and programs are based on fundamental beliefs and commitments about ultimate questions of purpose and meaning. Not all education systems, particularly those who claim secular neutrality and objectivity as defining characteristics, are equally transparent about that fact. The way forward is to be transparent about both the theologies (which I understand as the codification of belief systems) and the preferred civic skills animating our education endeavors. This section expands on the first three questions.

WHAT WORK IS DONE BY THE RELIGIOUS LITERACY AND ILLITERACY BINARY?

One way to approach the construction of a *religious literacy versus religious illiteracy* binary is to ask what is motivating the current interest in religious literacy. In other words, when did religious illiteracy become a problem and what was the problem? The point here is that the definition of a problem lays the path toward its resolution.

Religious Literacy and Illiteracy Are Not New Concerns

Interest in religious literacy and illiteracy is not new. In the Abrahamic traditions, Jews have identified themselves as *people of the book*,

Christians have engaged in religious education throughout the history of Christianity, Muslims are expected to know the Qur'an. Adherents in any tradition are expected to be literate in its beliefs, rituals, practices, and taboos, ignorance or willful violation of which can be dangerous. Further, people in any tradition dedicate time and resources to deliver religious literacy.

We can see one approach to religious literacy in the research by Cardus and the Canadian Bible Society conducted by Andrew Bennett. The problem driving the research is declining familiarity with the biblical sacred text among Christians.[10] Other research on religious literacy is based on a *world religions* model that foregrounds familiarity with religions in a more general sense. However, this leaves a question about the significance of religious literacy defined in terms of familiarity or lack of it with the sacred texts important in a particular religious tradition. What public difference might familiarity with, for example, the Bible or the Qur'an make in a secular society? In other words, so what?

The focus of this chapter is not the interests of religious groups in declining familiarity with their sacred texts. Rather, it is on state interests in religious literacy, which, on the face of it, is curious in states self-identifying as secular. Why might states be interested in religious literacy and then how might state interest in religious literacy shape the way it is conceptualized and operationalized?

State interest in religious literacy is not new, as we see from any number of examples, including the role of Emperor Constantine in convening the Council of Nicaea to settle the Athanasian-Arian controversy that threatened to tear apart his fragile empire back in the fourth century CE. Whether he actually cared about where the resolution might land is an open question. His primary problem was not theological purity and Christian orthodoxy, but rather the social and political tensions arising out of the disputes that had the potential to tear apart his empire. The important distinction at the time was between orthodoxy and heresy within a Christian framework rather than between religion and the secular, but the fundamental issue from a state point of view was social and political cohesion then as it is in the twenty-first century. State interest in *togetherness* is not a new problem, you might say.

In another example, the Protestant Reformation of the sixteenth century was linked to state interests, one notable example being Henry

---

10. Bennett, *Bible and Us*.

VIII's role in establishing the Church of England to achieve, among other things, state independence from the Roman Catholic Church. (His problem of divorce and remarriage is interesting, the political implications of succession being more important than love and affection among princes, but can be a distraction from a trend in Western Europe between princes and Rome, some of whom may have had issues in their marriages, marriage being what it is.) In yet another example, the King James Version of the Bible was designed to make it more widely accessible, but it occurred in a context marked by social tensions overseen by King James, ever aware of his political vulnerability. The *divine right of kings* was under scrutiny, and he wanted, among other things, to establish its legitimacy by foregrounding interpretations that supported his claims.[11]

The representation of modern states as secular does not mean they are not interested in religious literacy. Hussein Ali Agrama proposes three features of the relationship between religion and politics that "underscore the centrality of the modern state, and especially its legal power, for secularism." The first feature is *the active principle of secularism* by which he means "that the state has the power and authority to decide what should count as essentially religious and what scope it can have in social life." Agrama's argument about law has implications for education when he says, "One way to think about the active principle is to see the state as promoting an abstract notion of 'religion,' defining the spaces it should inhabit, authorizing the sensibilities proper to it and then working to discipline actual religious tradition so as to conform to this abstract notion, to fit those spaces and to express those sensibilities."[12]

My argument is that regulation of RE is the key persuasive and disciplinary strategy deployed to achieve state interest in religious literacy with a preferred religiously literate citizen as its outcome. The point is that state interest in religious literacy is not new, and it has not diminished in a secular age. Modern secular states do not require citizens to bow before a golden statue[13] and, in liberal states at least, citizens are not required to

---

11. My point here is not to question the King James Version of the Bible, which is brilliant, served to make the Bible accessible to a wider audience, and has had an enormous impact on literacy and the development of the English language. My focus is on King James's political interests in shaping the translation. See Nicolson, *God's Secretaries*, for more on the writing of the KJV.

12. Agrama, *Questioning*, 72.

13. See Dan 3:1–7 for the story of Nebuchadnezzar's golden statue. Like the Roman emperors, Nebuchadnezzar, ever nervous about the social order and his own survival, required expressions of ultimate loyalty, which in this story involved bowing before the

worship the emperor (although *cult-of-personality* projects are evident in states around the world). In that sense, religion and religious literacy are not important in themselves. Rather, religious literacy becomes important in wider state concerns over the definition and achievement of social or public order with the emergence of the modern state unified by nationalism in nineteenth-century Europe and subsequently in jurisdictions around the world.[14]

Interest in Religious Literacy Is Not Restricted to Beliefs and Practices Commonly Identified as Religious

If you expand the definition of religion to include nationalism as an imagined moral community, students are expected to know national anthems and other rituals associated with national pride and loyalty that transcend sectarian identities. We engage in rituals, for example standing for the singing of national anthems at events that, on the surface, have little to do with either religion or national loyalty. Anyone watching the spectacle of the Super Bowl or a professional hockey game sees emotional spectators and athletes with hands placed over their hearts, considered appropriate behaviors and reinforced by social pressure exercised in a variety of ways. Colin Kaepernick's football career took a sharp turn when he *took the knee* in 2016.[15] *Kneeling* is a common religious practice but, in his case, it was the wrong kind of religious expression, at least in the view of some important power interests.[16] Taking the knee continues to be controversial, including in European football, having been interpreted by some as a political gesture and therefore inappropriate to a public ritual represented as being above political and social controversies.

A BBC article on the topic includes this:

> Several Conservative politicians have said they oppose kneeling because they see it as a political statement. Before Euro 2020, the then Home Secretary Priti Patel said that she did not support "people participating in that type of gesture politics." Gillian Keegan, who is now the education secretary, has previously said

---

golden statue of him. However, the same principle is at play in modern states, where national rituals and cults of personality complicate the distinction between modern and not-so-modern states. Golden statues show up in any number of iterations.

14. Agrama, *Questioning*, 95.
15. McEvoy et al., "Colin Kaepernick."
16. One way to frame it is, "We stand for the flag, we kneel for the cross."

taking the knee is "creating division," and Tory MP Lee Anderson refused to watch England's Euro 2020 matches in protest, saying it was a political gesture with which he disagreed.[17]

Transgressors experience the consequences of not knowing or respecting taboos by, among other things, public shaming and legal complications. Colin Kaepernick is only one of those whose bodied expression exposed the idea that religion is not so easily disentangled from other ways of being in the world.

In another example, the young man who urinated on the Canadian War Memorial in July 2006 was charged with public mischief but even more, his action triggered moral outrage. He escaped severe punishment only by an act of repentance in the form of sincere apology and a ritual of forgiveness and community service, allowing him to return to a state of grace. "'The young man apologized to the Legion, the veterans of Canada and the citizens of Canada,' Bob Butt of the Royal Canadian Legion's headquarters told the Canadian Press. 'The apology was definitely heartfelt. I know that it was real, and I know it was heartfelt, and I know the young person was definitely sorry.' He added that the apology was accepted."[18] Given the fact that the young man was in a group of young men, one can guess the backstory, which included impaired judgment about consequences but, in the end, he learned he had violated a taboo in Canadian society. A teachable moment (a kairos moment, maybe?), you might say, in the development of the young man's literacy about the ultimate values of the society in which he lives and of which he is (still) a member.

Another example of the disciplines involved in the achievement of social order is the moral scrutiny of language in our social media world, something Professors Greg Patton and Verushka Lieutenant-Duval found out when their students were offended by their use of terms that crossed from purity into impurity.[19] Along with public repentance in the form of apologies and, in the case of Professor Patton, reinstatement to his position, there were questions about academic freedom and how much latitude is tolerable in a social environment that, paradoxically, also values free speech. The answer is, of course, it depends on which ultimate values have been blasphemed, who has been offended, and what

---

17. BBC, "Taking the Knee," paras. 8–10.
18. CBC News, "Teen," paras. 2–4.
19. McGahan, "Mild-Mannered USC Professor"; Pfeffer, "Ottawa Professor."

power can be mobilized either defending free speech or punishing the blasphemer.

In 2024, university presidents have been deposed (and cursed) over their remarks or silences interpreted as anti-Semitic, in an environment in which long-standing tensions between Israelis and Palestinians have once again burst onto the world stage. However, the controversies occur in a wider context of deepening political divisions in the United States, diminishing the space for nuanced conversation over complex issues.[20] Peter Beyer argues that "the blessed/cursed code, in spite of seeming perhaps too linguistically particular, applies to all important social formations that operate practically as religion in our contemporary world,"[21] adding that, although it "is still in a certain sense core, [it is] also often rather remote in the day-to-day reproduction of religious communication."[22] I would add that, although some traditional theological formulations of a blessed-cursed dynamic may be remote, its operation in a disciplinary society is immediate in its role in managing social diversity and deviations from preferred social order.

Groups, however organized, are inspired by ultimate values and concerns that transcend individual members. Social practices of enculturation and disciplinary practices ensure compliance, group solidarity, or *togetherness*. Literacy in a group includes information and knowledge, the intellectual content of belief, but, perhaps more, it includes loyalty to the overall values and purposes of the group. Getting the details wrong is tolerable and can be corrected by mentoring and education but deviation from transcendent values and commitment takes us to the boundary between *civility and barbarity*.

Religious Literacy and Illiteracy as Markers of Civility and Barbarism

Illiteracy becomes an assessment of deviation from a preferred literacy, including an assessment of behaviors and beliefs and what they indicate about familiarity with and loyalty to ultimate values. Public reaction to the young man relieving himself on the Canadian War Memorial suggested that he was engaging in an act of barbarism, having violated a

20. Tait, "What's Behind."
21. Beyer, *Global Society*, 85.
22. Beyer, *Global Society*, 173.

sacralized space. Given sober reflection before (and after) the event, he could probably have indicated intellectual literacy awareness, but his action was an example of bodied illiteracy.

In 2016, Presidential hopeful Hillary Clinton's "basket of deplorables" included people who could read, write, and speak. She was making an assessment, not about their literacy in a technical sense, but about their position in her *civility-barbarity* continuum. She said, "You know, to just be grossly generalistic, you could put half of Trump's supporters into what I call the basket of deplorables. Right?" She erased any doubt about what she meant, adding descriptors that included "racist, sexist, homophobic, xenophobic, Islamophobic—you name it. And unfortunately, there are people like that. And he [Donald Trump, her political nemesis] has lifted them up."[23] Her comment indicated bafflement like that expressed by Jerry Coyne in his frustration at the rejection of his evidence by his religious listeners. Both are reacting to people they have identified as barbarians and aliens who live among us and may, in fact, look like us.

Religious literacy becomes a term associated with social control when we think of it in terms of civility and barbarity because the wrong kind of religious literacy, from a state perspective (or the right kinds, depending on your point of view), empowers people to challenge existing networks of power, triggering social disorder. Some examples: The millennial movements in medieval and early modern Europe described by Norman Cohn challenged the authority of the Roman Catholic Church in various reform movements, one of which was the Protestant Reformation. They drew on particular readings of the Bible to narrate their social and economic distress so were not illiterate but, in the eyes of the religious authorities of the day, they did have to be schooled, by rough methods if necessary, to bring them back within the boundaries of civility.[24]

---

23. Reilly, "Hillary Clinton," para. 2.

24. Of course, some of the behaviors in Norman Cohn's story seem barbaric, at least to me, including disruptive violence to persons and property, but also to social and political orders. The attack on the US Capitol in January 2021, recorded in videos and photographs, seemed barbaric but then, to be fair, so do other forms of civil disobedience to which I am more sympathetic but which some of my friends think of in quite different terms. My university experience in Chicago between 1968 and 1973 included activities, forms of dress, and personal style that elicited assessments on the civility-barbarity scale. I thought I was on the side of social reform, but others were pretty sure that civilization was teetering on the edge of the abyss of barbarism, which led them to support the actions of police and National Guard that I thought barbaric.

References to God telling Moses that God would "utterly blot out the memory of Amalek from under heaven"[25] have provided a theological narrative justifying Israeli policy to secure national security, with devastating consequences for Palestinian men, women, and children. The passage goes on to suggest mortal enmity in perpetuity, saying, "And Moses built an altar and called the name of it Adonai-nissi. He said, 'It means, Hand upon the throne of the Lord. The Lord will be at war with Amalek throughout the ages.'"[26] Benjamin Netanyahu's use of the sacred text and the phrase "Remember what Amalek has done to you" has triggered counternarratives and interpretations by others, including "the Rev. Munther Isaac, pastor of the Lutheran Christmas Church in Bethlehem and academic dean at the Bethlehem Bible College, [who]rejects the application of the text to modern warfare. 'It is horrifying,' he said, adding that 'religious texts should be used to promote peace and justice, not genocide. This is ISIS-like.'"[27] After 2000 the Islamic state became an iconic symbol of barbarity with its theatrical use of atrocities, disseminated through the effective use of various media platforms. The link between Israeli policy and ISIS made by Rev. Isaac was potent in that context, but not because he was accusing both of lack of familiarity with sacred texts. ISIS and Netanyahu both draw on a reading of sacred texts, appealing to history to code their practices designed to purify the land. Both engaged in actions that can be described as barbaric, which could be seen to be evidence of moral illiteracy but not illiteracy in a technical sense.

In other examples, the African American civil rights movement challenging the caste system based on white supremacy is fueled by social tensions arising out of economic disparity and political oppression. Biblical interpretation has been an integral part of its narration, providing language for Black dissent and imaginary for a better world. The civil rights movement was and is socially disruptive, but it cannot be said to be based on illiteracy. The power of Islamic movements as a political force in global affairs are, in part at least, responses to Western imperialism and colonialism that cannot be seen apart from sophisticated scholarship in the Muslim world. The impact of an energized Hindu nationalism on minorities in India could be narrated in terms of an increased literacy of a particular kind, but the practices involved seem quite barbaric to an outsider. Debates over COVID-19 restrictions and the management of

25. Exod 17:14, NJPS.
26. Exod 17:15–16, NJPS.
27. Kuttab, "Court Decides," para. 6.

access to abortion services take us into interpretations of sacred national texts encoded in the American Constitution and the Canadian Charter of Rights and Freedoms. Those, like debates over Biblical interpretation, become contests over literacy and which interpretation is most true to an original intent with appeals to antiquity to give it transcendent authority.

While contests over literacy are usually and fortunately civil and healthy, conducted within commonly accepted rules of engagement, fears about a slippery slope into barbarism can trigger more intense, winner-take-all battles, ISIS being on the extreme end. Linda Wertheimer provides evidence of the intense local battles over textbooks and pedagogical practices in the United States, but her account is only one among so many characterizing our social interactions over literacy. She recounts stories of strong reactions against RE programs that encourage more open acceptance of the idea that Christianity is one religion among others, including Islam. Similar conflict is evident in jurisdictions around the world.

Schools can become battlegrounds over public space, the role of education, and specifically RE, in the delivery of a preferred graduate profile being vigorously contested. Jeffrey Salkin comments on book banning in Florida and in Texas triggered by fear, the high stakes including fears children might be contaminated by the wrong ideas or, conversely, that they might be deprived of access to the diversity of ideas that will equip them to live well in the modern world.[28] In the background is fear for the trajectory of the American story: on the one hand, that American civilization might be diluted by progressive religious relativism and, on the other hand, that regressive intolerance of religious diversity will impede progress. Both are seen by the other as un-American and illiterate. This is not unique to the United States, of course, the twenty-first century seeing global tensions over economic disparities triggering movements of people groups and political instability, taking us to intense engagement over our ultimate values and concerns. Religion, seen in a more comprehensive sense, is an interpretive category through which assessments are made about identity, attitudes, and behaviors on a civilization-barbarity continuum.

Writing about RE in post-communist Serbia, Zorica Kuburić and Milan Vukomanović say, "Religious Education, more than any other school subject, has been a conflict-prone field on many levels, especially

---

28. Salkin, "When They Came for the Books. . ."

in the education system. Its reception ranged from rejection to acceptance, from fear to the hope that it has the power to install or uproot a socio-political system."[29] Religious literacy and illiteracy are closely linked to the boundaries between social order and disorder. Literacy and illiteracy, as markers of the boundary between civility and barbarism, take us to consideration of our second question about the social context in which religion and religious literacy and illiteracy are conceptualized and operationalized.

WHAT IS THE SOCIAL CONTEXT IN WHICH AN OPPOSITIONAL RELATIONSHIP BETWEEN RELIGIOUS LITERACY AND RELIGIOUS ILLITERACY IS CONSTRUCTED AND IN WHICH IT IS GIVEN SIGNIFICANCE?

The social context in which religious literacy is conceptualized and operationalized in the late twentieth and early twenty-first centuries is marked by anxiety over diversity and conflict, either real or imagined (which creates its own reality). While most encounters are nonevents, resolved without drama, we are seeing hardening fault lines in which religion plays roles in our imaginative space and energy. The intellectual construction of a world divided between religion and the secular finds evidence for its legitimacy in the social tensions around religion because religious differences and their theological codifications and institutionalization really do make a difference, not all of which contributes to social cohesion and harmony. The question in this section is about the intersection of religious literacy and the social context in which it is defined and operationalized, marked as it is by fears of a breakdown of a preferred social order.

I have argued that the definition of religious literacy is contextual, occurring in a network of social relations to deliver a particular kind of literacy designed to serve a preferred social order represented as civilized. The question is not whether schools are religious or secular. Similarly, the binary between literacy and illiteracy is a distraction. Rather, the question is how religion and literacy are defined within social contexts that give definitions more and less traction in public policy and institutional practice. Religious literacy is defined and mobilized in contexts created

---

29. Kuburić and Vukomanović, "Religious Education: Serbia," 132.

by those networks, designed to deliver a graduate with a preferred profile of knowledge and commitments.

States have been granted authority over religion and religious diversity to manage social order and anxieties about its stability. Consider this recommendation in one policy proposal:

> We recommend that the best way to promote community cohesion across the school system is to make the kinds of curriculum change which we are proposing and to establish a strong inspection system to ensure that all schools, faith or not, *play a constructive role in their practice*. This will help ensure that Islamist and other extremist ideas are tackled by way of *serious critical discussion* in the classroom, in the context of a *proper engagement* with religious and non-religious traditions. We believe that this offers a more robust and effective way of dealing with extremist beliefs amongst young people than driving such ideas underground or presenting "British values" as a kind of "counter-propaganda." Values of respect, liberalism and democracy can then be promoted in practice as well as in theory.[30]

There are several things to note here. The first is that the national strategy will be overseen by state inspectors to ensure that all schools play a constructive role in the delivery of social cohesion. The target is "Islamist and other extremist ideas" and the educational strategy is "serious critical discussion" to achieve "British values." "British values" include "respect, liberalism and democracy" through a process of "proper engagement with religious and non-religious traditions" in a process of "counterpropaganda."[31]

I am not, in the first place, challenging the intent of this recommendation and, in fact, there is much about the *New Settlement* report that addresses complexities inherent in RE in a religiously diverse society undergoing profound changes. What I am saying is that there is a preferred outcome for an RE program that is not easily explained either by a literacy-illiteracy binary or a religious-secular one. I also do not intend to diminish the significance of the challenges of maintaining social cohesion and order in highly diverse societies in which individual freedom is a marker of liberal modernity. Education and the delivery of religious

---

30. Clarke and Woodhead, *New Settlement* (2015), 48; italics added.

31. There has been concern about *foreign schools* basing their legitimacy on British accreditation that do not conform to current interpretations of "British values." The question here is about the interpretation of these malleable terms and who owns the interpretations. Young and Adams, "Overseas Schools."

literacy have a role to play in equipping students to live well in a diverse society. However, what that means is open to interpretation about the nature of religion and its role in contributing to a good society.

Timothy McCowan, advocating for the BBP to deliver religious literacy, assumes a definition of religion when he comments on the link between religion and *problematic issues*. He suggests that "educators need to consider how they address problematic issues when they arise, such as the political conflict between Israel and Palestine, acts of terrorism by religious extremists, and negative media presentations of religious people or communities. In the BBP, teachers and facilitators insisted that the focus remain on each one's *personal story and experience not on politics or bigger global issues*, but dialog around *faith*, if it is to be honest, open, and worthwhile, needs a process for dealing with such issues at an appropriate level for the participants."[32] In other words, religion as individual, subjective experience, avoiding the social and political context in which religion occurs, is one way to keep religion and religious difference from disrupting social harmony. The issue of "problematic issues" comes up again in a recommendation that says, "Finally, as a means to address some of the more problematic issues around politics and extremists, consideration should be given to an 'advanced Building Bridges dialogue group' for approved graduates of the programme."[33]

The BBP proposal is arguing for a particular kind of religious literacy that includes knowing what topics to avoid in the interests of *building bridges*. The BBP and the Clarke and Woodhead proposal are among many around the world designed to deliver a particular kind of religious literacy, opposed to the wrong kinds. There are important assumptions in the language about what is and what is not proper engagement, about what a constructive role might be, and how serious critical discussion is to be applied and how far it is allowed to go. A further thing to note is that state and state actors are positioned as the arbiters of the boundary between religious literacy and illiteracy, what constitutes serious critical engagement, and what forms of religion align with respect, liberalism, and democracy. In effect, state and state actors are seen as religious authorities.

---

32. McCowan, "Bridges," 248; italics added.

33. McCowan, "Bridges," 251. McCowan alludes here to pedagogical consideration of the maturity of students and when they are ready to deal with complex political and social issues and where, in the curriculum scope and sequence, topics can most effectively be explored. I am foregrounding another issue, which is the view of religion and religious literacy in his proposal.

However, states are not neutral religious actors. Rather, they are religious authorities motivated by their own preferred forms of religion. What is not explicit is that, rather than being objective or neutral about religion, state and state actors are operating with their own religious esthetic that leans toward forms of religion that do not disrupt social order. What Dorothy Smith observes about gender in the world of sociology is applicable to consideration of the idea that RE can be neutral or objective. She says, "We are looking at a gender organization of the apparently neutral and impersonal rationality of the ruling apparatus. The male subtext concealed beneath its apparently impersonal forms is integral not accidental. Women were excluded from the practices of power within these textually mediated relations of ruling."[34] What I am arguing is that RE projects similarly occur within social networks to achieve preferred ways of thinking about religion and being religious, operating as a kind of *subtext*. We are not just addressing forms of harm linked to religious illiteracy, but we are being asked to consider and adopt particular resolutions to harm that are masked by the language of neutrality.

States as Actors in Religious Literacy and Illiteracy

State-sponsored RE projects designed to deliver religious literacy are less about intimate knowledge of any one form of religion and more about the civic and social codes around the boundaries and taboos about the boundaries constructed for religion. *Politeness* about religion plays a role, often conveyed in nuanced ways, something Schiffauer et al. examine in four schools in Europe and the UK. Among others, Dinham and Shaw refer to the highly sensitive nature of RE that, among other things, means schools in liberal societies want students to be polite about their forms of religion, using methods that are persuasive without being coercive. In other words, we do not want to be impolite to our students or violate their religious freedom rights, but we also do not want them to miss the message that they are expected to conform to a preferred model of how to be religious. Identification of the chronological age at which they reach maturity about appropriate behavior and choices is unique to the jurisdiction in which it occurs and can intersect with ideas about gender,

---

34. Smith, *Everyday World*, 4.

race, and other factors.[35] What is common to all jurisdictions is a level of alertness to beliefs and practices identified as threats to social order.

Examination of academic papers, policy proposals, and policy statements since the 1970s suggest that interest in religious literacy is fueled by anxiety over the fragility of social harmony in a religiously diverse world. After the mid-twentieth century, political movements narrated in the language of religion heightened the anxiety for a variety of reasons, not least of which were expressions of violence. Religion and religious diversity became a security problem to be managed.[36] Diane Moore argues that "first, there exists a widespread illiteracy about religion that spans the globe; second, one of the most troubling and urgent consequences of this illiteracy is that it often fuels prejudice and antagonism, thereby hindering efforts aimed at promoting respect for peaceful coexistence and cooperative endeavors in local, national and global arenas." Moore goes on to add her idea of a resolution, saying, "And third, it is possible to diminish religious illiteracy by teaching about religion from a non-sectarian perspective in primary and secondary schools."[37]

The foreword to the *Toledo Guiding Principles* refers to "recent events across the world, migratory processes and persistent misconceptions about religions and cultures [which] have underscored the importance of issues related to tolerance and non-discrimination and freedom of religion or belief for the Organization for Security and Co-operation in Europe (OSCE)." The statement goes on to propose the way forward, saying that "in the OSCE region, and indeed in many other parts of the world, it is becoming increasingly clear that a better understanding about religions and beliefs is needed. Misunderstandings, negative stereotypes, and provocative images used to depict others are leading to heightened antagonism and sometimes even violence."[38] However, management of religion lives in a state of creative tension with freedom of speech and thought in liberal societies. *Better understanding* finds its meaning in particular social and political contexts animated by the hope that it will deliver social harmony without harming individual freedoms.

---

35. Beaman, *Defining Harm*; Königsberger and Kubarth, "Austria."

36. Gearon and Prud'homme, *State Religious Education*; Bosco, *Securing*; Dinham et al., "Towards a Theory"; Agrama, *Questioning*.

37. Moore, "Overcoming Religious Illiteracy," para. 2.

38. ODIHR, *Toledo Guiding Principles*, 9.

Religious Literacy: Emancipation or Empowerment

Biesta et al. observe that "with regard to the question whether religious literacy can be a way forward for religious education it is, therefore, at least important to ponder the distinction between literacy education as empowerment (socialization) and literacy education as emancipation (subjectification) and not to assume that there is only one 'modality' of literacy education."[39] The issue in RE is that the ostensible goal of RE in a modern society is religious literacy, including the skills to engage in *serious critical discussion*. However, what is also clear is that in state RE projects, the goal is literacy that contributes to socialization with limits to emancipation that does not disrupt social cohesion. This is not unique to RE and religious literacy, of course. In chapter 4 I argued that education lives at the intersection of belief and doubt, the liminal space between the limitations inherent in socialization and the freedom of individuals to exercise critical thought.

Our problem with RE is not so different from the one faced by the authorities in the medieval church. The Inquisition, an instrument deployed by church authorities to address *heresy*, has a bad reputation in our time. However, the horror stories we tell about the medieval church are a distraction from the fact that modern states share a lot of anxious common ground with church authorities in medieval Europe.[40] Modern state interest in religious literacy is equally driven by anxiety about social cohesion around fundamental values and loyalties. Religious illiteracy is seen as those forms that are identified as threats to a preferred social order.

There is evidence that religious diversity is potentially disruptive, and that some forms of religion are more disruptive than others. Religious freedom is a great concept when it is expressed within a consensus about the limits of its expression within the boundaries of social order. However, religion, being the human capacity to reach for and embody ultimate values, can lead people to make commitments from which they are not easily budged, and which can be disruptive to social order. Freedom to express commitment to ultimate values must have boundaries

---

39. Biesta et al., *Religious Literacy*, 10.

40. The use of the historiographical descriptors the *Dark Ages* and the *Age of Faith* was deployed by subsequent generations to bolster the myth that they are more enlightened than their forebears. *History* and historical categories are often self-serving that way.

about which people have to be persuaded for a society or a group to have a future.[41]

It is also true that anxiety about religious diversity is not confined to states and state authorities represented as secular. Religious literacy defined within a theological and confessional framework is often marked by anxiety about viability of groups and traditions in a religiously diverse and competitive world. Religious literacy and illiteracy are defined by the distinction between insiders and outsiders, by theological orthodoxy and heresy, and by loyalty and disloyalty. Religious literacy becomes a way to achieve loyalty and equip adherents to engage competitor ideas without straying from the straight path as defined by dominant stakeholders.

There are good reasons to advocate for religious literacy but the construction of RE and religious literacy to achieve social and political ends might well be a form of *religious appropriation* designed to domesticate religion, to make it governable. Charles Taylor comments that "it is not defined as to what comes from properly ordered desire, but rather what disengaged reason demands of desire, to which desire has to be trained to be docile."[42] Religion education projects serve to address the complexities of religious diversity and the implications of devotion. Religion education projects can become a form of *religious tourism* that encourages our students to take religion less seriously, part of the point of religious literacy in a secular age. Decisions about religion and religious literacy become "politically strategic," as Liz Bucar says about developments in yoga in the shift from devotional yoga, the purpose of which is to "help the practitioner reunite with Brahman," to its being "promoted as part of a healthy lifestyle."[43]

The conundrum of RE is evident in Liz Bucar's reflections on her trips on the Camino de Santiago as part of her RE programs as a university professor. She says, "I don't see my job as to assist with my student's religious formation," but adds, "And yet, to reiterate, religion is not so

---

41. In the sacred texts central to Christianity, the letters attributed to the apostle Paul writing to the churches in various cities reflect similar concerns about the implications of "freedom in Christ." However, Robert M. Grant, placing Paul's writing in the context of the first-century-BCE Roman world, tells us that Roman authorities were equally worried about the excesses of Bacchanalian rites, which at least one group's slogan was "consider nothing wrong." Grant, *Paul in the Roman World*, 82. Religious frenzy and excess are not new, and state authorities do have the role of managing what can be tolerated.

42. Taylor, *Secular Age*, 614.

43. Bucar, *Stealing*, 152–53.

easily controlled, especially in a real-world setting."[44] I would add that any RE program contributes to our students' religious formation, even if it is to train them in how to take religion less seriously or to domesticate it. And RE programs, delivered in schools, are windows on more easily controlled environments encouraging students to adopt as normal the idea that what they believe is irrelevant, as long as they adhere to privatized and manageable versions of it.

However, there are important implications of state mobilization of RE for religious literacy. Bucar, distinguishing "respite" from "devotional" yoga, writes that "respite yoga depends on the appropriation of devotional yoga. It is just as much an invention of something new as the practice of something old." She goes on to say that "it makes me question whether the pursuit of personal health is as innocuous as I thought."[45] Her questions about yoga can be applied to religious literacy. To paraphrase, "the pursuit of religious literacy may not be as innocuous as I thought." I argue that we need to be transparent about the power relations in the social contexts in which it is defined and operationalized and the preferred "something new" emerging in those networks.

Religious Literacy as Enculturation in a Network of Power Relations

Here's a question: Were the leaders in the American Civil Rights movement extremists? Was Ayatollah Khomeini an extremist religious fundamentalist or was he a liberator leading the resistance to the corrupt regime of the last Shah, propped up as it was by self-serving Western powers?[46] Here's the thing: there is widespread use of the descriptive terms *extremist* and *fundamentalist* in the literature on RE and religious literacy, but like the term *heretic*, their meanings are malleable and contextual. Living as they do at the intersection of social cohesion and disruption (or civility and barbarity), their meanings indicate anxiety

---

44. Bucar, *Stealing*, 134.

45. Bucar, *Stealing*, 147–48.

46. Full disclosure here: I think the Iranian revolution and its aftermath have been awful on any number of levels. However, it cannot be fully understood apart from the geopolitical context of decolonization. In addition, focus on the horrors of the Iranian Revolution can be a distraction from the barbarities perpetrated by Europeans around the world. Colonizers may speak Latin and know which forks to use in what order at state dinners, but they are still extreme fundamentalists.

(and to be honest, sometimes outright and justifiable horror; I am not a relativist on these questions). Concern about social cohesion is evident in Schiffauer et al., in European schools, in Stephanie Gravel's study of the demands for teacher objectivity in Quebec's (now obsolete) ERC, and in Gregory Starrett's examination of Egyptian education. While I have questions about the role of states and state actors as religious authorities, my point here is that religious literacy projects *about* religion occur in social contexts serving purposes of achieving social cohesion and civic literacy rather than achieving literacy *in* religion. One outcome is a form of secularization with a built-in logic that privileges some forms of religion and marginalizes those that are identified as transgressing the bounds of tolerance.

L. Philip Barnes's arguments about the failures of multifaith RE in the UK can be disputed, but he rightly observes that "these professions of success should be seen for what they are: claims that are intended to confirm the existing structures of power and influence in British religious education; they tell us little, positive or otherwise, of the contribution of religious education to the school curriculum."[47] He goes on to argue for RE but one that takes religion itself seriously, not just as an instrument designed to deliver social harmony serving the interests of "existing structures of power and influence."

Barnes's concern, also raised by Adam Dinham and Martha Shaw, is that RE in England has increasingly been colonized by themes such as citizenship and cohesion, which overlap with, but are not in themselves, seen as religion, or belief.[48] In other words, RE in the UK is designed to persuade students to doubt some forms of religion while adopting others. However, the criteria are not, in the first place, explicitly theological but political, the preferred outcome being adaptation to a particular social order that masks its theological codification.

Justine Ellis, commenting on RE programs in the UK, observes that "in very recent years, religious literacy has stepped onto the scene as a possible re-branding strategy for RE. Increasingly entangled with concerns surrounding citizenship education in the form of so-called British values and growing, and widely contested, securitization and surveillance agenda, RE appears to have reached a pivotal moment in deciding and advancing a particular set of learning objectives. Although future

---

47. Barnes, "Time," para. 3.
48. Dinham and Shaw, *RE for Real*, 3.

directions for religion education remain uncertain, themes of social cohesion loom large."[49] Religion education motivated by anxiety about civil enculturation has implications for the way religious literacy is defined and operationalized in education.

Resistance to State and State Actors as Religious Authorities: Unintended Consequences

The identification of religion and religious diversity as a security problem and the mobilization of RE as a persuasive response has triggered resistance by groups whose heightened awareness of religion has led them to becoming more assertive about their religious identities. Strategies deployed by states and other authorities to deny space and voice has triggered tactical responses by groups who find their forms of religion and religious literacy categorized as harmful, having had their citizenship loyalties called into question.[50]

Gregory Starrett's examination of Egyptian state intervention in RE is a case study demonstrating the use of mass RE as a persuasive strategy to achieve a modern nation. However, mass education has had the paradoxical effect of heightening awareness of Islamic traditions. The unintended consequence has been self-awareness about religion and forms of religious literacy that eluded state control as citizens began to interpret sacred texts and draw their own conclusions that did not align with what government had envisioned. Resistance movements to state authority in Egypt have drawn on Islamic sacred texts, which have triggered coercive state responses to the failure of persuasion.

Christina Easton expresses a caution about the possible consequences of Philip Kitcher's robust embrace of indoctrination directed at what he identifies as "primitive forms of religion," saying, "Teaching didactically that a person's cherished beliefs (or the beliefs of their parents and community) are wrong is likely to whip up dissent."[51] Dissent may take any number of forms, including choices by parents to withdraw from state schools and enroll their children in schools sponsored by non-state actors, one consequence of which is that they may be subjected to "primitive forms of religion." Easton is cautious about Kitcher's proposal

---

49. Ellis, *Politics*, 17.
50. See Linda Woodhead, "Tactical and Strategic Religion."
51. Easton, *Religion and Religious Education*, 619.

that the freedom to opt out of state schools should be denied to parents. She tries to nuance Kitcher's promoting "didactic indoctrination" by suggesting a "more light-touch, non-didactic approach" akin to the distinction between coercion and persuasion, but I argue that people tend to recognize, and resist, attempts to undermine their most deeply held commitments and values. In fact, their resistance can deepen their resolve and their self-awareness of what they really believe and hold dear, for which we see evidence in jurisdictions around the world. Schools are so often sites of contestation between stakeholders and resistance to state-imposed forms of religion.

WHAT IS THE INTELLECTUAL CONTEXT IN WHICH RELIGIOUS LITERACY VS. RELIGIOUS ILLITERACY IS GIVEN ITS SIGNIFICANCE?

If the social context is about how we live and experience religious literacy and religion, the intellectual context is about how we think about and theorize it based on a preferred or normative intellectual order. While concerns about religious literacy and illiteracy are not new, what is new (or relatively new) is the social and intellectual context in which the religious-secular binary is basic to the normative intellectual order in which I am writing. The context is the *secular age* examined by Charles Taylor and many others, which means that the concept of the secular cannot be avoided in our conversations about religious literacy. Taylor says, "Secularity in this sense is a matter of the whole context of understanding in which our moral, spiritual or religious experience and search takes place."[52] His question is, "How did we move from a condition where, in Christendom, people lived naively within a theistic construal, to one in which we all shunt between two stances, in which everyone's construal shows up as such; and in which moreover, unbelief has become for many the major default option?"[53] *Unbelief* as a response to commonly understood definitions of religion is a feature of RE programs in twenty-first-century Europe and European settler states about which students must make a choice in ways that would not have been the case in the sixteenth century.

Secularization is not one thing, of course, and there is plenty of literature to complicate what we mean by it and its implications. For

---

52. Taylor, *Secular Age*, 3.
53. Taylor, *Secular Age*, 14.

example, secularization of state authority has opened up spaces for intellectual diversity in societies around the world, something Perry Glanzer and Joel Carpenter observe about the space created for Christian higher education in states around the world.[54] The rapid secularization in Quebec's Quiet Revolution in the 1960s was energized by pent-up frustration over, among other things, the grip of the Roman Catholic Church over all areas of social life. Subsequent developments indicate space for greater diversity, competing narratives, and creating a lively intellectual and social environment.

Intellectual Context One: Secularism and Secularization

However, the window for religious diversity in Quebec might well be narrowing as that jurisdiction adopts a more ideologically rigid form of secularization as secularism or *laïcité*. Like religion, secularization can mean a lot of different things, and it is never static. Charles Taylor acknowledges the complexities of secularization but he is getting at something more ideological, more productive, than developments that limited the social power of the church and produced its own religious and moral esthetic. Glanzer and Carpenter observe that "secularization has not been a natural and inevitable historical process, but instead it became a social movement among intellectuals, setting out to accomplish something akin to a political revolution." They link secularization and nationalization, arguing that states have mobilized the concept of secularization for their own purposes, promoting nationalism that, quoting Hans Kohn, is "a state of mind in which the supreme loyalty of the individual is felt to be due the nation-state."[55] Secularism, as a more comprehensive ideology or state of mind, works well for states in the sense that it normalizes the marginalization of religion as a possible competitor in the contest for the supreme loyalty of citizens. Religion education programs in state-sponsored school systems cannot be seen apart from that overall project.[56]

---

54. Glanzer and Carpenter, "Evaluating," 278.
55. Glanzer and Carpenter, "Evaluating," 279–80.
56. In Ontario public education, the phrase "Canadian values that transcend all other cultures and traditions" was used in Policy/Program Memorandum 112: Education About Religion in the Public Elementary and Secondary Schools (issued 1991; revoked 2009) to introduce education about religion programs, repeated in the 1994 program document *Education About Religion in Ontario Public Elementary Schools*.

Ideological secularism mobilized by states reflects common definitions of religion with important implications for the way religion and religious literacy are conceptualized. Current discussions about religious literacy and the implications of religious illiteracy take place in contexts in which religion indicates either something some of us *do* (or don't) or *believe* (or don't) about some form of vertical transcendence. In addition, the current context is characterized by a relatively unquestioned value of the freedom of the individual to make choices about what they do and believe, particularly in private times, spaces, and relationships. In a secular age there are educational questions about *how* we deliver religious literacy but the search for effective pedagogical strategies is not new. The prior question of *why* we should deliver it is also not new, but the intellectual context of a secular age creates a logic leading to the conclusion that there is no pressing *public* reason to do so. In fact, given the shift in ultimate loyalty to the nation-state and the representation of states as the exclusive custodians of public space, there are logical reasons *not* to do so.

Secularism carries its own logic regarding religion, establishing the ground for how something is identified as a problem and questions about it can be asked. Agrama argues that "secularism's power lies not only in the norms it imposes but also in the question it raises. Secularism is therefore a questioning power, involved in a process of continual questioning facilitated by the precariousness of its own normative categories."[57] I would add that its power is also in disallowing some questions. The questioning may be continual, but it is also strategic. Specifically, secularism assumes that questions of meaning, purpose, ultimate values, and truth are essentially matters of private interest and personal choice, the implication being that it creates neutral public spaces, with science providing a common language transcending private, sectarian differences. Secularism is seen as a characteristic of modernity leading to the conclusion that religion does not have a public role in modern societies. The prevailing questions arising out of a secular logic are about the line between religion and the secular with religion being the problem when it encroaches on secular space.

The Education About Religion initiative became redundant after the 2008 Character Education Program was introduced. I include it here for the revealing reference to "Canadian values that transcend," which is still operative but more hidden (neither document is available any longer).

57. Agrama, *Questioning*, 107.

The logic of secularism constructs religion in a way that puts religion on the defensive, having to explain itself and its role in a modern society. However, secularism is so foundational to our modern imaginary that it is hard to see, let alone to think about critically. Agrama argues that accepting the distinction between the religious and secular as normative leads to its "peculiar intractability," concluding that "it is more usefully approached as a historical problem space, that is, in terms of an ensemble of questions and attached stakes that seem indispensable to the practical intelligibility of political and social life."[58] Its intractability is due to the ways in which the religious-secular binary is embedded in law and the regulation of, among other things, education but also because its shape-shifting malleability allows the masking of privileging preferred forms of religion in public discourse and the marginalization of forms that threaten its construction. While there is considerable critical academic examination of secularism, there is less so in law and the regulation of public educational space in the achievement of a preferred public order.[59]

James Beckford comments on Peter Berger's examination of modernity and secularization and "the social, cultural and experiential implications of the process of rationalization" on religion. He says, "The main implications of rationality for modern Christian denominations were said to be pluralism, that is, the erosion of the monopoly which religious organizations had traditionally enjoyed over legitimate world-views, the progressive segmentation of religion and non-religious outlooks and the weakening of taken-for-granted assumptions on the life-world about self-identity, moral virtue and religious truth."[60] Religion is on the intellectual hot seat, in an environment that assumes the distinction between the private world of religion and the public world of the secular to be normative. One implication for religious literacy is that it is optional, a matter of private interest.

---

58. Agrama, *Questioning*, 71.

59. *Intractability* of any paradigm has another dimension, of course, which is that professional and institutional interests are invested in the maintenance of the paradigm and social arrangements in which they have found their niche. This is not the subject of this section, the point being that the factors contributing to intractability are complex, only one of which is intellectual. The link in this study is that the context in which religious literacy is conceptualized and operationalized is complex, including theory among other factors, some of them having to do with self-interest.

60. Beckford, *Industrial Society*, 89–90.

Intellectual Context Two: The Global Reach of Secularism

The Routledge International Handbook of Religious Education indicates the global influence of the European model for the role of religion in society. That influence includes a model of secularism in which the privatization of religion is closely tied to the concept of modernity. Religion education projects in state schools are designed to draw students into a common understanding of a boundary between religion and the secular as inherent in the development and maintenance of a modern society. How that plays out is contextual, dependent on factors—including the politics/power dynamics—unique to each situation. However, the principle of the contests among the actors is basically the same, which is that state actors, on the one hand, are identified as secular and non-state actors, on the other, tend to be identified as religious. A typical and case-specific example is the statement in a paper on Brazil that says, "In recent years there has been a strong debate on the harmony between the constitutional norm that assures religious education in public schools and the secular character of the state."[61]

In the introduction to the global survey of Christian higher education, Joel Carpenter writes, "Indeed, one of the themes in the history of higher education has been the secularization of religiously founded universities and we have found that this process happens not only in Europe and North America, but in Africa, Asia and Latin America as well." Further, he writes that, outside North America, "universities have been seen as the unique responsibility of the state, and the higher education sector is assumed to be secular, whether or not the nation's universities had their origins in the educational work of churches."[62] In short, there is plenty of evidence that secularism is fundamental to the intellectual context in which questions of religious literacy are framed.

Secularism and its acceptance as normative in common definitions of religion has several interrelated concepts. They include postmodernism or post-structuralism, functionalism, and the distinction between RE and religious education, each with implications for religion and religious literacy.

---

61. Gomes, "Brazil," 66.
62. Carpenter et al., *Christian Higher Education*, 3.

Intellectual Context Three: Postmodernism and Skepticism About Meta-Narratives

The skepticism of grand narratives in postmodernism has had important implications for religion. Religion and religious imaginations narrate meaning in terms of grand narratives, in which the great themes of origins and destiny, meaning, purpose, and truth are both universal and personal. Skepticism of meta-narratives includes a shift to more instrumental forms of education, which is having an impact on institutions identified as Christian but also more generally on funding for liberal arts.[63] There is evidence that the humanities and liberal arts are under increasing pressure, vulnerable to cost-cutting initiatives in colleges and universities, their social and public role under scrutiny in the logic of secularism, which includes the idea that a search for truth and meaning is private, individual, and irrelevant to state interests defined in terms of secular modernity.

In their introduction to a study of religion and education in the Western Balkans, Zorica Kuburić and Christian Moe offer a brief comment on the implications of truth and truth claims. They acknowledge that people with deep religious commitments usually get along well in religiously diverse societies but conclude that truth claims "seem incongruent with the general thrust of modern education, which stresses critical reflection and exposure to different points of view according to a common curriculum."[64] Religion, particularly the forms which make exclusive claims to universal truth that compete with state and economic interests, has a marginalized and privatized role in the model of secular modernity and becomes a matter of state interest as a management problem in the achievement of social order. Religious literacy will inevitably be defined in the framework of state interests in an intellectual context in which secularism provides the dominant discourse around religion. The perspective offered by Kuburić and Moe is that religion, as a confessional matter, is biased and always potentially socially divisive while the state is seen as an unbiased arbiter of public space and order.

---

63. Editorial Board, "Guardian View on Humanities."
64. Kuburić and Moe, *Religion and Pluralism*, 5.

Intellectual Context Four: A Crisis in Functionalism

Another way to think about the intellectual context in which religious literacy is defined, which has implications for its role and, as I argue below, its marginalization, is that we have a crisis of functionalism, not only in the sociology of religion as James Beckford argues, but more generally in religion as a legitimate knowledge category. The point here is that the value of religion in classical sociology was in its role as a source of social cohesion and commonly held transcendent values. It had a job and so, while those promoting religion may not have been themselves committed to any particular religion, they could still advocate for its continued role in society. Seen in terms of its social functions, religion can still play a valuable and even essential role in a society that identifies itself as modern and secular. Religious literacy is defined and operationalized to serve the social functions of religion in modern, diverse, and secular societies.

However, that raises the question of what happens to religion if its functional role in the construction and institutionalization of transcendent social values can be articulated and achieved without reference to religion? What happens if, for example, moral values can be achieved through a process of rational and scientific thinking to arrive at commonsense, shared commitments to social cohesion? Or, what happens if the quest for meaning and purpose is essentially meaningless, a search for fool's gold?

The question has important implications for religion and religious literacy. While religion may have had a role in earlier traditional societies, or even in some forms of secular societies, it would be hard to make a universal case for it if we have moved beyond both, embracing the idea that there exists no "objective reference point, separate from culture and politics, available to distinguish truth from ideology, fact from opinion, or representation from interpretation."[65] Thinking about religion or any other interpretive category as a source of meaning cannot rescue it in an intellectual context where secularism and its development in postmodernism are considered normative. Whatever religion might be and however it might be defined, do it and education about it deserve an uncontested place at the academic table where we meet our students? The logical conclusion is that it does not. Beckford's examination of the marginal role of the sociology of religion in the larger world of sociology parallels the marginalization of RE in education.

65. Purpel, *Crisis*, xiv.

Unless we address the definition of religion and the binaries inherent in the logic of secularism, advocacy for RE and religious literacy cannot be sustained.

Intellectual Context Five: Religious Education, Religion Education, and the Marginalization of Religion

The distinction between RE and religious education is an educational outcome of a secular-religious construction with implications for how religious literacy and illiteracy are defined.[66] It also indicates the idea that social sciences and theology are seen in a competitive and even hostile relationship over religious literacy. The binary distinction, I argue, serves political and social purposes but masks a much more complex and nuanced social and educational reality. Religion education and religious education share significant common ground because education is a social practice with a complex of strategies to persuade students in one direction or another.

However, the persuasive intent of RE is masked by the language of secularism, represented as religiously neutral and objective. It also deepens social divisions by suggesting that some of us are religious and some of us are not, suggesting that some of us are more attuned to the modern world and modern ways of thinking about the world or that some of us are more attuned to universal truth than those of us who are not in the preferred category. The binary reduces access to the information, knowledge, and wisdom generated by religion. By narrating religion in terms of either social sciences or theology, a religion-secular binary and its educational outcome, religion education-religious education, it narrows the registers in which religion can speak.

So What? What Is the Purpose of Religion Education and Religious Literacy in a Secular Age?

The question then is, What is the purpose of RE? Social sciences answers usually are that, even though not all of us are religious, religion is a fact

66. This distinction shows up in any number of forms, the common principle being that RE is represented as nonsectarian, objective, scientific, etc., while religious education is seen as sectarian, theologically embedded, and leading with faith rather than science (ignoring the meaning context in which science is conceptualized and practiced).

on the ground in our societies so we must deal with it. Our dealing with it includes some form of management to find the balance between freedom and social order, while on a personal and community level we need consensus about civic skills and attitudes so we can live well together.

However, this is less about religion itself and more about religion and religious diversity as a management problem, creating a social fault line between those of us who are religious in socially disruptive ways and those of us who are religious (or not) in ways that conform to social norms. In addition, a social sciences framework for religious literacy masks its own theology by presenting itself as religiously neutral or secular science with its own beliefs and practices.

A traditional theological answer to the question is that we are all religious in the sense that we all have some kind of belief system about some form of transcendent reality about which we should be literate, if for no other reason than the implications for eternal salvation. However, that leaves a further question of what that means conceptually but also what it means for religious literacy's social and public role. In a way different from a social sciences approach to religious literacy, this also creates social fault lines when we think about it in terms of true and false religion in which some of us are on the true religion side of the divide looking at those others of us who are on the false side.

Both the social sciences and theological approaches to religious literacy, accepting common definitions of religion, undermine its legitimacy as a source of public wisdom. However, we do not have to accept a binary opposition between them, which is inherent in an intellectual context that normalizes a religious-secular model. To answer the educational questions around religious literacy in a way that provides a more enduring rationale for it as essential in education, we need to reconsider the nature of information, knowledge, and wisdom foregrounded by and in the interpretive category of religion.

Conclusions About Questions One, Two, and Three

My conclusion for questions one, two, and three is that rather than thinking of religion as beliefs and practices constructed as a management problem, we think of it in terms of a human capacity that is socially constructed in a vast variety of ways. I propose that rather than thinking of literacy in opposition to illiteracy we think in terms of *multiple literacies*. Biesta et al. call for a "shift in stance amongst sociologists of education [which] has allowed for the proliferation of different types, including digital literacy, financial literacy, emotional literacy, physical health literacy (and of course religious literacy)."[67] Their observation that "literacy is a deeply political concept" applies to the definition of religion, which is that, among other things, definitions find their meaning and purpose in social, intellectual, and political contexts.

Debates about religion and its role in education do not occur in the abstract. They are embedded in particular historical and social contexts, occurring within networks of power that shape both the debates and their resolutions. My point is not to argue that this should not be so, power relations being inherent in any society and group and the social practices that sustain it. What I am arguing is that the contest between theology and the social sciences in a context that has normalized the marginalization of religion is counterproductive in making a case for religious literacy. We need another approach based on a different definition of religion to develop a sustainable argument for religious literacy as a public good, the topic of chapter 6.

---

67. Biesta et al., *Religious Literacy*, 7.

6

A Case for Religious Literacy as a Public Good

IN CHAPTER 6, WE ask the question previously introduced as question four: What might an alternative to a social sciences or a theological framework for religious literacy look like that would support a case for religious literacy as a public good? In chapter 6 I make the case that religion and religious literacy are a public good and an essential component of any educational endeavor. However, making the case requires us to think about both religion and religious literacy in a different way, including addressing the objections to religion identified in chapter 3. My argument is that religious literacy is essential to critical thinking because it equips students to identify and respond to the ultimate values and concerns embodied in the cultural practices and products in their everyday lives. It also equips them to think critically about their own spirit quests as they move into mature consideration of their moral tasks in the world. Borrowing from Dorothy Smith, you might say that religious literacy equips students to engage the *religious problematics* of their collective and individual worlds. Chapter 6 is organized in three steps.

First, *there is a consensus that religious literacy is preferable to religious illiteracy*. However, two things can be observed in the consensus about the importance of religious literacy. The first is the evidence that the consensus is limited to advocates for religious literacy. Second, there is a fault line dividing advocates about the definition and purpose of religious literacy. There is a consensus, but it is a contested one, which undermines the case for religious literacy as a public good. This takes us to the second step.

The second step in my argument examines the reality that, *beyond those advocating for religious literacy, religious literacy and RE continue to be a matter of marginal interest.* There is a fault line between advocates for religious literacy and those who are not persuaded. In this step, I provide evidence that RE and religious literacy live on the margins of educational respectability and I examine the logic of that marginalization.

Finally, I argue that *two gifts of religious literacy make it an essential component in any education endeavor.* The first is that religious knowing and a well-trained religious imagination are important components of critical thinking about the world in which our students find themselves. The second gift is that religion and religious literacy equip our students to engage their personal spirit quests. In short, building on the definitions of religion and literacy developed in previous chapters, the two gifts of religious literacy make it a public good and an essential component of any educational endeavor.

FIRST, THE CONSENSUS ABOUT THE IMPORTANCE OF RELIGIOUS LITERACY

Although there is considerable variation among advocates for religious literacy, there is a consensus among them about two things. First, religious literacy is accepted as a public good in societies characterized as modern and diverse. Second, there is a consensus that the primary difference between advocates for religious literacy is between social sciences and theological frameworks for religious literacy.

Voices in the consensus that religious literacy is preferable to religious illiteracy include the American Academy of Religion's *Religious Literacy Guidelines*, which state that "'religious literacy' helps us understand ourselves, one another, and the world in which we live."[1] Terry Muck agrees that the study of religion is important because it "helps us to understand the world better."[2] Arguing a case for religious literacy in the Canadian context, W. Y. Alice Chan et al. "formulate a conception of [religious literacy] that recognizes the regional and cultural nuances within differing belief groups across Canada, one that correlates to the

---

1. American Academy of Religion, "Guidelines," para. 4.
2. Muck, *Why Study*, xi.

historical, legal and social variances across the country. This recognition of the provincial context, as well as individual and communal experience, structures a cohesive [religious literacy] conception for Canada amidst its regional nuances and national similarities."[3]

In an Australian context, Gary Bouma and Anna Halafoff argue for multifaith education to "counter ignorance and advance a greater level of interreligious awareness, respect and understanding," for achievement of "a harmonious culturally and religiously diverse society," and that "it is in our national interest," delivering "social inclusion and common security." In their view, "ignorance about religion in general and about the religions of our neighbors increases the potential for the denigration of religion in general, the despising of those who are religious by those who are not, the demonization of those who are not religious by those who are and the vilification of those who are religiously different whether within the same group or of another group."[4]

In the UK, Charles Clarke and Linda Woodhead set their proposal for a national strategy for RE in the context of the changing role of religion from more traditional society to a more modern, diverse one. They argue that their recommendations will lead to more appropriate methods of delivering RE, "which can better foster genuine understanding of modern religion and belief and allow young people better to explore their own and other peoples' religious and non-religious beliefs and come to their own conclusions."[5] In other words, among many observers, religious literacy is linked to better understanding of religious differences, which will (hopefully) lead to a reduction in social tensions in religiously diverse societies.

Examining models of RE in Europe, Jean-Paul Willaime refers to "a European consensus about the need to strengthen the role of religious knowledge in public school education," the purpose of which is "to combat ignorance, stereotyping, and incomprehension of religions." The consensus has inspired a campaign based on the argument that "governments must also do more to guarantee freedom of conscience and religious expression, to encourage religious instruction, to promote dialogue with and between religions, and to further the cultural and social expression of religions" in order to "fight fanaticism, effectively." As part

---

3. Chan et al. "Recognition," 259.
4. Bouma and Halafoff, "Multifaith Education," 17.
5. Clarke and Woodhead, *New Settlement* (2015), 8.

of a student's religious literacy, "it is essential to understand the history of political conflicts in the name of religion."[6] However, within the consensus shared by member states of the EU, he also indicates serious differences about the nature of religion, its role in society, and assessments of threats to social order. Differences within the consensus have resulted in conflicting purposes and effectiveness of RE programs.

Educational Effectiveness and Religion Education

Another argument for religious literacy is its role in educational effectiveness. Charles Glenn provides evidence that religion is the basis for the educational success of students in Roman Catholic schools in the United States. Longitudinal studies supported by Cardus, a Canadian Christian think tank advocating for *public theology*, suggests that *faith-based* education has a positive effect on social values and civic values. While neither specifically link *religious literacy* to educational effectiveness, both do argue that an intentional religious framework provides a meaning-filled context that energizes and focuses educational endeavors.

In short, there is widespread consensus that religious literacy is preferable to religious illiteracy with, however, considerable diversity and even confusion about its meaning and purpose.

Religious Literacy, Theology, and Social Sciences

Besides a consensus that RE and religious literacy are important, another intellectual consensus is that there is a distinction between social sciences and theological approaches. Patricia Hannam observes a continuum "between two poles, one being more theological and the other more sociological."[7] Others see the continuum as evidence of a historical development from more traditional to more modern societies. Either way, discussion of religious literacy is dominated by theological and sociological frameworks.[8]

---

6. Willaime, "Different Models," 83–84.
7. Hannam, "Religious Education," 30.
8. Liam Gearon, in *On Holy Ground*, examines in more detail the theoretical models for competing conceptualizations of religious/religion education. I am limiting my analysis as indicated but the reader will see references to other analytical models.

The relationship between them can be theorized through the narrative lens of historical development of secular modernity in which the social sciences are seen to supersede theology. It assumes that a social sciences approach provides a framework for objective observation of religion to transcend subjective embeddedness in and commitment to a particular form of religion. Critical thinking about religion and belief is important in this context. Examination of overlapping concepts of secularization, diversity, and modernity demonstrates a sense of history linking religion to a traditional past marked by allegiance to sectarian interests and beliefs in nonscientific explanations for the world. While they are malleable concepts, secularization, diversity, and modernity provide a narrative framework for the shift from confessional to social sciences approaches to religious literacy.

In Ontario, the *Mackay Report* explicitly linked modern approaches to RE with the social sciences, which became the basis for provincial educational policy after 1988 and 1990. Dinham and Shaw argue that social sciences research provides *real information* about religion allowing religiously neutral and objective study of religion that avoids confessional indoctrination. Andrews Acquah says that the *phenomenological framework* for RE offered by Ninian Smart "presupposes that the researcher should approach the religion being studied in a more scientific way and the religion must be studied objectively with no biases in his or her judgments."[9] The quest has been to develop a theoretical framework for religious studies that avoids the biases embedded in theological frameworks.

An educational outcome of the contest between social sciences and theology in defining RE and religious literacy is some form of the distinction between *religious* education (or religious instruction or indoctrination) and *religion* education (or education about religion, religious studies, or multifaith education). Reforms of RE are framed as necessary in a historical sense, to move students and, indeed, societies from a traditional stage of social development to a modern one. However it is labeled, Bruce Grelle argues that a neutral, non-devotional, academic approach to teaching about religion in public schools can play an important role in promoting civic and religious literacy in pluralistic democratic societies. He says, "From this perspective, religion education is viewed as a means of preparing students to become more responsible citizens

---

9. Acquah, "Phenomenological Approach," 7.

in a world where multiple religious and non-religious worldviews exist side by side."[10] Grelle argues that "religion education is distinguished from catechism or theology, defined as the formal study of the nature of God and of the foundation of religious belief."[11] The point is the belief that, in the modern world, religious literacy is most effectively delivered in RE programs by the social sciences rather than theology.

In conclusion, there is consensus that religious literacy is preferable to religious illiteracy and that there is an important distinction between theological and social sciences approaches to answering questions about why that might be so. As a result, within the consensus, there is competition over what that means.

Competition Over Religious Literacy

L. Philip Barnes agrees that religious literacy is important because, for him, religion and morality are linked. However, he disagrees with the way it is conceptualized and operationalized in the UK, arguing that the shift away from a theological basis for religious literacy undermines the idea that religion provides a transcendent point of reference for morality.

He questions the confessional to non-confessional narrative, arguing that what we are seeing is one confessional framework being replaced by another. Referring to resistance by religious groups to the policy changes in the UK, he says, "The concern by faith community members about how their beliefs and practices are portrayed and treated in schools has been given further substance by the contention of Copley (2005) that Christian confessionalism in schools has largely been replaced by secular confessionalism."[12] Barnes's concern comes close to Talal Asad's argument that *secularism is a project*, and others who argue that secularism is not just the absence of religion but that it is a presence of something replacing what we usually think of as religion. As a result, what we have are competing presences.

Christina Easton tells us that Philip Kitcher's advocacy for religious literacy also links religion and morality in history, although in a different way from the one suggested by Barnes. Kitcher, she says, argues that "a primary aim of religious education is to recognize the defects of

---

10. Grelle, "Neutrality," 236.
11. Grelle, "Neutrality," 236.
12. Barnes, *Education, Religion and Diversity*, 18.

tribal and first-stage ecumenical religions" and that "it is the teacher's business—in a healthy society—to defend the three most progressive frameworks against the two more primitive ones." Further, "in particular, we should aim to entrench Kant's insight about the priority of secular morality."[13] In Easton's view, Kitcher's embracing the idea of indoctrination to achieve the ends he prefers are questionable, but she agrees with Barnes that religious literacy is important to a large degree because of the link between religion and morality. However, they land in different and competing places about the implications of the links based in part, at least, on their historiographies.

The competition over the implications of religious literacy can be fierce and sometimes ugly, but even in situations where it is not, it is still evident, both philosophically but also personally. Linda Wertheimer describes the tensions over the boundary between transgressive religious ideas and acceptable ones at local levels in several jurisdictions in the United States. Her account of the introduction of a core curriculum in Minneha School (Kansas) includes the reaction of a father, Mr. Ecklund, to his son's feeling "like an outsider because he knew so much less about Christianity than his classmates," but also that his son was beginning to think that Jesus was God.[14] Wertheimer documents fierce battles over control of school curricula, with traumatic effects for teachers, parents, and students.

Mr. Ecklund's worries echo the concerns of the Millingtons whose daughter Andrea was beginning to entertain the idea that the Bible stories delivered by Mr. Plum in an Elgin County public school (Ontario, Canada) might be true. Their concerns and testimony in the 1990 Elgin County case on religious instruction in public schools were pivotal in the court ruling that religious instruction was unconstitutional.[15] One way to read this is that the Millingtons were losing a contest over their daughter's religious literacy to the persuasive Mr. Plum in a way similar to the concerns expressed by Mr. Ecklund. A conceptual problem in debates about RE and religious literacy is that persuasion, even when it is "more light-touch, non-didactic" as recommended by Christina Easton,

---

13. Easton, *Religion and Religious Education*, 618.

14. Wertheimer, *Faith Ed.*, 114.

15. Corporation of the Canadian Civil Liberties Association v. Ontario (Minister of Education), [1990] 71 O.R. (2d) 341, 46 C.R.R. 316 (C.A.). Retrieved from Bayefsky and Waldman, *State Support for Religious Education*.

cannot hide the fact that we are dealing with competition over the hearts, minds, and loyalties of students.

The teacher delivering RE at Minneha was trying to find a balance between her own religious faith and the core curriculum described as progressive she was professionally obligated to deliver. It was designed to teach students that "no religion would be singled out in any way that suggested that it was superior or more correct than another," and that people "of different faiths believe different things to be true."[16] However, she did not quite believe it and, in addition, parents instinctively know that progressive education has its own truth about religion and its own conversion impulse that establishes boundaries between transgressive and acceptable ideas. I am not faulting the idea of a core curriculum identified as progressive. Rather, my interest here is in considering the idea that the competition over religious literacy exposes the questionable distinction between RE and religious education, the one being religiously neutral education, the other being sectarian indoctrination. No religious literacy program is neutral, and all have a preferred animating end.

In a similar case, school officials in Community Unit School District 300 were defendants in a case involving a teacher in Jacobs High School in Algonquin, Illinois, who was, allegedly, exercising influence when their daughter converted from Islam to Christianity. The judge dismissed the case against the school district, but the case of the teacher is ongoing at the time of this writing. This case, along with others, indicates that there is ongoing competition over the role of religion in public education systems, not just between intellectual systems, but equally because of the implications for students and their loyalties. The world religions teacher at Jacobs High School was doing his job within the parameters of his professional duties, "a popular teacher who was named Educator of the Year for Kane County, Illinois, in 2015."[17] Despite that, he eventually resigned his position, having crossed a boundary of what was considered acceptable in his role.

A Contested Consensus

A concluding comment about the complexities within the consensus about the importance of RE and religious literacy comes from John F.

---

16. Wertheimer, *Faith Ed.*, 113.
17. Smietana, "Judge Dismisses," para. 5.

Young's contribution to *The Routledge International Handbook of Religious Education*. Writing about RE in Canada, Young observes that "while the issue remains controversial, particularly given the tensions of the past, the U.S. National Council for Social Studies recognizes that 'knowing about religions is not only a characteristic of an educated person but is absolutely necessary for understanding and living in a world of diversity.'" He goes on to acknowledge the complexities of delivering RE and religious literacy when he adds, "Where secularism was once considered neutral ground in disputes between Catholics and Protestants, it has no neutrality in disputes between evangelicals and moral relativists, or between Catholics and secular humanists."[18] The lack of consensus within the consensus about RE in state-funded school systems lives on several levels, including broad questions of purpose and of pedagogy and in teacher responses to the requirement to deliver it. So, a consensus, but a tenuous and conflicted one.

HOWEVER, THE CONSENSUS THAT RELIGION EDUCATION AND RELIGIOUS LITERACY ARE IMPORTANT IS LIMITED TO ITS ADVOCATES

Here's a question for our advocates: Why does the advocacy for RE face such an uphill struggle? Why are religion and religious literacy marginalized in jurisdictions identified as secular and modern?

There are several ways to think about this, including seeing the status of RE as part of a more general trend in which the humanities are facing a precarious future in universities.[19] However, let's keep our focus on RE. Liam Gearon, thinking about RE, echoes Timothy Fitzgerald's conclusion that, deprived of its theological basis, religious studies are meaningless. He says, "The problem of modern religious education remains how to ground the subject when it is no longer grounded in the religious *life*, in the *life* of the holy."[20]

Developments in two Canadian jurisdictions and in Zambia illustrate both the consensus that religious literacy is important and, paradoxically, its marginalization. The question cannot be considered apart from the dominant discourse about religion framed in terms of the

18. Young, "Canada," 74–75.
19. Fernhout, "Quest," 242.
20. Gearon, *Holy Ground*, 8.

religion-secular binary. My argument in this section is that the ambiguous role of religion in liberal societies and its marginalization should not surprise anyone.

Marginalization of Religious Literacy: Case Studies

Religious literacy, defined within either theological or social sciences frameworks, is based on definitions of religion that cannot sustain an argument in favor of religious literacy as a public good. While both have their unique contributions to an argument for religious literacy, they are nested stories that, when isolated and imagined to be in competition defined by the logic of secularism represented as inevitable as part of modernity, lead to religious literacy being marginalized as a partner in generating public wisdom. Here are case studies to illustrate what I mean.

Ontario, Canada

We can see evidence for the marginalization of religious literacy in the contest between a theological approach and then, after the 1960s, a social sciences framework for RE in Ontario education history. Both resulted in policy decisions with the perhaps unintended consequence that religion and religious literacy were marginalized in public school programs. I am going to risk the historian's problem of knowing at what point in history to start the story by giving you some background with an arbitrary starting point. I recounted this history in chapter 4 on literacy where the focus was on the distinction between education and indoctrination. Here the story demonstrates the vulnerability of RE and religious literacy when defined in either theological or social sciences frameworks.

Back in the 1870s, Ontario established a *common school* system that, among other things, was designed to inculcate a *common (Protestant) Christianity* as the basis for a unifying social ethos in a society marked by, among other things, considerable social tension around religion. To avoid exacerbating those tensions among the Protestant groups participating in the common school project, religious instruction was confined to after-school hours, delivered by local church leaders. This compromise was designed to create space for sectarian confessional loyalty, the preferred outcome of religious instruction, without having those loyalties interfere with the project of nation building.

The competition for confessional loyalty among Protestant groups was serious enough to jeopardize the common school project and, indeed, the hopes for cohesive and harmonious social diversity. In the end, however, Protestant groups divided over theology and resistant to the idea of a common Christianity were unified by an even greater suspicion (hatred, actually, at least in some cases) of Roman Catholicism. Common Christianity was seen to be in the public interest with the theologically controversial (and arguably more interesting) bits that divided them delivered outside instructional times of the school day. While there were dissenting voices from groups who advocated for their own schools and from those who opposed diversity within the common schools (mainly animated by racism), there was broad consensus that common Christian (Protestant) theology was integral to Canadian identity and essential to social cohesion.[21]

Aside from a brief experiment in the 1890s, religious instruction was not part of the school curriculum until 1944 when the George Drew government made religious instruction a compulsory part of the program in the public school system.[22] Although this development was offensive to, among others, some Jewish groups, Ontario resisted calls for change until 1990 when the Ontario Court of Appeal, based on the Charter of Rights and Freedoms (Constitution Act, 1982),[23] ruled religious instruction in public schools to be a violation of the religious freedom and equality rights of students. In the same decision the court ruled that

21. As a way of managing political dissent and social tensions around schooling, there are three broad categories of schools in Ontario: public (formerly known as *common*), separate, and private. The separate school category included Roman Catholic, Protestant, and Colored. The most enduring of these is the now fully funded Roman Catholic system. Burkevale Protestant Separate School in Penetanguishene is the one remaining Protestant separate school, while the last of the Colored separate schools closed in 1965. There is a One School Movement with the objective of creating one public school system, eliminating any funding or other forms of state recognition for either separate or private schools; see Tedjo and Baak, *One School System*.

Jean-Paul Willaime, in "Different Models," 83, complicates the *private-public* categories detaching them from the distinction between *lay* and *religious* schools. The point is that distinctions between public and private education are situational adaptations to conditions unique to the jurisdictions in which they occur.

22. The Drew government was influenced by the anti-Catholic Orange Protestant movement, heightened by pro-British Empire nationalism during World War II. The right to deliver religious instruction in Roman Catholic separate schools had long been an irritant to some Protestant groups who chafed at the restrictions placed on their right to do so in the common schools. The Drew government initiative paralleled a similar one in Britain in 1944.

23. Government of Canada, "Constitution Act, 1982."

education about religion was acceptable, accepting arguments that it represented a nonsectarian, secular, and noncoercive way to include religion in Ontario public schools.[24]

The reasoning by the court in arriving at its decision was based in part on thinking expressed in the *Mackay Report*, which drew on the theories of developmental psychology by Lawrence Kohlberg.[25] The idea that *moral reasoning* could be detached from religion had gained traction but the transition away from Christianity toward a *world religions* model was controversial. Resistance to that idea and support for a theological framework for social cohesion was strong enough to motivate the government of the day and subsequent governments to shelve the *Report* until the court decision in 1990. The government response to the 1990 decision triggered several policy documents and memoranda introducing *education about religion* as a cross-curricular program as well as courses, particularly a world religions course.[26]

However, around 2000, developments in Ontario education history demonstrated the weakness in both theological and social sciences arguments for religious literacy as a public good. Documents referring to *education about religion* were removed from the Ministry of Education website, to be replaced by *character education* in 2008. The point is that, until 1990, Ontario public education had explicitly identified a (Judeo-Christian) confessional basis as essential to its identity. In 1950, the *Hope Commission Report* could confidently assert,

> We reiterate that the two essential allies of the school in this regard are the home and the church. By precept and by example gifted teachers can engender in their pupils certain immutable values accepted and indeed won by mankind as the expression of his highest ideals in terms of beauty, truth and goodness. Mankind has found in the practice of these ideals the deepest satisfaction as he seeks to serve his fellow-men, his country and his God. The importance of the individual and the significance of his obligations, which form part of our spiritual heritage, are the foundations of our democratic society. The meaning of life is made manifest in adherence and obedience to ideals that

---

24. Corporation of the Canadian Civil Liberties Association v. Ontario (Minister of Education), [1990] 71 O.R. (2d) 341, 46 C.R.R. 316 (C.A.). Retrieved from Bayefsky and Waldman, *State Support for Religious Education*.

25. Mackay et al., *Religious Information and Moral Development*.

26. One observation is that the court solved a political problem for the government of the day.

lie outside oneself and that transcend one's personal interests. Inspiration and aspiration are never self-centred. Without proclaiming any creed or doctrine we know that in our democracy the Christian ideals as personified and exemplified by Jesus have an appeal to all persons of good will and are the surest common ground for an educational programme related to the pupil as a person. The attitude of Jesus toward children, His understanding of human nature and behavior, His charity and loving kindness toward all men, form a perfect model for a true democracy in the classroom, the community, and the nation.[27]

Character and citizenship were the goals of the public school system, both narrated in terms of values embedded within a Judeo-Christian confessional tradition of thought. In addition, there was little doubt in the minds of the authors that we are all religious and that Protestant Christianity (or at least its common elements) was the best of all religions. Not only was a form of Protestant Christianity seen as common Canadian Christianity, it was also represented as the common or universal religion.

In 1990, education about religion based on social sciences research was ruled to be the modern way forward to replace the confessional model in the 1944 legislation and the *Hope Report*. However, by 2008 the ministry had concluded that the civic attitudes and skills essential to social harmony could be achieved without reference to religion at all. The 2008 decision to lead with *character* was not new, character having been a category seen to transcend sectarian differences throughout the history of the common school movement.[28] What the 2008 iteration of character demonstrates is that a preferred character profile, including civic attitudes and skills, can be achieved without reference to religion, defined either within a social sciences or a confessional rationale for RE. At the time of this writing, *religion* is evident in Ontario public education thinking mainly as a social management issue—for example, around bullying, providing prayer space for Muslim students in schools with a Muslim population, and religiously oriented student clubs during

27. Hope, *Royal Commission*, 36.

28. Ontario's adoption of *character* as the keystone to the idea of common Christianity in the late nineteenth and early twentieth century coincides with youth movements emerging in European nations at the same time. Robert Baden-Powell described the hugely influential Boy Scout movement as the *Character Factory*, designed to produce manly men prepared to serve the nation and the British Empire. The Boy Scout movement was rapidly adopted throughout the world, supported by states who liked its essentially conservative impulse and emphasis on *loyalty*. State-sponsored public schools were being established at around the same time.

noninstructional times. Religion and religious literacy are not serious factors in the Ontario public school academic program.

Quebec, Canada

In 2021 the government in Quebec made a similar change, replacing the Ethics and Religious Culture (ERC) program with one titled Culture and Citizenship in Quebec. The ERC was introduced in 2008, replacing *catechesis* in school programs. However, "in announcing a public consultation about what should replace the program, Education Minister Jean-Francois Roberge said there's still 'too much' religion in schools. This revision process 'is part of the government's desire to offer students a modern citizenship education course based on respect for oneself and others,' he said on January 10."[29] The shift in Quebec was not surprising, given the skepticism of the ERC among educators from the time it was introduced. Sabrina Jafralie and Arzina Zaver report that teachers of the ERC perceived "disdain over religious education courses carried forward from the time the Catholic- and Protestant-specific courses were taught, alongside Moral Education" and that "the ERC was still perceived as an unimportant course and therefore not taken seriously."

Answering their own question, "So why is such little value on the ERC?" Jafralie and Zaver suggest that lack of interest was not confined to teachers.[30] Lack of commitment started with the Ministry of Education that mandated the program and local boards of education in implementing it, despite the mandate and the perception among teachers that the ERC is a "filler course." In 2021, the government of Quebec took the next logical step, having seen that the political costs of accepting the marginalization of religion were negligible. The logic of the step is inherent in the framework of secularism, the political establishment in Quebec having moved to a more ideological form of *laïcité* like the French model.

The trajectory from catechesis to the ERC was like Ontario's shift from religious instruction to education about religion but there the stories diverge, Ontario opting for character while Quebec focused on citizenship, language replacing religion as the marker of Quebec citizenship. The cultural and historical backgrounds for the differences are outside the scope of this book, the point being that both jurisdictions have

29. Vaillancourt, "Quebec to Take Out," paras. 1–2.
30. Jafralie and Zaver, "Teaching Religious Education," 95–97.

decided that religion and religious literacy are not essential to achieve a citizen prepared to live in a modern, diverse society. In other words, by 2000 in Ontario and after 2008 in Quebec, we no longer believed that we are all religious and then, after 2000 in Ontario and in 2021 in Quebec, we no longer believed that we needed to teach students about religion.[31]

Zambia

Nelly Mwale et al. trace a similar shift in RE offered in Zambia, the confessionally oriented programs offered by European Christian missionaries giving way to *multifaith education* in the post-colonial, modern state. In both, RE and religious literacy are considered important to the project of nation building. However, the focus of the programs changed between 1964 and 2017 from one defined in a theological framework to one formulated in language of the social sciences. Both were political projects, the authors saying that "for most missionaries, especially Protestants, conversion required not only the acceptance of Christianity but most importantly the extirpation of existing traditional or primal religions." The postcolonial forms of RE are based on the idea that "Zambia is a pluralistic society in terms of religion," in which RE is seen as an important strategy in the challenge of building a unified nation. The two key outcomes of RE are the "promotion of moral uprightness" and "social cohesion."[32]

However, the authors describe a "disappointing end to the missionary era" that they link to a loss of energy in and commitment to RE program development and delivery. They say that "the driving force behind missionary work in relation to RE development was dedication and hard work by all the missionaries we have cited." They quote another scholar who argued that "missionaries had a great influence on RE in Zambia because they love RE and saw its great potential to enrich young Zambians."[33] In their view, the dedication and hard work evident in the religious educational efforts of missionaries seem to have dissipated.

What Mwale et al. identify as a "disappointing end," I see as the logical outcome of a fundamental contradiction in the Zambian RE

---

31. Readers interested in the Quebec government's rationale for the shift in policy can find it in the 2006 brief to the minister of education; Cadrin-Pelletier et al., *Secular Schools in Québec: A Necessary Change in Institutional Culture*.

32. Mwale et al., "Zambia," 38, 42.

33. Mwale et al., "Zambia," 55.

programs. Here's the problem: when RE and religious literacy are defined within a more sectarian theological framework, their contribution to public wisdom and social cohesion is diminished and, in Zambia, were seen as an impediment to the establishment of a modern, diverse, and inclusive society. However, RE outcomes defined in terms of civic skills and attitudes designed to serve nation-building projects render it irrelevant except perhaps as a discrete, optional area of study interesting only to a select audience.

Other cases

Linda Wertheimer, arguing for RE, acknowledges the dilemma facing RE advocates in the United States. She describes how, after initial enthusiasm for a more secular, objective approach to RE in the USA following *Abingdon v. Schempp* (1963), by "the 1980s efforts were fading" and "religion was being downplayed or ignored in most textbooks." However, interest in theologically based RE was rising as "Evangelical Christians were renewing pushes for lessons on creationism." Education about religion in the USA did get its biggest boost after the attacks on 9/11 but "there remains no concerted effort even though few educators and policy makers disagree whether students should learn about the world's religions as a part of history." She goes on to describe the advocacy for RE as "free-for-all movements."[34] In Germany, Joachim Willems observes a similar pattern, citing evidence that the education establishments are not really interested in RE and religious literacy. He concludes that RE ranks far below other subjects in education priorities.

Referring to the "use of a phenomenological, inquiring, and multi-religious perspective like 'Texts and Traditions' and 'Religion and Society'" in Australian schools, Timothy Ross McCowan says that "although these have been quite popular in faith-based schools including Catholic, Protestant and Jewish schools, barely a handful of government schools have taught them across the country (Rossiter, 2001). Therefore, most secondary students do not study religion in any form."[35] In fact, he reports resistance from schools to implement RE and that teachers who expressed initial interest in his research did not even return his requests

---

34. Wertheimer, *Faith Ed.*, 165–67.
35. McCowan, "Bridges," 8.

for follow up interviews.³⁶ He then goes on to say that "this research was also situated in the Australian educational context where religion in secondary schools is typically taught either one religious perspective alone (as in faith-based schools), or not at all (as in most Government schools). This perpetuates the divisions between religiously based and Government schools, and exacerbates the widespread ignorance, and the uninformed negative perceptions that exist among students about the religious other."³⁷

Reports by Adam Dinham and Martha Shaw; Adam Dinham, Matthew Francis, and Martha Shaw; and by Gordon Clarke and Linda Woodhead reflect concern about similar logic in education developments in the UK. Clarke and Woodhead report that "these concerns have been reinforced by the 2013 *All Party Parliamentary Group* report which concluded: RE has been the unintended victim of a combination of major policy changes rather than the subject of a deliberate attack. Nevertheless, the combined impact of so many severe setbacks in such a short time has been to convey the message that, even though it is a statutory subject, RE is of less value than other subjects."³⁸ Dinham and Shaw report that, aside from *faith schools*, RE has given way to other subjects. They observe that "the decision to exclude RE from the new English Baccalaureate Certificate (EBacc) is widely acknowledged as having led to a reduction in teaching time devoted to RE. Many schools have taken to delivering RE through tutor time, or occasional 'RE days' rather than as a discrete regular subject on the timetable."³⁹ Dinham, Francis, and Shaw, examining the marginal role of religion at the university level, cite research revealing "a trend found in other parts of the study—to allow religion in technical operational aspects of the university's life, but to disallow it when it comes anywhere near intellectual life."⁴⁰

Colin Bloom, reviewing the state of *faith education* in the UK, identifies the marginal role of RE as a key factor in the ineffectiveness of RE in the UK. He quotes one of the respondents in his research who said that "I believe the curriculum of most schools should be comprehensive enough, however, RE is one of the first lessons to be dropped in schools

---

36. McCowan, "Bridges," 201–2.
37. McCowan, "Bridges," 238–39.
38. Clarke and Woodhead, *New Settlement* (2015), 34; Dinham and Shaw identify Michael Gove, former Secretary of State for Education, as a source of this observation.
39. Dinham and Shaw, *RE for REal*, 2.
40. Dinham et al., "Towards a Theory," para. 23.

and in some places is barely on the timetable at all. Some faith-based schools don't cover enough RE for other religions."[41]

So, what's going on? Why is religious literacy being marginalized, and what is the logic in its marginalization? Five contributing factors are the topic for the next section

Five Contributing Factors

1. Marginalization of religion and religious literacy: Logic of secularism and objections to religion

Advocates for RE face the challenges of persuading reluctant school officials to include RE in the formal school program. However, in doing so, the concerns among advocates reflect the dilemma identified by Timothy Fitzgerald when he says that "the more the researcher distances himself or herself from the explicit or implicit theological domination of 'religion,' adopting for example sociological or anthropological critical perspective, the more irrelevant the concept of religion will become."[42] Daniel Moulin offers a similar argument in his assessment of RE in the UK.[43] He traces a shift to RE for instrumental purposes detached from the authority of the church and of the Bible, arguing that it is philosophically weak and difficult, if not impossible, to deliver without harm to children's identity formation. The point is that the *instrumental turn* away from a clear theological framework has undermined a coherent case for RE. Other advocates for RE offer similar concerns about religious illiteracy but do not answer the fundamental contradiction inherent in their proposals around the question of why we need religion and religious literacy to achieve social harmony.

The answer to the *why* question is evident in the logic of the choice made by school officials. From a school's point of view, religious literacy delivered within a theological framework is best left to private institutions with an interest in delivering familiarity with and loyalty to the confessional tradition in which it occurs. Given the pressures of limited resources, teacher expertise, and time, the question of *why* RE should be

---

41. Bloom, *Review*, 67.
42. Fitzgerald, *Ideology*, 8.
43. Moulin, "Doubts."

included cannot be adequately addressed in state school systems identified as secular.

I question Clarke and Woodhead's suggestion that RE has been the *unintended* victim of a combination of major policy changes rather than the subject of a deliberate attack. The description of the marginalization as *unintended* decontextualizes policy, suggesting it is religiously neutral. I argue that policy decisions are a form of RE, teaching students that religion is not important, except perhaps as a personal, private matter, provided it does not interfere with public time and space. The overall intent of this lesson by omission is an outcome of the logic of secularism that gives intellectual cover for avoidance of a pesky management problem. I am not faulting state actors developing and working within policy frameworks reflecting state priorities. States operate with their own preferences for forms of religion, privileging some forms of religion or marginalizing religion as an important interpretive category. What needs attention is the myth of religious neutrality in the language of secularism and the way the language of neutrality masks *education's religion*.

My conclusion is that, while there is general acceptance among its advocates that religious literacy is important, there is evidence that others are less convinced and that there is little agreement on its outcomes. The cases of Ontario, Quebec, and Zambia affirm what Dinham and Shaw, Clarke and Woodhead, and others suggest about lack of interest in RE in secular schools. However, lack of interest is not incidental, but rather is logical. Religion defined in terms of practices and beliefs associated with a vertically transcendent divinity has a marginal and ambiguous role in modern societies identified as secular. Defined within a confessional and theological framework, on the one hand, and within a social sciences framework, on the other, religion and RE do not enjoy the secure position shared by, for example, the maths and sciences.

No education is religiously neutral

The logic of secularism is that, outside the confines of RE, academic programs are religiously neutral. However, no teacher or education project equips their students with information and knowledge without a moral compass and without markers to guide them. To suggest otherwise misrepresents how education works, putting teachers in impossible positions, worrying as they do about student choices and hoping for good outcomes. The mythology of scientific and professional detachment is dishonest, masking a story in which we are invested. Teachers do not operate with the *absolute indifference* Hussein Ali Agrama observes about "the strict application of the principle [of legal equality which] requires that citizens be treated with absolute indifference." Agrama questions the supposed neutrality of law and "elaborate principles of proof," saying they are less about finding facts and more about providing "moral comfort" for judges and jurors when they establish guilt and assign punishment.[44] I am not making a comment about individual teachers and school administrators, who I know lose sleep over any number of things, including the students in their care. However, the construction of secular education delivering objective neutrality in matters of religion and ultimate destiny is a way of providing moral comfort to education systems while depriving educators of shared language for their deepest concerns and commitments.

However, while the logic of secularism is key to understanding the reasons for the marginalization of religious literacy, there are other related factors at play.

2. The marginalization of religion: Religion as fundamentally irrational and socially harmful

One of the factors at play in the marginalization of religion and religious literacy are assessments of the knowledge generated by religion. Assessments of the social role of religion, its rationality, and harm are not, in the first place, theoretical or abstract, but are socially and politically situated in social and intellectual contexts. *Context* is socially constructed, with some things being identified as important while others fade into the background, some things identified as a threat and some things given space and voice in public discourse. For example, one, or rather two ghosts in the context of Tim Breen's 2015 study of the experience of teachers of RE in Manitoba, narrated to illustrate the ever-present threat of indoctrination, are Jim Keegstra[45] and Malcolm Ross.[46] Both were teachers convicted of promoting views of history interpreted as examples of religion gone awry. However, although religion was a factor,

---

44. Agrama, *Questioning*, 124.
45. Brean, "Jim Keegstra."
46. Jewish Telegraphic Agency, "Anti-Semitic Teacher."

foregrounding it as the most important one allows other factors in the stories to be placed in the background of the context, which then reinforces the representation of religion as threat to a society of otherwise reasonable citizens. The Canadian story is not unique in the world. Globally, RE became important in the latter part of the twentieth century because it was given a role of managing religion in an emerging story of globalization and diversity, which included identifying what forms of it are potential public partners, which are tolerable, and which represent threats. The ghosts of harmful forms of religion hover over the histories of European and European settler states. Stories of harm are important as part of our truth telling, but they can also be strategic in the project of delivering and rationalizing narratives of progressive secular modernity.

The characterization of religion as a fundamentally irrational source of harm to individual development and social harmony has been examined in chapter 3 as one objection to religion. Here it is sufficient to say that educators having to navigate religion make a logical choice. Not only does religion carry considerable risks but, in a context identified as secular, the costs far exceed the benefits of a mode of thought and practice considered private and out of step with modernity. Foregrounding stories of religion as a source of harm provides a way of states and state actors to position themselves as protectors against primitive and traditional forms of religion.

The purpose (or one of the purposes) of RE designed and delivered in systems identified as secular is to detach students from their traditional modes of thought and commitments and reattach them to something else. This is evident in Doret de Ruyter and Michael Merry's advocacy for RE as a strategy to deliver *reasonable citizens*. Their assertion that they have "pushed the discussion of religious toleration and reasonable pluralism much further along" is questionable for two reasons. First, their distinction is an iteration of the *education about religion and religious education* binary that has been a feature of conversations since the 1960s. Second, their idea that state-sponsored education projects serve to mitigate harm to children by their families is evident in literature about schooling as a state strategy since the nineteenth century.[47] In its earliest expressions, the point was to inculcate a common Christianity as the highest expression of religious ideals with the irrational parts left out in the interests of delivering reasonable citizens. Their proposal reiterates

---

47. De Ruyter and Merry, "Religious Ideals," 308–9.

both ideas, indicating long-standing ambiguity about the role of religion as a potentially harmful mode of thought and the religious citizens who practice it.

There is evidence that the idea of religion as a source of harm in the modern world is pervasive in the world of education. Dinham, Francis, and Shaw observe that "this is problematic because of a tension between global and local prevalence of religion and belief on the one hand, and widespread assumptions of secularity in universities on the other."[48] One source of resistance to RE in schools is that university campuses are where teachers are educated so it is not entirely surprising that they enter the profession with, at best, ambivalence about religion.[49]

Objections to religion, summarized in chapter 3, include the charge that religion is basically irrational, leading to the logical conclusion that any resources and time spent on delivering religious literacy in schools identified as secular must be explained in ways that other disciplines rarely face. Schools are institutionalized strategic sites for enculturation, an important part of which is to equip students to think well. Thinking well about religion has received more attention than thinking well religiously but, as the evidence above suggests, even thinking about religion in a systematic and disciplined way is rarely a priority and usually delivered as an absence.

At worst, religion is seen as a source of harm to social cohesion because it is seen to rely on irrational thinking processes and social exclusion relying on truth claims that cannot be falsified. These are, in Philip Kitcher's words, forms of "primitive religion" that, along with "first stage ecumenical religion," should be proscribed as sources of harm.[50] This is exactly what education, at least in contexts self-identifying as secular, is designed to address, education being seen as an important strategy to counter irrational modes of thought and practice. While RE is seen as one way to address harmful forms of religion, the more logical way to do it is to ignore it altogether. Religious people are seen to rely on irrational

---

48. Dinham et al., "Towards a Theory," 276.

49. There is evidence that universities are being caught up in the more general political divisions, intensified by a kind of religious and nationalist populism. It can show up in any number of ways under the rubric of free speech and academic freedom, but like God and religion, universities are on the hot seat in ways they have not been for a long time. In the United States, critical questions are being asked about the "separation between church and state," which is a more context-specific way of framing the question of the role of religion in (secular) education.

50. Easton, *Religion and Religious Education*, 609.

thinking and commitments to sources of authority that are not easily amenable to rational, public discourse and, although their right to do so is protected in law, it has no claim on limited public resources. The purpose of RE in a context identified as secular is to teach students to keep religion and its expression confined to private times and spaces and, in some cases, to leave religion behind on a trajectory of mature, rational thought.

3. Marginalization of religious literacy: Confusion among educators and professional risk

Along with the pervasive idea that religion is anachronistic and the professional risks inherent in dealing with it in schools, there is considerable confusion among advocates for RE about its preferred outcomes and its purpose. Clarke and Woodhead say that "debate about religion in schools is bedevilled by what is meant by 'religious education.'"[51] Confusion occurs quite a lot in their description of the state of RE in the UK, also evident in research by Tim Breen, and in Sabrina Jafralie and Arzina Zaver, who research the implications for teachers of RE in Manitoba and Quebec (identified as EAR, Education About Religion, in Manitoba and ERC, Ethics and Religious Culture, in Quebec). They observe that confusion about the subject puts teachers at increased professional and personal risk. The confusion includes lack of clarity about the purpose of RE, inconsistent administrative support, lack of resources and professional training, and a sense of professional isolation with colleagues who are indifferent at best and hostile at worst. There is repeated acknowledgment that teachers' personal knowledge and commitments are important but, at the same time, teachers must avoid being seen to have strong opinions that might be interpreted as indoctrination. Religion education is required by the province but practices identified as indoctrination in public schools is a violation of students' constitutional and legal rights. However, because religious illiteracy is seen as "one of the contributing factors to religious intolerance" there is hope that "teaching students about world religions can help correct this, helping them find common ground between faiths."[52] However, for teachers, the vague outcomes and

---

51. Clarke and Woodhead, *New Settlement* (2015), 32.
52. Breen, "Teachers' Approaches," 139.

the sensitivities around religion give RE risks and burdens not so evident in other subjects.

In addition, teachers have their own beliefs that might well conflict with the idea that what is most important about religions is the common ground among them. Religion education is conceptualized by a *world religions* model that includes the idea that it must be delivered in an objective manner while avoiding giving any one religion preferential treatment. However, that raises questions about what should be included in the program without giving offense in an ever-changing demographic.[53] Diversity lives in creative tension with the purpose of finding common ground that, in the context of state education projects, is the real point of RE. Teachers in RE are never sure where the lines might lie between what is required and what is forbidden, the key concepts in their professional lives being malleable and subject to interpretation.

4. The marginalization of religion education: Religion as text

Another challenge to advocacy for religious literacy projects is that literacy tends to privilege text while backgrounding other aspects of religion. Thomas Lewis observes that, although there was increased interest in religion, especially after the attacks on the World Trade Center in 2001, "scholars of religion have frequently lamented that this interest in religion among colleagues in other fields has rarely generated a corresponding level of interest in religious studies." The reason is that literacy leaves unexamined other and arguably more important aspects of religion. While he agrees with Stephen Prothero that "an informed public needs to understand religion more than it does" he also says that "religious literacy as conceived by Prothero sets back, rather than advances, that goal." The point for Lewis is not that religion and its management are unimportant. Rather, he argues "that understanding of religion leaves us dramatically unprepared to comprehend the myriad, complex ways that religion functions in people's lives."[54] In other words, knowledge about religion is not what moves people, either to fly planes into buildings or to be more tolerant of religious diversity. Something else is going on that challenges the idea that literacy will address our social fault lines.

---

53. Eric Sharpe, in the preface to *Comparative Religion*, xii, refers to the confidence that characterized early studies in the study of religion, saying, "Today we look back, not without a certain nostalgia, at the age which produced such a confident definition."

54. Lewis, "Against," 119–20, 122.

Justine Ellis and Megan Watkins address the limitations of religious literacy defined by text drawing on affective theory to argue that religious knowing is bodied and complex. Affective theory encourages us to see text as the codification of a long conversation over a long time about the big questions of origins, meaning, and destiny. Text reduced to intellectual propositions misses the dynamic nature of traditions of thought, struggles with big questions, contested, tested over time among real people with their own foibles, limitations, and blind spots. In frameworks of vertical transcendence, sacred texts emerge in communities and traditions over time and space but are also codified and written conversations with the divine in which truth is revealed, giving text an elevated authoritative source and weight. Seen as dynamic conversations in community and with the divine, disputes over hermeneutics can become energized.

There is potential for misunderstanding and hostility between vertical and horizontal models of truth, both of which have their authoritative sacred texts. The satirizing of Islamic sacred texts by *Charlie Hebdo* triggered a debate over free speech and blasphemy, but among other things, freedom of speech arguments masked the fact that one religious tradition was held in contempt by another.[55] This was about more than an argument about textual interpretation; this was a winner-take-all fight for air, for life, between contestants who felt their backs were against the wall, whose life principles were being called into question. In that sense, contempt is life threatening. Contempt is evident in the stories told by J. Edward Chamberlin about the inability of Canadian courts to hear indigenous groups speaking of their land and traditions, sacred to them. Their religious traditions are bodied and therefore do not count as evidence in European settler public discourse that tends to privilege a narrower understanding of text.

The idea that text establishes and fixes essential truths is problematic for advocates and for skeptics in any knowledge category, including religion, because truth about anything is messy. Life is messy, something Dinham, Francis, and Shaw suggest when, developing their argument for the purpose of religious literacy they say, "To understand dispositions— the emotional and atavistic dimensions which are brought, often subconsciously, to the conversation, especially those which are indifferent or hostile on the one hand, and those which result in the evangelical on

---

55. Paris (AFP), "10 Years After Attack." See also Asad et al., *Is Critique Secular?* for a critical examination of the Danish cartoon controversy; and McGraw and Warner, "Danish Cartoon Crisis," for further commentary.

the other."[56] Text is not nothing and needs to be taken seriously as part of religious literacy projects. However, it tends to be detached from human experience, made to seem objective, ahistorical, and apolitical, either to fix its legitimacy as a codified expression of universal truth or to serve as evidence of religion's irrationality and irrelevance.[57] Either way, text can be an impediment to wisdom, because wisdom embraces the messiness of human experience and relationships. The realities of classroom teaching, with their limitations of time, resources, biases, and prejudices, tend to reduce the space for patient, reflective, and communal listening to sacred texts that make them come alive and relevant. Religion is a wild card in human consciousness, not easily accounted for when detached reading of text as its most accurate representation is foregrounded.

5. Marginalization of religious literacy: Shifts in priorities among stakeholders to technical research and national interests

Yet another challenge to advocacy for religious literacy is a shift in priorities in state-sponsored education that has implications, not only for religion and religious literacy, but also more generally for the humanities and liberal arts. In the United States, George Marsden observes that "the federal government invests huge amounts in higher education for technical research, so that most of higher education is oriented toward technical areas. Furthermore, something like two-thirds of all students take degrees in career-oriented fields rather than in the traditional arts and sciences."[58]

While the trend toward technical education as a state priority is not the subject of this research, it is important to note that the goals of education have shifted away from critical thought about ultimate values and commitments. The marginalization of RE occurs in that context, which is given little critical attention for two reasons. First, the tendency to see religion as a sui generis category has meant that it is not seen as

---

56. Dinham et al., "Towards a Theory," para. 10.

57. Schofield, "Charlie Hebdo." I am not condoning the violent reaction to the Charlie Hebdo satire. The point here is that the protection of satire in the name of free speech masked contempt for the deeply held convictions of religious groups that their texts have sacred status and "an inability to understand the sense of injury expressed by so many Muslims." Mahmood, "Religious Reason," 64. At the same time, deeply held religious convictions that give permission to violence also masks destructive power dynamics.

58. Marsden, "Renaissance," 272.

a legitimate partner in the liberal arts and humanities. The second reason is that religion is defined in terms of embodied beliefs and practices rather than as a knowledge category with its own legitimate information, knowledge, and wisdom. The logic of secularism is that religion, in its embodied forms, is a matter of private and sectarian interests that cannot and should not contribute to education. The acceptance of religion as a legitimate knowledge category undermines the logic of secularism, which has important implications for institutions organized around that very principle.

A couple of observations: I agree that the domination of Christianity, particularly its European forms, has needed critical reassessment given its global reach, not all of which has been benign. However, the idea that the decolonization of religion must include rejecting it as a knowledge category means that learning, literacy, and critical thought are deprived of an important partner. Besides the philosophical reasons for objecting to religion, there are also strategic considerations. The strategic considerations include reluctance to focus critical thought on the ultimate values and concerns driving our institutions and practices, something Anthony Pinn observes in his examination of religion. The shift toward technical education in the context of global capitalism, facilitated by nation-states, is presented as objective and instrumental, masking the fact that they are operating with comprehensive ideologies that cannot tolerate serious dissent.

Technical education has an important role to play in equipping students to live well in modern societies, but it becomes strategic when it is represented as the key to a good society and social cohesion. Marsden says that "the percentage of those majoring in the humanities (where Christian perspectives have traditionally made the most conspicuous difference) has been in single digits." While it is tempting to ignore Marsden's observations as being narrowly focused on Christian higher education, his argument has wider implications that should attract critical attention when he says, "If exposure to the humanities and even the more critically attuned social sciences disappears from most students' higher education, then it is unlikely that those students will have substantial opportunities to gain broadly humane, not to mention Christian, perspectives from their collegiate experience."[59]

Concern about the trend toward technological thinking is not new. David Purpel argues that the crisis in American education is

---

59. Marsden, "Renaissance," 272–73.

fundamentally *spiritual* and *moral*, which cannot be addressed through technical means without dealing with purposes and ultimate meaning. Alan Bloom raised concerns about the shift away from the liberal arts with implications for critical thought. He does not identify religion as key to identifying the challenges and resolutions, focusing on the humanities in the context of a liberal arts tradition, unlike Purpel who argues that religion can be a source of critical thought. Referring to liberation theology and the moral majority, he says, "In addition to their obvious differences" that "both are active political movements which work within religious boundaries, and both work outside the conventional political apparatus." He adds that "both represent *serious criticism* of the fundamental structure of contemporary society."[60] Purpel observes "an even greater emphasis on the pragmatic and functional nature of schools—extraordinary emphasis on job training, meeting the needs of industry and the school's relationship to American foreign policy."[61] The shift to technical education and alignment with state interests that Marsden and other authors argued about in Christian higher education around the globe in 2014, Purpel was observing back in the 1980s.

The marginalization of religious literacy is a kind of canary in the coal mine, an early warning indicator of the shrinking status of the humanities and the liberal arts in higher education.[62] The logic of secularism has implications for the role of religion defined in terms of its embodied sectarian forms but equally for religion as an interpretive category equipping students to ask questions about ultimate purposes that can be socially and economically disruptive. Global capitalism wants the trains to run efficiently no matter what they are carrying and at what costs. The logic of secularism includes toleration of forms of religion that know their place and stay there, that do not ask questions about the destination of trains and the freight they carry. Adolf Eichmann's obsession with technical skills, scheduling, and efficiency is a cautionary tale for us.

---

60. Purpel, *Crisis*, 26.

61. Purpel, *Crisis*, 17.

62. For an example see Fazackerley, "New University Job Cuts." Note that the cuts to academic programs consistently target the arts and humanities.

Conclusions: The Marginalization of Religious Literacy and the Dubious Benefits of Tolerance

In environments identified as secular, religion is tolerated rather than embraced. Critical assessment of tolerance by Wendy Brown and Lori Beaman demonstrates the ambiguities around tolerance that, they argue, masks aversion, organized to protect power relations. Tolerance is marked by attentiveness to a somewhat unpredictable guest who should be taught manners but who might well embarrass the table when it speaks out of turn about things best left to the adults. Charles Clarke and Linda Woodhead's calling for a "strong inspection system to ensure that all schools, faith or not, play a constructive role in their practice" through "proper engagement" is revealing in this context.[63] Hussein Ali Agrama argues that "secularism must be crucially understood as a questioning power, a modality of power that operates through the activity of question that it animates," making "religion into an object of politics," one consequence of which is that "any use of religion for politics becomes an inauthentic use." He goes on to say that "religious claims are therefore up for special scrutiny, objects of characteristic suspicion and ongoing anxiety."[64] The tolerated but eccentric table guests include those who might express "Islamist and other extremist ideas" who must be schooled in "values of respect, liberalism and democracy."

Religion is an ambiguous presence in liberal societies and education has a role in its management. However, as indicated earlier, other jurisdictions and authorities have decided that the civic values and skills essential to social harmony can be delivered without reference to religion (and, increasingly to the humanities and the arts). In this context, advocacy for RE and religious literacy amounts to a kind of special pleading that has little traction in a secular age.

Choice in liberal societies and in education

In liberal societies, religion is seen as a matter of personal choice to be protected, not because religion is a legitimate source of public and personal wisdom, but rather because it is a matter of personal *choice*. While the choice to marginalize religion in public school systems identifying as

---

63. Clarke and Woodhead, *New Settlement* (2015), 48.
64. Agrama, *Questioning*, 33.

secular can be interpreted through the lens of administrative and organizational efficiency, what is equally true is distaste or aversion inherent in tolerance of religion.

In liberal societies, choice is its own justification. The *Mackay Report* made student choice about religion central to its case against coercive indoctrination. Clarke and Woodhead made choice explicit in calling for reforms in RE "which can better foster genuine understanding of modern religion and belief and allow young people better to explore their own and other peoples' religious and non-religious beliefs and come to their own conclusions."[65]

However, the context in which choices are made and the options made available to students through policy decisions is never neutral. A social and intellectual context that constructs religion as a matter of private interest creates its own choice logic for students facing time and career pressures. The logical result is that religious literacy may equip students to make their own choices about religion, but students may also choose not to engage RE and religious literacy. Either way, what they choose does not really matter, or should not, to states and state actors identified as secular.

However, choices do matter, evident in debates over students' right to *opt out* of RE courses. The creative tension is in finding the balance between the *right to exit* as a human right to be protected and ensuring that students are guided toward outcomes considered essential. While I acknowledge the challenges inherent in managing the logistics around opting out, the point here is that opting out is only partly about the protection of human rights. In schools identified as faith-based, education in the faith is considered essential to the purpose of the school, one policy outcome of which is that the right of exit might well be limited. In schools identified as *secular*, RE is seen as one strategy among others to transmit common civic values, in which case RE might well become optional since the preferred values can be achieved in other ways. In other words, policy decisions about the right to opt out are selective, reflecting the graduate profile animating the school. Marios Koukounaras-Liagis argues that RE is "indispensable to a contemporary curriculum" and is one "which is attended by all the students regardless of their beliefs or non beliefs."[66] However, his argument is not entirely persuasive in the world of education

---

65. Clarke and Woodhead, *New Settlement* (2015), 8; (2018), 9, 14, 43.
66. Koukounaras-Liagis, "Post-Modern Era," 1373.

where RE is optional, if it is offered at all. In addition, the goals of RE and its delivery in achieving those goals might well conflict with the deeply held convictions of parents and students, if they interpret the program as a strategy to marginalize their beliefs and traditions. Like so much else in RE, opting out is not a straightforward matter.[67]

The fond hopes of advocates for religious literacy are likely to founder on the logic of secularism along with other factors at play in schools identified as secular. Despite the argument by Clarke and Woodhead that religion be treated like any other subject, the fact is that it has a marginal role in a modern imaginary. The choice by students and schools not to take and deliver courses in religion is therefore not surprising, leaving advocates with arguments that amount to a kind of special pleading. The paradox in RE's ambiguous status to which I want to draw our attention is due, in part at least, to how both religion and literacy are defined by its advocates. In societies represented as modern, advocates for religious literacy are engaged in special pleading for a place for an eccentric family member at the public educational table, demonstrating our tolerance for diversity but being nervous about it when it shows up in all its embodied messiness.

And yet I argue for religious literacy as a public good that should be included in all education delivery systems. My argument depends on thinking about the question, What kind of information, knowledge, and wisdom is foregrounded by religion about which we want our students to be literate? That's the educational question. A further question is, What contribution does religious literacy make to public wisdom? In educational terms, religious literacy equips students in a particular cluster of skills and knowledge, knowledge skills if you like. However, that leaves questions about what those might be, at the heart of which is the question of the definition of religious literacy.

Beyond tolerance and special pleading: Religion education as story telling

To move beyond special pleading for religious literacy, we must engage the question of what public good is delivered by religious literacy and what we lose by marginalizing it. One obvious answer is that religious

---

67. See for example Clarke and Woodhead, *New Settlement* (2015), 24–27, on "obligation," "compulsion," and opting out of collective worship.

literacy includes information about religion and the civic skills and attitudes essential for living well together. The context in which religious literacy is defined almost always includes references to religious diversity but also that people are generally suspicious of and hostile to unfamiliar forms of diversity. Education, including education about religion, has a role in introducing and guiding students through ideas with which they are unfamiliar.

My argument acknowledges religious diversity and its role in religious literacy projects in the sense that students need to understand what's religiously active in their everyday worlds. In other words, religious literacy projects must include information and knowledge about the world they inhabit and that includes information about their religious landscape. However, context does not provide adequate rationale for a specific resolution—in this case, information and knowledge about religion as a response to the challenges inherent in the global movement of people and the management of socially and religiously diverse societies.

GIFTS OF RELIGIOUS LITERACY

Charles Taylor, examining the human quest for *fulfillment* in the secular age, asks us to consider "two dimensions of Utopia, which correspond to the two facets of modern moral/ethical consciousness; not just the harmony between body and spirit, or bodily desire and our highest aspirations; but also the harmony between all human beings so harmonized which brings us to our attachment to the ethic of universal rights and well-being."[68] In this section I invite us to think about the implications of what he is saying for religious literacy.

Taylor places the tension between the two dimensions of Utopia in "excarnation,"[69] one of the outcomes of the rationalist tendencies in the Protestant Reformation and the Enlightenment. The question, he says, drawing on Friedrich Schiller's resistance to rationalist excarnation, is, "What does it mean to achieve wholeness by rescuing the body?"[70] Thinking about religious literacy, I expand the "harmony between all human beings" to include harmony with the earth. One of the implications of excarnation is that we have a long (and complicated) relationship, not only

---

68. Taylor, *Secular Age*, 616.
69. Taylor, *Secular Age*, 554.
70. Taylor, *Secular Age*, 615.

with our individual bodied existence but also with our collective bodies and the earth. So, let's think about the two gifts of religious literacy in a secular age, which is, among other things, one of the descendants of the Protestant Reformation via the Enlightenment.

Religious literacy, although it includes information and knowledge about the religious landscape important in the lives of our students, does its most valuable public work when it is mobilized to speak to two key areas. You might say there are two gifts of religious literacy that will be valuable for our students in their life journeys.

First, it equips students to make sense of their worlds by tracing the ultimate values and concerns embodied in social structures, power relations, land use, cultural products, and anything else they may encounter, the second dimension of Utopia suggested by Charles Taylor. Social constructions of the world are not arbitrary, but rather they are embodiments of dreams and visions of a preferred future world, with their own logic that can be traced to rarely examined *presuppositions*.[71] Our students need to know what those dreams, visions, and presuppositions are, equipping them to make responsible, sometimes critical decisions about their moral tasks in the world in which they find themselves.

Second, religious literacy equips students to embrace their own bodied spirit quests, and to be self-aware about their own ultimate values and concerns, identified by Taylor as the "first dimension of Utopia." Deep commitments stabilize and orient them in the ever-shifting landscapes in which they find themselves and it can help them define their moral tasks in the world. However, deep commitments can also create blind spots of which we (and our students) need to be critically aware. Another way of saying it is that, as an essential element in identity formation, students need to be aware of the deepest loves and longings driving the society in which they are members and of their own deepest loves and longings in their quest for fulfillment and wholeness.

José Mejia's argument for Christian higher education in Mexico applies here. He says, "An integral Christian higher education should include space for reflection on the spiritual dimension of a person, but it should also be pertinent, relevant, and adequate to the reality that the professional will face in the marketplace."[72] Education is transforma-

---

71. Fernhout, "Quest," 234. Fernhout's use of *presupposition* is close to Benjamin Berger's use of *aesthetic*, and Charles Taylor's use of *picture*. *Metaphysics* is another formulation of the same thing.

72. Mejia, "Mexico," 205.

tional, both in an individual spirit quest and for navigating the world. Religion education delivering religious literacy has a unique contribution to that big task.

Commenting on the challenges facing Christian universities in South Korea, Kuk-Won Shin calls for a more robust model of RE based on a more comprehensive "Christian worldview foundations for all of life, especially for education."[73] What Shin argues about Christian identity I broaden to include religion as a knowledge category, that is neither so closely linked to a particular theological tradition nor limited by social sciences frameworks about religion, either one of which follows a logic of secularization in which religion is inevitably marginalized.

Here's the question for the next section: How might RE and religious literacy contribute to identity formation and to public wisdom?

Gift One: Religious Literacy Is Essential to our Navigating the World

I have argued that the way forward is to define religion as a shared human capacity to reach for a transcendent point of reference in our ever-shifting sense of time. Our cultural activities are, in the end, embodiments of our points of transcendence, reflecting our deepest values, our longings, and our hopes. They are our expressions of what lasts as ultimately significant in our collective spirit quests. Our embodied cultural markers provide standing stones marking our journeys in time and space.

Here's a mythological story from the sacred texts important in the Jewish and Christian tradition of the Israelites crossing the Jordan River after their forty-three-year sojourn in the wilderness: their leader, Joshua, is instructed by God to build a commemorative monument to the event constructed of twelve stones on the west bank of the river, one for each of the Hebrew tribes. The story, in part, reads: "When the entire nation had finished crossing the Jordan, the Lord said to Joshua, 'Select twelve men from among the people, one from each tribe, and instruct them as follows: Pick up twelve stones from the spot exactly in the middle of the Jordan, where the priests' feet are standing; take them along with you and deposit them in the place where you will spend the night.'" The

---

73. Shin, "History, Tasks, and Vision," 103.

instruction was carried out and the passage then goes on to say, "And so these stones shall serve the people of Israel as a memorial for all time."[74]

This is part of a story of a quest in time and space that tells the Israelites who they are, where they came from, and what they must now do to preserve what they have been given. It identifies them as actors, not in just any story, but in a mighty story, a story that must be passed on to generations not yet born. Their story may not be ours and the monument they constructed may not resonate in our memories and imaginations. In fact, given the divinely commanded ethnic cleansing of their promised land inherent in the story, we may and probably should be horrified by what it meant for the *heathens* on the receiving end of the divine commands and for the ways the story has been used and abused throughout history. (I remind the reader of the reference above to Benjamin Netanyahu's recalling the perpetual enmity between Israel and Amalek, drawing on the account of Israel's journey from slavery to their promised land in the book of Exodus.) Not surprised, perhaps, and given the human propensity to engage in violence to secure promised lands, this could well serve as a cautionary tale rather than the triumphalist one I learned as a child. A conversation for another time, perhaps.[75] The point is not to agree or disagree with the story or to argue its historicity. Rather, the point here is to argue that groups construct monuments to enduring mythological narratives.

Our markers are social constructions that we see and live in a vast variety of ways. There is an element of cultural arbitrariness in our constructions about which we can exercise critical awareness and, at the same time, be matter of fact. The point is that our cultural and social constructions are not random accidents or driven by survivor necessity. They tell a story about life, about what's important, what's not, what's good and what's evil, who we are and who we are meant to be. What is not socially constructed is our story-telling *capacity* embodied in standing stones guiding our individual and collective spirit quests.

Being socially constructed, markers are malleable, and they are contested, destroyed, removed as we reinterpret our stories. That does not make them meaningless. In fact, the energy with which we reimagine

---

74. Josh 4, NJPS.

75. This issue has taken on new urgency in 2024 with Israeli policy on Palestinians being explicitly narrated in the language of the Old Testament and the conquest of the *Holy Land*. It raises lots of questions about the use of sacred texts to justify current practices of domination.

our cultural markers tells us that the stories they carry are powerful. Education is one important way we do it and the resources dedicated to it provide evidence of its importance.[76] Education is the social practice of storytelling, reminding our students that our urban landscapes, our great buildings, our art, and our sciences mean something. Some of those things cause us to grieve and some of them we celebrate. Statues of our former heroes come down and are put into storage, away from public viewing, which does not render them meaningless. Rather, they take on new significance in the story we want to tell about ourselves and about who we no longer want to be. That includes our stories about religion.

The significance of the marginalization of religion, our putting it into storage, does not make religion meaningless. What it does tell us is that we no longer want to think of ourselves as religious. We might think about religion, and we might have to think about how to manage it, but, in a secular progressive trajectory, we also want to imagine ourselves as adults who have outgrown it. Leaving religion behind is proving to be easier said than actually accomplished, which is where we experience some ambiguities, our religious inheritances being a complicated mix with which we continue to struggle. However, putting religion into storage does not remove the human capacity to construct meaning stories embodied in standing stones.

We construct standing stones that embody our shared values, our hopes, and dreams for a life that we hope will endure, reflecting universals that transcend time. That's where the distinction between the religious and the secular breaks down. I argue that our complicated religious inheritance does not mean that we no longer reach for transcendence or that we are no longer religious. We continue to seek and embody transcendence because to do so is an essential and defining characteristic of our humanity. Religious literacy equips students to understand that aspect of their shared humanity and of the humanity in whatever they encounter in their everyday lives. Religious literacy takes students into the meaning of the standing stones they encounter in their lives in the form of political and social structures, electrical transmission lines,

---

76. Debates about textbooks and curriculum are interesting and revealing in this regard. Romero, "Heroes or Enslavers?"

In Canada, Ryerson University is now Toronto Metropolitan University, Egerton Ryerson having become persona non grata in the Canadian story: Toronto Metropolitan University, "Ryerson University." He joins John A. Macdonald in our national rogue's gallery: Purdon and Palleja, "Death Threats."

networks of superhighways, impressive skyscrapers and cell phones, dramas played out on the stages of their lives, music and art.

Literacy includes the 3 R's, which take their meaning and purpose when seen in the context of knowledge and the brass ring of wisdom. This takes us to the conclusion that religious literacy includes information about religion, but information detached from its meaning and embodied moral task leads to the disappointment expressed by Mwale et al. in the marginalization of RE in Zambia and to Lewis's conclusion that it leaves us ill-equipped to deal with religion as we encounter it in all its messy diversity. Mwale et al. say,

> In addition to the lack of missionary drive and investment in RE today, there is no ZARET [Zambia Association of Religious Education Teachers] and there are only recycled, "copy and paste" RE syllabi and textbooks that do not make a religious experience central to the learners. Consequently, as Bro. Poirier lamented, "The RE of today has watered down the moral and spiritual components to please everybody . . . I am not sure it has a holistic integral approach to the formation of personality for students. It seems very watered down and therefore may give information and nothing else."[77]

I am not making an argument to return to "missionary drive and investment" as it occurred in its colonial and imperialist context and, like the Joshua story, carries its own baggage. However, the disappointment expressed is significant in its similarity to other expressions, among them by L. Philip Barnes who argues that the current trend in RE development in the UK is less successful than it was hoped to be. Missionary drive and investment indicate confidence in a great, transforming story that answers fundamental questions about human destiny in time and space. The trend in education away from the humanities in general and RE in particular toward more instrumental forms of education may indicate that we have lost confidence in a great story that anchors us as we navigate the world. Perhaps there are questions we do not want our students to ask, and one way to avoid them is to put religion into storage, pretend it does not exist as something to be taken seriously in a modern world. Another way is to mobilize and domesticate it so the questions and answers are more crafted and controlled.

---

77. Mwale et al., "Zambia," 56.

Religious literacy is critically important in that context. Religion is not an anthropological survivor, a historical anachronism, or a social curiosity. It is an interpretive category foregrounding one way in which we know the world. Religious literacy equips students to trace the ultimate values and commitments in the cultural products and patterns that have been normalized in their lives. Religious literacy also equips them to understand the rational thought and logic inherent in the cultural products and social patterns that can seem alien. It alerts them to multiple levels of knowing and the nested stories that carry our knowing and our being known. Educators are never neutral about what students know and how they understand what they know. Religion education delivers religious literacy as a gift of life to students equipping them as they navigate their landscape dotted with standing stones. Doing so may be hard work but then, any learning worth its time is. Hard work, that is.

Religious literacy and critical thought;
Religious literacy as critical thought

Religion education equips students with critical thinking skills to call out destructive meaning stories embodied in cultural and social practices, tracing their logic back to their spiritual origins. In the context of RE, this means following a straight path from evidence of what they see to ultimate values and commitments embodied in what they see. Here's why this is important: social and personal differences are relatively easy to negotiate but become increasingly difficult when they require reassessment of our ultimate commitments. Religious literacy equips students with the language to follow a straight path, even when their doing so requires courage in the face of opposition, normalizing discomfort necessary to follow a path of truth. Isabel Wilkerson starts her examination of caste by calling to mind "the man in the crowd" who refused to raise his arm in a Nazi salute, the one person who folded his arms in a great crowd of worshippers. She asks, "What would it take to be him in any era? What would it take to be him now?"[78] One thing it takes is discernment about the spiritual roots of what we might call the idolatries of our time, normalized by familiarity, social pressure to conform to what has come to be accepted as common sense.

---

78. Wilkerson, *Caste*, xvii.

Other examples: it has taken a great deal of courage for women to call out patriarchy so entrenched and normalized that feminists were and often still are considered abnormal. Another example is systemic caste hierarchies, one form of which is racism, one of humanity's original sins, which needs to be called out even if it risks life and security. In the United States, negotiation around gun ownership is almost impossible because guns have been fetishized so that, more than tools, they are symbols of identity and of a deeply entrenched story about America about which there seems to be little room for discussion. In Ontario, discussions about education reform become highly animated when the link between social cohesion, public education, and the state-funded public school system is questioned. You can supply your own examples of willful and inadvertent blind spots from contexts with which you are familiar. Following a straight path of evidence is not unique to RE, of course. The achievement of disciplined thought is one of the points of education in any discipline, although each has its own rules of engagement within its field. What is unique about RE is that it foregrounds the search for ultimate values and commitments as embodied in our everyday lives.

The metaphor of the *straight path* delivered in the Islamic schools in Jasmin Zine's study leads to God as the ultimate end of education and, indeed, of life. The explicit understanding of God as the ultimate end of education makes it relatively easy to marginalize the idea of a straight path as unique to religious schools who practice indoctrination rather than true education. However, my argument is that any education system is animated by a graduate profile with pedagogical practices marking the straight path to achieve it and then setting them free to engage the ultimate commitments and values of their societies. Justine Ellis observes that Diane Moore's "religious literacy focuses self-consciously on forming students who have the ability to participate as active moral agents in the conscious social reproduction of society."[79] I agree, but cautiously, adding the idea that *social reproduction*, which suggests faith in current practices, must be balanced by critical assessment of what might have become accepted as *normal*, a first step in social reform. The first gift of RE and religious literacy includes equipping our students with the skills and commitments to serve their societies and their world by following a straight evidentiary path from their reading of the world to the ultimate commitments of the societies that animate their constructions of it.

79. Ellis, *Politics*, 91.

Gift Two: Religious Literacy as Essential to Our Spirit Quests

Here's a news flash: the world does not work the way it should. It is not getting better. I am processing the implications for education of the idea that the world is not getting better. If the world is not getting better, the next question for our students is, So, what's the point?

The first gift of religious literacy is to equip students with the skills to follow a straight path of evidence from what they see and experience in their everyday lives to the ultimate values and commitments embodied in those things, many of which are so ubiquitous and familiar that they are almost invisible. Another way to think of it is to encourage and equip students to see that what has come to be accepted as normal is socially constructed and might well be abnormal.

The meaning of suffering and death: An educational problem

But that leaves us with a problem. The problem is that a straight path of evidence, if consistently followed, can be deeply troubling, destabilizing, and sometimes appalling.[80] This is especially true in our world in which students have access to stories coming at them from all over the world and to competing wisdom and opinions all claiming to have access to *truth*. Where do we find a place to rest, a place where our students can find a secure platform on which they can build their lives? One thing we know, and they do now or will know in their life journey, is that their world includes suffering, loss, and grief. It will also include joy, success, and sheer happiness, but I want to draw our attention to the loss and suffering theme, because it most challenges a progressive personal and collective

---

80. A friend once recounted the time he realized that his German heritage included the Nazi period and the industrialized murder of Jews to purify the nation. He was undone and much of his life story included coming to terms with what he discovered at about the age of twelve. While his story seems extreme, I came to see that his quest is more common than you might think, our students having to find their way toward a stable platform for meaning in a noisy and confusing world. My own Dutch Calvinist heritage includes colonialism, racism, and other features that have complicated my world. Our family stories include secrets and lies. A straight path of evidence can take us into places we would prefer not to go, and we need to find a way to embrace the truths hidden there and places where we can place our hope and energy for redemptive action. At the same time, a straight path of evidence can lead us to see a trajectory of benefits—in my case, an inherited stable personal history, political environment, and social context that have protected me. And that needs to be protected. Our students need to see both sides of their inherited stories.

story. One enduring question is about the meaning of grief and loss, of suffering. In a secular age, an immanent framework of reference is normal, one implication of which is that suffering is seen as a problem to be addressed by some form of therapy. However, no amount of therapy can take away our existential questions of meaning in the face of loss and grief.

Therapy leaves a question of the *meaning* of suffering and death unanswered. It might blunt its sting, but temporary relief does not make it go away, and our students know it. Ernest Becker tells us that "this whole book is a network of arguments based on the universality of the fear of death, or 'terror' as I prefer to call it, in order to convey how all consuming it is when we look it full in the face." He quotes William James who says, "Let sanguine healthy-mindedness do its best with its strange power of living in the moment and ignoring and forgetting, still the evil background is really there to be thought of, and the skull will grin in at the banquet."[81] Ouch! Not a great dinner conversation, something those of us not gifted with the skill of small talk might want to keep in mind.

But is it an *educational* problem and if so, why? I argue that it is. First, our students are thinking about suffering and death, which has implications for education. The educational question is, If the evidence of their everyday lives undermines a progressive view of history, then what will be their source of hope? Our students' lived reality is that death and suffering are not going away, that Miroslav Volf's contention that *evil is irremediable* is closer to the truth.

The problem, as I argued in chapter 4, is built into education and literacy, which lives at the intersection of doubt and belief. Our students, if they are going to successfully navigate the world successfully, will need the skills, attitudes, character traits, and robust identities necessary to find their place in the liminal space between doubt and belief. Suffering and death have a way of creating doubt in our beliefs about how the world should work. They should do that, since doubt, in that sense, can lead to deeper and more enduring wisdom. The educational question is, *Will our students have the language of hope to navigate those places of doubt, and a place to land from which they can continue to be people who can serve the world, deepened by their suffering rather than destroyed by it? What does it take to become the persons in the crowd who do not raise their arms in a sea of arms raised to salute evil power, and not be destroyed by it?*

---

81. Becker, *Denial*, 15–16.

Charles Taylor reflects on the *moral source* that will avoid *misanthropy*, by which he means the disappointment, anger, and contempt to which we are attracted when our benevolence does not yield its promised results. His question, "How can we become agents on whom misanthropy has no hold, in whom it awakens no connivance?"[82] occurs in the context of his examination of the *ethical predicament* inherent in a secular age. I am asking the question about education, our students living that predicament and will do so as they engage their futures. Taylor draws on his Christian tradition for an enduring moral source, an argument I understand but is not the point of what I am suggesting here. My point is that all education, to be meaningful, draws on a moral source for its energy and purpose.

Asking about how we become the *person in the crowd*, Miroslav Volf says, "Theologians should concentrate less on social arrangements and more on *fostering the kind of social agents capable of envisioning and creating just, truthful, and peaceful societies and on shaping a cultural climate in which such agents will thrive.*"[83] I would add that Volf is offering a good word for educators about the spiritual nature of education. The question of the moral source that will guide and sustain our students as they engage the truth of the world is an educational one.

The role of teachers and schools is to guide students through and toward a sustainable moral source and to be the kind of person described by Volf. There is no easy answer to how that might happen, at what age, and under what circumstances. (There are developmental issues involved, not the subject of this book.) It is not really a process with a guaranteed outcome, education as I argued being one of our social practices with unintended consequences. I am drawing on Miroslav Volf to argue that education, in any meaningful sense, comes about in a relationship he describes as *embrace*. However, embrace in life and in education is not control. Nor should it be. Volf says, "Built into the very structure of embrace is a multifinality that rests on the systematic underdetermination of outcomes."[84] Education is inherently risky and playful in the best sense that the outcomes are not guaranteed. An uncertainty principle in education, you might say. That's true of RE as well wherever it is delivered.

While it is the role of educators to guide students, modeling for them a preferred outcome and alert them to harmful outcomes, a spirit

---

82. Taylor, *Secular Age*, 701.
83. Volf, *Embrace*, 10; italics original.
84. Volf, *Embrace*, 150.

quest is deeply personal. Education, in that sense, is a spirit quest in which teachers walk alongside but also stand back, in developmentally appropriate ways. The gift of SBNR is to foreground the deeply personal nature of religion. Meredith McGuire and others point out that, while institutions, among them states, create the context for spirit quests, how individuals respond and construct their own interpretations of those contexts is deeply personal, eclectic, and idiosyncratic.

Religious literacy equips students to embrace their own spirit quests in response to a view of the world and the role of religion preferred by authorities in their lives. Authorities might include those we more typically identify as religious but in the twenty-first century they are as likely to include *influencers* who might have only tangential relationships with religion as it is commonly defined. Influencers shape our imaginations around what it means to live a good life, achieved through the right clothing, skin care products, ways of thinking and behaving, or any number of things. Our students live in a world in which they navigate the often-conflicting voices claiming access to unique authoritative knowledge and wisdom about the world. They make their decisions about who they will trust and what advice they will follow. However, they are following a path constructed by authorities they often do not know for reasons that may not be immediately obvious.

In chapters 2 and 3 I argued that a limitation of the SBNR formulation of religion is that it constructs spirituality as an individual, private, ahistorical, and apolitical aspect of humanity that is opposed to its institutionalized religious forms with a history and tradition. Further, it can lead to a conclusion that there are no universal truths or absolutes not of our making and that truth in any meaningful way is individual and self-created. While I am cautious about meta-narratives, I am equally cautious about the idea that there are no transcendent stories that can anchor us in time. Meta-narratives can serve to gloss over the messy bits of our stories but, at their best, they are stories that carry meaning, purpose, and moral task. One of the gifts of critical theory is a call to honesty about the world and about the meta-narratives in their lives. One of the traps of meta-narratives is that our students will come to believe that theirs is the only one worth considering. However, another dead end is that they may come to believe that there is no meaning story for them that can provide context and meaning for their own story.

I argue that this *either-or* construction is an unnecessary distraction from the lived reality of our students. Students do exercise their critical assessments of the contexts in which they find themselves and they make their own decisions about those contexts. However, they are not autonomous and atomistic individuals detached from their contexts. They live in networks of relationships and realities not of their own making. And they have the freedom to make choices, some of them life affirming and some of them destructive. Teachers, even the most committed and skilled ones, delivering well-designed programs in optimal conditions, do not control the outcomes. That does not mean the guidance of teachers is meaningless. Rather, students are looking for guides and mentors who they can trust but who trust them in return. The embrace in which education occurs is hope-filled, faith-based guidance, not control.

Spirit quests, among other things, include self-awareness of their own ultimate values and concerns and their capacity to live their lives guided by a transcendent polestar. Their transcendent star can be imagined within a horizontal framework or a vertical one but, either way, it is deeply human to live in pursuit of a straight path guided by a reality that is bigger than our lived experience. We need to navigate *the world outside our heads*, but an equally important journey is the one we take into our interior landscapes as we work out our ultimate values, concerns, and destinies. Deep understanding and enduring commitments can stabilize and orient our students in the ever-shifting landscapes in which they find themselves and it can help them define their moral tasks in the world. However, they do not invent their own polestars out of thin air, but rather draw on language, accumulated wisdom, and an imaginary that they inherit from the network of relationships in which their lives take shape. The second gift of religious literacy is that it equips students to trace and contextualize their own spirit quests in a bigger story that transcends their own.

Spirituality, religion education, and schools

Education is a social practice delivered in a network of relationships designed to pass on accumulated wisdom, including about religion, most commonly institutionalized in schools. Religion and RE have an ambiguous role in the social practice of education in modern societies self-identifying as secular. The most common way to address the ambiguities around religion in secular schools is to separate religion from spirituality and then to suggest that education about religion can be delivered in an objective and religiously neutral manner. The idea is that the spirit quests of students are private matters for which the school might want to make room but for which it does not take responsibility.

However, my main objection to RE represented as objective and religiously neutral is that it isn't. We do our students a disservice if we pretend that their spirit quests are not important to us, asking them to live a split existence, divided between a private spiritual life and a public secular one. Their choices do make a difference to their teachers and any teacher who does not care should get out of the education business. Teachers provide guidance about life, shaped by their own values, concerns, and commitments because they love their students, and they love the world into and through which their students are journeying.

Teachers do not take off their spiritual selves when they put on their professional clothing. Teachers are influencers. To pretend otherwise renders us less able to exercise our pedagogical power in appropriate ways. Schools are not religiously neutral places. They create times and spaces that give permission for preferred forms of religion and withhold permission for forms of religion that deviate from what is considered normal.

That's not a problem if two questions are on the table. The first is if the school is fulfilling its public obligation in relationship to the social covenant providing common ground for social harmony and public wisdom. The second is the transparency with which schools exercise their authority in the delivery of their preferred graduate profile. However, issues around the social covenant are challenges that require constant negotiation and transparency. The issue of transparency is important in addressing the language of secularism that tends to mask the religious esthetic of organizations and contexts identified as religiously neutral and objective.

Living by bread alone

The gift of religious literacy is to equip our students with the language for the spirituality of their everyday lives. They *do not live by bread alone*,[85] even bread packaged so attractively in new phones, shoes, and perfumes. We are mammals who need bread, but we are also irresistibly drawn to the meaning of our lives, to a straight path of truth. Our students are drawn to and repelled by truth in the sense that they cannot live without

---

85. Matt 4:4.

reliable truths. Often and irritatingly, truth confronts us with realities not of our own making. We may have elevated the idea of individual autonomy, even more so with the ever more sophisticated constructions of virtual realities. However, there are inescapable truths about human limitations that present themselves in consequences that we cannot control, one of which is that, like all living things, we die. Unlike most living things, we struggle with what that means.

I argue that RE, when it is given full, robust meaning, can give our students the language of a redemptive meaning narrative, both for their own lives and for the world. They need to embrace their own meaning narrative, the great story in which they are actors and which gives their lives a transcendent purpose. Their meaning narratives intersect, finding expression in a world rich in meaning potential. There is an *aha* moment in which it all comes together, which is what Otto calls the numinous, the *mysterium tremendum*. This is not irrational, but it is nonrational. It is not detached from reality in some sui generis category. Rather, it is the star by which we navigate reality. It is to fall in love with a transformative reality that will transcend our life stages, our encounters with deep pain and grief that are inherent in a life lived fully on the earth.

Here's what religious literacy does not do

Religious literacy does not necessarily make us better people and sometimes it makes people more intentionally and intelligently evil. There is not a predictable link between religious literacy and morality, morality being a socially constructed code of behavior that embodies values. The capacity to construct moral codes is universal, inherent in human nature, but how it is embodied can take any number of forms, some of which can be shocking to outsiders. One gift of religious critical thinking is its capacity to trace what we see in moral codes to their spiritual sources, leading to deeper insights, both of our own values and moral codes and of those which are unfamiliar. Sometimes that deeper understanding can lead to appreciation of diversity and sometimes it can inspire change.

However, not always. Religious literacy does not make us more tolerant of diversity and sometimes it makes us less tolerant. There are times when it should make us intolerant. However, productive intolerance is based on more than discomfort due to lack of familiarity or ideology. Religious literacy can equip our students to trace the evidence of what they see to its sources, allowing their capacity to see to be expanded, broadened, and deepened by embracing insights of people who see differently. Schools that embrace differences can provide a valuable service by bringing together students who see differently and live in the world in different ways. The point of that kind of diversity is not to increase tolerance in a general sense, but rather create the possibility of encounters that sharpen critical sensitivities to the way the world works for people for whom it does not work so well.

Some examples: abuses of power and the marginalization of people practiced on an individual and collective level and normalized in caste structures and religious discourses are simply wrong. Our students know it, and we should not play games with them by pretending otherwise; short-term economic gain at the expense of people trapped in poverty, having children bought and sold, and dumping plastic in the oceans are rooted in evil impulses, even if that evil has become banal and normalized.[86] Child marriage justified by religion is wrong. My assessment that it is wrong is guided by but not based on my Christianity, but rather it is based on the evidence of its impact on the bodies of young girls. Free market capitalism, driven by fear and greed, is wrong. The evidence is available to us in the cries of pain we hear in the poor, the animals, plants, and other members of our earthy community, drowning as we are in the discarded stuff we call trash, an inevitable consequence of our belief that uncontrolled consumption is essential to our model of a good life. Unrestricted access to high-powered weaponry is wrong. The impact of gun violence and poverty have created national health crises around the world. You can add your own lines in the sand beyond which you will not go. We can argue the details but, in fact, we are not objective about a lot of things, and we are intolerant of many of them. The promise of religious literacy is that it equips students to drill down below surfaces to see the ultimate commitments, values, and imaginaries, if you like, that give evil social practices their meaning and energy.

In short, education is not therapy in the sense Charles Taylor talks about it, making the distinction between *ethical* and *therapeutic* transformation.[87] Education confronts students with what they do not know, what they cannot do, where they must grow and change. It also confronts them with truths about the world that can challenge their preconceptions

---

86. Arendt, *Eichmann in Jerusalem*.
87. Taylor, *Secular Age*, ch. 17.

and illusions. The world is not Disneyland or the virtual realities that we enter and think we can control, in which the consequences of what we do are virtual.[88] Sometimes our students feel worse and sometimes they should. Sometimes they need to repent, change course, rethink. While I endorse the idea of schools being safe learning spaces, educators need to define what that means in an educational context. Arbitrary pain and abuses of pedagogical power serve no purpose and are harmful. Classrooms must be safe spaces where ideas and practices are tested, reformulated, rejected as dead ends, or adopted as reliable. The process involves mistakes and sometimes embarrassment, possible in safe spaces where the consequences are limited. Strategically and carefully planned discomfort and risk (aka, *cognitive dissonance*) are essential to growth. Sometimes that means reassessing the parameters of what is considered normal. Learning, in any meaningful sense, is hard work and not safe, although the environment in which risks are taken must be safe in order for it to work well.

Here's what religious literacy does

What religious literacy does is equip us to trace the evidence of what's on the surface to the ultimate commitments energizing and normalizing what we see. Religious literacy can give us appreciation for what needs to be protected for future generations and insight into what needs to be discarded in acts of repentance, even if it costs us to do so and even if we do not want to pay the costs. The refusal to hear cries of pain, to listen to testimony of those being hurt, and to seriously consider evidence is not just a matter of illiteracy. It is evidence of what, in my religious tradition, is called *idolatry*, the worship of and ultimate commitments to something that, in the end, is going to eat us and our children.

Besides equipping us to identify the ultimate commitments and values of our everyday lives, religious literacy also brings us to a place of robust identity as social actors. While I question Ontario's Character Development initiative on several grounds, it is motivated by the idea that the ultimate purpose of education is to guide students toward a robust

---

88. One of my younger acquaintances spends time in his virtual world in which he can enthusiastically blow up worlds, kill people and be killed. He can drive with joyous abandon, running over pedestrians, crashing into other cars, all without real-life consequences. He is now in the process of driver training, hoping to get his driver's licence. Suddenly, and thankfully, he is very careful, very conscious of consequences.

identity that will contribute to a good society. I disagree that *character* is religiously neutral, the language in the 2008 documents being reminiscent of the common religion language going back to the nineteenth century. Rather than marginalizing religion using masking strategies represented as religiously neutral, I argue that religious literacy, in partnership with other literacies, can lead our students to believe in a great story to which they can commit themselves. Our students need great stories in which they can be actors, giving meaning to their lives that transcends their immediate circumstances. Religion and religious literacy, at their best, can lead us to be socially disruptive, difficult citizens if that's what is needed. It can also lead us to astonishing acts of generosity and good citizenship in service of a society marked by *shalom*.

Religious literacy equips us to speak prophetically, to die intelligently if we must speak truths about networks of power that want to stay masked. Prophets, William James tells us, are sometimes impolite and sometimes they are unbalanced. Here's a little something from the great man given to us back in the early twentieth century: "There can be no doubt that as a matter of fact a religious life, exclusively pursued, does tend to make the person exceptional and eccentric."[89] While I want my students to live good and happy lives, I would encourage them to be exceptional and eccentric if their straight path takes them to the hearts of darkness masked by what has come to be accepted as normal and inevitable. I argue that deep commitments can give them the spiritual backbone they need to resist evil, to call out abuses of power. Religious literacy and a disciplined religious imagination can equip them to do so intelligently and lovingly. A religious imagination, at its best, is *queer* in the sense that it creates a "third [imaginative] space," being "neither state nor corporation."[90] Religion opens possibilities for loves detached from networks of power, allowing critical assessment of power relations by following a path of evidence to their ultimate commitments. We want our students to be the people in the crowd who refuse to bow to evil powers, and, of course, we cannot expect our students to be that if we, the adults in their lives, are not prepared to lead the way.

Religious literacy is a key element in critical thought. Our students must become critically aware of their own ultimate values, concerns, loves, and hates. For that they need others who can guide them to take

---

89. James, *Varieties*, 8.
90. Watkin, *Biblical Critical Theory*, 461–62.

distance from what they see as normal, which does not mean they necessarily reject it. It does mean that they can choose to live more thoughtfully, maybe even humbly. It can also lead them to treat others with the care they would like to be treated. There are truths on which they base their lives, transmitted in traditions of thought and practice that anchor them. They will find things in their lives that are nonnegotiable. But, again paradoxically, their living well and confidently in an enduring story allows them to engage others with confidence and with respect. If the first gift equips students with loving critical thought about the deepest loves and commitments animating the society in which they find themselves, it also equips them to simultaneously embrace and take critical distance from their own life journeys and commitments.

SOME COMPLICATIONS IN THE DELIVERY OF RELIGIOUS LITERACY

Complication One: How Do We Know Religiously?

Living a great story takes us to places of deep love and enchantment. However, here's a problem: what do enchantment, a great story, hope, and redemption have to do with the hard stuff of education in a modern world? Aren't we straying into some murky territory here, marked by cognitive impairment and rationality deficits? Aren't enchantment and belief best kept to private times and spaces, leaving the public activities of education uncluttered for real thinking? Well, as you may have guessed from previous chapters, bifurcated constructions of the world do useful political and regulatory work but do not stand up to closer scrutiny.

For one thing, the death of enchantment has been exaggerated. For example, the world of entertainment draws us into places of enchantment that can also push the boundaries of our comfort zone. Enchantment, like religion, may have an ambiguous role in our world but education projects are animated by love for students and for the world. In a way, we want them to be horrified by abuses of power, and we want them to develop skills essential for success, but we also want them to be drawn into places of enchantment about the wondrous ways in which the universe works: by astonishing art, by the human struggle for justice, by our bodies. We want them to live in a world of wonders, watch and be overwhelmed by a lunar eclipse and the Perseid meteor showers, rather than accepting a monochromatic world of necessity and instrumental thinking. We have faith that our efforts will guide them on a straight path to a preferred future for which we reach but cannot yet see. All schools are faith-based, delivering education that encourages our students to reach for the stars. We do not want them to be cynical, jaded, or too smart to be enchanted, but we also want them to be grounded in the real world. Religious literacy puts us into the double paradox created by the paradoxes inherent in both religion and literacy, in the liminal space of uncertainty and knowing. Religion takes us into questions of transcendent values, knowing and faith, final answers to which often elude us and draw us into places of wonder. But how do we *know* religiously? And, what is the answer, the real, dependable one on which we can base our lives and to which we can lead our students?

Of course, this is not unique to religion. Ask any couple how they knew that they were really in love and you get a sense of wonder that goes beyond rationally compiled evidence. Knowing is central to our religious literacy discussion. We are, after all, talking about literacy and education, which lead with knowing. What it is to know religiously usually lands somewhere on a continuum between propositionally codified theological answers on the one extreme and emotional and intuitive ways of knowing.

The affective: Emotion, bodied experience, and knowing in religion

What is often foregrounded in religion and religious knowing is *feeling* and *emotion* rather than knowing in a more rationalist sense. Emotions such as love or awe, a sense of the mystery experienced by individuals as they contemplate, for example, the passage of time, the stars, the beauty of a sunset, or the mysteries of love are often associated with religion. Feelings are often what bind groups into a mysterious unity or agreement that eludes rational explanation. Rudolph Otto refers to the "contrast between rationalism and profounder religion."[91] While he does not dismiss the rational elements of religion, he argues that it is the *numen* and the *numinous* that, "strictly speaking, cannot be taught, it can only be evoked, awakened in the mind; as everything that comes 'of the spirit' must be awakened."[92]

---

91. Otto, *Idea*, 2.
92. Otto, *Idea*, 7.

Justine Ellis foregrounds the *affective* in thinking about the politics of religious literacy, drawing on Megan Watkins who examines the bodied nature of learning. The focus on the affective offers an alternative and balance to the tradition of rational and propositional formulations of religion and religious truth.

I am cautious about what might be overconfidence in the affective as a source of truth. However, there is a creative tension inherent in religious knowing, something Taylor identifies when he links certain forms of religion, among them Reformed Christianity, to *disenchantment*, which deny, or perhaps background, the bodied nature of our religious and spiritual lives. Setting the tension in historical context he says, "We can look at the 'enlightened ethics' of today. On one side we have a Humean stream, which does indeed, have a place for feeling in ethics, the reaction of sympathy, but accords this no power to discern its good or bad uses. This calculating reason must determine. And in certain extreme variants, even the most basic 'gut' feeling, like our horror at infanticide, are ruled irrelevant. On the other side, we have the Kantian stream, which derives our moral obligations from a consideration of ourselves as pure rational agents."[93]

While the focus on feelings and the bodied nature of religion encourages us to think more broadly about how we know anything, it can also limit the ways we might think about religion. The emphasis on feelings can lead to the conclusion that religion is irrational or, at best, nonrational and therefore not a dependable source of public information, knowledge, and wisdom. Rather, I argue that religious knowing includes, but is not limited to, feelings. Andrew Lang, making *belief in a transcendent intelligence* the defining feature of religion, argues that belief has implications for all of life, saying that by *religion* he means "the belief in the existence of an Intelligence or Intelligences not human, and not dependent on a material mechanism of brain and nerves, which may, or may not, powerfully control men's fortunes and the nature of things."[94] I am not sure I agree with Lang that our religious knowing is not dependent on "a material mechanism of brain and nerves," since all our knowing is bodied. And I am cautious about Lang's leading with "intelligence" and the language of "control." However, where I do agree with Lang is that our imagined transcendent realities do powerfully animate

---

93. Taylor, *Secular Age*, 554.
94. Lang, *Making*, 50.

our fortunes and our understanding of the "nature of things." But how do we *know* a transcendent reality—that is, a reality that transcends our bodied realities?

Religious knowing is complex, including intuition, bodily practices, and rational processes that occur in social contexts. Religion is a mode of knowing the world and the human journey in time and space. Religion as knowing includes rational thought and construction, but it does not begin and end there. Of course, the same could be said for other forms of knowing, such as science, the arts, or law, that include rational constructions along with intuition, feeling, and group think. Although religion has its own unique contribution to our knowing the world, it is, at the same time, not a sui generis category living off in a parallel universe with its own inscrutable rules of engagement. This is central to what follows and gets more treatment further along.

However, previous generations (pre–*secular age*, that is) might observe that we may be overthinking this. Taylor examines the historical trajectory in which transcendence became a problem we had to think about, which has resulted in religion's ambiguous status in the modern imagination. One outcome of the trajectory is that transcendence and transcendent realities became detached from our everyday experience and from the real world that we can access through our senses, rationally codifying its truths in propositional and falsifiable statements. However, our lived realities are not governed by abstract, falsifiable codes. Writing about the paradoxes in the concept of *rule of law*, Hussein Ali Agrama identifies law's *indeterminacy* and our suspicion of law and, at the same time, our dependence on it to create social order distinct from *justice*. However, he says, "That everyday life is suffused with the potential for indeterminacy does not therefore mean that it is continuously lived in anxious uncertainty. Only under specific historical conditions do the potential uncertainties of a particular practice become a source of perceived paradox, a focus of collective anxiety, and an object of systematic elaboration in relation to power."[95] We experience the world in multiple, nuanced ways that we can codify but are not reduced to propositions that can be continually questioned. We live with some *basic trust*, places where we can find rest and peace that we find in *clustered reliances* and *testimony* of lived, collective wisdom. However, how we get there is complex and not easily defined in rational, propositional terms.

---

95. Agrama, *Questioning*, 110.

Reflections on Religious Literacy

Telling stories from and about experience

One way to think about religious knowing in a way that bypasses the assessment of its essential irrationality is to frame it in terms of *religious experience*. You cannot argue with someone's account of a deeply personal experience. It may not have traction in public discourse or have authoritative status in a broader sense, but it would be impolite to argue that someone's experience is not real in some way. There's a challenge inherent in our secular age where a commonsense acceptance of religion, defined in terms of vertical transcendence, is a thing of the past. The implication is that religious experience may be interesting but without public significance unless, of course, it becomes a management problem. Some of us may still believe that it has authoritative status, but it must be defended and rationalized in the twenty-first century in a way that it did not have to be back in 1500.[96] *Experience* does not have to answer questions about its rationality because it simply is what it is (well, maybe not all that simply in real life). But does experience have authoritative knowledge status, and can it sustain an argument for religious literacy as a public good? Another way to ask it is, Are accounts of religious experience a reliable source of information and knowledge? I accept the problem and have some questions.

Theoretically we can foreground religion in our experiences, identifying an experience as *religious*. However, what we are doing is foregrounding a particular way of describing an experience. The foregrounding of language (our hermeneutical problem) suggests that we do not have *religious* experiences; what we have are experiences we narrate in particular ways, including the language of religion. Our being human means that our nested stories or our multiple interpretive categories do not tell the whole story but a particular way of remembering, assigning meaning to our experiences. Christopher Watkin illustrates this with a story when he says, "Take G. E. M. Anscombe's example of a man pumping to fill a cistern that provides drinking water for a house. What is he doing? Performing

---

96. Readers might be interested in the account of Lucrecia de Léon, whose dreams landed her in the Inquisition courts in sixteenth-century Spain. Dreams were taken seriously enough to attract attention from civic and religious authorities, and her trial was a test (or a series of tests) of their source (of the devil, or God, or her fevered womanly imagination). The point is that, in the pre-secular world of the sixteenth century, religious experience had knowledge consequences in ways that it tends not to have in our world. See Kagan, *Lucrecia's Dreams*, for an interesting and thought-provoking story.

geometrical movements? Sending electrical signals from his brain to his muscles? Providing for his family? Being a good citizen? Earning a living? Serving his God? All these descriptions are possible, along with many more besides. And none of them rules out the others."[97]

However, thinking about religious experience through the lens of language and narrative can lead to skepticism about its status as source of information, knowledge, and wisdom. Justine Ellis shares a caution about the multiple narratives idea, when she identifies the *linguistic fallacy* of classic liberalism. The idea is that decision-making results directly from language "which misunderstands religion as merely a byproduct of language." Her "focus on embodiment shifts the emphasis from cognitivist to materialist strands within religious studies."[98] Saba Mahmood, while not dismissing semiotics, raises a similar caution when she says that "many dimensions of practice—both linguistic and nonlinguistic—cannot be grasped in terms of a theory of representation alone."[99] In fact, people do have experiences of love that you can narrate in terms of body chemistry, social pressure, a biological drive to reproduce, and economics but reducing love to its component narrative parts does not do justice to love itself. The conclusion is that *experience* tells us something but is not uncomplicated when thinking about religious knowing.

Revisiting rationality and religion

The objection that religion is irrational or, at best, nonrational, seen as a questionable and even harmful source of information, knowledge, and wisdom, needs to be addressed if the case for religious literacy is going to withstand critical scrutiny. Affective theory, foregrounding emotion and bodied experience, invites consideration of how we know religiously but leaves us with some questions inherent in education, living as it does in the liminal territory between critical thought and belief. Thinking well finds its place in that sweet spot between reliable truth and critical thinking skills without landing in an untenable and anarchic relativism or rigid fundamentalism. Our educational problem is how to get our students to land there. Another way of putting it is that we want our students to develop the

---

97. Watkin, *Biblical Critical Theory*, 336.
98. Ellis, *Politics*, 96–97.
99. Mahmood, *Politics of Piety*, xi.

skills equipping them to construct a reliable meaning narrative out of the astonishing array of information with which they are immersed.

The process by which that happens is complex and can be described in any number of ways. It is shaped by any number of factors as well. Education usually happens in pretty standard ways, but teachers also know that *special needs* students draw the complexity of the process to our attention. I do not address the fascinating and complex world of learning diversity, brain and neurological functioning, and learning disabilities here.[100] Rather, I am concentrating on religion as a mode of knowing, with particular attention to the charge of religion being inherently irrational.

Thinking well and evidence in religion education

What is religious knowing and how do you know that what you know is *true*? This is a problem in religion more generally but is so especially for forms of religion based on vertical transcendence or transcendence realism. The educational question is, How does evidence work for forms of religion structured around transcendence realism? Remember that God is on the evidentiary hot seat in modern societies that rely on falsifiable propositions as the source of reliable public information, knowledge, and wisdom.

Religion and rationality deficit

The reliance of dependable knowledge on falsifiable *propositions* leaves transcendence realists with a *rationality deficit* that accounts, in part at least, for its ambiguous place in modern imaginaries. Justine Ellis, arguing for affective theory, and Charles Taylor, drawing our attention to intuition, invite us to think in other ways about knowing that nuance dependable knowledge. Taylor refers to a *leap of faith* we make, suggesting that we come to our conclusions not as the result of a linear decision-making process but, rather, intuitively in the context of what we believe about the world. In other words, rational thinking occurs but that's not where we start. And where we start comes out of what we have inherited

---

100. I entered the profession of teaching in the early 1970s when research in learning was entering a new and exciting phase that fundamentally changed the way we thought about learning success and failure. We became better equipped to respond to learning diversity, which, on the whole, my younger colleagues now take for granted and are more skilled in delivering. Very encouraging! But not the subject of this book.

through a process most of which is unconscious, not remembered, not articulated unless it must be defended against challenges, either by changing circumstances or by people who see the world quite differently from what we have assumed to be true.

Nicholas Wolterstorff, writing about religion on university campuses (specifically Yale where he taught), points out that, "beginning some forty years ago, philosophers of religion have asked whether it's true, as the critic assumes, that not holding one's religious beliefs on the basis of arguments that adequately support those beliefs represents a deficiency in the functioning or use of one's capacity for reasoning."[101] The idea that dependable knowledge can have a variety of sources established by a variety of processes has been backgrounded in historiographies based on a model of knowing that privileges a linear reasoning process preferred in the European Enlightenment tradition. The question is not whether a linear reasoning process is a legitimate way of knowing. The question is whether it represents a pinnacle of human intellectual development or if it represents a marginalization of other ways of knowing for purposes that have little to do with the achievement of truth in a more nuanced and complex sense.

Wolterstorff asks if religion has been asked to meet an evidentiary standard we do not demand of other interpretive categories of knowing. He says, "Those who challenged the demand for propositional evidence pointed to the fact that we all hold many beliefs immediately without anybody taking that to be a deficiency of rationality on our part. So why insist that holding religious beliefs immediately always and everywhere indicates a deficiency of rationality? What is it about religious beliefs that makes them different?"[102]

Charles Taylor, identifying a similar prejudice, observes that "modern enlightened culture is very theory-oriented. We tend to live in our heads, trusting our disengaged understandings: of experience, of beauty (we can't really accept that it's telling us anything, unless about our own feelings); even the ethical: we think that the only valid form of ethical self-direction is through rational maxims or understanding. We can't accept that part of being good is opening ourselves to certain feelings; either the horror at infanticide, or agape as a gut feeling. But the effect

---

101. Wolterstorff, *Religion in the University*, 83.
102. Wolterstorff, *Religion in the University*, 84.

of Reform has been that much of modern Western Christianity has been following the same path."[103]

Jerry Coyne argues that religion and religious knowing do indicate a deficiency of rationality. Reflecting on a debate with a Lutheran theologian he says, "The toolkit of science, based on reason and empirical study, is reliable, while that of religion—including faith, dogma and revelation—is unreliable and leads to incorrect, untestable, or conflicting conclusions. Indeed, by relying on faith rather than evidence, religion renders itself *incapable* of finding the truth." This is no marginal matter of intellectual differences of opinion between equals. Rather, his book "deals with the conflict between religion and science" that is "only one battle in a wider war—a war between rationality and superstition."[104]

This sets the theorizing about rationality and religion in a much more profound context. We are at war with each other, in Coyne's mind at least, in which there is no room for *accommodationists* who look for common ground between science and religion. His language of war is reminiscent of the language in the Ark Encounter, and both have gained a certain kind of public legitimacy in the social fault lines constructed as a culture war. Coyne is described as a *New Atheist* with all the evangelistic fervor of that old new movement. He has written extensively, the author of a *New York Times* bestseller (*Why Evolution Is True*), and is a professor emeritus of the University of Chicago. No marginal thinker, in other words, and, like Ken Ham of the Ark Encounter, a good person with whom to think.

One of the things that has irked Coyne is that religious people are not convinced by his arguments. He says, "It didn't take me long to realize the futility of using evidence to sell evolution to Americans for faith led them to discount and reject the facts right before their noses." Recounting "an aha moment" in a talk he gave to a "group of businessmen in a ritzy suburb of Chicago" after which one of the attendees "shook

---

103. Taylor, *Secular Age*, 555. While I think Taylor is legitimately foregrounding the theme of rational thought and disenchantment, he is oversimplifying the Protestant Reformation that was a complex development. For example, John Calvin's writings reflect brilliant systematic rationality (he was a lawyer by profession, and it shows), they also show him to be a complex human being with a great depth of pastoral concern and passionate feeling. However, there is no doubt that rational thought was the dominant theme of the *Enlightenment*, which picked up on part of the Protestant Reformation and which continues to shape the way we think about religion as rationally defective. In addition, some branches of Calvinism would have given the great man heartburn.

104. Coyne, *Faith vs. Fact*, xii; italics original.

my hand and said, 'Dr. Coyne, I found your evidence for evolution very convincing—but I still don't believe it.'" He describes himself as "flabbergasted" but finds the explanation in that fact that it "was that his religion had immunized him against my evidence."[105]

There is a great deal to unpack here, among which is Coyne's tone of indignation that his *facts* failed to convince his audience. He sounds not unlike Ken Ham, speaking in the voice of Noah who delivers God's indignation expressed in dramatic ways. Besides our being somewhat entertained by Coyne's tone, his being flabbergasted reveals a more important issue, which is the problem of how we arrive at a common basis for understanding the world and for organizing our collective lives. If we can't appeal to God and divine revealed truth, on the one hand, or if facts are not convincing, on the other, where does that leave us? Religion in any traditional sense might work for individuals and the sectarian tribes in which they find themselves but no longer creates a common authoritative platform for all of us. It may have done so at one time but has been sidelined to the margins of public life.

However, as noted before, religion is not going anywhere, even though some of us might long for a flood that would take care of its problematic forms once and for all. And anyone engaging in RE is entering contested territory because education is about the development of knowing in all its variety and complexity, the extremes of which are occupied by Ken Ham and Jerry Coyne. So, back to the future where we must think about religion and the problem of evidence in religious knowing, at a time when our consensus about secularism and knowing are being contested.

Transcendence, rationality, and group think: Problems in education

Let's go back to the problem of *evidence* and rationality in thinking about transcendence in the context of a progressive historiography. The idea that religion is basically irrational is linked to the idea that religion is essentially a matter of group indoctrination effective with people who do not think for themselves. Jeff Spinner-Halev says of religious conservatives, "The religious conservative is not the model Millian character; he may choose his life, but he has little individuality. The person is autonomous, but only in a limited way. He has chosen a life, but it is a

---

105. Coyne, *Faith vs. Fact*, xiv–xv.

life of little choice, at least in many important spheres."[106] According to Spinner-Halev, the modern liberal makes free choices based on evidence, while religious conservatives, who he describes as those who "believe in an external transcendental authority," are limited by tradition and group cohesion whose "institutions are centered around something powerful that few ethnic groups can match: a certain belief in God."[107] This description of themselves might be surprising to "the religious conservative" but Zehavit Gross observes something similar in his category of *heritable religiosity*.[108] Among other things, their comments suggest that they are less aware of the elitism in their positions than maybe would be useful to them. But let's leave that for now and continue with the link between rationality and group think.[109]

Consensus gentium

The technical term for what is negatively thought of as group think is *consensus gentium*, which essentially means that much of what we know comes to us from and through the groups in which we live.[110] The point here is that there is a whole lot about the world that I take as given. A simple example is my working understanding of the earth as a sphere rotating along with eight or nine other planets around the sun, which is one star among who knows how many other stars in a galaxy, which is only one among so many out there that it makes my head spin. At least, that's what astronomers tell us, having done work I am not prepared to do. I accept the even more astonishing theory of general relativity, which I do not really understand, and the evidence for black holes that I have not personally seen. I have not actually done the research on this in any great depth and what I have read comes from sources who claim to have evidence. Not everyone believes these things, and you can go online to

---

106. Spinner-Halev, *Surviving Diversity*, 5.

107. Spinner-Halev, *Surviving Diversity*, 9–10.

108. Gross, "Religious Education," 268.

109. Wandering around the religion section in the *Gutenberg Project* I came across *The Sex Worship and Symbolism of Primitive Races: An Interpretation* by Sanger Brown II published in 1916. He freely refers to *savages* and, among his statements is one that parallels observations by Spinner-Halev and Gross about the "religious conservative" and "heritable religion." Brown says, "To properly interpret these beliefs and conduct, certain facts must be kept in mind. One is that with primitive races the group stands for the unit, and the individual has little if any personality distinct from the group." 19.

110. Kelly, "*Consensus gentium*."

become acquainted with a fascinating world of flat-earthers if you would like.[111] I am writing this using a computer that works in ways less easy to explain than the virgin birth and when I sit down to turn it on in the morning it mostly works due to a vast array of mechanisms the operation of which is opaque to me. These include electricity, which is another one of those things that I trust will work and can talk about fairly intelligently without really knowing what I am talking about. To be honest, most of my life depends on a kind of *consensus gentium* about all kinds of things.

Our societies are based on *consensus gentium*, which includes our agreement about how money works, our traffic patterns, and the fact that I have a deed to my house that is protected by law so I can say to anyone coming up my driveway "So far and no further" if I suspect their visit may be unwelcome, and I trust that if I call 911, I will get support for my command. Thinking about how money works and the faith on which it depends makes me shudder, my comforts depending on most of humanity holding to the consensus that it actually means something. I do not even want to think about cryptocurrency, so I don't. The providence of God is a stretch, but I can get there. Bitcoin, not so much.

Consensus gentium and indoctrination

In the dynamic world of education politics, group agreement and belief, or *consensus gentium*, is often described as *indoctrination* and *coercion*. However, in his examination of "uncompelled belief," James Ross claims that *belief* is not necessarily the result of a coercive process. He argues that anyone's life depends on "clustered reliances," most of which are unexamined.[112] In that sense everyone is a believer in something. Without "the silent presence [of] basic trust,"[113] life cannot work, either on a micro or a macro level. Thomas Kelly argues that "outside of the philosophy seminar room, we regularly treat the beliefs of others as evidence for the truth of what they believe, revising our own views in the light of what they think, and that (often enough) it is reasonable for us to do so."[114] My world is built on *clustered reliances* that can, of course, be shaken by unexpected developments, such as a global pandemic the overall effects

111. www.tfes.org
112. Ross, "Willing Belief."
113. Rizutto, *Birth*, 203.
114. Kelly, "*Consensus gentium*," 138.

of which we are still assessing in 2025. To think of myself as an autonomous, free-thinking individual might be good for my self-esteem but cannot really withstand close scrutiny.

Consensus gentium, clustered reliances, and autonomy

That's the rub, of course. A Western understanding of what it means to be a fully realized human being in the modern world is closely linked to autonomy, agency, and freedom narrated with the atomistic individual as the primary actor. Collective forms of religion practiced by true believers are associated with social disruption and violence, impediments to social progress and personal freedom. Even more fundamental, however, is that in educational terms fundamentalist modes of thought are seen to be harmful to achieving full humanity. Clustered reliances are seen as an affront to personal autonomy but the paradox is that if we ignore the network of relationships within which knowledge is developed, we fail to do justice to the complexity of what we know and how we got there. Our obsession with autonomy can draw us into an anxious world that we have to constantly reinvent because we can never completely trust the clustered reliances passed on to us by others.

Alan Bloom observes about his students that "there is one thing a professor can be absolutely certain of: almost every student entering the university believes, or says he believes, that truth is relative."[115] His point is that our freedom of choice and autonomy are illusions or articles of faith that get in the way of critical self-awareness. His book was a challenge to an emerging generation to be critically self-aware of its clustered reliances (although he does not use that term). We rely on frameworks of reference that any educated person should question but rarely does or is required to do, which is the basis of Bloom's critique of university education in the late twentieth century.

Clustered reliances and critical thought: The ambiguous role of the kid who calls out the emperor on the issue of clothing

We do not like having our clustered reliances questioned too much, which is one of the reasons graduate students are such a pain sometimes (often, actually) because they must add to knowledge, which means

---

115. Bloom, *Closing*, 25.

questioning the knowledge that exists. Other examples include family solidarity, which depends on our knowing when to stop asking questions, but the same thing is true of societies. The captain of a naval vessel can be demoted for raising the alarm about COVID-19 on his ship[116] and a doctor can be imprisoned for doing the same thing in the jurisdiction in which she is working.[117] In both cases, the decisions were revisited by others in the bureaucracies where the sanctions occurred, and both the officer and the doctor have been vindicated. In general, though, we tend to be uneasy around emperor-has-no-clothes whistleblowers, the point being that information is never just information.[118] Nevertheless, Thomas Kelly observes that "one might very well date the beginning of the Western philosophical tradition from Socrates' adamant insistence that the mere fact that certain views and practices are dominant among his fellow Athenians is not itself a good reason for accepting those views and practices."[119] The point for RE is that it gives students the information and knowledge, critical thinking skills, and courage to assess the clustered alliances on which our lives depend and, paradoxically, from which we need to take distance. Sometimes our clustered alliances are wrong, and we need our whistleblowers even if we don't like them all that much all the time.

Historiography, rationality, and religion

The view that religion is basically irrational is linked to the ideas associating religion with less-developed premodern or traditional societies and with earlier stages of personal development in which the individual had not yet fully emerged. In this view, religion is something that a society leaves behind in a process of secularization with advances in science and other marks of modernity and the maturing of the free individual. Further, as people mature, they no longer need the crutch that religion may provide and that religion among adults represents a kind of pathology. Erik Erikson argued that "religion is the necessary basis for the achievement of personal identity in adolescence" doing what it "must do for the young person what the mother did for the infant; provide nutriment for

---

116. Wade, "Navy Captain."
117. Kuo, "Coronavirus."
118. Cohn et al., "Unusual"; Bloomberg, "China Honors."
119. Kelly, *Consensus gentium*, 137.

the soul as well as for the stomach and screen the environment so that vigorous growth may meet what it can manage."[120]

Back in the heyday of enthusiasm for an enlightenment narrative, David Hume "notoriously claimed that belief in miracles is more common among 'ignorant and barbarous' peoples."[121] He was not the only one, of course, our progressive historiographies constructed in such a way as to make us look smarter than people who went before us. For example, Matthew Sweet demonstrates how the Victorians fell "victim to the enormous condescension of posterity," having been reimagined by the "Bloomsbury set" to their own advantage.[122] A progressive history places religion along a continuum that has a built-in elitism, some of us having attained rational maturity while others are still somewhere behind us.[123]

A progressive historiography that assumes secularism as inherent in modernism represents religion as a problem to be examined, which has real-life consequences in how religion is theorized and regulated. Thinking of "secularism as a historical problem space" in his examination of the evolving use of *hisba* in Egyptian courts, Hussein Ali Agrama "sees secularism as a set of processes and structures of power wherein the *question* of where to draw a line between religion and politics continually arises and acquires a *distinctive salience*" which "is ineluctably invested with high stakes, having to do with the definition and distribution of the fundamental rights and freedoms of citizens and subjects."[124] His insight has implications for how religion in education systems is regulated by state and state actors.

The Supreme Court of Ontario explicitly based its reasoning leading to the removal of Christian school opening exercises in public schools on a progressive historiography linking individualized and choice-based forms of religion to modernity when it said,

> In an earlier time, when people believed in the collective responsibility of the community toward some deity, the enforcement of

---

120. Osmer and Schweitzer, *Between Modernization*, 255.
121. Zagzebski, "Epistemic Self-Trust," 35.
122. Sweet, *Inventing*, xv.
123. Claire Dederer shows how this works to absolve people in the past of their monstrosity, by suggesting that, as people of their time, they did not know any better. She disputes that, arguing that this is designed to let them off the hook, but also that it represents subsequent generations (us, me) as morally more sophisticated and mature.
124. Agrama, *Questioning*, 27; italics original.

religious conformity may have been a legitimate object of government, but since the Charter, it is no longer legitimate. With the Charter, it has become the right of every Canadian to work out for himself or herself what his or her religious obligations, if any, should be and it is not for the State to dictate otherwise. The State shall not use the criminal sanctions at its disposal to achieve a religious purpose, namely, the uniform observance of the day chosen by the Christian religion as its day of rest.[125]

There is quite a lot to see in this reference, but noteworthy is the contrast between the court contrasting what we used to believe "in an earlier time" with the more enlightened understanding exemplified in the Canadian Charter of Rights and Freedoms adopted in 1982. The contrast is between "religious obligations" as a "collective responsibility" and "the right of every Canadian to work out for himself or herself." *Consensus gentium* did not figure into the court's imagined future for Canada as a legitimate basis for information, knowledge, and wisdom in a modern, secular society. At least, not the particular one under scrutiny by the groups challenging the constitutionality of Christian school opening exercises in Ontario public schools. While I support the removal of explicitly Christian school opening exercises in state schools, my point here is that the court seemed less attentive to its own group think that included a progressive historical trajectory. In doing so, it was making a statement about the role of religion in society, a much bigger issue than the legitimate one of justice and inclusion for non-Christian students in public schools. However, the court's reasoning reflected a more widely accepted consensus, associating religion with a traditional past characterized by group think that is seen as an impediment to a march-of-progressive civilization. Zehavit Gross says something similar in his description of the Middle Ages in contrast with the Renaissance and the Enlightenment when he says,

> Until the Middle Ages, religious definitions were uniform, comprehensive, and monistic and subject to the social control of the relevant religious institutions. In contrast, the Renaissance—especially the Enlightenment and the subsequent Age of Emancipation—enabled religious definitions to develop and flourish and granted legitimacy to a certain differential

---

125. Zylberberg v. Sudbury Board of Education (Director) (Ont. C.A.) 65 O.R. (2d) 641, [1988] O.J. No. 1488, CanLII 189 (ON CA), 12, https://www.canlii.org/en/on/onca/doc/1988/1988canlii189/1988canlii189.pdf.

character, enabling people to adopt or ignore various components of their respective religions.[126]

Gross's characterization of the Middle Ages deserves critical evaluation as it assumes a historical trajectory in which we see growing self-awareness and individuality, of which individual critical and rational thought are essential components, unique to modernity. It does not do justice to the complexity of the Middle Ages, which is itself a historiographical construct. It does support the idea that we have left *consensus gentium* behind, along with other patterns of thought and knowing more characteristic of an earlier, less enlightened period of human history. But is this true or is it a self-serving narrative?

Consensus gentium and evidence based on testimony

As a source of evidence, *consensus gentium* is in part at least based on *testimony*. We believe something, not because of our having tested it personally, but because we believe the testimony of trusted sources of information. Testimony plays an important role in, for example, court cases where juries and judges must figure out which testimony is reliable, much of their process of making their determinations resting on their assessment of the people giving the testimony. However, according to Nicholas Wolterstorff, the "epistemology of testimony" has received relatively little attention, describing it as "an undeveloped area in philosophy generally, and in philosophy of religion in particular."[127]

Chris Tucker distinguishes between "doxastic justification" or "well foundedness" and "propositional justification." Doxastic justification, he says, is a "property of beliefs" while propositional justification is inherent in a linear logical process of arriving at conclusions.[128] The distinction is important, not for arguing that one is inherently superior in generating truth, but rather that each has a legitimate role in accounting for the multiple ways we know the world.

Here's a question in the religious tradition in which I find myself and with which I have struggled: Was the resurrection of Jesus Christ real or is it a metaphor? Did he really rise from the dead? The Gospel of Luke starts out with the author's assertion that he interviewed witnesses,

---

126. Gross, "Religious Education," 271.
127. Wolterstorff, *Religion in the University*, 82.
128. Tucker, "Phenomenal Conservatism," 53.

weighed the evidence, and concluded that it is real and not fake news. He writes that,

> Many have undertaken to draw up an account of the things that have been fulfilled among us, just as they were handed down to us by those who from the first were eyewitnesses and servants of the word. With this in mind, since I myself have carefully investigated everything from the beginning, I too decided to write an orderly account for you, most excellent Theophilus, so that you may know the certainty of the things you have been taught.[129]

His letter to Theophilus, which we know as the book of Acts of the Apostles, is his account of what he learned from his research (and from his personal relationship with Paul, after they met in Derbe, after which they traveled together and must have done a lot of talking[130]). But here's the question: Do you believe his account, which depends on the testimony of his interviewees? Orthodox Christian belief depends on the testimony summarized in the Gospels and the rest of the New Testament, which Nicky Gumbel, founder of Alpha, a popular evangelistic program, found convincing enough to lead to his conversion to Christianity.[131] He was a barrister, an atheist, and a skeptic and then, he tells us, he started to read the Bible and decided that the story it tells about the resurrection is true, well founded on evidence that he has found persuasive. But do you believe Gumbel? Lee Strobel argues that we accept the truth of other historical events on much slimmer documentary evidence. Strobel, an investigative journalist in the world of crime, consulted with scholars who approach the stories of Jesus's death and resurrection from medical, historical, theological, and philosophical perspectives and concludes that the evidence is convincing. He concludes that the stories have withstood critical examination and, although he started out as a skeptic, was persuaded of their truth. Francis Collins and Alister McGrath tell their stories of coming to a position of transcendence realism, specifically Christianity, having rejected their previous atheism and coming to accept God as the divine author of a finely tuned universe because of their work as scientists.

John Gray identifies the issue of historical evidence as "the true threat to monotheism," saying that "the real conflict is not between

---

129. Luke 1, NIV.
130. Acts 16:1–5.
131. Ritchie, "Conversation with Nicky Gumbel."

religion and science but between Christianity and history." He concludes that, "if Jesus was not crucified and did not return form the dead, the Christian religion is seriously compromised."[132] The apostle Paul states it even more strongly, saying that "we are of all people most to be pitied" if the resurrection were not historically real and true.[133] However, Gray, unlike Paul, is not persuaded, arguing that the story, like much of the Bible, is myth. It is myth in the best sense of the word, providing a powerful and enduring story that has inspired life-giving and affirming truths. Its value does not depend on it having happened in history in the sense that orthodox Christianity asserts, but in Gray's interpretation religion as myth is not a threat to secular time, in contrast with Paul's claims that challenge Gray's skepticism.

It would be hard to argue that Paul's spiritual descendants, including Gumbel, Strobel, Collins, and McGrath, are not part of the modern world or that they are less sophisticated in their thinking processes than religious skeptics. Paul was certainly a bright guy and well educated in Jewish traditions of thought and in the Hellenistic philosophies ubiquitous in the first century CE. A bit maladjusted, maybe, but he saw something, figured out what it was, and spread the word that has influenced the history of the world. Besides, can you really argue that skeptics do not rely on their own sources of testimony based on a kind of group think or that they are more rational than transcendence realists? And isn't much of the work of education, including RE, the transmission of knowledge derived from testimony and *consensus gentium*?

Rational thinking in religion: A gift of religious literacy

There is lots of evidence that the rationality inherent in scientific thinking has delivered a great many benefits to humanity's welfare. Advances

---

132. Gray, *Seven Types*, 14.

133. The passage reads: "But if it is preached that Christ has been raised from the dead, how can some of you say that there is no resurrection of the dead? If there is no resurrection of the dead, then not even Christ has been raised. And if Christ has not been raised, our preaching is useless and so is your faith. More than that, we are then found to be false witnesses about God, for we have testified about God that he raised Christ from the dead. But he did not raise him if in fact the dead are not raised. For if the dead are not raised, then Christ has not been raised either. And if Christ has not been raised, your faith is futile; you are still in your sins. Then those also who have fallen asleep in Christ are lost. If only for this life we have hope in Christ, we are of all people most to be pitied" (1 Cor 15:12–19, NIV).

in medical technology are so called for good reasons. Our lives are better than the lives of many of our forebears—at least, those of us who are winners in the competition for access to advanced medical technologies. We figured out that cholera and bubonic plague have causes that can be identified, isolated, and addressed by, among other things, clean water, efficient treatment of human waste, and vaccinations. Just think modern dentistry and you need go no further.

There is also lots of evidence of religious thinking that conflicts with and denies science. Some of us still believe that the correct religion can make us immune to COVID-19,[134] the equivalent of some of the human family who believed that the right application of magic could turn bullets into water.[135] The religious leaders who reject the advice of medical experts are engaging in magical thinking that places religion out of reach of other modes of thought. In short, conclusions that religion is irrational have evidence to support them, among which is the magical thinking that includes the idea that Donald Trump is God's agent who is going to make America great again.[136] And it is also true that groups can talk themselves into almost anything, something of which Jon Krakauer and Olga Tokarczuk remind us. *Consensus gentium* is not benign and there is a valuable role for whistleblowers who tell us that our emperors have no clothes, or at least that their clothes cover a multitude of sins they would prefer to keep out of sight.

My point here is that RE and the delivery of religious literacy must include the realities of abuses of power and destructive nonrationality narrated in the language of religion. Bad religious thinking is a thing. However, the marginalization of religion and religious knowing on the basis that religion inherently suffers from a rationality deficit and group think does not withstand critical scrutiny. Religion has its own kind of rationality, in the same way that legal, political, ethical, and any other kind knowing are unique with their own kind of rationality. Religion education programs delivering religious literacy invite students to understand and practice the rationality in religious thought.

---

134. Lewis, "Religious Extremists."
135. TomP, "Maji Maji Rebellion."
136. I am picking on Donald Trump, but similar magical thinking was evident in the support of Barack Obama who was also seen as a political messiah, oversold as someone who would usher in a new world of equality and harmony based on enlightened thinking.

Complication Two: Education, Indoctrination, and the Three Objections to Religion

The distinction between education and indoctrination is often considered a key boundary marker between education about religion and religious education. Education about religion is described as objective, delivering religiously neutral information about which students can then make informed choices. It is represented as true education, as opposed to religious education, religious instruction, and religious indoctrination, which are not truly education because they are seen to reduce student agency and freedom of choice. Indoctrination is associated with coercion while education is not. Religious instruction is associated with exclusion while RE is seen to be inclusive. Religious education is associated with regressive group think and therefore out of step with modernity, which is imagined as a stage of human development in which the rational individual can be fully realized. The legal and regulatory implications include the distinction between public and private education that has further implications for what forms of education are funded and at what levels.

While I question the distinction between RE and indoctrination, I want to consider the issues of pedagogical power and its abuses to which the distinction alerts us. The issues to which it alerts us can be accessed by considering the objection that religion is institutionalized and codified spirituality. In its institutionalized and codified forms, it seems to have greater potential to interfere with education. What I mean is that the purpose of education in liberal societies is to persuade students to make intelligent choices as free-thinking individuals contributing to the social good. In modern liberal societies that place a high, even sacralized value on individual autonomy tempered by rationality to achieve social cohesion, religion and education are, at best, uneasy neighbors.

Education is seen as the way forward in two ways. The first is that education is seen to present students with information and knowledge in an objective manner that respects their freedoms to make rational choices. Second, hope in education depends on students making rational choices that will do no harm, either to themselves or to the social body. However, the representation of education that puts individual rational choice at its center brings us to the conundrum of unintended consequences outlined in chapter 4.

Saba Mahmood and Talal Asad address the problem by contrasting Kantian and Aristotelian models of learning, examining the role of bodily practice in religion and belief. In the Ontario Ministry of Education documents, a shift between 1990 and 2008 includes the adoption of bodily practice as an integral element of students adopting the preferred universal traits of good character. The point is that the distinction between education and indoctrination serves important political purposes of legitimization but cannot withstand closer examination when it is identified as unique to religion and religious knowing.

Religion, education, and public space

This takes us into the distinction between public and private space as a way of managing ambiguities inherent in both religion and education. One way in which the ambiguities around religion have been managed is a social model based on the distinction between the religious and the secular, the boundary between them being identified as private and public space, which is policed in ways that are unique to the jurisdiction in which they happen. In Quebec, for example, people delivering public services are prohibited from wearing religious symbols. In August of 2025, the Quebec government is considering legislation to ban prayers in public spaces to further "strengthen secularism."[137]

Quebec's regulation of religion takes forms unique to its history, but forms of a religious-secular boundary are maintained in all other Canadian jurisdictions in ways unique to them. In Ontario, the distinction between public, separate, and private education are closely linked to religion with important implications for access to public resources. In Alberta, the Hutterian Brethren of Wilson Colony were unsuccessful in their bid for exemption from photo identification requirements for driver licences.[138] Outside Canada, controversies over clothing for women occur in jurisdictions around the world. In short, boundaries around religion depend on a categorical distinction between public and private spaces.

While the boundary markers may be unique to the jurisdictions in which they occur and therefore strange to outsiders, there is less commentary about the boundary itself. In fact, closer examination of the boundary between public and private spaces, like the boundary between religion and the secular and between education and indoctrination,

137. Lapierre, "Quebec Plans," para. 3.
138. Young, "Alberta v. Hutterian Brethren."

tends to reveal ambiguities rather than clarity about the distinctions. Regulation and case law depend on clarity, but the language of regulation and case law often does not reflect the messiness of the family, of neighborhoods, of the classroom.

I question the boundary between public and private spaces, particularly when it is deployed to create boundaries between the religious and secular that are then linked to the distinction between indoctrination and education. My doing so does not ignore the abuses of religion that it is designed to address, which are deeply embedded in the Christian history of liberal societies. However, what also needs critical examination are the networks of power served by doing two things in constructing boundaries between religion and non-religion or the secular, identifying religion as private and the secular as public. One is that institutions and modes of thought, including the boundaries between public and private spaces, are socially constructed rather than universally normative, which is often how they are represented. The other is that the reification of religion as private is seen as normative and, indeed, necessary to the achievement of a modern society. Quebec's Bill 21 is an example of the marginalization of religion as necessary to achieve a preferred social outcome. In Ontario, the rigid boundaries between public, separate, and private education have given public schools a status sacralized by the malleable but powerful concept of secular education that needs to be protected from incursions by religious minorities. The legal and regulatory interpretation of the boundary between public and private spaces can be useful by marginalizing and punishing ways of thought and practice considered intolerable expressions of religious diversity and threats to social harmony. It can also serve to protect institutions and practices seen to deliver values essential to dominant social constructions.

The distinction between the religious and the secular also serves to construct boundaries between what is considered legitimate public knowledge. The distinction between religion and knowledge does several things, including protecting religion from public accountability but it also marginalizes religion as a potential public partner in the delivery of education. The idea that religion generates knowledge is not controversial. What is controversial is the status of the knowledge foregrounded by religion, religion being seen as irrational, exclusive institutionalized spirituality.

I suggest that the distinction between private religious knowledge and secular public knowledge deserves critical attention around two issues. First, considering a more nuanced understanding of literacy we can conclude that information delivered without reference to a meaning narrative is, well, meaningless. It begs the *Why do we have to take this stuff?* question asked by our grade ten students. Instrumental answers to the question only go so far because what students are looking for is where they and their learning fit into a big picture. The Ontario Ministry of Education acknowledges this in its advice to teachers to encourage and embrace big questions. We are back to considering religious literacy, which includes information about religion; knowledge about religious systems of thought; the kind of information and knowledge foregrounded in and by religion; and how ultimate values, loves, and longings work in the lives of individuals, in groups, and in societies. However, wisdom includes leading our students to understand their own religions, by which I mean their ultimate loves and longings. Their lives are enriched when they embrace the multiple registers in which they hear, see, and know the world.

At the same time, teachers live their own religious lives in their teaching. It is their professional duty to be self-aware and self-critical of the source of their moral energy, their sense of right and wrong, their hopes for their students. The work of teachers and schools is faith based and it is public, as I argued in chapter 4, in any educational endeavor. That, I am saying, blurs the distinction between public and private space and the layering of secular and religious on top of that distinction. Further, it makes religion and religious literacy matters of public interest, even as they are embodied in deeply personal and private ways.

Education's religion

Literacy and religious literacy projects are always framed in terms of a preferred outcome as a proper way of critically engaging religion, to promote forms of religion that encourage inclusivity as opposed to exclusivity. This is not unique to religion, of course. All education is a form of enculturation in which we draw our students into a way of seeing the world. Religion education is no different in the sense that we want our students to see and understand religion in a particular way. Education is animated by big questions of meaning and purpose, both for the individuals engaged in it and for society.

The distinction between education and indoctrination places teachers in an impossible situation when they are expected to deliver information about religion in an objective manner.[139] Linda Wertheimer, researching RE in Minneha School, says, "I sensed tension between teachers' deep fondness for their faith and the goal to treat several religions equally."[140] Affect theory encourages us to think in nuanced ways about the educational process in religion, with a conclusion that teachers do not leave their religious selves at the door of their classrooms.[141] Educators are guided by a preferred graduate profile that is anything but neutral. If, as I am arguing, one gift of religious literacy is that it equips students to be intentional about their meaning narratives, they are guided by teachers who have a preferred future for them based on their own transcendent meaning narratives. Teachers are passionate about how their students move into their futures and all of us who have been in the business for a while have heart-breaking stories of students who committed suicide or in other ways engaged in self-destruction. We want them to commit themselves to lives energized by a big story and redemptive activity. Teachers model for their students a life marked by hope and purpose, which blurs the distinction between indoctrination and education.

Education and indoctrination: A problem of pedagogical power rather than religion

In conclusion, the distinctions between education and indoctrination and between education about religion and religious education are less clear than their representation in law and in education politics. Linking the distinction between education and indoctrination to religion is a distraction from the issue of pedagogical power, which is inherent in the relationship between teachers and students. Of course, teachers in religion need to be critically aware of their use of power, but so do teachers in history, the sciences, technology, athletics, and any other academic discipline. Education's religion can be seen in legal and regulatory frameworks, policy, and program documents, in classroom practices, in lessons, and assessment and evaluation tools. We believe in our students'

---

139. Gravel, "Impartiality"; Breen, "Teachers' Approaches."

140. Wertheimer, *Faith Ed.*, 110.

141. Ellis, *Politics*; Watkins, "Gauging"; Jafralie and Zaver, "Teaching Religious Education."

futures, and we are distressed when they leave the straight path, however defined and imagined. However, we also live with the ambiguities in the pedagogical embrace that accepts the "underdetermination of the outcome."[142] The illusion of determination of outcome is the abuse of pedagogical power, the temptation inherent in any educational endeavor.

CONCLUSION

In this chapter I have argued that RE, designed to deliver religious literacy, leads students to distinguish two broad areas of educational concern. The first of these is the human capacity to reach for, imagine, and construct meaning narratives around a point of either vertical or horizontal transcendence. The second topic is the astonishing diversity in the ways meaning narratives are constructed. Although the ways in which religion is embodied are socially constructed, the human capacity to do so is not.

Religious literacy includes consideration of the objections to religion and the abuses of power narrated in the language of religion. However, it also includes the context in which abuses of power are narrated so that students are equipped to distinguish between religion as a human capacity and it embodied expressions. This is not unique to religion, of course, since the same problem presents itself in other academic disciplines.

Religious literacy includes disciplined consideration of what it means to think well in religion. What this means is the ability to see the world our students navigate in terms of the ultimate values and commitments animating their everyday worlds. The two gifts of religious literacy for our students include the ability to see the religious problematics of the everyday world and of their own spirit quests. In that sense, religious literacy is one kind of literacy among others enriching their critical thinking capacities and their abilities to love deeply and intentionally.

The case for religious literacy includes the development of civic skills and attitudes equipping our students to live well in the societies in which they find themselves and it may encourage commitment to a particular transcendence narrative. However, for religious literacy to achieve its promise as a partner in generating public wisdom, it must be based on a definition of religion as a universal shared human capacity that generates its own unique nested story about the world and our spirit quests in our brief journey in time and space.

142. Volf, *Embrace*, 150.

7

Education as a Spiritual Exercise

I hope you have a vision of life that will sustain you in the moments on the pavement. There will likely be a day when the world stops, and your heart breaks and you will need a vision of a life worth living that can survive the storm. Surely, your vision will be deepened, transformed, sharpened by the days on the pavement, but I hope your vision already has a compass that can orient you or, better yet, an anchor that will hold you.

—Miroslav Volf et al., *Life Worth Living*

She also explained the purpose of religion and how people used it today to answer questions that may seem unanswerable, such as "Why do we die?"

—Linda Wertheimer, *Faith Ed.*

It's not that unbelief shuns Christian ideas of fullness for nothing at all; it has its own versions. The swirling debate between belief and unbelief as well as between different versions of each, can therefore be seen as a debate about what real fullness consists in.

—Charles Taylor, *A Secular Age*

Here are two education and literacy questions:
    What is the chief end of man?

EDUCATION AS A SPIRITUAL EXERCISE

And, What is your only comfort in life and in death?

A traditional answer to the first one is, "Man's chief end is to glorify God, and to enjoy Him forever," while the answer to the second one is,

> That I am not my own, but belong with body and soul, both in life and in death, to my faithful Savior Jesus Christ.
>
> He has fully paid for all my sins with his precious blood and has set me free from all the power of the devil.
>
> He also preserves me in such a way that without the will of my heavenly Father not a hair can fall from my head; indeed, all things must work together for my salvation.
>
> Therefore, by his Holy Spirit, he also assures me of eternal life and makes me heartily willing and ready from now on to live for him.

No doubt you recognize the source of the first as the Westminster Shorter Catechism[1] and the second as the Heidelberg Catechism.[2] OK, we usually do not think of them as school questions but I am inviting you to consider their implications for education and for religious literacy. Here's why.

Religious literacy lives at the intersection of religion as a human capacity and its innumerable embodied forms. Focus on its embodied social practices and beliefs in the social sciences and theology has distracted consideration of religion as a way of knowing and a source of public wisdom. Seen through the lens of the social sciences, its embodied forms are often expressed in language, metaphors, and practices that seem archaic and anachronistic in a modern imaginary. Theological frameworks for religion, especially its theistic forms, engage questions, concerns, and arguments that seem to have little relevance for the stuff of everyday life or that could as well be addressed without reference to religion.

Many of us do not reference *my faithful Savior Jesus Christ* as we consider the meaning of our life and death. Among other things, the traditions in which the catechisms are located carry a lot of cultural and historical baggage. For example, the Westminster Catechism asks about the *chief end of man*, using gender-exclusive language that leaves out about half of humanity. Further, Canadian leaders who subscribed to it as fundamental to their faith also designed and operated residential schools for indigenous children with their terrible consequences. The Heidelberg Catechism was recited by Dutch Calvinists who also designed the colonial

1. Bible Presbyterian Church, "Westminster," Q1.
2. Christian Reformed Church, "Heidelberg," Q&A 1.

policies that have left their dreadful legacy in South Africa and Southeast Asia. Both find inspiration in the writings of the great apostle Paul who argues that women should keep quiet in assembly and slaves should obey their masters, cheerfully. In short, there is much about institutionalized theological traditions and sacred texts that lead some of us to walk away from religion.[3] There are good reasons to doubt the relevance of religion in a modern, progressive imaginary and even to see it as an impediment to social harmony.

However, critical reconsideration of and skepticism about religion in its codified and embodied forms does not address questions about our chief end and our only comfort in life and in death. Their embodied forms take us to socially constructed and historically specific answers to the questions but not to the questions themselves. Charles Taylor refers to "conceptions of our ethical predicament," asking the question of whether "materialist reductionism" can account for "our being active, creative agents; our being moral subjects; our ability to respond to beauty." Taylor agrees that we can find "space for our esthetic experience (for both beauty and the sublime) within an immanentist ontology; in the case of Dawkins and Hamilton, even a materialist one," but, he adds, "only in part."[4]

In the Allahabad Address delivered in 1930, Muhammad Iqbal says something similar when he argues for the legitimacy of the theory of evolution to explain the mechanisms of life. His purpose in delivering the lectures was to address the apparent conflict between traditional Islam and modern ways of thinking about how the world works, specifically the theory of evolution. His argument that the theory of evolution has its roots in Islam is not entirely persuasive, but he does address a point like one made by others. The point is that the purpose of life and death are matters that elude mechanistic explanations. In other words, the theory of evolution can explain the world but, in Taylor's words, "only in part."

---

3. There are important questions of interpretation in reading Paul's letters, including understanding the context, which allows us to distinguish between what is case specific from the universal principles he is developing. Paul, and any ancient text, is easy to misunderstand because his twenty-first-century readers are reading someone else's mail. His letters were responses to requests for advice about specific situations, so we are stepping into a longer conversation, most of which refers to problems that seem quite alien to us. So, it takes some patient reading and consulting with other sources, including scholars who know a lot more about this than I do, to do justice to what Paul is saying here. So, when you are reading him, hang in there. There is good stuff there. Not unlike Shakespeare, for example.

4. Taylor, *Secular Age*, 604–7.

The problem with mechanistic explanations being asked to do more than they can is that they become traps of necessity. Iqbal says, "Prayer in Islam is the ego's escape from mechanism to freedom."[5] His point is that human life and the human ego find true freedom only by transcending the mechanisms of necessity of *chronos* time, including death. The human quest for freedom is more than a struggle for political and social space, important as those are. Freedom is more profoundly a quest to transcend *chronos* time and experience *kairotic* time, those moments of meaning in relationship to eternity or to that which truly lasts.

In her examination of religious appropriation, Liz Bucar argues that we cannot fully understand the meaning of our practices without reference to their transcendent origins. Her assessment of the detachment of *yoga*, the *Camino de Santiago*, and the *niqab* from their religious roots and sources of meaning suggests that their therapeutic uses reflect understanding of their purposes only in part. Here my point is that it is deeply and fundamentally human to conceptualize beauty and the sublime and ultimate questions of meaning and purpose. The answers to our questions and our understanding of the source and meaning of beauty and the sublime can be formulated within a vertical or horizontal framework but the point is that we are wired to consider them.

Here's another answer to questions of ultimate meaning and destiny: "He who dies with the most toys wins." This one, attributed to Malcolm Forbes, might have been ironic but there is evidence in our consumer-driven, free-market, increasingly predatory capitalist model of society that it isn't.[6] Here the answer to our great questions, the point of life and the evaluation of a successful life, our chief end you might say, is the accumulation of wealth and the things to which wealthy people have access.

Common definitions of the term *religion* take us to the answers, in the forms of confessions and practices, but not to the questions that inspire the answers. Common definitions, with their focus on embodied forms of religion, have tended to marginalize consideration of the universal human capacity to ask questions about our only comfort that remains after everything else has been stripped away by illness, death, or the realization that our striving has not brought us happiness and satisfaction. We do not have to wait for extreme circumstances for the

---

5. Iqbal, *Reconstruction*, 87.
6. Forbes, "My Father," para. 20.

questions to emerge. Our students really do wonder what they are doing here on this earth. We want them to weep with Lady Macbeth's crisis as she cries "out, damned spot, out,"[7] and we want them to be enchanted by the laws of thermodynamics in a way that opens up worlds of meaning and purpose about which they wonder. OK, I know that sometimes we are just getting through a lesson, but still, every encounter has the potential to open up worlds of possibility to see beyond.

I understand Timothy McCowan to be getting at a distinction between questions as universal and socially constructed answers that are, by the very fact of their being socially constructed, more provisional when he says, "Even if not all agree with the conclusions, these ultimate questions need to be asked as part of one's education: why are we here, what is the purpose to life, how can humans live together harmoniously, and what do humans share in common?"[8]

Christopher Watkin proposes a model for critical thought he calls *biblical critical theory* based on his reading of the Bible, including creation, the fall into sin, and the life, death, and resurrection of Jesus Christ. Christian models of reality have been enormously influential in the ways we think about the world, but they are not the only ones out there (obviously). Watkin proposes one theory in a particular historical context to universal questions, among them the meaning of our lives in time, the nature of time, and the problem of living well in a network of power relations that demand our ultimate allegiances and commitments.

Watkin's is a socially constructed framework of answers to universal questions, in a Christian tradition of critical thought. He may not agree with the assessment that it is particular and socially constructed, his book suggesting that the Bible and his reading of it is the one source of universal truth. I have not talked with him, so I don't know, but that's not the problem I am addressing here. Not being an evangelist or an apologist, I leave the question about the Bible or any other sacred text as an ultimate source of truth to others to debate. What I am arguing is that the problems of living well, among which are questions of ultimate meaning and destiny, are universal. And I am arguing that the capacity to ask universal questions and to offer answers is at the heart of religion as an analytical category.

---

7. Shakespeare, *Macbeth*, 5.1.37.
8. McCowan, "Bridges," 12–13.

I am not advocating for a particular answer to the question about my only comfort in life and death and my chief end although, having grown up in a Christian subtradition, the answer given in the Heidelberg Catechism has guided and anchored me, increasingly so as I have aged. At the same time, the answers that have enriched my life are not universal, despite what my more committed Christian friends assert. While I do not doubt that Christianity has its unique contribution to religion, I do not share the confidence of some of my coreligionists that Christianity provides the only answers to the universal human problem of living well in time and space.

However, I am committed to the idea that the questions that sparked great (and not so great) texts are universal and central to the conceptualization and delivery of literacy. Religion education and religious literacy live in the liminal space between questions and their answers. When restricted to only the questions, religious literacy loses its relevance, remaining a matter of philosophical speculation detached from our bodied realities or detached observation of interesting human behavior. When restricted to only the answers, religious literacy becomes relevant only to those within the tribe for whom they have provided a way of navigating time, space, and relationships or to anyone interested in observing or managing religious diversity.

EDUCATION, LITERACY, AND THE GREAT COMMANDMENT

Another example of the difference in status between a question and its answer is found in a story told in the Gospel written by Matthew. The context is Matthew's account of a debate between Jesus and the Pharisees, the religious authorities of his day. The question posed is, "Teacher, what is the great commandment in the law?" Jesus's answer is, "'Love the Lord your God with all your heart and with all your soul and with all your mind.' This is the first and greatest commandment. And the second is like it: 'Love your neighbor as yourself.' All the Law and the Prophets hang on these two commandments."[9]

While it would be easy to dismiss this exchange as religious and therefore irrelevant to education, the general acceptance of the *Golden Rule* (Do unto others as you would have done unto you) calls for a more

---

9. Matt 22:36–40, NIV.

nuanced reaction. The element to which I draw your attention is the more general pedagogical issue and its implications for literacy. Here's the thing: the question here is asked in a particular historical context and the answer speaks to that context. The Bible, like many ancient texts, was not written for a twenty-first-century audience so understanding it takes time and a kind of patient, silent listening. Besides the obvious Golden Rule answer, I suggest that the question is one driving all literacy projects. The question for education is, What is the great commandment on which all our learning depends for its meaning? Roy Rappaport's *hierarchy of values* is getting at the same thing.[10] The question, in other words, is universal while the answers are socially constructed in particular historical and social contexts because we do not encounter the universal questions in the abstract. The earth itself speaks to us, with both great possibilities and limitations.

Another way of saying it is that students need to be aware of the great commandment, the deepest loves and the longings driving the society in which they are members, and of their own deepest loves and longings. The great commandment summarized in the Gospel of Matthew is not, in the first place, about a list of demands and restrictions. There are demands and restrictions, but they find their meaning in love (of God and of neighbor). The question for education is, What is the great love animating all the demands and expectations inherent in learning and in life? The question is universal, even if we land in different places in our answers. The question is key to the sacramental nature of all of reality and to the idea of *learning as a spiritual exercise*. All reality is sacramental in the sense that it calls for a response animated by a great commandment. The spirituality of education is that it guides students toward a great commandment. We don't all see the great commandment in the same way, but we are all guided by one.

CONCLUDING THOUGHTS

Being an educator and an academic I have wondered about the implications for education and literacy of the distinction between question and answer. Religion education framed by the social sciences to achieve civic

---

10. Rappaport, *Ritual*, 426. Rappaport illustrates this by describing the difference between American and Chinese understandings of the meaning context of wheat farming. While at the lower levels wheat farming is what it is, a path of reasoning takes one to the level of *ideology* as the source of its meaning in the universe and in society.

skills and values, on the one hand, and a particular theological tradition, on the other, have been unsatisfying because they do not sufficiently engage a further question about the public implications of both the question and its answer. Public policy is designed to deliver a good society in which the fully realized person can find a home. However, definitions of a good society and the fully realized human being occur within a framework of meaning and destiny. We guide our students toward a fully realized life, and we want them to engage with a good society, contributing to it and resisting the decisions, practices and institutions that represent outcomes we do not want. We want them to embrace some answers to the questions of their chief end and we want them to doubt others. We want them to embrace a great commandment that will give their moral framework its coherence and we want them to reject other, competing commandments.

Religious literacy includes sophisticated thinking about how answers are developed and the human capacity to ask them. We want our students to embrace a tradition of answers so they are not left without a reliable conceptual platform on which they can base their life decisions but, paradoxically, we also want them to be able to take critical distance from that tradition so they can make intelligent choices about what they will embrace and what needs to be modified or even rejected. This comes close to what others have described as a stance of objectivity although objectivity suggests a lack of detachment about outcomes and commitments that does not reflect the ways in which education actually works. Religious literacy at its best is love with wise intelligence that takes a lifetime to acquire, with teachers serving as partners and guides in laying a foundation for that lifelong learning.

There are developmental issues to be considered in taking our students into the liminal space between doubt and belief that are not the subject of this book. Educators meet their students at stages of development in their life journeys, shaping their content and strategies to appropriately meet the needs of the students under their care. However, teachers nurturing students at every stage of development work with an end in mind that they will likely never see. As a general principle, students need a platform of belief from which to engage their critical thought. They need to believe before they can doubt. Education, including RE, is animated by faith that students will achieve intelligent, loving wisdom that includes critical awareness of evil, however attractively packaged, and a firm platform of belief and hope. Religion education and religious literacy live at the intersection of deep commitments and critical thinking. Living well in that space is one of the things that keeps teachers awake at night and is, also, the best thing imaginable when we see our students on the straight path through it.

I have argued that religious literacy is an important component of critical thought in the sense that it equips our students to see the meaning story told by the everyday things in their lives. That includes contest and conflict over human rights, the distribution of resources, and the networks of power within which things are decided. Contest and conflict in society can usually be traced to ultimate values and concerns.

In Canada, the discovery of unmarked graves at residential schools has been traumatic evidence that the achievement of a European-style society involved the destruction of Indigenous ways of life, wisdom, and social practices. This was not just because Europeans did not like the indigenous peoples who were on the land long before those fateful Atlantic Ocean voyages. Dislike may have been a factor, and probably was, but not necessarily in the personal, individual sense we usually think of it. Rather, the point is that Indigenous people were in the way of what was imagined as a good society and had to be removed, destroyed if necessary, including by the weaponization of education. The fully realized human being in the new society imagined by Europeans was not an Indigenous man or woman but a European one of a particular class, religion, and gender. The engagement between Europeans and Indigenous people was a mortal combat over land, the ideal society, and who was fully human. Matters of ultimate value and concern, you might say. Our students need to know the details but equally important, they need to know the deep spiritual commitments that gave the details their meaning and energy. We need to do better but doing better must be animated by repentance, a fundamental reorientation of our deepest values. Repentance is the process by which we embrace the other.

I have argued that religion lives in that place of ultimate concerns and values on which we build our lives. In that sense, religion is not some category living off by itself in a parallel, private universe that we tolerate as long as it stays there. While we make personal decisions in our spirit quests about ultimate values and concerns, the distinction between our private and public realities and our religious and secular selves may be less meaningful than is sometimes suggested. While education's religion means that matters of ultimate concern and value add analytical depth to each discipline, RE is where our students get to think religiously—that is, drawing their attention to the universal human capacity to ask the big questions, thinking critically about the big questions.

CONCLUDING QUESTIONS

My questions for my academic and professional colleagues are, Are our education systems and practices equipped to honor the spiritual nature of what we do in our schools? What are the public implications in education for our chief-end, only-comfort, and greatest-commandment questions?

Can we think of our education practices as spirit-quest guidance and, if they are, can we consider the implications for our categorizing some schools as faith schools in contrast with secular schools? Within school programs, does the distinction between religious and secular subject areas make sense? Does it mean that some of our subjects do not engage the questions of ultimate meaning, that the big questions are restricted to RE? Does that mean that some subjects are essentially meaningless or, at best, important only because of their instrumental outcomes such as getting a job? Don't we want our students to *get a life* that includes jobs and professions but also so much more? Or do we marginalize this most essential capacity in our students to suggest that their spirit quests are private and therefore of little public interest? Are we prepared to equip them to read their cultures and their worlds as embodiments of a collective spirit quest? And then guide them as they test ideas, different formulations of answers to the big questions, walk with them as part of our own spirit quests, so they emerge as loving critical thinkers, even if it leads them to become difficult citizens?

The arguments here beg the question of where, in schools, religious literacy should be delivered. At risk of over simplifying, there are two options. The first model is that RE could be seen as a discrete subject area, like maths or history. The second is if it could be considered an across-the-curriculum subject that deserves consideration in all other subject areas. While the specifics, including developmental issues, are not the subject of this book, I would argue for both. I am going to draw on *language* to illustrate. Should *language* be taught as a discrete subject or is it more broadly across the curriculum? Well, both, of course. Students need to be taught the basic rules of spelling and grammar, but those same rules will be reinforced in other subject areas.[11] Effective writing is a discrete

---

11. A note on limitations here: I am writing here in the English-speaking Canadian

subject involving training in specific skills, but a poorly written essay on the French Revolution needs attention, not only to the ideas at play but also to the matter of clear writing and logical thought. Similarly, students might need discrete classes in *ethics*, but the principles learned there will be reinforced across the curriculum and in noninstructional activities.

Religion, the human capacity to seek answers to ultimate questions, shows up in socially constructed forms with which students need familiarity, which can be delivered in discrete classes. It is also an organizational and communal stance, any school having its religious esthetic. Teachers, administrators, regulators, and school staff are energized by the hope that students in their care will adopt preferred lives, values, and practices, which will be reinforced across the curriculum and in noninstructional activities. Office staff, for example, greet students in distress with kindness and care, custodial staff keep the plant clean and functioning efficiently, bus drivers, being the first school staff students see in the morning, honor their passengers by modelling preferred social and civic skills, including careful and responsible driving practices. Why? Because they are all part of the scaffolding of care that students see, hear, experience, and, hopefully, adopt. We usually do not think of these activities as religious but, in fact, they are evidence of the ultimate values and concerns of schools. Teachers in science share their wonder and amazement at the structure of molecules but they also are storytellers in a great story evident in what they teach about those molecules and what they mean in the lives of their students and their world. Religion, in short, is both the legitimate subject of disciplined investigation and an interpretive category through which we see the world.

Our students are crying out for standing stones to guide them through what often seems like a trackless wilderness of information. Or a wilderness with too many tracks created by influencers presenting themselves as sources of true wisdom. This is not a new problem, as we hear in the question posed by the psalmist: "How shall the young direct their way? What light shall be their perfect guide?" The answer—"Your word, O Lord, will safely lead, if in its wisdom they confide"[12]—will not be the

---

context where spelling and grammar are necessary, given the vagaries of the English language. There are rules but the exceptions have been the source of frustration, confusion, and irritation to untold numbers of students. My friends in other jurisdictions view this with curiosity, enjoying more rational and predictable linguistic patterns. I also grew up in a pre-autocorrect world, in which proper grammar and spelling marked the educated (and civilized?) person.

12. "How Shall the Young."

one for all of us but the question is another universal one that continues to animate education and literacy projects. School systems are designed to guide students along a straight path to a life-giving end. That's education's religion and it is what makes education a spiritual exercise.

Bibliography

Acquah, Andrews. "Phenomenological Approach to the Teaching of Religious Education: Sharing Knowledge to Benefit Religious Educators." *Journal of Philosophy, Culture and Religion* 29 (2017) 7–11.

Agrama, Hussein Ali. *Questioning Secularism: Islam, Sovereignty and the Rule of Law in Modern Egypt*. Chicago Studies in Practices of Meaning. Chicago: University of Chicago Press, 2012.

Alberta Education. "What Is Literacy?" https://education.alberta.ca/literacy-and-numeracy/literacy/everyone/what-is-literacy/.

Alberta, Tim. *The Kingdom, the Power, and the Glory: American Evangelicals in an Age of Extremism*. New York: Harper-Collins, 2023.

Ambedkar, Bhimrao Ramji. *The Annihilation of Caste*. New Delhi: Rupa, 2018.

American Academy of Religion (AAR). "AAR Religious Literacy Guidelines." Updated October 3, 2019. https://aarweb.org/resource/aar-religious-literacy-guidelines-2/.

Anderson, Benedict. *Imagined Communities*. London: Verso, 2006.

Arendt, Hannah. *Eichmann in Jerusalem: A Report on the Banality of Evil*. New York: Penguin, 1994.

Ark Encounter. "The Door: The Ark and the Good News." https://arkencounter.com/about/good-news/.

Armstrong, Karen. *The Battle for God*. New York: Random House, 2000.

———. *A History of God: The 4000-Year Quest of Judaism, Christianity and Islam*. New York: Ballantine, 1993.

Asad, Talal. *Formations of the Secular: Christianity, Islam, Modernity*. Cultural Memory in the Present. Stanford: Stanford University Press, 2003.

———. *Genealogies of Religion: Discipline and Reasons of Power in Christianity and Islam*. Baltimore: Johns Hopkins University Press, 1993.

Asad, Talal, et al. *Is Critique Secular? Blasphemy, Injury and Free Speech*. Berkeley: University of California Press, 2009.

Augustine. *The City of God*. New York: Modern Library, 1950.

Baggott, Jim. "What Einstein Meant by 'God Does Not Play Dice.'" Edited by Nigel Warburton. Aeon, November 21, 2018. https://aeon.co/ideas/what-einstein-meant-by-god-does-not-play-dice.

Barna Group. "Meet Those Who 'Love Jesus but Not the Church.'" March 30, 2017. https://www.barna.com/research/meet-love-jesus-not-church/.

Barnes, L. Philip. *Education, Religion and Diversity: Developing a New Model of Religious Education*. London: Routledge, 2014.

———. "Time for a New Model RE." *Guardian*, March 16, 2009. https://www.theguardian.com/commentisfree/2009/mar/11/religious-education-religion.

Basden, Andrew. "A Presentation of Herman Dooyeweerd's Aspects of Temporal Reality." *International Journal of Multi-Aspectual Practice* 1 (2011) 1–28. https://www.researchgate.net/profile/Andrew-Basden/publication/266279899_A_Presentation_of_Herman_Dooyeweerd%27s_Aspects_of_Temporal_Reality/links/55b250e908aec0e5f4317a89/A-Presentation-of-Herman-Dooyeweerds-Aspects-of-Temporal-Reality.pdf.

Bayefsky, Anne, and Arieh Waldman. *State Support for Religious Education: Canada Versus the United Nations*. Studies in Religion, Secular Beliefs and Human Rights 3. Leiden: Brill, 2006.

BBC. "What's Taking the Knee and Why Is It Important?" November 21, 2022. https://www.bbc.com/news/explainers-53098516.

Beaman, Lori G. *Deep Equality in an Era of Religious Diversity*. Oxford: Oxford University Press, 2017.

———. *Defining Harm: Religious Freedom and the Limits of the Law*. Law and Society. Vancouver: University of British Columbia Press, 2008.

———, ed. *Reasonable Accommodation: Managing Religious Diversity*. Vancouver: University of British Columbia Press, 2012.

———. *The Transition of Religion to Culture in Law and Public Discourse*. ICLARS Series on Law And Religion. London: Routledge, 2020.

Becker, Carl L. *The Heavenly City of the Eighteenth-Century Philosophers*. New Haven: Yale University Press, 1967.

Becker, Ernest. *The Denial of Death*. New York: Simon & Schuster, 1997.

Beckford, James A. *Religion and Advanced Industrial Society*. Routledge Library Editions: Sociology of Religion 9. Abingdon, UK: Routledge, 2019.

———. *Social Theory and Religion*. Cambridge: Cambridge University Press, 2003.

Bennett, Andrew. *The Bible and Us: Canadians and Their Relationship with Scripture*. Ontario, Can.: Cardus, 2023. https://biblesociety.ca/wp-content/uploads/2023/05/CBS_Cardus_Report_2023_The_Bible_and_Us.pdf.

Berger, Benjamin L. *Law's Religion: Religious Difference and the Claims of Constitutionalism*. Toronto: University of Toronto Press, 2015.

Berger, Peter. *The Sacred Canopy: Elements of a Sociological Theory of Religion*. New York: Random House, 1967.

Berger, Peter, and Anton Zijderveld. *In Praise of Doubt: How to Have Convictions Without Becoming a Fanatic*. New York: HarperOne, 2009.

Beyer, Peter. *Religions in Global Society*. London: Routledge, 2006.

Bible Presbyterian Church. "Westminster Shorter Catechism." https://bpc.org/shorter-catechism.

Bick, Angela Reitsma, and Peter Schuurman. *Blessed Are the Undone: Testimonies of the Quiet Deconstruction of Faith in Canada*. Saskatoon: New Leaf, 2024.

Biesta, Gert, et al. *Religious Literacy: A Way Forward for Religious Education?* London: Culham St. Gabriel's Trust, Brunel University London, and Hampshire Inspection and Advisory Service, 2019. https://www.reonline.org.uk/news/religious-literacy-a-way-forward-for-religious-education/.

BIBLIOGRAPHY

Blake, William. "Auguries of Innocence." Poets.org. https://poets.org/poem/auguries-innocence.

Bloom, Allan. *The Closing of the American Mind: How Higher Education Has Failed Democracy and Impoverished the Souls of Today's Students*. New York: Simon & Schuster, 1987.

Bloom, Colin. *The Bloom Review: Does Government "Do God"? An Independent Review of How Government Engages with Faith*. London, 2023. https://assets.publishing.service.gov.uk/media/64478b4f529eda00123b0397/The_Bloom_Review.pdf.

Bloomberg News. "China Honors Whistle-Blowing Doctor Whose Death Fueled Anger." March 5, 2020. https://www.bloomberg.com/news/articles/2020-03-05/china-honors-whistle-blowing-doctor-whose-death-fueled-anger.

Bosco, Robert M. *Securing the Sacred: Religion, National Security, and the Western State*. Ann Arbor: University of Michigan Press, 2014.

Bouma, Gary, and Anna Halafoff. "Multifaith Education and Social Inclusion in Australia." *Journal of Religious Education* 57 (2009) 17–25.

Bourdieu, Pierre, and Jean-Claude Passeron. *Reproduction in Education, Society and Culture*. Translated by Richard Nice. 2nd ed. Theory, Culture & Society. Thousand Oaks: Sage, 1990.

Brean, Joseph. "Jim Keegstra, Holocaust Denier Who Took Hate Speech Battle to Supreme Court, Dead at 80." National Post, June 13, 2014. https://nationalpost.com/news/canada/jim-keegstra-holocaust-denier-who-took-hate-speech-battle-to-supreme-court-dead-at-80.

Breen, Tim. "Teachers' Approaches to, and Experiences with, World Religions in the Grade 8 Social Studies Curriculum." MA thesis, University of Manitoba, 2015. https://mspace.lib.umanitoba.ca/server/api/core/bitstreams/cec8d950-2626-47b5-bcc5-a1e3cc8bdf75/content.

Brown, Sanger, II. *The Sex Worship and Symbolism of Primitive Races: An Interpretation*. Boston: Badger, 1916. Produced by Bryan Ness et al. Project Gutenberg, 2009. https://www.gutenberg.org/ebooks/30750.

Brown, Wendy. *Regulating Aversion: Tolerance in the Age of Identity and Empire*. Princeton: Princeton University Press, 2006.

Buber, Martin. *Between Man and Man*. Translated by Ronald Gregor Smith. New York: Collier, 1965.

Bucar, Liz. *Stealing My Religion: Not Just Any Cultural Appropriation*. Cambridge: Harvard University Press, 2022.

Bulka, Reuven. "It's a Matter of Fairness." *National Post*, August 29, 2007. https://nationalpost.newspapers.com/newspage/514183018/.

Bullard, Gabe. "The World's Newest Major Religion: No Religion." *National Geographic*, April 22, 2016. https://www.nationalgeographic.com/culture/article/160422-atheism-agnostic-secular-nones-rising-religion.

Bullivant, Stephen, et al. *Understanding Unbelief: Atheists and Agnostics Around the World*. Tuckenman, UK: St. Mary's University, 2019. https://www.stmarys.ac.uk/research/centres/benedict-xvi/docs/benedict-centre-understanding-unbelief-report.pdf.

Burlington Post. "March Through Downtown Burlington Honoured Animal Rights Activist Struck and Killed by Pig Transport Truck." Inside Halton, August 9, 2020. https://www.insidehalton.com/news/march-through-downtown-burlington-honoured-animal-rights-activist-struck-and-killed-by-pig-transport-truck/article_a0c38059-8d59-58d2-96d2-9798fad36814.html?.

Cadrin-Pelletier, Christine, et al. *Secular Schools in Québec: A Necessary Change in Institutional Culture*. Québec: Ministère de l'Éducation, du Loisir et du Sport, 2007. https://www.education.gouv.qc.ca/fileadmin/site_web/documents/ministere/organismes/CAR_Avis_LaiciteScolaire_ang.pdf.

Canadian Museum of Nature. "Water Gallery." https://nature.ca/en/visit-us/whats-on/listing/water-gallery/.

Carpenter, Joel, et al., eds. *Christian Higher Education: A Global Reconnaissance*. Grand Rapids: Eerdmans, 2014.

Carwana, Brian. "Emotions, Politics & Religion—with Donovan Schaefer." Religions Geek, January 28, 2021. https://religionsgeek.com/index.php/2021/01/28/emotions-politics-religion-with-donovan-schaefer/.

———. "How Religious Literacy Helps Us See One Another." Religions Geek, February 11, 2021. https://religionsgeek.com/index.php/2021/02/11/how-religious-literacy-helps-us-see-one-another/.

Casanova, José. *Public Religions in the Modern World*. Chicago: University of Chicago Press, 1994.

Cavanaugh, William. *The Myth of Religious Violence: Secular Ideology and the Roots of Modern Conflicts*. Oxford: University of Oxford Press, 2009.

CBC News. "Teen Offers 'Heartfelt' Apology for Urinating on National War Memorial." July 7, 2006. https://www.cbc.ca/news/canada/ottawa/teen-offers-heartfelt-apology-for-urinating-on-national-war-memorial-1.573944.

Centers for Disease Control (CDC). "Firearm Mortality." August 20, 2025. https://www.cdc.gov/nchs/state-stats/deaths/firearms.html?CDC_AAref_Val=https://www.cdc.gov/nchs/pressroom/sosmap/firearm_mortality/firearm.htm.

———. "The Untreated Syphilis Study at Tuskegee Timeline." September 4, 2024. https://www.cdc.gov/tuskegee/about/timeline.html?CDC_AAref_Val=https://www.cdc.gov/tuskegee/timeline.htm.

Chamberlin, J. Edward. *If This Is Your Land, Where Are Your Stories? Reimagining Home and Sacred Space*. Cleveland: Pilgrim, 2003.

Chan, W. Y Alice, et al. "Recognition of Context and Experience: A Civic-Based Canadian Conception of Religious Literacy." *Journal of Beliefs and Values* 41 (2020) 255–71. https://www.tandfonline.com/doi/full/10.1080/13617672.2019.1587902.

Christian Aboriginal Infrastructure Developments (CAID). "An Act to Amend and Consolidate the Laws Respecting Indians." April 12, 1876. https://caid.ca/IndAct1876.pdf.

———. "An Act to Encourage the Gradual Civilization of the Indian Tribes in This Province, and to Amend the Laws Respecting Indians." June 10, 1857. https://caid.ca/GraCivAct1857.pdf.

Christian Reformed Church. "Heidelberg Catechism." https://www.crcna.org/welcome/beliefs/confessions/heidelberg-catechism.

Clark, Kelly James, and Andrew Samuel. "Morality and Happiness." In *Evidence and Religious Belief*, edited by Kelly Clark and Raymond J. VanArragon, 157–74. Oxford: Oxford University Press, 2011.

Clark, Kelly James, and Raymond J. VanArragon, eds. *Evidence and Religious Belief*. Oxford: Oxford University Press, 2011.

BIBLIOGRAPHY

Clarke, Charles, and Linda Woodhead. *A New Settlement: Religion and Belief in Schools*. Westminster Faith Debates, 2015. https://faithdebates.org.uk/files/wp-content/uploads/2015/06/a-new-settlement-for-religion-and-belief-in-schools-2.pdf.

———. *A New Settlement Revised: Religion and Belief in Schools*. Westminster Faith Debates, 2018. https://faithdebates.org.uk/files/wp-content/uploads/2018/07/clarke-woodhead-a-new-settlement-revised.pdf.

Cohn, Lindsay, et al. "This Is What Was So Unusual About the U.S. Navy Making Captain Brett Crozier Step Down." *Washington Post*, April 5, 2020. https://www.washingtonpost.com/politics/2020/04/05/this-is-what-was-so-unusual-about-us-navy-making-captain-brett-crozier-step-down/.

Cohn, Norman. *The Pursuit of the Millennium*. Rev. ed. New York: Oxford University Press, 1970.

Collins, Francis S. *The Language of God: A Scientist Presents Evidence for Belief*. New York: Free, 2006.

Commission on Religious Education (CORE). *Religion and Worldviews: The Way Forward; A National Plan for RE*. 2018. https://www.commissiononre.org.uk/wp-content/uploads/2018/09/Final-Report-of-the-Commission-on-RE.pdf.

Conkin, Paul K., and Roland N. Stromberg. *Heritage and Challenge: The History and Theory of History*. Arlington Heights, IL: Forum, 1989.

Connolly, William E. *Pluralism*. Durham, UK: Duke University Press, 2005.

Cosper, Mike, host. *The Rise and Fall of Mars Hill*. Christianity Today, podcast, 2022–2024. https://www.christianitytoday.com/podcasts/the-rise-and-fall-of-mars-hill/.

Cowper, Willliam. "God Moves in a Mysterious Way." Timeless Truths, 1774. https://library.timelesstruths.org/music/God_Moves_in_a_Mysterious_Way/.

Coyne, Jerry A. *Faith vs. Fact: Why Science and Religion Are Incompatible*. New York: Penguin, 2016.

Crawford, Matthew B. *The World Beyond Your Head: On Becoming an Individual in an Age of Distraction*. Toronto: Penguin, 2015.

Davis, Derek H., and Elena Miroshnikova, eds. *The Routledge International Handbook of Religious Education*. Routledge International Handbook Series. London: Routledge, 2013.

Dederer, Claire. *Monsters: A Fan's Dilemma*. New York: Vintage, 2023.

De Ruyter, Doret J., and Michael S. Merry. "Why Education in Public Schools Should Include Religious Ideals." *Studies in Philosophy and Education* 28 (2009) 295–311. https://link.springer.com/article/10.1007/s11217-008-9120-4.

Dessing, Nathal, et al., eds. *Everyday Lived Islam in Europe*. AHRC/ESRC Religion and Society Series. London: Routledge, 2013.

Dinham, Adam, and Martha Shaw. *RE for REal: The Future of Teaching and Learning About Religion and Belief*. London: Goldsmiths, University of London, 2015. https://www.gold.ac.uk/media/documents-by-section/departments/research-centres-and-units/research-units/faiths-and-civil-society/REforREal-web-b.pdf.

Dinham, Adam, et al. "Towards a Theory and Practice of Religious Literacy: A Case Study of Religion and Belief Engagement in a UK University." *Religions* 8 (2017). https://doi.org/10.3390/rel8120276.

Dooyeweerd, Herman. *A New Critique of Theoretical Thought*. Translated by David H. Freeman and William S. Young. 4 vols. Phillipsburg, NJ: Presbyterian and Reformed, 1969.

BIBLIOGRAPHY

Douglas, Mary. *Leviticus as Literature*. Oxford: Oxford University Press, 1999.

———. *Purity and Danger: An Analysis of Concept of Pollution and Taboo*. London: Routledge, 2004.

Douthat, Ross. *Bad Religion: How We Became a Nation of Heretics*. New York: Free, 2012.

Durkheim, Émile. *The Elementary Forms of the Religious Life*. Translated by Joseph Ward Swain. London: Allen & Unwin, 1915. https://www.gutenberg.org/files/41360/41360-h/41360-h.htm.

Eagleton, Terry. *After Theory*. New York: Basic, 2003.

Easton, Christina. *Religion and Religious Education on the Journey to the Ideal Society*. Analysis 84 (2024) 609–21. https://doi.org/10.1093/analys/anad073.

Editorial Board. "The Guardian View on Humanities in Universities: Closing English Literature Courses Signals a Crisis." *Guardian*, December 5, 2024. https://www.theguardian.com/education/2024/dec/05/the-guardian-view-on-humanities-in-universities-closing-english-literature-courses-signals-a-crisis.

Eikelman, Dale F. "Mass Higher Education and the Religious Imagination in Contemporary Arab Societies." *American Ethnologist* 19 (1992) 643–55.

Eliade, Mircea. *The Myth of the Eternal Return, or Cosmos and History*. Translated by Willard R. Trask. Princeton: Princeton University Press, 1974.

———. *The Sacred and the Profane: The Nature of Religion*. San Diego: Harcourt Brace Jovanovich, 1987.

Ellis, Justine Esta. *The Politics of Religious Literacy: Education and Emotion in a Secular Age*. Political and Public Theologies 2. Leiden: Brill, 2023.

Fabian, Johannes. *Time and the Other: How Anthropology Makes Its Object*. New York: Columbia University Press, 1983.

Fairclough, Norman. "The Discourse of New Labour: Critical Discourse Analysis." In *Discourse as Data: A Guide for Analysis*, edited by Margaret Wetherell et al., 229–66. London: Sage, 2001.

Fazackerley, Anna. "New University Job Cuts Fuel Rising Outrage on Campuses." *Guardian*, October 24, 2021. https://www.theguardian.com/education/2021/oct/24/new-university-job-cuts-fuel-rising-outrage-on-campuses.

Fernhout, Harry. "Quest for Identity and Place: Christian University Education in Canada." In *Christian Higher Education: A Global Reconnaissance*, edited by Joel Carpenter et al., 230–56. Grand Rapids: Eerdmans, 2014.

Fitzgerald, Timothy. *Discourse on Civility and Barbarity: A Critical History of Religion and Related Categories*. Oxford: Oxford University Press, 2007.

———. *The Ideology of Religious Studies*. New York: Oxford University Press, 2000.

Forbes, Robert. "My Father, Malcolm Forbes: A Never-Ending Adventure." *Forbes*, August 19, 2019. https://www.forbes.com/sites/forbesdigitalcovers/2019/08/19/my-father-malcolm-forbes-a-never-ending-adventure/?sh=628559c519fb.

Foucault, Michel. *The Archaeology of Knowledge and the Discourse on Language*. Translated by A. M. Sheridan Smith. New York: Pantheon, 1972.

———. *Discipline and Punish: The Birth of the Prison*. Translated by Alan Sheridan. New York: Vintage, 1995.

Frankl, Viktor E. *Man's Search for Meaning: An Introduction to Logotherapy*. Translated by Ilse Lasch. New York: Pocket, 1963.

Gauchet, Marcel. *The Disenchantment of the World: A Political History of Religion*. Translated by Oscar Burge. Princeton: Princeton University Press, 1997.

Gearon, Liam. *On Holy Ground: The Theory and Practice of Religious Education*. New York: Routledge, 2014.
Gearon, Liam, and Joseph Prud'homme. *State Religious Education and the State of Religious Life*. Eugene, OR: Pickwick, 2018.
Giberson, Karl W., and Francis S. Collins. *The Language of Science and Faith*. Downers Grove, IL: Intervarsity, 2011.
Gillmor, Don. "Why the Baby Boomer Generation Presents a Unique Risk for Suicide." Zoomer, January 28, 2021. https://zoomer.com/health/2021/01/28/why-baby-boomers-present-a-unique-risk-for-suicide.
Ginzburg, Carlo. *The Cheese and the Worms: The Cosmos of a Sixteenth-Century Miller*. Translated by John and Anne Tedeschi. Baltimore: Johns Hopkins University Press, 1980.
Glanzer, Perry L. "Resurrecting Universities with Soul: Christian Higher Education in Post-Communist Europe." In *Christian Higher Education: A Global Reconnaissance*, edited by Joel Carpenter et al., 163–90. Grand Rapids: Eerdmans, 2014.
Glanzer, Perry L., and Joel Carpenter. "Conclusion: Evaluating the Health of Christian Higher Education Around the Globe." In *Christian Higher Education: A Global Reconnaissance*, edited by Joel Carpenter et al., 277–305. Grand Rapids: Eerdmans, 2014.
Glenn, Charles. *The Ambiguous Embrace: Government and Faith-Based Schools and Social Agencies*. New Forum Books. Princeton: Princeton University Press, 2000.
Glenn, Charles L., and Jan De Groof. *Balancing Freedom, Autonomy and Accountability in Education*. Vol 1. Nijmegen: Wolf Legal, 2005.
Gomes, Evaldo Xavier. "Religious Education in Brazil." In *The Routledge International Handbook of Religious Education*, edited by Derek H. Davis and Elena Miroshnikova, 62–68. Routledge International Handbook Series. London: Routledge, 2013.
Goodenough, Ursula. "Vertical and Horizontal Transcendence." *Biology Faculty Publications & Presentations* 93 (2001) 1–16. https://openscholarship.wustl.edu/cgi/viewcontent.cgi?params=/context/bio_facpubs/article/1094/&path_info=Vertical_and_Horizontal_Transcendence__Goodenough_Zygon_2001.pdf.
Got Questions. "What Is the Seven Mountain Mandate, and Is It Biblical?" https://www.gotquestions.org/seven-mountain-mandate.html.
Government of Canada. "Constitution Act, 1982." Last modified November 10, 2025. https://laws-lois.justice.gc.ca/eng/const/page-12.html.
Grant, Robert McQueen. *Paul in the Roman World: The Conflict at Corinth*. Louisville: Westminster John Knox, 2001.
Gravel, Stephanie. "Impartiality of Teachers in Quebec's Non-Denominational Ethics and Religious Culture Program." In *Issues in Religion and Education: Whose Religion?*, edited by Lori G. Beaman and Leo Van Arragon, 367–88. International Studies in Religion and Society 25. Leiden: Brill, 2015.
Gray, John. *Seven Types of Atheism*. New York: Picador, 2018.
Greene, Brian. *Until the End of Time: Mind, Matter, and Our Search for Meaning in an Evolving Universe*. New York: Knopf, 2020.
Grelle, Bruce. "Neutrality in Public School Religion Education: Theory and Politics." In *Issues in Religion and Education: Whose Religion?*, edited by Lori G. Beaman and Leo Van Arragon, 231–56. International Studies in Religion and Society 25. Leiden: Brill, 2015.

Gross, Zehavit. "Religious Education: Definitions, Dilemmas, Challenges, and Future Horizons." *International Journal of Educational Reform* 20 (2011) 257–76.

Hadot, Pierre. *Philosophy as a Way of Life: Spiritual Exercises from Socrates to Foucault*. Edited by Arnold I. Davidson, translated by Michael Chase. Malden, MA: Blackwell, 1995.

Halberstam, David. *The Best and the Brightest*. New York: Random House, 1972.

Hannam, Patricia. "What Should Religious Education Aim to Achieve? An Investigation into the Purpose of Religious Education in the Public Sphere." PhD diss., University of Stirling, 2016.

Hanson, Erin. "The Indian Act." Indigenous Foundations. https://indigenousfoundations.arts.ubc.ca/the_indian_act/.

Harris, Kathleen. "Trinity Western Loses Fight for Christian Law School as Court Rules Limits on Religious Freedom 'Reasonable.'" CBC, June 15, 2018. https://www.cbc.ca/news/politics/trinity-western-supreme-court-decision-1.4707240.

Hawking, Stephen. *A Brief History of Time*. Toronto: Bantam, 1988.

Hedges, Chris. *American Fascists: The Christian Right and the War on America*. New York: Simon & Schuster, 2006.

Heelas, Paul, and Linda Woodhead. *The Spiritual Revolution: Why Religion Is Giving Way to Spirituality*. Religion in the Modern World. Oxford: Blackwell, 2005.

Hershey, Doug. "The True Meaning of Shalom." FIRM, January 3, 2020. https://firmisrael.org/learn/the-meaning-of-shalom/.

Hervieu-Léger, Danièle. *Religion as a Chain of Memory*. Translated by Simon Lee. New Brunswick, NJ: Rutgers University Press, 2000.

Hristova, Bobby. "Private Christian University Says No Sex Outside Heterosexual Marriage. LGBTQ Alumni Say That Discriminates." CBC, August 4, 2020. https://www.cbc.ca/news/canada/hamilton/redeemer-university-discrimination-lgbtq-1.5651627.

Holtmann, Catherine, ed. *Exploring Religion and Diversity in Canada: People, Practice and Possibility*. Cham, Switzerland: Springer, 2018.

Hope, John, chairman. *Report of the Royal Commission on Education in Ontario*. Toronto: Baptist Johnston, 1950.

Hossenfelder, Sabine. *Existential Physics: A Scientist's Guide to Life's Biggest Questions*. New York: Viking, 2022.

"How Shall the Young Direct Their Way?" In *Trinity Psalter Hymnal*, 119B. Tune DUANE STREET composed by George Coles, 1835. Hymnary. https://hymnary.org/hymn/TPH2018/119B.

Humanists UK. "Non-Religious Beliefs." https://humanists.uk/humanism/humanism-today/non-religious-beliefs/.

Interights. "Lautsi v Italy." March 18, 2011. https://www.interights.org/lautsi/index.html.

Iqbal, Muhammad. *The Reconstruction of Religious Thought in Islam*. Stanford: Stanford University Press, 2013.

Jackson, Robert. *Rethinking Religious Education and Plurality: Issues in Diversity and Pedagogy*. London: RoutledgeFalmer, 2004.

———. *Signposts—Policy and Practice for Teaching About Religions and Non-Religious World Views in Intercultural Education*. Strasbourg: Council of Europe, 2014.

BIBLIOGRAPHY

Jackson, Robert, et al., eds. *Religion in Education: A Contribution to Dialogue or a Factor of Conflict in Transforming Societies of European Countries*. Hamburg: REDCo, 2006.

Jafralie, Sabrina, and Arzina Zaver. "Teaching Religious Education: The Ethics and Religious Culture Program; A Case Study." *Forum for International Research in Education* 5 (2019) 89–106.

Jakobsen, Janet R. and Ann Pelligrini. *Love the Sin: Sexual Regulation and the Limits of Religious Tolerance*. Boston: Beacon, 2004.

Jamal, Hebh. "The French Government Wants to 'Save' Muslim Women by Controlling Them." Al Jazeera, October 2, 2023. https://www.aljazeera.com/opinions/2023/10/2/the-french-government-wants-to-save-muslim-women-by-controlling-them.

James, William. *The Varieties of Religious Experience*. Toronto: Random House, 1994.

Jenkins, Jack. "New Survey Points to Correlation Between Christian Nationalism and Authoritarian Views." Religion News Service, September 16, 2024. https://religionnews.com/2024/09/16/new-survey-points-to-correlation-between-christian-nationalism-and-authoritarian-views/?utm_source=RNS+Updates&utm_campaign=11ebe48e82-EMAIL_CAMPAIGN_2024_09_17_01_56&utm_medium=email&utm_term=0_c5356cb657%E2%80%9311ebe48e82-%5BLIST_EMAIL_ID%5D.

Jewish Telegraphic Agency. "Anti-Semitic Teacher Banned from Classrooms in Canada." September 4, 1991. https://www.jta.org/archive/anti-semitic-teacher-banned-from-classrooms-in-canada.

Johnson, Byron R. "Can a Faith-Based Prison Reduce Recidivism?" *Corrections Today* 73 (2012) 60–62. http://www.baylorisr.org/wp-content/uploads/Johnson_Jan2012-CT-3.pdf.

Jones, Allison. "Cursive Is Making a Comeback: Ontario to Make Learning Script Mandatory in School." CBC, June 22, 2023. https://www.cbc.ca/news/canada/toronto/cursive-writing-ontario-1.6885628.

Kagan, Richard L. *Lucrecia's Dreams: Politics and Prophecy in Sixteenth-Century Spain*. Berkeley: University of California Press, 1990.

Kelly, Thomas. "*Consensus gentium*: Reflections on the 'Common Consent' Argument for the Existence of God." In *Evidence and Religious Belief*, edited by Kelly James Clark and Raymond J. VanArragon, 135–56. Oxford: Oxford University Press, 2011.

Khouri, Rami G. "Watching the Watchdogs: Babies and Truth Die Together in Israel-Palestine." Al Jazeera, October 13, 2023. https://www.aljazeera.com/opinions/2023/10/13/watching-the-watchdogs-babies-and-truth-die-together-in-israel-palestine.

Kobes-DuMez, Kristin. *Jesus and John Wayne: How White Evangelicals Corrupted a Faith and Fractured a Nation*. New York: Liveright, 2020.

Königsberger, Georg, and Louis Kubarth. "Religious Education in Austria." In *The Routledge Book of Religious Education*, edited by Derek H. Davis and Elena Miroshnikova, 32–37. Routledge International Handbook Series. Abingdon: Routledge, 2013.

Koukounaras-Liagis, Marios. "Religion in the Curriculum in the Post-Modern Era: Why Young People Should Know About Religion." *International Journal for Cross-Disciplinary Subjects in Education* 3 (2013) 1373–78.

Krakauer, Jon. *Under the Banner of Heaven: A Story of Violent Faith*. New York: Doubleday, 2003.
Kuburić, Zorica, and Christian Moe, eds. *Religion and Pluralism in Education: Comparative Approaches in the Western Balkans*. Novi Sad, Serbia: CEIR and The Kotor Network, 2006.
Kuburić, Zorica, and Milan Vukomanović. "Religious Education: The Case of Serbia." In *Religion and Pluralism in Education: Comparative Approaches in the Western Balkans*, edited by Zorica Kuburić and Christian Moe, 107–38. Novi Sad, Serbia: CEIR and The Kotor Network, 2006.
Kuhn, Thomas. *The Structure of Scientific Revolutions*. Chicago: University of Chicago Press, 1962.
Kuo, Lily. "Coronavirus: Wuhan Doctor Speaks Out Against Authorities." *Guardian*, March 11, 2020. https://www.theguardian.com/world/2020/mar/11/coronavirus-wuhan-doctor-ai-fen-speaks-out-against-authorities.
Kuttab, Daoud. "As Court Decides on Genocide Charge, Netanyahu's Use of a Bible Passage Haunts Him." January 25, 2024. https://religionnews.com/2024/01/25/as-court-decides-on-genocide-charge-netanyahus-use-of-a-bible-passage-haunts-him/.
Lang, Andrew. *The Making of Religion*. London: Paternoster Row, 1898.
Lapierre, Matthew. "Quebec Plans to Table Bill Banning Prayer in Public." CBC, August 28, 2025. https://www.cbc.ca/news/canada/montreal/public-prayer-ban-quebec-1.7619985.
Lavietes, Matt. "Here's What Florida's 'Don't Say Gay' Bill Would Do and What It Wouldn't Do." NBC News, March 16, 2022. https://www.nbcnews.com/nbc-out/out-politics-and-policy/floridas-dont-say-gay-bill-actually-says-rcna19929
Lévi-Strauss, Claude. *The Savage Mind*. Chicago: The University of Chicago Press, 1966.
Lewin, David. "After Religious Education: Lessons from Continental Pedagogy." *Journal of Religious Education* 71 (2023) 197–211.
Lewis, Charles. "Charles Lewis: Religious Extremists Who Flout COVID-19 Rules Are Doing a Disservice to God's Creation." National Post, April 2, 2020. https://nationalpost.com/opinion/charles-lewis-religious-extremists-who-flout-covid-19-rules-are-doing-a-disservice-to-gods-creation.
Lewis, C. S. *The Abolition of Man*. San Francisco: HarperSanFrancisco, 1974.
Lewis, Thomas A. "Against Religious Literacy." In *Why Philosophy Matters for Religion—and Vice Versa*, 119–43. Oxford: Oxford University Press, 2015.
Lundin, Roger. *The Culture of Interpretation: Christian Faith and the Postmodern World*. Grand Rapids: Eerdmans, 1993.
Mackay, J. Keiller, et al. *Religious Information and Moral Development: The Report of the Committee on Religious Education in the Public Schools of the Province of Ontario*. Ontario Department of Education, 1969.
Mahmood, Saba. *The Politics of Piety: The Islamic Revival and the Feminist Subject*. Princeton: Princeton University Press, 2005.
———. "Religious Reason and Secular Affect: An Incommensurable Divide?" In *Is Critique Secular? Blasphemy, Injury and Free Speech*, edited by Talal Asad et al., 64–100. Berkeley: University of California Press, 2009.
Marsden, George. "A Renaissance of Christian Higher Education in the United States." In *Christian Higher Education: A Global Reconnaissance*, edited by Joel Carpenter et al., 257–76. Grand Rapids: Eerdmans, 2014.

BIBLIOGRAPHY

Masuzawa, Tomoko. *The Invention of World Religions: Or, How European Universalism Was Preserved in the Language of Pluralism*. Chicago: University of Chicago Press, 2005.

Matevski, Zoran, et al. "Introducing Religious Education in Macedonia." In *Religion and Pluralism in Education: Comparative Approaches in the Western Balkans*, edited by Zorica Kuburić and Christian Moe, 139–58. Novi Sad, Serbia: CEIR and The Kotor Network, 2006.

Matthews-King, Alex. "Who Is Andrew Wakefield and What Did the Disgraced MMR Doctor Do?" Independent, May 4, 2018. https://www.independent.co.uk/news/health/andrew-wakefield-who-is-mmr-doctor-anti-vaccine-anti-vaxxer-us-a8328326.html.

McCowan, Timothy Ross. "The Building Bridges Through Interfaith Dialogue in Schools Programme: An Investigation into the Effectiveness of a Model of Interfaith Education." PhD diss., School of Religious Education, Australian Catholic University–St. Patrick's Campus, 2013.

McCutcheon, Russell T. *Manufacturing Religion: The Discourse on Sui Generis Religion and the Politics of Nostalgia*. New York: Oxford University Press, 1997.

McDonald's. "Our Mission and Values." https://corporate.mcdonalds.com/corpmcd/our-company/who-we-are/our-values.html.

McEvoy, Colin, et al. "Colin Kaepernick." Biography, last updated September 27, 2023. https://www.biography.com/athletes/colin-kaepernick.

McGahan, Jason. "How a Mild-Mannered USC Professor Accidentally Ignited Academia's Latest Culture War." *Los Angeles Magazine*, October 22, 2020. https://lamag.com/education/usc-professor-slur/.

McGrath, Alister. *Surprised By Meaning: Science, Faith and How We Make Sense of Things*. Louisville: Westminster John Knox, 2011.

McGraw, Peter, and Joel Warner. "The Danish Cartoon Crisis of 2005 and 2006: 10 Things You Didn't Know About the Original Muhammad Controversy." Huffpost, September 25, 2012, updated December 6, 2017. https://www.huffpost.com/entry/muhammad-cartoons_b_1907545.

McGuire, Meredith B. *Lived Religion: Faith and Practice in Everyday Life*. Oxford: University of Oxford Press, 2008.

Mejia, José. "Christian Higher Education in Mexico." In *Christian Higher Education: A Global Reconnaissance*, edited by Joel Carpenter et al., 191–206. Grand Rapids: Eerdmans, 2014.

Merriam-Webster. "Numeracy." https://www.merriam-webster.com/dictionary/numeracy.

———. "Pistic." https://www.merriam-webster.com/dictionary/pistic.

Ministry of Education. *Finding Common Ground: Character Development in Ontoario Schools, K-12*. June 2008. https://schoolweb.tdsb.on.ca/Portals/greenholme/images/Finding_Common_Ground.pdf.

———. *Inquiry-Based Learning*. Capacity Building Series. May 2013. https://www.brainreach.ca/uploads/1/1/2/0/112061741/cbs_inquirybased_9.pdf.

Mooney, Margarita A. *Faith Makes Us Live: Surviving and Thriving in the Haitian Diaspora*. Berkeley: University of California Press, 2009.

Moore, Diane L. "Overcoming Religious Illiteracy: A Cultural Studies Approach." World History Connected, November 2006. https://worldhistoryconnected.press.uillinois.edu/4.1/moore.html.

Moulin, Daniel. "Doubts About Religious Education in Public Schooling." *International Journal of Christianity & Education* 19 (2015) 135–45. https://doi.org/10.1177/2056997115583583.

Mouw, Richard J. *Adventures in Evangelical Civility: A Lifelong Quest for Common Ground*. Grand Rapids: Brazos, 2016.

Muck, Terry C. *Why Study Religion? Understanding Humanity's Pursuit of the Divine*. Grand Rapids: Baker, 2016.

Museka, Godfrey. "Toward the Implementation of a Multifaith Approach in Religious Education: A Phenomenological Guide." *Religious Education* 114 (2019) 130–42.

Mwale, Nelly, et al. "Accounting for the Shift Towards 'Multifaith' Religious Education in Zambia, 1964–2017." *Zambia Social Science Journal* 5 (2017) 37–60. https://scholarship.law.cornell.edu/zssj/vol5/iss2/5.

Netland, Harold. *Christianity and Religious Diversity: Clarifying Christian Commitments in a Globalizing Age*. Grand Rapids: Baker Academic, 2015.

Nicolson, Adam. *God's Secretaries: The Making of the King James Bible*. New York: HarperCollins, 2003.

Nisbet, Robert A. *The Quest for Community*. London: Oxford University Press, 1976.

Norris, Kathleen. *Acedia & Me: A Marriage, Monks, and a Writer's Life*. New York: Riverhead, 2008.

Numbers, Ronald L. *The Creationists: The Evolution of Scientific Creationism*. New York: Knopf, 1992.

ODIHR Advisory Council of Experts on Freedom of Religion or Belief. *Toledo Guiding Principles on Teaching About Religions nad Beliefs in Public Schools*. Warsaw: OSCE/ODIHR, 2007. https://www.osce.org/files/f/documents/c/e/29154.pdf.

Ontario Ministry of Education. *Finding Common Ground: Character Development in Ontario Schools, K–12*. 2008. https://schoolweb.tdsb.on.ca/Portals/greenholme/images/Finding_Common_Ground.pdf.

Orsi, Robert. *Between Heaven and Earth: The Religious Worlds People Make and the Scholars Who Study Them*. Princeton: Princeton University Press, 2005.

Osmer, Richard R., and Friedrich Schweitzer. *Religious Education Between Modernization and Globalization: New Perspectives on the United States and Germany*. Grand Rapids: Eerdmans, 2003.

Otto, Rudolph. *The Idea of the Holy*. London: Oxford University Press, 1950.

Padilla, Norberto. "Religious Education in Argentina." In *The Routledge International Handbook of Religious Education*, edited by Derek H. Davis and Elena Miroshnikova, 13–18. Routledge International Handbook Series. London: Routledge, 2013.

Paikin, Steve. "Brian Greene: From the Big Bang to the End of Time." *TVO Today*, April 14, 2020. https://www.tvo.org/video/brian-greene-from-the-big-bang-to-the-end-of-time.

Palmer, Parker. *To Know as We Are Known: Education as a Spiritual Journey*. San Francisco: HarperSanFrancisco, 1993.

Paris (AFP). "10 Years After Attack, *Charlie Hebdo* Is Uncowed and Still Provoking." *France 24*, March 1, 2025. https://www.france24.com/en/live-news/20250103-10-years-after-attack-charlie-hebdo-is-uncowed-and-still-provoking-1.

Patrick, Margaretta L., et al. "A Call for Teacher Professional Learning and the Study of Religion in Social Studies." *Canadian Journal of Education / Revue canadienne de l'éducation* 40 (2017) 603–37. https://journals.sfu.ca/cje/index.php/cje-rce/article/view/3111/2465.

Perlman, Susan. "What Is Shalom: The True Meaning." Inherit, August 27, 2018. https://inheritmag.com/articles/what-is-shalom-the-true-meaning.

Pfeffer, Amanda. "Ottawa Professor Apologizes for Using N-Word, Regrets Growing Controversy." CBC, October 21, 2020. https://www.cbc.ca/news/canada/ottawa/professor-apologizes-university-of-ottawa-1.5770946.

PhilJ925. "This will Strengthen your Faith!" Ark Encounter review, Trip Advisor, July 7, 2016. https://www.tripadvisor.ca/ShowUserReviews-g39995-d101110346-r390061126-Ark_Encounter-Williamstown_Kentucky.html.

Pinn, Anthony B. *Interplay of Things: Religion, Art and Presence Together.* Durham: Duke University Press, 2021.

Postmedia News. "Canada's Polygamy Law Will Be Tested in Court for the First Time in 127 Years on an Indictment with 24 Women." *National Post*, April 17, 2017. https://nationalpost.com/news/canadian-polygamy-law-tested-in-court-for-the-first-time-in-127-years.

Prison Fellowship. "What We Do." https://www.prisonfellowship.org/about/.

Prothero, Stephen. *Religious Literacy: What Every American Needs to Know—And Doesn't.* New York: HarperCollins, 2007.

PRRI Staff. "Wedding Cakes, Same-Sex Marriage, and the Future of LGBT Rights in America." PRRI, August 2, 2018. https://prri.org/research/wedding-cakes-same-sex-lgbt-marriage/.

Purdon, Nick, and Leonardo Palleja. "Death Threats and Burning Effigies: Sir John A. Macdonald Controversy Gets Extreme." CBC, November 10, 2018. https://www.cbc.ca/news/canada/sir-john-a-macdonald-history-controversy-1.4859448.

Purpel, David. *The Moral and Spiritual Crisis in Education: A Curriculum for Justice and Compassion in Education.* New York: Bergin and Garvey, 1989.

Raboteau, Albert J. *Slave Religion: The "Invisible Institution" in the Antebellum South.* New York: Oxford University Press, 2004.

Rappaport, Roy. *Ritual and Religion in the Making of Humanity.* Cambridge: Cambridge University Press, 1999.

Reilly, Katie. "Read Hillary Clinton's 'Basket of Deplorables' Remarks About Donald Trump Supporters." *Time*, September 10, 2016. https://time.com/4486502/hillary-clinton-basket-of-deplorables-transcript/.

Remington. "About Remington." https://www.remington.com/about-us.html#event-about-us-this-is-remington-country.

Reuters. "Kentucky Clerk Who Refused Gay Marriage Licenses Can Be Sued." NBC News, August 26, 2019. https://www.nbcnews.com/feature/nbc-out/kentucky-clerk-who-refused-gay-marriage-licenses-can-be-sued-n1046306.

Ritchie, Flyn. "A Conversation with Nicky Gumbel, Who Still Loves to Introduce People to Jesus." Church for Vancouver, March 21, 2024. https://churchforvancouver.ca/a-conversation-with-nicky-gumbel-who-still-loves-to-introduce-people-to-jesus/.

Rizzuto, Ana-Maria. *The Birth of the Living God: A Psychoanalytic Study.* Chicago: University of Chicago Press, 1979.

Roetzel, Calvin J. *The Letters of Paul: Conversations in Context.* Louisville: Westminster John Knox, 1998.

BIBLIOGRAPHY

Romero, Simon. "Heroes or Enslavers? Texas Eyes Laws to Shield Its Founders from Scorn." *New York Times*, May 20, 2021. https://www.nytimes.com/2021/05/20/us/texas-history-1836-project.html.

Rosenthal, Michael. *The Character Factory: Baden-Powell and the Origins of the Movement*. New York: Pantheon, 1986.

Ross, James. "Willing Belief and Rational Faith." In *Evidence and Religious Belief*, edited by Kelly Clark and Raymond J. VanArragon, 13–21. Oxford: Oxford University Press, 2011.

Roy, Arundhati. *The Doctor and the Saint: Caste, Race and the Annihilation of Caste; The Debate Between R. R. Ambedkar and M. K. Gandhi*. Chicago: Haymarket, 2017.

Said, Edward. *Culture and Imperialism*. New York: Vintage, 1993.

———. *Orientalism*. Toronto: Random House, 1979.

Salkin, Jeffrey. "When They Came for the Books . . ." Religion News Service, February 10, 2023. https://religionnews.com/2023/02/10/florida-book-banning/.

Sandle, Mark, and William Van Arragon. *Re-Forming History*. Eugene, OR: Cascade, 2019.

Schäfer, Heinrich. "The Janus Face of Religion: On the Religious Factor in the 'New Wars.'" *Numen* 51 (2004) 407–31.

Schaeffer, Francis. *How Should We Then Live? The Rise and Decline of Western Thought and Culture*. Grand Rapids: Revell, 1976.

Schama, Simon. *The Embarrassment of Riches: An Interpretation of Dutch Culture in the Golden Age*. London: Collins, 1987.

Scharer, Matthias. "'Learning Religion' in the Presence of the Other: Provocation and Gift in Public Education." In *The Future of Religious Education in Europe*, edited by in Katrina Stoeckl, 39–43. Luxembourg: European University Institute, 2015.

Schiffauer, Werner, et al., eds. *Civil Enculturation: Nation-State, School and Ethnic Difference in the Netherlands, Britain, Germany and France*. New York: Berghahn, 2004.

Schrödinger, Erwin. *"What Is Life? The Physical Aspect of the Living Cell" with "Mind and Matter" and "Autobiographical Sketches."* Cambridge: Cambridge University Press, 2019.

Scurr, Ruth. *Fatal Purity: Robespierre and the French Revolution*. New York: Owl, 2006.

Shakespeare, William. *Hamlet*. Edited by Barbara Mowat et al. Washington, DC: Folger Shakespeare Library, n.d. https://www.folger.edu/explore/shakespeares-works/hamlet/read/.

———. *Macbeth*. Edited by Barbara Mowat et al. Washington, DC: Folger Shakespeare Library, n.d. https://www.folger.edu/explore/shakespeares-works/macbeth/read/.

Sharpe, Eric J. *Comparative Religion: A History*. 2nd ed. London: Duckworth, 2003.

Shin, Kuk-Won. "Christian Higher Education: History, Tasks, and Vision." In *Christian Higher Education: A Global Reconnaissance*, edited by Joel Carpenter et al., 90–110. Grand Rapids: Eerdmans, 2014.

Simpson, Peter. "Newman's Revenge: The Value of *Voice of Fire* Is Scorching Hot." Ottawa Citizen, July 31, 2014. https://ottawacitizen.com/entertainment/local-arts/newmans-revenge-the-value-of-voice-of-fire-is-scorching-hot.

Skinner, B. F. *Walden Two*. Indianapolis: Hackett, 1948.

Smart, Carol. *Feminism and the Power of Law*. Sociology of Law and Crime. London: Routledge, 1989.

Smietana, Bob. "Judge Dismisses Muslim Couple's Lawsuit Against School Where Daughter Converted to Christianity." Religion News Service, January 4, 2024. https://religionnews.com/2024/01/04/a-muslim-couple-sued-a-public-school-after-their-daughter-converted-to-christianity-a-judge-dismissed-the-case/?utm_source=pushly.

Smith, Dorothy E. *The Everyday World as Problematic: A Feminist Sociology.* Toronto: University of Toronto Press, 1987.

Smith, James K. A. *You Are What You Love: The Spiritual Power of Habit.* Grand Rapids: Brazos, 2016.

Smith, Wilfred Cantwell. *The Meaning and End of Religion.* Minneapolis: Fortress, 1991.

Southon, Emma. *A Fatal Thing Happened On the Way to the Forum: Murder in Ancient Rome.* New York: Abrams, 2021.

Spafford, Horatio G. "It is Well with My Soul." Timeless Truths, 1873. https://library.timelesstruths.org/music/It_Is_Well_with_My_Soul/.

Spektor, Brandon. "Stephen Hawking's Final Book Says There's 'No Possibility' of God in Our Universe." LiveScience, October 17, 2018. https://www.livescience.com/63854-stephen-hawking-says-no-god.html.

Spencer, Nick. "Did Albert Einstein Believe in God?" Prospect, December 4, 2018. https://www.prospectmagazine.co.uk/ideas/philosophy/42002/did-albert-einstein-believe-in-god.

Spielberg, Steven, dir. *E.T.* Amblin Entertainment and Universal Pictures, 1982.

Spinner-Halev, Jeff. *Surviving Diversity: Religion and Democratic Citizenship.* Baltimore: Johns Hopkins University Press, 2000.

Spitz, Lewis W. *The Renaissance and Reformation Movements.* 2 vols. St. Louis: Concordia, 1987.

Stabile, Angelica. "Book Banning Efforts Are on a Record-High Trajectory for 2022: Report." Fox News, September 19, 2022. https://www.foxnews.com/lifestyle/book-ban-efforts-record-high-trajectory-2022-report.

Stacey, Timothy. *Saving Liberalism from Itself: The Spirit of Political Participation.* Bristol: Bristol University Press, 2022.

Stack, Liam. "A Brief History of Deadly Attacks on Abortion Providers." *New York Times*, November, 29, 2015. https://www.nytimes.com/interactive/2015/11/29/us/30abortion-clinic-violence.html#:~:text=The%20First%20Abortion%20Doctor%20Killed%3A%20David%20Gunn%20Dr.,to%20the%20National%20Abortion%20Federation%2C%20an%20advocacy%20group.

Starrett, Gregory. *Putting Islam to Work: Education, Politics and Religious Transformation in Egypt.* Comparative Studies on Muslim Societies. Berkeley: University of California Press, 1998.

St. John the Evangelist Anglican Church. "37 Church Street Youth Centre." https://anglicanstrathroy.com/ministries/37-frank-street-youth-centre.

Stoeckl, Katrina, ed. *The Future of Religious Education in Europe.* Luxembourg: European University Institute, 2015.

Strobel, Lee. *The Case for Christ: A Journalist's Personal Investigation of the Evidence for Jesus.* Grand Rapids: Zondervan, 1998.

Suleiman, Omar. "France's Laïcité in the Name of Secularism Is Really Only Supremacist Legacy of Colonialism." Religion News Service, September 6, 2023. https://

religionnews.com/2023/09/06/frances-laicite-in-the-name-of-secularism-is-really-only-supremacist-legacy-of-colonialism/?utm_source=pushly.

Sullivan, Randall. *The Miracle Detectives*. New York: Grove, 2004.

Sullivan, Winnifred Fallers. *The Impossibility of Religious Freedom*. Princeton: Princeton University Press, 2005.

———. *Prison Religion: Faith-Based Reform and the Constitution*. Princeton: Princeton University Press, 2009.

———. "We Are All Religious Now. Again." *Social Research* 76 (2009) 1181–98.

Swaner, Lynn E., et al. *School-Sector Influence on Graduate Outcomes and Flourishing: Findings from the 2023 Cardus Education Survey*. Cardus, 2024. https://www.cardus.ca/research/education/reports/school-sector-influence-on-graduate-outcomes-and-flourishing/.

Sweet, Matthew. *Inventing the Victorians*. London: Faber and Faber, 2001.

Tait, Robert. "What's Behind the Antisemitism Furor over College Presidents' Testimony?" *Guardian*, December 12, 2023. https://www.theguardian.com/us-news/2023/dec/12/university-president-antisemitism-israel-palestine-explained-harvard-penn.

Taves, Ann. "What Is Nonreligion? On the Virtues of a Meaning Systems Framework for Studying Nonreligious and Religious Worldviews in the Context of Everyday Life." *Secularism and Nonreligion* 7 (2018) art. 9. https://doi.org/10.5334/snr.104.

Taylor, Charles. *The Malaise of Modernity*. Toronto: Anansi, 1991.

———. *Modern Social Imaginaries*. Public Planet Books. Durham: Duke University Press, 2005.

———. *A Secular Age*. Cambridge: Harvard University Press, 2007.

———. *Varieties of Religion Today: William James Revisited*. Cambridge: Harvard University Press, 2002.

Tedjo, Alvin, and Leonard Baak. *A One School System in Ontario*. Humanist Canada, 2021. https://www.humanistcanada.ca/webinar-series-2021-a-one-school-system-in-ontario/.

Ten Boom, Corrie, et al. *The Hiding Place*. 35th ann. ed. Grand Rapids: Chosen, 2006.

Terpstra, Nicholas. *Religious Refugees in the Early Modern World: An Alternative History of the Reformation*. Cambridge: Cambridge University Press, 2015.

Theoi Project. "Kairos." https://www.theoi.com/Daimon/Kairos.html.

Thoman, Bret. "Pilgrimage to Orvieto: The Eucharistic Miracle of Bolsena." Aleteia, January 27, 2021. https://aleteia.org/2021/01/27/pilgrimage-to-orvieto-the-eucharistic-miracle-of-bolsena/.

Thurman, Howard. *Jesus and the Disinherited*. Boston: Beacon, 1976.

Tillson, John. "Rival Conceptions of Religious Education." Forthcoming in *International Handbook Of Philosophy of Education*, edited by Paul Smeyers. Springer International Handbooks of Education. Dort, Netherlands: Springer, 2018.

Tokarczuk, Olga. *The Books of Jacob*. Translated by Jennifer Croft. London: Fitzgerald Editions, 2021.

———. *Drive Your Plow Over the Bones of the Dead*. Translated by Antonia Lloyd-Jones. London: Fitzgerald Editions, 2019.

Tolentino, Jia. *Trick Mirror: Reflections on Self Delusion*. New York: Random House, 2020.

TomP. "The Maji Maji Rebellion in German East Africa When Bullets Did Not Turn Into Water." Daily Kos, September 8, 2017. https://www.dailykos.com/

stories/2017/9/8/1697011/-The-Maji-Maji-Rebellion-in-German-East-Africa-When-Bullets-Did-Not-Turn-Into-Water.
Toronto Metropolitan University. "Ryerson University Changing Its Name to Toronto Metropolitan University." April 26, 2022. https://www.torontomu.ca/media/releases/2022/04/ryerson-university-changing-its-name-to-toronto-metropolitan-uni/.
Trueman, Carl. "Robust Biblical Theology Runs Along Diagonal Lines." The Gospel Coalition, December 6, 2023. https://www.thegospelcoalition.org/article/biblical-critical-theory-review/.

Tuchman, Barbara W. *A Distant Mirror: The Calamitous 14th Century*. New York: Ballantine Books, 1978.
———. *The March of Folly from Troy to Vietnam*. New York: Knopf, 1984.
Tucker, Chris. "Phenomenal Conservatism and Evidentialism in Religious Epistemology." In *Evidence and Religious Belief*, edited by Kelly Clark and Raymond J. VanArragon, 52–76. Oxford: Oxford University Press, 2011.
UNESCO. "Literacy." https://www.unesco.org/en/literacy.
University of Waterloo. "Institute for Religion, Culture, and Societal Futures." https://uwaterloo.ca/st-jeromes/academics/research/institute-religion-culture-and-societal-futures.
Vaillancourt, Philippe. "Quebec to Take Ethics and Religious Culture Out of School Curriculum." America, January 15, 2020. https://www.americamagazine.org/politics-society/2020/01/15/quebec-take-ethics-and-religious-culture-out-school-curriculum/?gclid=CjoKCQiAtJeNBhCVARIsANJUJ2E2Bmv4lTcjM2yuBH4yoF2NUl5_uoiGKgv7n-4kqbbRa-NYHR3Jd-UaAvo6EALw_wcB.
Van Arragon, Leo. "Epistemology, Religion, and the Politics of Inclusion in Ontario Public Education." In *What Teachers Need to Know: Topics in Diversity and Inclusion*, edited by Matthew Etherington, 301–19. Eugene, OR: Wipf and Stock, 2017.
———. "Religion and Education in Ontario Public Education: Contested Borders and Uneasy Truces." In *Issues in Religion and Education: Whose Religion?*, edited by Lori G. Beaman and Leo Van Arragon, 34–58. International Studies in Religion and Society 25. Leiden: Brill, 2015.
———. "Religion and Education: The Story of a Conflicted Canadian Partnership." In *Exploring Religion and Diversity in Canada: People, Practice and Possibility*, edited by Catherine Holtmann, 81–106. Cham, Switzerland: Springer, 2018.
———. "We Educate, They Indoctrinate: Religion and the Politics of Togetherness in Ontario Public Schools." PhD diss., University of Ottawa, 2015.
VanArragon, Raymond J. *Key Terms in Philosophy of Religion*. London: Continuum International, 2010.
Van Brummelen, Harold. *Stepping Stones to Curriculum: A Biblical Path*. 2nd ed. Colorado Springs: Purposeful Design, 2002.
Vaters, Karl. "11 Ways to Be the Church for Those Who Don't Go to Church." *Christianity Today*, October 2, 2015. https://web.archive.org/web/20151006022440/https://www.christianitytoday.com/karl-vaters/2015/october/11-ways-to-be-church-for-those-who-dont-go-to-church.html.
Visser, Margaret. *Beyond Fate*. Toronto: Anansi, 2002.

BIBLIOGRAPHY

Volf, Miroslav. *Exclusion and Embrace: A Theological Exploration of Identity, Otherness, and Reconciliation.* Nashville: Abingdon, 2019.

Volf, Miroslav, et al. *Life Worth Living: A Guide to What Matters Most.* New York: Viking, 2023.

Wade, Peter. "Navy Captain Fired for Sounding Alarm About Coronavirus Outbreak Tests Positive." *Rolling Stone*, April 5, 2020. https://www.rollingstone.com/politics/politics-news/fired-navy-captain-crozier-coronavirus-tests-positive-978693/.

Wainwright, William J. "Theistic Proofs, Person Relativity, and the Rationality of Religious Belief." In *Evidence and Religious Belief*, edited by Kelly Clark and Raymond J. VanArragon, 77–94. Oxford: Oxford University Press, 2011.

Walters-Sleyon, George. "Studies on Religion and Recidivism: Focus on Roxbury, Dorchester, and Mattapan." *Trotter Review* 21 (2013) art. 4. https://scholarworks.umb.edu/trotter_review/vol21/iss1/4/.

Watkin, Christopher. *Biblical Critical Theory: How the Bible's Unfolding Story Makes Sense of Modern Life and Culture.* Grand Rapids: Zondervan, 2022.

Watkins, Megan. "Gauging the Affective: Becoming Attuned to Its Impact in Education." In *Methodological Advances in Research on Emotion and Education*, edited by Michalinos Zembylas and Paul A. Schutz, 71–79. Cham, Switzerland: Springer International, 2016.

Wertheimer, Linda. *Faith Ed.: Teaching About Religion in an Age of Intolerance.* Boston: Beacon, 2015.

Westacott, Emrys. "Summary and Analysis of Plato's *Euthyphro*." ThoughtCo, October 5, 2024. https://www.thoughtco.com/platos-euthyphro-2670341.

Whitehead, Andrew L., and Samuel L. Perry. *Taking America Back for God: Christian Nationalism in the United States.* New York: Oxford University Press, 2020.

Wikipedia. "Book Banning in the United States (2021–Present)." Last edited November 4, 2025. https://en.wikipedia.org/wiki/Book_banning_in_the_United_States_(2021%E2%80%93present).

Wilkerson, Isabelle. *Caste: The Origins of our Discontents.* New York: Penguin, 2023.

Willaime, Jean Paul. "Different Models for Religion and Education in Europe." In *Religion in Education: A Contribution to Dialogue or a Factor of Conflict in Transforming Societies of European Countries*, edited by Robert Jackson et al., 81–93. Hamburg: REDCo, 2006.

Willems, Joachim. "Religious Education and the Student's Fundamental Right to Freedom of Religion—Some Lessons and Questions from Germany." In *The Future of Religious Education in Europe*, edited by in Katrina Stoeckl, 27–39. Luxembourg: European University Institute, 2015.

Wolterstorff, Nicholas. *Religion in the University.* New Haven: Yale University Press, 2019.

Woodhead, Linda. "Tactical and Strategic Religion." In *Everyday Lived Islam in Europe*, edited By Nathal Dessing et al., 9–22. AHRC/ESRC Religion and Society Series. London: Routledge, 2013.

York Catholic District School Board. "York Catholic Communities of Faith." https://www.ycdsb.ca/wp-content/uploads/Communities_Faith_Poster.pdf.

Young, Charles, and Richard Adams. "Overseas Schools Given 'British' Accreditation Despite Anti-Equality Curriculum." *Guardian*, May 26, 2024. https://www.theguardian.com/education/article/2024/may/26/overseas-schools-given-british-accreditation-despite-anti-equality-curriculum.

BIBLIOGRAPHY

Young, Jim. "Alberta v. Hutterian Brethren of Wilson Colony (2009)." Centre for Constitutional Studies, July 31, 2009. https://www.constitutionalstudies. ca/2009/07/alberta-v-hutterian-brethren-of-wilson-colony-2009/.

Young, John F. "Religious Education in Canada." In *The Routledge International Handbook of Religious Education*, edited by Derek H. Davis and Elena Miroshnikova, 69–75. Routledge International Handbook Series. London: Routledge, 2013.

Yun, Tom. "Trudeau Defends Liberal Campaign Video Flagged by Twitter as 'Manipulated media.'" CTVNews, August 23, 2021. https://web.archive.org/web/20210823155946/https://www.ctvnews.ca/politics/federal-election-2021/trudeau-defends-liberal-campaign-video-flagged-by-twitter-as-manipulated-media-1.5557657.

Zagzebski, Linda. "Epistemic Self-Trust and the *Consensus gentium* Argument." In *Evidence and Religious Belief*, edited by Kelly Clark and Raymond J. VanArragon, 22–36. Oxford: Oxford University Press, 2011.

Zine, Jasmin. *Canadian Islamic Schools: Unravelling the Politics of Faith, Gender, Knowledge and Identity*. Toronto: University of Toronto Press, 2008.

Zwilling, Anne-Laure. "Are the 'Non-Religious' Becoming the New Religion?" The Conversation, October 25, 2018. https://theconversation.com/are-the-non-religious-becoming-the-new-religion-105446.

www.ingramcontent.com/pod-product-compliance
Lightning Source LLC
Chambersburg PA
CBHW061423300426
44114CB00014B/1518